Coordination and the Syntax–Discourse Interface

OXFORD SURVEYS IN SYNTAX AND MORPHOLOGY

General Editor
Robert D Van Valin, Jr.
Heinrich-Heine University and the University at Buffalo, State University of New York

Advisory Editors
Guglielmo Cinque, *University of Venice*
Daniel Everett, *Illinois State University*
Adele Goldberg, *Princeton University*
Kees Hengeveld, *University of Amsterdam*
Caroline Heycock, *University of Edinburgh*
David Pesetsky, *Massachusetts Institute of Technology*
Ian Roberts, *University of Cambridge*
Masayoshi Shibatani, *Rice University*
Andrew Spencer, *University of Essex*
Tom Wasow, *Stanford University*

For a complete list of titles published and in preparation for the series, see p. 316.

Coordination and the Syntax–Discourse Interface

DANIEL ALTSHULER AND ROBERT TRUSWELL

OXFORD
UNIVERSITY PRESS

OXFORD
UNIVERSITY PRESS

Great Clarendon Street, Oxford, OX2 6DP,
United Kingdom

Oxford University Press is a department of the University of Oxford.
It furthers the University's objective of excellence in research, scholarship,
and education by publishing worldwide. Oxford is a registered trade mark of
Oxford University Press in the UK and in certain other countries

Published in the United States of America by Oxford University Press
198 Madison Avenue, New York, NY 10016, United States of America

British Library Cataloguing in Publication Data
Data available

Library of Congress Control Number: 2021950249

ISBN 978–0–19–880423–9 (hbk)

ISBN 978–0–19–880424–6 (pbk)

DOI: 10.1093/oso/9780198804239.001.0001

Printed and bound by
CPI Group (UK) Ltd, Croydon, CR0 4YY

Contents

General Preface

Oxford Surveys in Syntax and Morphology provides overviews of the major approaches to subjects and questions at the centre of linguistic research in morphology and syntax. The volumes are accessible, critical, and up to date. Individually and collectively, they aim to reveal the field's intellectual history and theoretical diversity. Each book published in the series will characteristically contain: (1) a brief historical overview of relevant research in the subject; (2) a critical presentation of approaches from relevant (but usually seen as competing) theoretical perspectives to the phenomena and issues at hand, including an objective evaluation of the strengths and weaknesses of each approach to the central problems and issues; (3) a balanced account of the current issues, problems, and opportunities relating to the topic, showing the degree of consensus or otherwise in each case. The volumes will thus provide researchers and graduate students concerned with syntax, morphology, and related aspects of semantics with a vital source of information and reference.

Coordination and the Syntax–Discourse Interface investigates one of the fundamental issues in linguistic theory over the past half century, namely the role of discourse in explaining syntactic phenomena. The authors examine displacement out of coordinate structures, and ask the question, 'what is the better explanation for the phenomena observed, purely syntactic constraints or discourse-motivated restrictions?'. The answer is not simple and straightforward, as befits the complexity of these phenomena, and it challenges assumptions many theories make regarding the syntax–discourse interface.

Robert D. Van Valin, Jr
General Editor

University at Buffalo,
The State University of New York

Heinrich Heine University,
Düsseldorf

Acknowledgments

We thank students and colleagues for their shared wisdom throughout this project. For critical input related to Chapters 2–4, we thank Mark Steedman and an audience at ZAS. For critical input related to Chapters 5–6, we thank Alex Lascarides and Julian Schlöder. Thanks also to Roger Schwarzschild, Richard Stockwell, and Károly Varasdi for discussing various aspects of this work with us at different stages of the project (Károly, in particular, was instrumental in getting the project off the ground). Thanks also to Scott AnderBois, Nils Franzén, Lisa Gotthard, Dag Haug, Jet Hoek, Aoi Kawakita, Alex Lorson, Kilu von Prince, Andreas Stokke, Tobias Ungerer, Hans Wilke, and Nairan Wu for their contribution and discussion of crosslinguistic data. Thanks to Carolyn Anderson and Kimberly Johnson for their judgments on thorny English data. Finally, we thank Robert Van Valin for inviting us to write this survey, as well as Vicki Sunter and the OUP staff for their encouragement, patience, and belief in this project.

List of Abbreviations

1/2/3	first/second/third person
I/II/III/IV	noun class 1–4
ABS	absolutive
ACC	accusative
ACC2	accusative 2 (A'ingae)
ADV	adverbializer
Agr	agreement
AI	artificial intelligence
ANA	anaphoric
ANDAT	andative
AP	adjective phrase
ASP	aspectual marker
ATB	Across-The-Board
ATTR	attributive
AUX	auxiliary
B	Boolean head
C	complementizer
CCG	Combinatory Categorial Grammar
CDU	complex discourse unit
CED	Condition on Extraction Domain
CL	classifier
CL	cleft marker (Palauan)
CNPC	Complex Noun Phrase Constraint
CNTR	contrastive topic
COM	comitative
COMP	complementizer
COND	conditional
Conj	conjunction
ConjP	conjunction phrase
CP	complementizer phrase
CSC	Coordinate Structure Constraint
CT	contrastive topic
D-linked	discourse-linked
DAT	dative
DECL	declarative
DEF	definite
DP	determiner phrase
DREF	discourse referent
DRS	discourse representation structure
DRT	Discourse Representation Theory
DS	different subject
DU	dual

DU	discourse unit
ECP	Empty Category Principle
EDU	elementary discourse unit
EST	Extended Standard Theory
EXCL	exclusive
F	focus
f-structure	functional structure
FBP	foreground–background pair
FOC	focus
GB	Government and Binding theory
GPSG	Generalized Phrase Structure Grammar
HAB	habitual
HPSG	Head-driven Phrase Structure Grammar
HUM	human
I	inflection
INESS	inessive
INF	infinitive
INFL	inflection
IP	inflection phrase
IPFV	imperfective
IRR	irrealis
KH1/2	Kehler's Hypothesis 1/2
LF	Logical Form
LFG	Lexical–Functional Grammar
LNK	linker
LOC	locative
MANN	manner
MCT	maximal common theme
MDC	Maximize Discourse Coherence
N	noun
NEG	negation
NMLZ	nominalizer
NOM	nominative
NP	noun phrase
NPI	negative polarity item
O	object
P	preposition
PCC	Path Containment Condition
PFV	perfective
PL	plural
PLS	plural subject agreement
PP	prepositional phrase
PRED	predicate
PRES	present
PRT	particle
PST	past

Q	question marker
QAP	question–answer pair
QR	Quantifier Raising
QUD	question under discussion
REAL	realis
REL	relativizer
RPT	reportative
S	sentence
S	subject
SBJV	subjunctive
SDRS	segmented discourse representation structure
SDRT	Segmented Discourse Representation Theory
SG	singular
SGF	subject gap in finite/fronted
SIMIL	similative
SLF	Subjektlücke in finiten Sätzen
SMC	Shortest Move Condition
SS	same subject
t	trace
TOP	topic
TP	tense phrase
UCA	Uniformity Corollary on Adjunction
ULF	underspecified logical form
V	verb
V2	verb-second
VM	verb modifier
VP	verb phrase
VPE	verb phrase ellipsis
WCO	Weak crossover

1

Introduction

The goal of this volume is to explore interactions between syntactic structure and discourse structure, through a case study of patterns of extraction from coordinate structures. It is not a typical survey monograph because the primary empirical focus is a fairly obscure and recalcitrant corner of locality theory. However, this obscure and recalcitrant corner serves us well as a microcosm, and allows us to illustrate fundamental methodological points about the interactions between syntax and discourse.

As is typical for a survey, there is not much original research in what follows. Nevertheless, we believe that this is the most complete account of extraction from coordinate structures to date. This is a consequence of the theoretical breadth of the survey: extraction from coordinate structures is, at first blush, a syntactic matter, but the survey ranges far beyond syntax, and this breadth raises theoretical and empirical questions across syntax, semantics, pragmatics, and discourse structure. A complete survey of extraction from coordinate structure must pay attention to all of these domains, and their interactions.

It will quickly become clear that we are not aiming to promote a single analysis. Instead, we want to motivate reasonable hypotheses which allow us to reason deductively from empirical facts to theoretical conclusions. The theoretical conclusions are likely to be significant in scope: we aim to show that this empirical area has the potential to enable us to discriminate between current syntactic theories, and to inform work on the interfaces between the domains just listed. However, in many cases, the necessary empirical work has not yet been done, and too much of the literature revolves around the same handful of examples, mainly in English. We hope that this survey will inspire further work on extraction from coordinate structures, particularly in understudied languages, and provide a guide to how to tease out the theoretical implications of empirical findings.

In the rest of this introduction, we introduce some overarching issues concerning syntax–discourse interactions, and then motivate our choice of case study.

1.1 Syntax, semantics, and discourse

Although it is now common to see the term 'syntax–discourse interface' in the literature (see, for instance, Avrutin 1999, Burkhardt 2005, and Erteschik-Shir 2007), the term is surprising, because such an interface seems to straddle the divide between competence and performance. Syntax, as part of competence grammar, should interface with other parts of competence grammar (morphophonology and semantics), while discourse effects are usually analyzed, with pragmatics, as performance phenomena, concerned with language use in context.

Coordination and the Syntax–Discourse Interface. Daniel Altshuler and Robert Truswell, Oxford University Press.
© Daniel Altshuler and Robert Truswell (2022). DOI: 10.1093/oso/9780198804239.003.0001

This means that we should be alert to the possibility of fundamental differences between the syntax–discourse interface and, say, the syntax–phonology interface, because the latter, as a mapping between two declarative 'competence' representations, is of a different nature from the former, with one foot in competence and one foot in performance.

There are two overly simple responses to this challenge, which we will not pursue seriously. The first is to say that empirical phenomena involving the 'syntax–discourse interface' are all performance phenomena. It will be hard to take this seriously because the empirical facts laid out in Chapters 3 and 4 in particular are too intimately related to locality phenomena which are central to the study of syntax in competence grammar.

The second simple response is to say that the syntax–discourse interface is somehow prefigured in syntactic structure, through syntactic counterparts of discourse relations. An example of this approach would be the cartographic syntax of Rizzi (1997), where syntactic [TOPIC] and [FOCUS] features derive syntactic restrictions (for instance on word order) with correlates in discourse structure. The gist of the problem with this approach, regardless of its general merits, is that syntactic structure demonstrably is not discourse structure, and it will turn out that we need to refer to both, and find a vocabulary for describing the interactions between the two structures.

This survey instead follows a separate path, one which is possible only because the landscape around representations of meaning above the sentence level has changed. Research into cross-sentential binding phenomena by Kamp (1981) and Heim (1982) led to the development of formal semantic theories in which the status of semantic correlates of the sentence is diminished, and sentence meanings are compositionally integrated into larger representations of discourse-level information. In short, this body of work motivates a redrawing of the line between competence and performance, and a conceptualization of part of the syntax–discourse interface as belonging within competence grammar, as a component of the syntax–semantics interface.

In Chapter 6, we will focus on a particular extension of Kamp's Discourse Representation Theory (DRT), namely SDRT, or Segmented Discourse Representation Theory (Asher and Lascarides 2003), which embodies rich hypotheses about discourse structure. As we shall see, representations of discourse structure share certain properties with representations of syntactic structure (e.g. both make use of a relation of hierarchical embedding, or **subordination**), but are incommensurate in various ways (for instance, discourse subordination relations do not always map onto syntactic subordination relations).

This approach to the syntax–discourse interface gives rise to several foundational questions, including the following:

- Are certain theories of syntactic structure more congenial to theories of discourse structure, and vice versa?
- Which structures represent which empirical phenomena?

Questions like these are familiar from other work on linguistic interfaces. Linguistic theory is a long way from providing definitive answers to them, so the best way to make progress is through case studies such as this one, chosen with one eye on empirical tractability and one eye on theoretical richness across subdisciplines. The latter consideration is important because progress in linguistics can become encapsulated within subdisciplinary communities, such as 'syntactic theory' or 'discourse semantics'. Working on an interface like this one necessarily involves drawing out connections between those subdisciplines. Perhaps unsurprisingly, the empirical discoveries that those subdisciplines have made, and the conclusions that researchers have drawn on the basis of those discoveries, don't always translate across disciplinary boundaries. Articulating what a realistic synthesis looks like, therefore, is a difficult challenge. This volume illustrates that challenge, as well as the virtues of meeting the challenge.

Instead of tackling questions like the above head on, we will identify a series of choice points in the course of this survey (collated in Appendix for easy reference). These choice points are interrelated, and range across syntax and discourse. Ultimately, they are all empirical questions, but in our opinion we do not yet have the data to resolve them. We hope that the choice points set an agenda for future research on extraction from coordinate structures, and on the syntax–discourse interface, by identifying the core questions, the relationships between them, and ways in which answers to these questions might be found.

1.2 Extraction from coordinate structures

Our case study concerns correlations between the interpretation of coordinate structures and patterns of extraction from those structures. Extraction from coordinate structures is limited. In fact, Ross (1967) proposed the **Coordinate Structure Constraint**, or CSC, which prohibits extraction of conjuncts, and extraction out of conjuncts. The effects of these two parts of the CSC are illustrated in (1) and (2), respectively.

(1)   a.   Who did you meet __ ?
       b.   *Who did you meet [__ and Sue]?

(2)   a.   What did you eat __ ?
       b.   *What did you [[eat __] and [drink water]]?

There are several known classes of counterexample to the CSC. Some can be characterized in purely syntactic terms. For instance, we will see in Chapter 3 that some languages do, in fact, allow extraction of initial conjuncts, of precisely the sort which (1b) shows to be ungrammatical in English. These examples are interesting in their own right, but not particularly illuminating for the study of the syntax–discourse interface, so we will draw a line around them and leave them to one side, for the attention of specialists in 'pure' comparative syntax.

We focus instead on patterns of extraction from one or more conjuncts, each apparently correlated with a particular interpretation of the coordinate structure. The first, and most discussed, pattern is **Across-The-Board movement**, or ATB extraction, also first observed by Ross. In ATB extraction, a single moved phrase corresponds to a gap in each conjunct. Often, but not always, ATB extractions correspond to **parallel** or **contrastive** interpretations. For instance, in (3), *Kim* and *Sally* contrast, as do *enjoy* and *hate*.

(3)   What did [[Kim enjoy __] but [Sally hate __]]?

Three more correlations were established by Lakoff (1986), building on observations amassed by researchers over the previous twenty years. In (4) (Lakoff's 'Type A'), the coordinate structure is interpreted as a **narration** and gaps are located in one or more typically noninitial conjuncts.

(4)   What did you [[go to the store] and [buy __]]?

In (5) (Lakoff's 'Type B'), the interpretation involves a **violated expectation**, and the gap is in the initial conjunct only.

(5)   How much can you [[drink __] and [still stay sober]]?

In (6) (Lakoff's 'Type C'), the interpretation is that the state of affairs described in the second conjunct is a **result** of the state of affairs described in the first conjunct, and extraction is again from the first conjunct only.

(6)   What do people [[eat __ here] and [then get sick]]?

Lakoff develops an analysis of these correlations with the following two main components:

- Conjunctions such as English *and* are interpreted as expressing a variety of discourse relations between propositions.
- Patterns of extraction from coordinate structures are conditioned by the discourse relation expressed by the conjunction.

This is a radically different approach to Ross's, because the acceptable patterns of movement are described not in syntactic terms like 'coordinate structure' or 'conjunct', but in terms of descriptions of interpretations like 'result' or 'narration'. However, Lakoff only actually describes correlations between certain interpretations and certain patterns of extraction. These correlations (even if empirically accurate) are only a step toward a full theory, because we don't know why the correlations should be this way, or why they should be visible in this empirical domain.

We might hope that established theories of syntax and of discourse structure could help answer these 'why' questions. However, we then encounter a further property of this empirical domain:

- Different syntactic theories have very different analyses of coordinate structures, and make significantly different predictions about extraction from coordinate structures. No theory currently makes fully accurate predictions for the attested data.
- Different theories of discourse structure make significantly different predictions about the interpretation of conjunctions like *and*. No theory currently makes fully accurate predictions for the attested data.

We will see in Chapter 2 that there is an almost embarrassingly wide range of analyses of the syntax of coordination under active current development. Chapter 3 shows that most theories don't predict the noted diversity of extraction patterns, and that we have a choice between analyses which are too restrictive, or which are too liberal.

Formal theories of discourse are newer, and the range of analyses is narrower as a consequence, but there are still several approaches under current development. The labels we used above ('parallel', 'contrast', 'narration', 'violated expectation', 'result') are fairly widespread, and, in fact, have been defined in several slightly different ways (see

Chapter 5), but only one work (Kehler 2002) has attempted to relate reasonably explicit definitions of those labels directly to patterns of extraction. Kehler (2002), therefore, is the most direct antecedent of the discourse research reported in this monograph, but we will diverge from Kehler in several important respects, particularly in Chapters 5 and 6.

Because neither the syntactic theory nor the discourse theory has stabilized, there are many moving parts to consider when attempting to build a unified account of syntax and discourse in this empirical domain. This problem has sometimes been underestimated on both sides: syntacticians have often been content with a demonstration that extraction from coordinate structures is semantically conditioned, without attempting to show *how* semantics influences a syntactic phenomenon like nonlocal dependencies (e.g. Munn 1993, Johannessen 1998). And the question of extraction from coordinate structures barely registers in many works on discourse semantics (with the notable exception of Kehler 2002), because, well, that's syntax.

Perhaps as a result of this disconnect, there have been two main approaches to extraction from coordinate structures in recent work. One, which we will refer to as 'syntax calls the shots', aims to reduce patterns of extraction from coordinate structures to principled statements about constraints on unbounded dependencies in syntax. The other, which we will call 'discourse calls the shots', aims to explain restrictions on extraction from coordinate structures in terms of asyntactic statements about the interpretation of unbounded dependency constructions in specific discourse contexts. We will survey research to date in these two approaches in Chapters 4 and 5 respectively. The following is a very brief summary of our findings.

- Certain variants of the syntax-calls-the-shots approach can offer real insight into data related to (3)–(6), but this approach offers no real hope for addressing the heart of Lakoff's challenge, namely the relationship between extraction patterns and interpretation of coordinate structures.
- Claims, such as Lakoff's or Kehler's, that extraction patterns correlate with discourse relations such as 'narration' or 'violated expectation' are approximately correct, but no more than that. Accordingly, variants of the discourse-calls-the-shots approach such as Lakoff's (which build directly on such relations) cannot address the relationship between extraction and interpretation in detail, despite their initial promise. These approaches also cannot capture certain patterns which admit explanations in a syntax-calls-the-shots vein.

The summary just given is largely negative, but all is not lost. There are two ways forward, which jointly offer potential for preserving the strengths of the two approaches while avoiding the weaknesses. The first is simple: divide and conquer. The syntax-calls-the-shots approach can explain some patterns quite naturally, in ways which are beyond the scope of the discourse-calls-the-shots approach. So we should let syntax take care of those patterns. To give one example, there is some crosslinguistic variation with respect to the extraction patterns in (3)–(6). The most important variation concerns the availability of extraction from noninitial conjuncts that are interpreted as being part of a narrative, like (4). For instance, English allows this pattern, but French and German do not. A syntactic explanation of this difference will be sketched in Chapter 4, but it is unclear how this crosslinguistic difference could be pinned on an invariant fact about discourse structure, such as the availability of narration-like readings for VP coordination structures, which is common to all three languages.

The second way forward comes from examining the theoretical status of discourse relations. Lakoff treated the different interpretations of coordinate structures as unanalyzed primitives, but there have been attempts since then to look for a principled reason why these particular relations feature in the way that they do. Kehler (2002) attempted this, but we will conclude in Chapter 5 that his approach is incomplete. We develop an approach in Chapter 6 that we believe to be more promising. This approach takes SDRT's analysis of discourse relations (Asher 1993, Lascarides and Asher 1993, Asher 1999, Asher and Lascarides 2003, Asher and Vieu 2005, inter alia) and coordination (Txurruka 2003) to generate hypotheses about common properties of interpretations of coordinate structures, and information-structural differences between these interpretations. These information-structural differences motivate the different extraction patterns that Lakoff noticed, as well as many nuances that are beyond his, or Kehler's, approach.

In sum, the questions that motivate this monograph have been investigated from a number of angles, for over fifty years, but to our knowledge, no previous work offers a truly integrative perspective on these questions, covering syntax, semantics, discourse, and the relations between these domains. We hope to demonstrate that progress in this area requires this integrative perspective. Our attempt to synthesize work across these domains has made us confront critical opportunities for comparison among established current syntactic and semantic theories. It has also substantially sharpened previous research questions, and implied a novel research agenda.

1.3 Structure of the volume

The first two chapters lay out the empirical focus of the monograph more precisely. **Chapter 2** begins by searching for definitions of 'coordination' and 'coordinate structure'. Section 2.2 proposes a first pass, roughly following Chomsky (1957), based on the propositional connectives ∧ and ∨, with subsentential coordination being derived from sentential coordination by ellipsis. However, Section 2.3 reviews evidence that not all coordinate structures can be reduced to sentential, or propositional, coordination, for instance because 'group-forming' NP coordination does not have a propositional analog (*Mary and John hugged* is not derived from *#Mary hugged and John hugged*). This suggests that coordinate structures are not semantically uniform: some are interpreted in ways which can be paraphrased as propositional conjunction or disjunction, while others are interpreted as groups.

In response to this, Section 2.4 discusses a range of analyses of the morphosyntax of coordination, developed on grounds independent of extraction. However, this section fails to identify a clear morphosyntactic 'hallmark' of coordination: no necessary and sufficient properties for distinguishing coordinate structures are identified. This conclusion chimes with the semantic map proposed by Haspelmath (2004), in which a range of different coordinate structures may be distinguished within a language, and certain types of coordinate structure may shade into adverbial and compounding structures.

Chapter 3 introduces data on patterns of extraction from coordinate structures. It is sometimes suggested that the patterns, and particularly the Coordinate Structure Constraint introduced in Section 1.2, is just the kind of hallmark of coordinate structures that

Chapter 2 failed to identify. Section 3.2 gives a fuller introduction to the CSC, and Section 3.3 describes many documented classes of counterexamples, which problematize the notion that the CSC is a hallmark of coordinate structures. Section 3.4 aims to dispel the possible impression that the patterns described in this chapter relate specifically to *and* and similar lexical items in Western European languages. While a proper typological survey of the CSC and its exceptions is not possible at this time (in part because descriptive grammars typically do not address such issues at all, and certainly not in the necessary depth), we can nevertheless show that similar patterns hold across multiple conjunctions in several genetically and areally unrelated languages. Section 3.5 discusses the scope of the CSC and its counterexamples across A', A, and head movement. Finally, Section 3.6 introduces a particularly complex case, the **SLF** construction found in many languages, but most widely discussed with reference to German and Dutch. This construction involves the interaction of syntactic and interpretive phenomena, which are informative about the syntax and discourse semantics of coordinate structures. Although there is a large literature on this construction, it is often ignored in discussions of Lakoff-style effects, so we devote extra space to it here.

The survey in Chapter 3 suggests that almost all cases of asymmetric extraction are specifically from VP coordination. This entails that, in order to make sense of Lakoff's data and the challenge that the data pose, we need to strike a proper balance between the general validity of the CSC and the range of apparent counterexamples concentrated in the special case of VP conjunction. In turn, this raises a general question, discussed in Section 1.2 and articulated more fully in Section 3.8: what kind of explanation should we seek for these patterns? The CSC, as formulated by Ross, clearly contains more than a grain of truth, but is strictly falsified by the patterns discussed in the second half of Chapter 3. On the other hand, discourse-based accounts such as Lakoff's suffer from several shortcomings. The question, then, is: who (if anyone) calls the shots?

Chapters 4 and 5 discuss this question from the perspective of syntax and discourse, respectively. **Chapter 4** begins with a discussion of the desiderata for a syntactic account in Section 4.2, and a brief introduction to mainstream locality theory, the theoretical context for the CSC, in Section 4.3. The main point, articulated in Section 4.4, is that mainstream locality theory has 'moved away' from the CSC since Ross's thesis. The processes of unification and generalization of locality theory in Chomsky (1973, 1981) implied increasingly clearly that the CSC was different. In response to this, Section 4.5 discusses locality theories which aim to incorporate the CSC and derive it from more general principles.

This establishes a choice point. Chomskyan locality theory essentially ignores the CSC, but the theories discussed in Section 4.5 integrate the CSC so tightly with the foundations of locality theory that there is only limited scope for addressing counterexamples. Hence, we need a third way. Section 4.6 discusses one possibility in detail, namely the possibility of relating patterns of extraction from coordinate structures to patterns of extraction from adjunction structures. The leading idea in this approach is to capitalize on similarities between ATB extraction and **parasitic gaps**, the other major class of cases in which a single moved element corresponds to multiple gaps. The approach has had a rocky history, mainly because Postal (1993) gave a thorough account of the many *dis*similarities between ATB extraction and parasitic gaps. Our estimation is that Hornstein and Nunes (2002) provides the outline of a viable response to Postal's argument: parasitic gaps are more restricted than ATB extraction, and these additional restrictions are due to an additional syntactic factor superimposed on an essentially identical movement configuration. The rest of Section 4.6 develops further predictions of this conjuncts-as-adjuncts analysis. The broad outline of these predictions (a slight reformulation of ideas in Postal 1998) is that extraction from initial conjuncts should be syntactically unrestricted, while extraction from noninitial conjuncts in VP conjunction structures should be as restricted, crosslinguistically and intralinguistically, as extraction from VP adjuncts. We show in this section that those predictions have some validity, but leave a string of unanswered questions.

The upshot of Chapter 4 is that certain options within syntactic theory can predict patterns of extraction from coordinate structures with greater subtlety than Ross could, without resorting to treating extraction from coordinate structures as sui generis. However, this does not, in itself, constitute a response to Lakoff's challenge. In fact, the patterns described in Section 4.6 are strictly orthogonal to those described by Lakoff. That is, it is a syntactic fact that extraction from initial conjuncts is often easier than extraction from noninitial conjuncts, and that noninitial conjuncts (even when they allow extraction) behave like weak islands. On the other hand, if Lakoff (1986) is correct, it is a nonsyntactic fact that 'narration'-like coordinate structures allow extraction from noninitial conjuncts, while 'violated expectation' and 'result' allow only extraction from initial conjuncts. These two types of observation appear to have irreducibly different statuses, but they both pertain to the same set of empirical phenomena.

Chapter 5 investigates Lakoff's analysis on its own terms. The heart of the analysis is a series of correlations between discourse relations and patterns of extraction. In Section 5.2, we outline Kehler's (2002) taxonomy of discourse relations. This taxonomy is based on seminal work by Hobbs (1979, 1985, 1990), who extends David Hume's philosophical ideas about the association of ideas to natural language discourse. We also provide a brief glimpse of how the Hobbs/Kehler program—originally intended for AI research—has led to fruitful research in semantics and pragmatics. Subsequently, in Section 5.3, we consider Kehler's (2002) formal definitions of some well-studied discourse relations that are relevant to Lakoff's analysis, namely OCCASION, RESULT, VIOLATED EXPECTATION, PARALLEL, and BACKGROUND. We discuss the challenges and shortcomings of Kehler's (2002) definitions and provide a glimpse of steps that have been taken to address some of these challenges.

Against this background, Section 5.4 evaluates the fit between these independently defined discourse relations and patterns of extraction from coordinate structures. Our conclusion is that there is no real scope for analyzing discourse relations as direct causal factors explaining the different extraction patterns that Lakoff identifies. There are two reasons. The first is that Lakoff's correlations don't give any immediate way to explain why VP conjunction allows this range of interpretations, but not others. The second, and more challenging, is that once we have explicit and reasonable definitions of NARRATION and RESULT, it becomes apparent that these relations do not stand in opposition to each other. Rather, they stand in an entailment relation: RESULT is a special case of NARRATION. This drastically limits the scope for explaining Lakoff's patterns in these terms: if RESULT is a special case of NARRATION, how are we to explain the apparent fact that RESULT doesn't allow the same extraction patterns as NARRATION? We conclude that discourse relations in their own right could not explain Lakoff's correlations, even though those correlations were originally stated in terms of discourse relations.

In the light of this conclusion, **Chapter 6** develops a hypothesis mentioned briefly by Kehler (2002), namely that the distribution of **topics** mediates the relationship between discourse relations and extraction patterns, because only topics can be extracted from co-ordinate structures. Section 6.2 introduces, fleshes out, and critiques Kehler's hypothesis. The most important criticism is that Kehler overstates the role of topics. In some cases, particularly the examples with a 'narration' interpretation and extraction from a noninitial conjunct, topicality seems to drive patterns of extraction, but in most other cases, examples can be found where an element which is clearly not a topic can nonetheless extract.

This leads us to introduce SDRT, as a formal, integrated theory of discourse structure with well-developed analyses of discourse relations, topicality, and coordination. SDRT gives us the resources to state hypotheses about why topicality is important with some discourse relations, but not others.

In Section 6.3, we spell out the graph-theoretic basics that underlie SDRT's analysis of discourse structure, focusing on a property of discourse relations that is especially important: the distinction between **subordination** and **coordination**. Section 6.4 then introduces Txurruka's (2003) groundbreaking hypothesis that *and* is only compatible with coordinating discourse relations.

Next, in Section 6.5, we consider how logical forms of discourses are constructed according to SDRT, focusing on how discourse relations factor into the construction of topics, and a broadly similar object called a **common theme**. The crucial point is that some discourse relations create discourse units that stand in a particular structural relation to a (possibly implicit) discourse topic, and others give a particular structural status to the common theme, while still others have no explicit discourse topic or common theme.

With all of these elements in place, Section 6.6 considers the prospects of working out an SDRT-based analysis of extraction from coordinate structures, and Section 6.7 extends this analysis to coordinate structures with more than two conjuncts. In particular, we propose that there are four patterns to consider, corresponding to four classes of relation just described:

1. Subordinating relations cannot be expressed by coordinate structures in the first place;
2. discourse relations which refer in their semantics to a common theme require ATB movement in the syntax;
3. all other relations also permit asymmetric extraction from initial conjuncts;
4. discourse relations which stand in a structural relation to a discourse topic allow extraction of topical elements from noninitial conjuncts.

Chapter 7 rounds off the survey with an evaluation of the strengths and weaknesses of the different approaches surveyed, focusing on a comparison of syntactic analyses from Chapter 4 and the SDRT-based approach developed in Chapter 6. We also give a summary of the choice points and their interrelationships, and a series of open questions, intended as a stimulus to further research. The new SDRT-based approach to extraction from coordinate structures developed in Chapter 6 has implications for everything from the syntax of coordination through to the relationship between information structure and extraction. We think that it is a new way of stitching together pieces of syntactic and discourse-semantic analysis to give a promising unified whole. However, several questions need to be answered in future research before it can be properly evaluated. These include the following:

- What are the implications of this analysis for the rest of syntactic locality theory?
- What can we learn about the nature of islands from this approach?
- What is the bridging hypothesis linking information structure and patterns of movement?
- What are the possible loci of crosslinguistic variation of extraction, on this analysis?

1.4 What this volume is, and isn't

Although the empirical scope of the survey is narrower than those of many other surveys in the series, we believe that this is necessary in view of the theoretical breadth that the topic requires.

As surveys go, this one is quite opinionated. We have endeavored to do justice to the range of current theories of relevant areas of syntax and discourse semantics, as well as to the history of these ideas, but we have also chosen to focus on theoretical choices that, in our opinion, hold real descriptive advantages. There is a limited amount of original research in the survey, in the service of these opinions.

There are many things that this book is not a survey of. It is not a survey of:

- Coordination. Van Oirsouw (1987) is an excellent survey of the early work on the syntax of coordination, not yet surpassed in its coverage despite the significant advances in understanding since 1987. More recent monographs with a survey aspect include Zhang (2009), while Progovac (1998a,b) briefly surveys the range of then-current proposed coordinate structures, and Haspelmath (2004, 2007) are particularly useful as chapter-length typological overviews.
- Locality. Recent surveys of locality effects and locality theories include Rizzi (2013) and Boeckx (2012), as well as Chapter 2 of Truswell (2011).
- Information structure. Among others, the survey in this series by Erteschik-Shir (2007) is a comprehensive introduction to information structure and its interface with syntax.
- The relationship between competence and performance. There is a large body of work on sentence processing and island constraints (see many chapters in Goodluck and Rochemont 1992), and Harris (2011) has demonstrated that processing studies can help us understand the syntax and semantics of extraction from coordinate structures.
- Discourse structure. Zeevat (2011) and Jasinskaja and Karagjosova (2020) are excellent surveys of work on discourse relations, with the latter also discussing their impact on discourse structure. For an overview of discourse structure within SDRT, see Asher and Vieu (2005). For a basic guide to SDRT, see, e.g., Lascarides and Asher (2007), Altshuler and Schlöder (2019).

We will truncate discussions in all of these areas in order to keep our eye on the prize. We will see that some elegant and parsimonious current syntactic theories leave empirical holes that may be fillable by a discourse-semantic analysis of coordination. Discourse theorists, for their part, are just trying to develop theories of discourse structure, without paying particular attention to what syntactic theory would like it to do. How close can we get to a complete account just by joining the dots between bodies of research that don't typically interact enough? How well do the different theories articulate? Where are the gaps, and what are the prospects for filling those gaps? These are the questions that we *do* aim to cover.

Finally, there are several other putatively syntactic phenomena where similar questions arise, including gapping and other ellipsis phenomena, and other 'island' effects. Any of these in principle could have been chosen as the empirical domain for this survey. We hope that the approach we take here to joining the dots can inspire similar work in those other areas.

2

What is coordination?

2.1 Introduction

Ideally, a survey such as this one would begin with a clear definition of its object of study. However, the simplest definitions of coordination, whether morphosyntactic or semantic, very quickly prove to be unsatisfactory. Over the course of this chapter, our first-pass definitions are iteratively refined, and our understanding of the object of study becomes more subtle. Nevertheless, we do not settle on a definition.

In fact, by the end of this chapter, and even by the end of this monograph, we will not have an adequate definition of 'coordination' or 'coordinate structure', which is able at once to capture the full range of structures that we would expect to fall under that definition, and exclude structures like adverbial modification and compounding, which share some properties with coordination but are normally excluded from the class of coordinate structures.

It is easy enough, however, to give an informal characterization of the object of study. We are interested in aspects of the syntactic and semantic behavior of forms like English *and* and *or*. These are often given as natural-language translations of the propositional logic connectives, with the former translated as ∧, and the latter as ∨. A natural initial hypothesis is therefore that coordination is a syntactic relation that corresponds to propositional ∧ or ∨. Section 2.2 elaborates on this initial hypothesis, including some preliminary discussion of *but*, which (like *and*) is often translated as ∧.

The simplicity of this hypothesis makes it straightforward to identify its limitations. Those limitations include the following:

- Lexical items like *and* and *or* need not relate propositions.
- When such lexical items do relate propositions, the interpretation is not always particularly close to that of ∧ or ∨.
- The basis for grouping *and* and *or* as a natural class, to the exclusion of other functional elements, is not clear, requiring further justification.

Section 2.3 elaborates on those limitations. An analytical choice arises already at this point, between building more elaborate syntactic and semantic structures on the foundation of ∧ and ∨, or considering analyses that have quite distinct logical properties.

Section 2.4 summarizes major proposals concerning the syntax of coordinate structures. Section 2.4.1 covers analyses which are more or less symmetrical, in that each conjunct has approximately the same status vis-à-vis the whole coordinate structure. An important point that emerges in this section is the diversity of coordinate structures. This was emphasized within English by Gazdar et al. (1985), and from a typological perspective by Haspelmath

Coordination and the Syntax–Discourse Interface. Daniel Altshuler and Robert Truswell, Oxford University Press.
© Daniel Altshuler and Robert Truswell (2022). DOI: 10.1093/oso/9780198804239.003.0002

(2004, 2007). Section 2.4.2 motivates an approach which includes both base-generation of subsentential coordinate structures and derivation of subsentential coordinate structures from sentential coordination by ellipsis. Finally, Section 2.4.3 discusses asymmetrical analyses of coordination, in which the conjuncts have different phrase-structural status (for instance, as specifier and complement, or in an adjunction relation). An interesting property of these approaches is that they tend to be reductionist. In particular, they integrate coordinate structures into the core of X'-theoretic phrase structure. We will see that some such approaches are quite promising and far-reaching: if the properties of coordination were reducible to the properties of, say, adjunction, we would have the germ of an argument that coordination is not a natural syntactic class, but diverse, with some coordinate structures being reducible to noncoordinate structures.

The conclusion of this chapter is therefore negative: we learn a lot about the properties of certain coordinate structures, but even as we do, the monolithic notion of 'coordinate structure' begins to fragment.

2.2 *And*, ∧, and conjunction reduction

The simplest hypothesis about the semantics of coordination can be found in propositional logic. The basic elements of propositional logic are a set of elementary propositions, and a set of **connectives**, ∧, ∨, →, and ¬. We can define the set of well-formed expressions of propositional logic as follows.

(1) a. Any elementary proposition P is a well-formed expression of propositional logic.
    b. If P and Q are well-formed expressions of propositional logic, then:
       (i) $(P \wedge Q)$, $(P \vee Q)$, and $(P \rightarrow Q)$ are well-formed expressions of propositional logic.
      (ii) $(\neg P)$ is a well-formed expression of propositional logic.

We now define a semantics to accompany the syntax. We assume that the truth value of an elementary proposition is given, and provide rules for recursively determining the truth value of a complex proposition on the basis of its internal structure:

(2) a. If P is true and Q is true, then $(P \wedge Q)$ is true. Otherwise $(P \wedge Q)$ is false.
    b. If P is false and Q is false, then $(P \vee Q)$ is false. Otherwise $(P \vee Q)$ is true.
    c. If P is true and Q is false, then $(P \rightarrow Q)$ is false. Otherwise $(P \rightarrow Q)$ is true.
    d. If P is true then $(\neg P)$ is false. Otherwise $(\neg P)$ is true.

There are approximate English translations for each of these connectives. *And* behaves roughly like ∧: (3a) is true iff (3b) and (3c) are independently true.

(3) a. Horses fear unicorns and dogs adore goldfish.
    b. Horses fear unicorns.
    c. Dogs adore goldfish.

(Either…) or is a crude approximation of ∨: (4a) is false if both (4b) and (4c) are false, but true if one of (4b) and (4c) is true.

(4)   a.   Either horses fear unicorns or dogs adore goldfish.
        b.   Horses fear unicorns.
        c.   Dogs adore goldfish.

People are often reluctant to admit that (4a) is true if *both* (4b) and (4c) are true, but that may be explained away as a pragmatic phenomenon: in contexts where both (4b) and (4c) are true, the more informative (3a) is typically preferred over (4a). Because of examples like (5), the use of *or* is still taken to yield a true sentence where both (4b) and (4c) are true.

(5)   If horses fear unicorns or dogs adore goldfish, I win the bet. In fact, horses fear unicorns *and* dogs adore goldfish, so I win easily.

$(P \rightarrow Q)$ corresponds roughly to *if… then*, although here, the correspondence is quite imprecise. While (6a) is certainly false if (6b) is true and (6c) is false, the truth of (6b) and (6c) is felt to be insufficient to guarantee the truth of (6a). Moreover, if (6b) is false then bets are off.

(6)   a.   If horses fear unicorns then dogs adore goldfish.
        b.   Horses fear unicorns.
        c.   Dogs adore goldfish.

Instead, *if P then Q* implies some causal or other relation between *P* and *Q* beyond the contingent fact of the truth or falsity of those propositions, which is all that → relies on. Still, → as a model of *if… then* is the best that propositional logic can do.

   Finally, $(\neg P)$ corresponds to *not*, or slightly more long-windedly, *it is not the case that*: if (7a) is true then (7b) is false, and vice versa.

(7)   a.   It is not the case that horses fear unicorns.
        b.   Horses fear unicorns.

Among these four connectives, only ∧ and ∨ are **binary** (they take two arguments) and **symmetrical** (switching the two arguments does not affect truth conditions). If $P \wedge Q$ is true, then so is $Q \wedge P$, and the same goes for $P \vee Q$ and $P \vee Q$. In contrast, it is possible for $P \rightarrow Q$ to be true, but $Q \rightarrow P$ to be false (specifically, if P is false but Q is true).

   At least at first sight, these properties appear to be shared by their approximate natural language equivalents: (8a) and (8b) are truth-conditionally identical, as are (9a) and (9b), but the same is not the case for (10a) and (10b).

(8)   a.   Horses fear unicorns and dogs adore goldfish.
        b.   Dogs adore goldfish and horses fear unicorns.

(9)   a.   Either horses fear unicorns or dogs adore goldfish.
        b.   Either dogs adore goldfish or horses fear unicorns.

(10)   a.   If horses fear unicorns then dogs adore goldfish.
         b.   If dogs adore goldfish then horses fear unicorns.

Building on this insight, (11) is a first-pass characterization of coordination. As we shall see, the reference to 'symmetry' will be a recurring point of discussion for the syntax and semantics of coordination in what follows.[1]

(11)   **What is coordination?** (First pass)
    a. A **coordinating conjunction** is a natural language expression that denotes one of the symmetrical propositional connectives ∧ or ∨.
    b. **Coordination** is the relationship between a coordinating conjunction and its arguments.
    c. A **coordinate structure** is a syntactic structure interpreted as a coordination.

In addition to *and* and *or*, a third English word which meets this definition is *but*. Like *and*, *P but Q* requires that both of its conjuncts be true. The examples in (12) differ from equivalent examples with *and* not so much in terms of their truth conditions, but in terms of an implication that the two conjuncts contrast, in a sense that we will make more precise in Chapter 6.[2]

(12)   a. Horses fear unicorns but dogs adore goldfish.
    b. Dogs adore goldfish but horses fear unicorns.

Now consider the mini-discourses in (13), which appear to be truth-conditionally equivalent to the sentences in (8).

(13)   a. Horses fear unicorns. Dogs adore goldfish.
    b. Dogs adore goldfish. Horses fear unicorns.

One possible way of explaining this observation is to assume a Ø-coordinator (truth-conditionally equivalent to *and*) relating the sentences in (13). However, we will reject this move, because it is unlikely that intersentential (discourse) semantic relations can be adequately modeled using ∧ in the general case, and we don't want to build a whole family of null intersentential connectives. We will put aside the nature and extent of the similarity between (8) and (13) until Chapters 5 and 6.

In some cases, we might be able to extend the characterization above to cover the interpretation of words like *and* or *or* when they relate subsentential constituents, as in (14), or even nonconstituents, as in (15).

(14)   a. Mary [$_{VP}$ [$_{VP}$ laughed] and [$_{VP}$ cried]].
    b. [$_{NP}$ [$_{NP}$ John] and [$_{NP}$ Mary]] jumped.

(15)   I gave [[a policeman a flower] and [a rioter a donut]].

This was in fact assumed in the earliest generative work on coordination, such as Chomsky (1957) and Gleitman (1965). The broad idea, often referred to as **conjunction reduction**,

---

[1] It is also a central element of Haspelmath (2004) typologically oriented characterization of coordinating constructions.

[2] We will see presently that *but* is also syntactically distinct from *and*, in that it is limited to two conjuncts (*She swore, screamed, but apologized*), and cannot directly conjoin NPs (*John but Mary came*).

is that the sentences in (14) and (15) can be derived from their equivalents with sentential coordination by deletion of material repeated across conjuncts.[3]

Following Partee and Rooth (1983), the connective-based approach to coordination can be extended to cases like (14) if the subsentential coordinations they contain can be related to propositional coordination.

(16)   a. *Mary laughed and cried* is true iff *Mary laughed* is true and *Mary cried* is true.
       b. *John and Mary jumped* is true iff *John jumped* is true and *Mary jumped* is true.

The procedure is recursive: in (16), the semantics of coordinated 1-place predicates is related to the semantics of coordinated propositions. In the same way, the semantics of coordinated 2-place predicates can be related to the semantics of coordinated 1-place predicates. Partee and Rooth give a general truth-conditional treatment for conjunction of types 'ending in t' (that is, propositions of type t, 1-place predicates of type $\langle e, t \rangle$, 2-place predicates of type $\langle e, \langle e, t \rangle \rangle$, modifiers of type $\langle \langle e, t \rangle, \langle e, t \rangle \rangle$, etc.), ultimately in terms of propositional coordination.

A challenge for the procedure just noted comes from 'nonconstituent' coordination in examples like (15). One must determine how those strings behave like constituents of types 'ending in t'. In fact, the relevant strings are predicted to be constituents on any syntactic theory adopting the VP-shell structure of Larson (1988). However, **Combinatory Categorial Grammar**, or CCG (Steedman 1985, 2000), goes much further in this direction, and treats essentially any coordinatable strings as constituents. In other words, compared to classical generative grammar, CCG takes very seriously the idea that coordination is a constituency test. This leads not only to the conclusion that 'a policeman a flower' and 'a rioter a donut' in (15) are constituents, but also that: (i) subject and verb form a (base-generated) constituent to the exclusion of the object in **Right Node Raising** constructions like (17), and even (ii) subject and object form a constituent to the exclusion of the verb in **Gapping** structures like (18) (which Steedman 1990 analyzes, in essence, as coordination of subject–object clusters in the scope of a single verb).

(17)   [[Mary likes], but [John detests]], donuts.

(18)   [[Mary likes donuts], and [John, gruel]].

The virtues of the conjunction reduction approach to the syntax and semantics of coordination are simplicity and explicitness. However, it is universally accepted that ∧ and ∨, and sentential coordination, do not exhaust the empirical terrain of coordination. The next section describes two problems for this propositional approach. The first concerns **collective** predicates, which show straightforwardly that coordination is not just propositional. The second comes from asymmetric interpretations of *and*. Here, the analysis is more nuanced, and will occupy us for much of this survey.

---

[3] In the early generative literature, this deletion operation bore several different names, and indeed 'conjunction reduction' referred to different operations in different works. The use of this term for this kind of analysis appears to have stabilized by the late 1970s.

2.3 Limitations of ∧ and ∨

Section 2.2 has shown the scope of a propositional analysis of the semantics of coordination, including coordination of subsentential constituents of types 'ending in *t*'. For all its virtues, this analysis is clearly incomplete (see already an appendix in Partee and Rooth 1983). Something more is needed for (19), where the most salient reading is that there is a single event of Mary and John hugging each other.

(19)   Mary and John hugged.

This is truth-conditionally distinct from (20): if (20) is interpretable at all, it probably means something like *Mary hugged the individual in question and John also hugged that individual.*

(20)   #Mary hugged and John hugged.

This is a straightforward indication that *and* does not just denote ∧, and that the semantics of noun phrase coordination need not, or even cannot be derived from ∧. In other words, coordination of individual-denoting noun phrases works differently from Partee and Rooth's schema for coordination of types 'ending in *t*'. *And* in (19) is often described as a 'group-forming' operator: *Mary and John* denotes the group composed of the individuals Mary and John (the group itself may still be an individual, if one adopts the approach of Link 1983, but that is not our concern here). This group is capable of acting as the argument to a collective predicate, like other group-denoting NPs:

(21)   The team hugged.

Earlier arguments, aiming to demonstrate the insufficiency of conjunction reduction as a general theory of the syntax of coordination, reinforce this conclusion (see Lakoff and Peters 1967, and Dougherty 1970a,b for a summary of related work). Those arguments revolved around interpretive differences like those between (22a) and (22b), or (23a) and (23b) (the latter pair attributed to Chomsky).

(22)   a. Mary and John are in love.
        b. Mary is in love with John.   (Dougherty 1970a: 858)

(23)   a. The drunk and the lamppost embraced.
        b. The drunk embraced the lamppost.

Despite the ingenuity of many syntactic analyses of such pairs, no analysis proved capable in the general case of reducing the (a)-sentences (with coordinate structures) to conjunction of sentences like the (b)-sentences (without coordinate structures); see Dong (1971) for discussion. Once again, this leads to the conclusion that (22a) and (23a) are genuine instances of NP coordination, not reduced sentential coordination.

In fact, further arguments against conjunction reduction motivate direct (unreduced) coordination of VPs, as well as sentences and NPs. For instance, it is not viable to analyze (24a) as derived from (24b) by ellipsis, because the two sentences are truth-conditionally distinct: if someone sang and someone else danced, then (24a) may be true, but (24b) is false.

(24)   a. No one sang and danced.
      b. No one sang and no one danced.

Even without (for now) venturing an opinion about the semantics of VP coordination in (24a),[4] the immediate implication of these facts should be clear: a general definition of 'coordinate structure' cannot be built on propositional connectives like $\wedge$ and $\vee$, because not all coordinate structures have denotations derivable from such formulae of propositional logic.

    A different challenge comes from cases where *and* has uses that go beyond the meaning usually assigned to Boolean conjunction. One of the most often-discussed differences concerns the fact that whereas logical conjunction is a symmetrical operation, natural language *and* has certain **asymmetric** uses, such as (25).

(25)   a. I started to type and the power went off.
      b. The lights were off and I couldn't see.   (Bar-Lev and Palacas 1980)

In these examples, the order of the clauses affects the interpretation: although both (25a) and (26) require both of their conjuncts to be true, (25a) and (26) are judged to be true in different situations, a defining property of an asymmetric interpretation.

(26)   The power went off and I started to type.

In this respect, *and* is like *but* (see (12)), and in fact asymmetric uses of *or* can also be found, as in (27). (27a) is naturally interpreted as a threat (this use was labeled as 'threat-*or*' by Culicover and Jackendoff 1997). The threat can seem asymmetric because it can be paraphrased as a conditional: *If you don't return the money then I call the cops.* In contrast, (27b) lacks such a salient asymmetric interpretation.

(27)   a. You return the money or I call the cops.
      b. I call the cops or you return the money.

Faced with asymmetric uses of all three coordinating conjunctions, researchers have adopted two general strategies. We illustrate these here with respect to *and*, the most widely discussed of the three (see Posner 1980), but similar considerations apply to the others.

    The first approach is the **meaning-minimalist** strategy (Grice 1975, Gazdar 1979, Kempson 1975, Schmerling 1975, Schriffin 1986, Carston 1993, Blakemore and Carston

---

[4] We are being deliberately evasive here, because a more complex analysis using propositional coordination can handle (24a), and is in fact widely assumed. This involves quantifier raising of *no one* from both conjuncts, to derive a logical form like $\neg \exists x.\,(\text{person}'(x) \wedge x \text{ sang} \wedge x \text{ danced})$. It will become clear that this isn't a viable complete analysis of VP coordination, but for now, this QR-based analysis could be seen as a reason to rephrase the lesson from (24): (24a) and (24b) must mean different things, so some constraint must prevent the derivation of (24a) from (24b) by ellipsis of *no one*. On any account which treats sentential coordination as basic, the necessity of that constraint is surprising.

2005). This strategy works by claiming that the meaning of *and* is symmetrical logical conjunction, but pragmatic principles allow the derivation of the asymmetric use. In contrast, according to the **meaning-maximalist** strategy (most notably Bar-Lev and Palacas 1980), *and* has a rich lexical meaning, including various temporal and causal relations, but under appropriate circumstances may also be interpreted as logical conjunction. Chapter 3 will discuss correlations between asymmetric interpretations and asymmetric extraction patterns, and Chapter 6 will return to the tension between these two strategies. For this chapter, the simple point is that it is not automatically the case that any coordinating conjunction unambiguously denotes a symmetrical propositional connective.

2.4 The syntax of coordination

2.4.1 Ross and GPSG

The discussion in the previous section suggests that there may be no unified semantic characterization of coordination. Coordinate structures sometimes correspond to propositional relations like conjunction or disjunction in the semantics. Coordinate structures may also correspond to group-formation, and perhaps to other relations, e.g. in VP coordination. It is not clear that there is any semantic unity to these different relations.

Consequently, it is natural to turn to morphosyntax to look for a unified definition of coordinate structures. Introductory syntax classes frequently tell students that there is something syntactically distinctive about coordination: take multiple phrases of the same category, add in a conjunction, and you get a larger phrase of the same category. Other pieces of syntactic structure don't (or at least, don't often) work this way, and this is what licenses the use of coordination as a constituency test (Chomsky 1957: Ch. 5).[5]

That distinctive syntactic property of coordination suggests a first-pass syntactic structure for coordination where the mother (the coordinate structure) has the same category as at least two daughters (the conjuncts), with conjunctions appearing at designated positions between the conjuncts, as in (28), where '(Conj)' represents places where we may or may not find conjunctions.

(28)

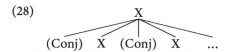

For English binary sentential conjunction (the first case we discussed in this chapter), this structure would be fleshed out as in (29).

(29)

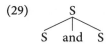

---

[5] Coordination is also known to give quite different results from other constituency tests. We won't worry about this, as the first-pass structure we're developing here will soon be superseded anyway.

For cases with more than two conjuncts, the structure in (29) could be generalized to (30a). This would cover sentences like (30b), which contains one or more *ands*.[6]

(30)   a.

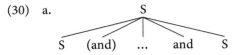

   b.   Horses fear unicorns, (and) dogs adore goldfish, and cats hate people.

Likewise, group-forming NP coordination is symmetrical in the same sense, so we could represent group-forming NP coordination as in (31).

(31)

One initially attractive property of these structures is that they are symmetrical: all conjuncts have equal status with respect to hierarchical relations such as c-command. This could be argued to reflect the fact that Boolean ∧ is symmetrical, and also that all conjuncts have equal status with respect to a worked-out semantics of group-formation. This kind of reasoning motivates the LFG analysis of coordination (Kaplan and Maxwell 1988, Peterson 2004), for instance, where conjuncts all feature equally as members of a set.

However, we have just seen that there is no English coordinating conjunction which always projects a fully semantically symmetrical semantic structure, and there are also morphological, prosodic, and syntactic asymmetries among conjuncts in coordinate structures. In fact, Haspelmath (2007: 9) goes so far as to state that 'monosyndetic coordination appears to be universally asymmetric'. It is therefore no surprise that all current syntactic theories that we are aware of have rejected a fully symmetrical structure for coordination.

Evidence against the symmetrical structure above was first presented by Ross (1967), who argued that *and* forms a phonological and syntactic unit with the following conjunct, to the exclusion of the preceding conjunct. He gave several pieces of suggestive evidence in favor of this conclusion. The first was the sentence boundary in (32): *and* can be sentence-initial, but not sentence-final.

(32)   a.   John left. And he didn't even say goodbye.
   b.   *John left and. He didn't even say goodbye.   (Ross 1967: 163)

Secondly, clitic coordinators like Latin *-que* can occur within a final conjunct, as in (33), but not within an initial conjunct.

(33)   vitam   salutemque
   life   safety-and
   'the life and safety'   (Cicero, Divinatio against Quintus Caecilius, 1.3)

---

[6] The propositional connectives corresponding to coordinate structures are only defined for pairs of propositions. However, it would be straightforward to define extensions of ∧ and ∨ for arbitrarily large sets of propositions: for a set of propositions $\mathcal{P} = \{P_1, ..., P_n\}$, $\wedge(\mathcal{P}) = T$ iff every $P \in \mathcal{P} = T$, and $\vee(\mathcal{P}) = F$ iff every $P \in \mathcal{P} = F$. A semantics for coordination along these lines is assumed in Gazdar (1981). Similar considerations would apply to group-forming *and*, discussed in Section 2.3.

Thirdly, *and* can introduce a parenthentical appositive clause, but cannot be stranded by one. That is, (34a) and (34b) are both grammatical and approximately semantically equivalent, while (34c) is ungrammatical.

(34) a. Even Harold failed, and he is the smartest boy in our class.
      b. Even Harold, and he is the smartest boy in our class, failed.   (Ross 1967: 164)
      c. *Even Harold, he is the smartest boy in our class, failed and.

Finally, the prosodic grouping of multiple coordination in English can indicate association of *and* with following, but not preceding, conjuncts.

(35) a. ((Tom) (and Dick) (and Harry)) all love watermelon.
      b. *((Tom and) (Dick and) (Harry)) all love watermelon.   (Ross 1967: 164–5)

Ross (citing joint work with Lakoff) proposed a deep structure of the form $[_S \text{CONJ } S^n]$, where $n \geq 2$ (p. 165), followed by a transformational derivation in which the conjunction is Chomsky-adjoined to each conjunct, and then deleted according to language-particular rules. This has the effect of grouping *and* with following, rather than preceding, conjuncts, as required. This was clearly intended as a general treatment for coordinate structures.

   Elements of Ross's treatment can be discerned in the analysis of coordination in Gazdar (1981). Gazdar proposed the two rules in (36), where the first member of the triple is an index, the second member states that a certain local configuration of categories is admissible, and the third member indicates the compositional combination of the denotations of elements of the second member. The subscript $[\beta]$ in (36a) is essentially a diacritic feature on α, whose value ranges over *and*, *or*, etc. This diacritic is then spelled out by the rule in (36b).

(36) a. $\langle 2, [_\alpha \, \alpha_1, ..., \alpha_n], \beta'(\alpha_1', ..., \alpha_n') \rangle$
          $_{[\beta]}$
      b. $\langle 3, [_\alpha \, \beta \, \alpha], \alpha' \rangle$
          $_{[\beta]}$

These two rules jointly generate structures like those in (37).

(37) a.

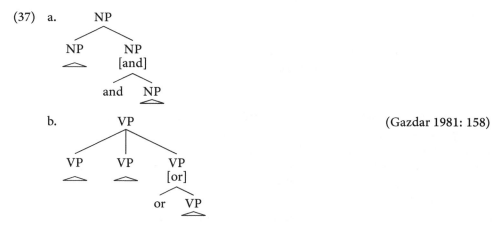

(Gazdar 1981: 158)

In these structures, the coordinating conjunction is adjoined to the final conjunct. However, the denotation of the coordinating conjunction is an operator which takes the conjuncts as arguments, as described in footnote 6. This approach imposes a semantic symmetry, in keeping with the meaning-minimalist approach, while incorporating the morphosyntactic and phonological asymmetries that Ross observed.

The rules in (36) were intended as general-purpose rules for building English coordinate structures. However, there is clearly a large amount of low-level variation in the morphosyntax of specific coordinate structures, even within English. Two dimensions of variation were discussed in later work in Generalized Phrase Structure Grammar (Gazdar et al. 1985, Sag et al. 1985, Klein and Sag 1985). The first is that some 'iterating' coordinate structures allow arbitrarily many conjuncts, while other 'binomial' coordinate structures allow precisely two. The binomial coordinate structures in English include those generated by *but*, and those generated by pairs of correlative conjunctions such as *both ... and* or *either ... or*. Gazdar et al. claim that binomial and iterating coordination are the only attested possibilities: there is no strictly ternary coordination in any natural language, for instance.

(38)   a.   The director made a speech but made no sense.
       b.   *The director gathered her thoughts, made a speech, but made no sense.

(39)   a.   She either solved the problem or asked for help.
       b.   *She either solved the problem, asked for help, or refused to participate.

The other dimension of variation, mentioned briefly in Gazdar et al. (1985) but developed more fully in typological work by Haspelmath (2004, 2007), is that certain coordinating conjunctions can only conjoin certain categories. In English, *and* and *or* are very flexible in the categories that they conjoin: although the full extent of this flexibility depends on the extent to which we rely on ellipsis in our analyses of coordinate structures, we have seen evidence (in the previous section) that these coordinating conjunctions conjoin clauses, NPs, and probably VPs. Gazdar et al., and Sag et al. (1985), make a convincing argument that *and* can also coordinate less traditional syntactic categories such as 'predicate' (see Bruening and Al Khalaf 2020 for more nuanced recent discussion). The argument concerns the contrast in (40).

(40)   a.   His father ... was [[$_{AP}$ well known to the police] and [$_{NP}$ a devout catholic]].
                                                          (credited to Monty Python)
       b.   *The [[well known] and [a catholic]] man was my father.
       c.   *Soon [[well known] and [a catholic]] started shouting again.
                                                          (Gazdar et al. 1985: 174–5)

(40a) involves coordination of unlike categories, an AP and an NP. This is surprising in itself, given the considerations mentioned at the start of this section. Perhaps more surprisingly, this coordinate structure does not have the distribution of an AP or an NP: it is ungrammatical in (40b), in a context which accepts APs, and in (40c), in a context which accepts NPs. Gazdar et al.'s analysis of this is that the category of the coordinate structure in (40a) is PRED, a feature common to the predicative uses of AP and NP. This category is licit in postcopular position but not the other two positions, because the postcopular position selects for a predicate but not for a more specific syntactic category. This analysis serves as an indirect argument that *and* is very permissive in the categories it can conjoin.

Even in English, though, according to Gazdar et al. (fn. 9, p. 180), other coordinating conjunctions are less permissive. *Both ... and ...* cannot conjoin sentences (see (41)), and *but* cannot conjoin NPs (see (42)). This indicates that we must be able to state restrictions on which conjunctions associate with which categories.

(41)   *Both Kim sang and Sandy danced.

(42)   *Kim but Sandy stuttered.

Haspelmath (2004, 2007) developed observations like these into a semantic map for co-ordination. He observes (2007: 20–1) that, if languages have two distinct coordinating conjunctions, they usually have one conjunction for NP coordination and another for 'event coordination' (S coordination or VP coordination in our terms). For instance, Korean has *-kwa* for NP coordination and *-ko* for event coordination, and Turkish has *-la* and *-ıp* respectively for these two functions. However, some languages make further distinctions, such as Somali, which uses *iyo* for NP coordination, *oo* for VP coordination, and *-na* for clausal coordination, as in (43).

(43)   a. rooti   iyo   khudrat
           bread   and   fruit
           'bread and fruit'
        b. Suuqa   tag   oo   soo   iibi   rooti.
           market   go   and   ANDAT buy   bread
           'Go to the market and buy bread!'
        c. Carrur-ti   waxay   joogaan   dugsi-ga   waxay-na   bartaan
           children-ART   3PL.FOC   be   school-ART   3PL.FOC-and   learn
           Ah-Soomaali.
           language-Somali
           'The children are in school, and they learn Somali.'   (Haspelmath 2007: 21)

Haspelmath (2004) also mentions Xârâcùù, a language of New Caledonia, in which NP coordination and VP coordination use a different morpheme from that used in sentential coordination, as in (44).

(44)   a. gu   mê   gè
           2SG   and   1SG
           'you and I'
        b. Ru   cha   mê   mara.
           3DU   clear.bush   and   work.in.fields
           'They cleared the bush and worked in the fields.'
        c. È   nä   fädë   nä   è   nä   bare   tèpe.
           3SG   IPFV   walk   and   3SG   IPFV   also   talk.
           'He speaks as he is walking.'   (Haspelmath 2004)

In addition to cases which demonstrate an interrelationship between the morphosyntax of the coordinate structure and the choice of conjunction, there are cases in which the semantic relation between conjuncts affects the syntax of the coordinate structure. An example of this is the distinction between what Wälchli (2005) calls **natural** and **accidental coordination**, where in natural coordination 'the parts express semantically closely associated concepts' (Wälchli 2005: 1). In many languages there is some formal distinction between these two cases; an extreme example is Malagasy, which has different coordinate structures for natural coordination (see (45a)) and accidental coordination (in (45b)).[7]

(45) a. ny   ray   aman-dreny
      DEF   father   CONJ-mother
      'father and mother'
    b. ny   lehilahy   sy   ny   vehivahy
      DEF   man   and   DEF   woman
      'men and women'   (Wälchli 2005: 47)

In other cases, the internal syntax of natural and accidental coordination may be identical, but the two coordination types may participate in different external morphosyntactic relations. For instance, in Finnish (Dalrymple and Nikolaeva 2006), a plural adjective is allowed with naturally, but not accidentally, coordinated singular nouns (compare (46a) and (46b)).

(46) a. Iloiset   [mies   ja   poika]   lähtivät   yhdessä   käsi   kädessä.
      happy.PL   man   and   boy   left.3PL   together hand   hand.INESS
      'The happy man and boy left together hand in hand.'
    b. *Han   osti   uudet   [talon   ja   auton].
      he   bought.3SG   new.ACC.PL   house.ACC   and   car.ACC
      'He bought a new house and car.'   (Dalrymple and Nikolaeva 2006: 825)

Wälchli is particularly interested in 'co-compounds' (more commonly called '*dvandva* compounds') as a means of expressing natural coordination. Co-compounds expressing natural coordination are not limited to coordination of Ns or NPs. (47) gives an example of a verbal co-compound expressing a natural coordination relation, from Erźa Mordvin.

(47) At'a-ś   kil'd-ś-povod-ś   alaša.
    old.man-DEF   harness-3SG.PST-bridle-3SG.PST   horse
    'The old man harnessed and bridled the horse.'   (Wälchli 2005: 1)

All of these morphosyntactically specialized coordinate structures constitute further evidence, complementing the semantic evidence from (24) in the previous section, that there may be many distinct coordinate structures in a language, beyond the basic cases of sentential coordination and NP coordination.

2.4.2 Ellipsis in coordinate structures

The possibility that base-generated coordinate structures may belong to several different categories suggests that coordinate structures may often be ambiguous: what looks on the

---

[7] Of course, men and women, as in (45b), are a prime example of a natural coordination. The point is that in (45b), the *syntax* is not specific to natural coordination. In other words, in Malagasy there is one structure which is only used for natural coordination, and another which can be used for any coordination, natural or accidental. This is generally the case.

surface like VP coordination could be either genuine VP coordination or reduced sentential coordination; what looks on the surface like NP coordination could really be NP coordination, but could also be reduced S coordination or VP coordination. This possibility was largely dismissed in the GPSG literature, as part of the GPSG program was the elimination of null elements (including the output of ellipsis processes) from syntactic structure. However, clear arguments have been given for an operation of conjunction reduction, as a form of ellipsis.

For instance, Rögnvaldsson (1982) discusses cases like (48) in Icelandic, in which the case on the subject is determined uniquely by the case of the verb in the first conjunct, even when the verbs in the two conjuncts select different cases (this can still be seen in (48) by looking at the patterns of agreement on the verbs: nominative subjects trigger full agreement, while non-nominative subjects instead co-occur with default 3sg agreement). This is surprising if (48) is analyzed as VP coordination, but straightforward if (48) is analyzed as sentential coordination, with deletion of the subject of the second sentence under identity with that of the first sentence.[8]

(48) a. Þeir   sjá   stúlkuna   og   finnst   / *finnast   hún
          they.NOM see.3PL   girl.DEF   and   find.3SG   find.3PL   she.nom
          álitleg.
          attractive
          'They see the girl and find her attractive.'
      b. Þeim   líkar   maturinn   og   borða   / *borðar   mikið.
          them.DAT likes.3SG food.DEF   and   eat.3PL   eat.3SG   much
          'They like the food and eat much.'   (Rögnvaldsson 1982: 559–60)

Further arguments pointing to the same conclusion have accumulated in the more recent literature, starting with van Oirsouw (1987) and Wilder (1994). A very simple argument for the availability of ellipsis processes within coordinate structures comes from van Oirsouw, who pointed out that the existence of Gapping (illustrated in (49)) and nonconstituent coordination (in (50)) more or less forces the conclusion that ellipsis within sentential coordinate structures is possible.

(49)   [[John likes Bill], and [Fred, Sue]].

(50)   Mary spoke [[[$_{PP}$ to Sue] [$_{PP}$ on Wednesday]] and [[$_{PP}$ to Fred] [$_{PP}$ on Thursday]]].

If *Fred, Sue* in (49) or the strings of PPs in (50) cannot be base-generated as constituents, they must be derived by ellipsis from larger constituents, such as clauses in the case of Gapping, and clauses or VPs in the case of nonconstituent coordination.

A full nontransformational treatment of Gapping was arguably never developed within GPSG, although the GPSG literature frequently cites Stump (1978) in this context. The major challenge in this area comes from Ross's (1970a) demonstration of a relationship between order of subject, object, and verb, and direction of Gapping. Ross showed that English allows only forward Gapping, as in (51), while Russian allows forward or backward

---

[8] As van Oirsouw (1987) emphasizes, the notion of 'identity' here is slippery: clearly morphological distinctions such as that between nominative and dative are insufficient to block deletion under identity.

Gapping, depending on whether the object has been scrambled past the verb, as in (52). Strictly SOV Japanese allows only backward Gapping, as in (53).

(51)　a.　I ate fish, and Bill rice.
　　　b.　*I fish, and Bill ate rice.

(52)　a. Ja　pil　　vodu,　i　　Anna　vodku.
　　　　 I　 drank　water　and　Anna　vodka
　　　b. Ja　vodu,　i　　Anna　vodku　pila.
　　　　 I　 water　and　Anna　vodka　drank
　　　　　'I drank water, and Anna vodka.'　　　　　　　　　　(Ross 1970a: 251)

(53)　Watakusi-wa　sakana-o,　Biru-wa　gohan-o　tabeta.
　　　 I　　　　　　　fish　　　　Bill　　　rice　　　ate
　　　　'I ate fish, and Bill rice.'　　　　　　　　　　　　　(Ross 1970a: 251)

Ross's claim is that deletion under identity of material on left branches proceeds left-to-right (so the leftmost copy is not deleted—this is the forward Gapping pattern), while deletion of material on right branches proceeds right-to-left (so the rightmost copy remains—the backward Gapping pattern). Although the details of Ross's proposal were soon demonstrated to be inaccurate, the broader point behind Ross's analysis has been widely accepted: the operation of Gapping in a language can be predicted on the basis of other syntactic properties in that language. As a consequence, interpretive, postsyntactic theories of Gapping such as Stump's are doomed to miss a generalization.

Within GB and Minimalist syntactic theories, the conclusion that ellipsis is widespread within coordinate structures has been widely accepted (see, for instance, Johnson 2014). It follows from this conclusion that many coordinate structures are ambiguous between base-generation and ellipsis analyses. However, the CCG treatment of Gapping by Steedman (1990) offers an intriguing alternative, treating Gapping constructions essentially as coordination of argument clusters in the scope of a single verbal head. This results in a narrowly syntactic yet deletion-free approach to Gapping, a combination of properties that can't easily be matched in other theories. To our knowledge, a close comparison of the empirical predictions of the GB/Minimalist and CCG analyses of Gapping has not been undertaken, but clearly such a project would have real potential as an exercise in theory comparison.

2.4.3 Asymmetrical syntactic analyses

We consider the GPSG analysis as a **symmetrical** analysis of coordination, in the sense that each coordinated XP stands in the same relation to the coordinate structure as a whole (disregarding the diacritic on the final conjunct, which is subsequently spelled out as a conjunction). This approach contrasts with three prominent **asymmetrical** theories of the syntax of coordination, due to Zoerner (1995), Johannessen (1998), and Munn (1993). These analyses have long, and intertwined, histories: Johannessen's monograph is a revised version of her 1992 dissertation, while Munn's dissertation is itself related to several papers in the late 1980s, in which he adopted essentially Johannessen's proposed structure.

Zoerner's dissertation developed many similar arguments to Johannessen, apparently independently and slightly later. We focus on Johannessen and Munn next, except where Zoerner diverges significantly from Johannessen.

The Johannessen/Zoerner structure

The structure in (54) represents the analysis of coordination in Johannessen (1998) and Zoerner (1995). In it, two conjuncts appear as specifier and complement of a 'Conj' head (we use this label in preference to Munn's 'B', or 'Boolean' head).

(54)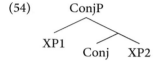

For constructions with more than two conjuncts, these authors suggest that one of the conjuncts is itself a ConjP, as in (55), a structure that Zoerner describes in terms analogous to those used by Larson (1988) in delineating his shell structures.

(55)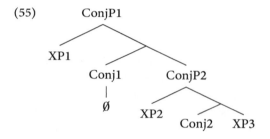

This differs from a symmetrical analysis in that some conjuncts have a different phrase-structural status from those of others (for instance, the first conjunct asymmetrically c-commands all the others; the first is a specifier while the others are contained with the complement). For Johannessen and Zoerner, working within the Minimalist Program, there is an immediate conceptual advantage to this analysis, because the symmetrical analysis developed in GPSG is incompatible with certain fundamental Minimalist assumptions about phrase structure, in particular with respect to projection and binary branching (Kayne 1994, Chomsky 1995). Johannessen and Zoerner's structure, in contrast, is identical to the structure of any other maximal projection.

Several empirical arguments have also been given in favor of an asymmetrical structure. A persuasive argument comes from the survey of agreement patterns in Dutch dialects by van Koppen (2005). Van Koppen's analysis rests on the following definitions of locality:

(56) **More local**

Y is more local to X than Z iff:
(i)   X c-commands both Y and Z;
(ii) the set of nodes that c-command Y is a proper subset of the set of nodes that c-command Z.

(57) **Equally local**

Y and Z are equally to X iff:

(i)   X c-commands both Y and Z;

(ii) the set of nodes that c-command Y is identical to the set of nodes that c-command Z.   (van Koppen 2005: 14–15)

According to these definitions, on an asymmetric structure like Johannessen and Zoerner's, the first conjunct is more local to a c-commanding head than the second conjunct, and, in fact, the first conjunct and the whole coordinate structure are equally local to a c-commanding head. In (58), only C c-commands ConjP and only C c-commands NP1, so ConjP and NP1 are equally local to C.[9] However, NP1 c-commands NP2, so NP1 and ConjP are both more local to C than NP2.

(58)

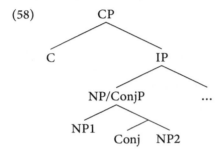

Van Koppen argues that Dutch complementizer agreement is constrained by locality: NP can only agree with C if there is no more local NP. But agreement with coordinated NPs is underdetermined by this constraint, because the first conjunct and the whole coordinate structure are equally local. Van Koppen argues that this is as it should be, and in fact agreement with either the whole coordinate structure or the first conjunct is attested.[10] For instance, (59a) shows first conjunct agreement in Tegelen Dutch (compare the agreement with the simple pronoun in (59b)).

(59) a. Ich dink de-s   doow   en   ich   ôs   treff-e.
        I   think that-2SG you.SG and   I   each.other meet-PL
        'I think that you and I will meet.'

     b. Ich dink de-s   doow   morge   kum-s.
        I   think that-2SG you.SG tomorrow come-2SG
        'I think that you will come tomorrow.'   (van Koppen 2005: 40)

Meanwhile, (60), from Lapscheure Dutch, shows full agreement with the coordinate structure: both conjuncts are singular, but the agreement is plural.

(60) Kpeinzen da-n   Valère en   Pol morgen   goa-n.
     I.think   that-3PL Valère and   Pol tomorrow go-PL
     'I think that Valère and Pol will go tomorrow.'   (van Koppen 2005: 48)

---

[9] This characterization of locality would make different predictions on other definitions of c-command, such as that of Kayne (1994).

[10] In fact, van Koppen argues that morphological competition, rather than locality, determines the precise agreement pattern in these cases, but this is irrelevant to our syntactic concerns.

Moreover, verbs also vary between first conjunct agreement and full agreement in VS orders, while they only permit full agreement in SV orders. In van Koppen's analysis, this is related to the fact that, in SV orders, the verb does not c-command the subject on the surface in SV orders.

Again on the assumption that c-command constrains agreement, all of this is out of reach of symmetrical structures for coordination, where van Koppen's definition of 'more local' would be inoperative because each conjunct c-commands the other. However, it is explained by an asymmetrical structure like Johannessen and Zoerner's.

Johannessen (1998) presents another argument from agreement patterns which aims to support her claim that the first conjunct is a specifier of ConjP and the second is a complement (this is a more specific claim than simply claiming that the first conjunct asymmetrically c-commands the second). Her argument concerns the phenomenon of **unbalanced coordination**, where only one of the conjuncts could grammatically take the place of the whole coordinate structure. Replacing the coordinate structure with any other conjunct would lead to ungrammaticality. Examples are in (61) and (62).

(61) a. Han   og   meg   var   sammen   om   det.
          he.NOM   and   me.ACC were   together about   it
          'He and I were in it together.'   (Norwegian)
      b. Han var sammen on det.
      c. *Meg var sammen om det.

(62) a. Půjdu   tam   já   a   ty.
          will.go.1SG there I   and   you
          'You and I will go there.'   (Czech)
      b. Půjdu tam já.
      c. *Půjdu tam ty.

Although the existence of unbalanced coordination was already reasonably well-known, Johannessen's key claims are that unbalanced coordination is ubiquitous in natural languages, and that it is possible to predict *which* conjunct would be the unbalanced one: in a head-initial language, it is the initial conjunct, and in a head-final language, it is the final conjunct. Johannessen explains this pattern by analyzing the two conjuncts as specifier and complement of the Conj head: the properties of the specifier determine the properties of the whole ConjP through Spec–head agreement, while the properties of the complement are able to differ.

Johannessen's structure also accommodates **extraordinary balanced conjunction**, where no individual conjunct can substitute for the whole coordinate structure, as in (63).

(63) a. Me and him will go.
      b. (i)   *Me will go.
          (ii)   *Him will go.

The essence of Johannessen's account of extraordinary balanced conjunction is that the coordinate structure is a projection of the conjunction, and there is scope for the ϕ-features of this phrase to diverge from the features of the individual conjuncts in specifier and complement. However, although it is clear that labeling the whole coordinate structure as a projection of the conjunction allows for divergence between properties of the conjuncts and properties of the whole, it is not clear that Johannessen's structure allows any kind of predictive account of extraordinary balanced conjunction.

Johannessen's analysis was the subject of a critique by Borsley (2005) which raises several serious challenges for her analysis. Borsley's criticisms apply equally to Zoerner (1995), as far as we can see (though see de Vries 2005 for a more skeptical evaluation of the scale of the challenge that Borsley poses). The most acute challenges target the assumptions that the conjunction is the head of the coordinate structure, and that iterated conjunction arises from treating a ConjP as an argument of a further conjunction. These assumptions entail that (64a) and (64b) are predicted to behave identically, as they both have the structure in (65), with the only difference being the presence or absence of *and* under the higher Conj head.

(64)   a. Hobbs and Rhodes and Barnes
       b. Hobbs, Rhodes, and Barnes

(65)

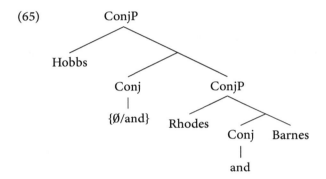

This prediction is not borne out: (64a) and (64b) behave differently in various respects. The first is with respect to *both*, which requires precisely two conjuncts. The sentences in (66) are acceptable if taken to range over, for example, the individual Hobbs and the group composed of Rhodes and Barnes in (66a).

(66)   a. both Hobbs, and Rhodes and Barnes
       b. both Hobbs and Rhodes, and Barnes

However, (67) is unacceptable even on such readings. This suggests that the structure underpinning (66) is not available in (67).

(67)   *both Hobbs, Rhodes, and Barnes

The sentences in (68) show a similar contrast with *respectively*, which enforces identity of cardinality between two sets (here denoted by *the two girls* and the coordinate structure). We can infer that *Hobbs and Rhodes and Barnes* can denote a two-member set, while *Hobbs, Rhodes, and Barnes* cannot.

(68)   a. The two girls were seen by Hobbs and Rhodes and Barnes, respectively.
       b. #The two girls were seen by Hobbs, Rhodes, and Barnes, respectively.

Finally, the contrast in (69) reveals a difference in behavior with respect to distributivity. (69a) can be used to describe four distinct situations: (i) each individual lifted the rock (the distributive interpretation), (ii) the three people lifted the rock together (the collective interpretation), (iii) Hobbs lifted the rock alone, and Rhodes and Barnes collectively, and (iv) Hobbs and Rhodes lifted the rock together but Barnes lifted it alone. In contrast, (69b) can only be used to describe (i) and (ii).

(69)   a. Hobbs and Rhodes and Barnes lifted the rock.
        b. Hobbs, Rhodes, and Barnes lifted the rock.

Our interpretation of these facts is as follows. It is similar to Borsley's, but with adjustments to take the findings of Schwarzschild (1992, 1996) into account. The patterns of distributive and collective interpretations in these pairs of examples reflect the prominence of certain (singular and plural) discourse referents in the discourse context. For instance, the interpretation of (69a) on which Hobbs lifted the rock alone, and Rhodes and Barnes lifted it together, requires those discourse referents (one that stands for Hobbs, and one that stands for Rhodes and Barnes) to be prominent. If this interpretation is readily available for (69a), but not for (69b), when the two examples are composed of the same lexical material, we should infer that a difference between the syntactic structures of these two sentences is responsible for this interpretive difference. This allows us to infer that the structure in (65) cannot be the correct structure for both coordinate structures.

Munn's structure
Munn (1993) proposed the asymmetric structure in (70), in which the conjunction takes the second conjunct as complement, producing a ConjP which adjoins to the first conjunct.[11]

(70)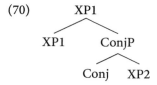

Munn suggests that further conjuncts are adjoined to the ConjP, as in (71).

(71)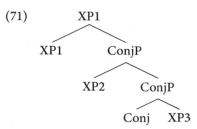

---

[11] Within the framework of Sign-Based Construction Grammar, Chaves (2012) proposes a similar structure which doesn't have a single distinguished head. We do not discuss Chaves's proposal at length because his proposal is quite incomplete with respect to the extraction patterns that will be our main focus. Moreover, it is unclear precisely what Chaves would propose to handle the different kinds of multiple coordination structure that we will discuss immediately below with reference to Borsley (2005).

This is an asymmetric structure in the same sense in which Johannessen's and Zoerner's structure is asymmetric: the first conjunct asymmetrically c-commands the second. Because this geometric asymmetry is all that is required to capture van Koppen's Dutch agreement data, Munn's analysis is equally capable of accounting for van Koppen's generalizations (although no one has accounted for all of van Koppen's data within Munn's framework, Munn 1999, 2000 argues for an analysis of first-conjunct agreement based on his structure for coordination). Moreover, Munn's structure escapes the worst of Borsley's criticisms of Johannessen, because on Munn's analysis, the two coordinate structures at issue have different structures, as illustrated in (72).

(72)   a.

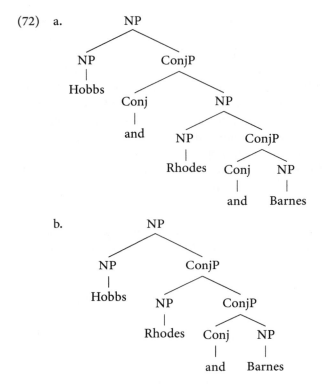

It is not immediately clear how to build a theory of the differences just listed on the basis of these syntactic differences, because it is not obvious how to interpret the structure in (72b) compositionally, but the fact remains that there *are* syntactic differences, which is sufficient to avoid the problematic prediction derived from Johannessen's and Zoerner's structure, that the two coordinate structures should behave identically.

Munn's structure cannot reproduce Johannessen's analysis of extraordinary balanced coordination.[12] In fact, though, Munn presents arguments which weigh against this analysis. He notes that no head selects for a ConjP, which is mysterious if the conjunction is the head

---

[12] Unbalanced coordination probably *can* be captured by Munn, at least in head-initial languages, as the noninitial conjuncts are adjuncts to the initial conjunct and therefore wouldn't usually determine agreement patterns.

of the coordinate structure. This is predicted by Munn, because the category of the first conjunct is identical to that of the whole coordinate structure, and ConjPs are unselected adjuncts. In short, each of the asymmetric analyses has strengths which are unmatched by those of the other, but our impression is the Munn's adjunction structure has more strengths, and is less compromised by Borsley's critique.

Munn also gave binding-theoretic arguments in favor of an asymmetric analysis, concerning Principle C (see (73)) and variable binding (see (74)).

(73)   a.   John$_i$'s dog and him$_i$ went for a walk.
       b.   *He$_i$ and John$_i$'s dog went for a walk.

(74)   a.   Every man$_i$ and his$_i$ dog went to mow a meadow.
       b.   *His$_i$ dog and every man$_i$ went to mow a meadow.

On approaches to binding based on c-command, as in theories deriving from Chomsky (1981), these pairs suggest that the first conjunct asymmetrically c-commands the second. For instance, (73a) suggests that the second conjunct does not c-command the first, because otherwise there would be a Principle C violation and the sentence would be ungrammatical. Munn claims that the ungrammaticality of (73b) follows from just such a violation. If this is correct (but we will return presently to an alternative analysis of (73b)), then the first conjunct must c-command the second. That would be sufficient to mandate an asymmetric analysis.

In fact, though, these arguments were convincingly challenged by Progovac (1998a). Progovac argues that the contrast in (73) follows not from Principle C, but from whatever pragmatic principles rule out the same pattern intersententially, as in (75).

(75)   *He$_i$ finally arrived. John$_i$'s dog went for a walk.   (Progovac 1998a: 3)

As for the variable-binding pattern in (74), Progovac agrees that this indicates that the quantifier occupies a position at LF from which it c-commands *his*, but that this does not reflect the surface position of the quantifier. Rather, Progovac claims that the quantifier raises to this position at LF, and that this operation of Quantifier Raising is possible out of the first conjunct but not the second, because QR out of the second conjunct would be an instance of Weak Crossover.[13] In other words, bound variable anaphora and Principle C are uninformative about the syntax of coordination, according to Progovac. This effectively nullifies Munn's binding-theoretic arguments for an asymmetric analysis.

Arguments against either asymmetric analysis
Borsley (2005) gave other arguments which apply equally to Munn (1993), Zoerner (1995), and Johannessen (1998). The most important arguments (for our purposes) bear on evidence that coordination isn't always phrasal, in contradiction to both asymmetric analyses.

---

[13] Essentially the same argument is presented in Neeleman and Tanaka (2020), building on Ruys (1992).

Borsley gives (76a) as an example, with the point being that this cannot be derived by deletion from the semantically anomalous (76b).

(76)   a.   Hobbs whistled and hummed the same tune.
       b.   #Hobbs whistled the same tune and hummed the same tune.

Borsley argues that this must instead be treated as a conjunction of heads, which on an asymmetric approach would lead to highly unusual trees such as those in (77).

(77)   a.

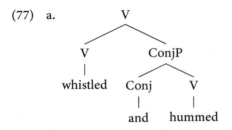

       b.

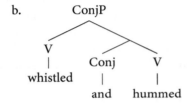

This conclusion, however, seems premature, given that the same pattern is found in extraposition from relative clauses, as in (78).

(78)   a.   [A man __] came in and [a woman __] walked out [who went to the same school].
       b.   #A man who went to the same school came in and a woman who went to the same school walked out.

Whatever the explanation of these facts is, it will not be unique to the syntax of coordination, and hence unlikely to shed new light.

The data in (79) are more revealing. It exemplifies conjunction of prefixes (see also Artstein 2005).

(79)   Bill and Martha are ortho and periodontists.

This cannot be derived from (80) because the two sentences have distinct truth-conditions.

(80)   Bill and Martha are orthodontists and periodontists.

If Bill is an orthodontist and Martha is a periodontist, but not vice versa, then (79) is true and (80) is false. (80) requires that Bill be both an orthodontist and a periodontist, and the same for Martha.

It would appear, then, to be an inescapable conclusion that coordinate structures exist at all scales from the subword level to at least the sentence, and so structures like Munn's, Zoerner's, and Johannessen's cannot be completely general structures covering all types of coordination, tied as they are to phrasal coordination. However, we have already noted that there is no reason to expect there to be a single universal coordinate structure. Nothing in Borsley (2005) appears to us to constitute a persuasive argument against Munn's structure as an analysis of specifically phrasal and sentential coordination.[14]

Further challenges to Johannessen's, Zoerner's, and Munn's structures can be found in Progovac (1998a). Progovac gives two pieces of evidence that the first conjunct in a coordinate structure does not c-command the second. The first piece of evidence concerns Principle A. Patterns of reflexive binding in English like (81) suggest that the first conjunct may asymmetrically c-command the second.

(81)   a.   There was a disagreement between Michael$_i$ and himself$_i$.
       b.   *There was a disagreement between himself$_i$ and Michael.

However, English -*self*-forms are notoriously unreliable, because they allow logophor-like interpretations sometimes called **exempt anaphors** (see Pollard and Sag 1992, Reinhart and Reuland 1993, and Büring 2005 for discussion). In languages where reflexives do not have logophoric uses, such as Serbo-Croatian in (82), equivalents of (81a) are ungrammatical.

(82)   *Jovan$_i$ i   svoja$_i$ žena   su   stigli.
        John   and   self's   wife   are   arrived
        'John and his wife have arrived.'   (Progovac 1998a: 3)

Failure to bind a reflexive in such contexts suggests that the first conjunct does not c-command the second.

The failure of NPI-licensing in (84) suggests the same conclusion. *Any* needs a c-commanding licenser, like *nobody*. The failure to license *any* in (82) therefore suggests an absence of c-command.

(83)   *He chased nobody and any dogs.   (Progovac 1998a: 3)

Recent symmetrical analyses

The evidence just reproduced from Progovac (1998a) argues not only against Johannessen's, Zoerner's, and Munn's asymmetric structures, but also against the flat, symmetrical structure proposed by Gazdar (1981). On that structure, conjuncts mutually c-command each other, so reflexive binding and NPI-licensing would be incorrectly predicted from any conjunct to any other.[15]

As a structure for coordination where no conjunct c-commanded any other conjunct, Progovac tentatively proposed the structure in (84) (see also Cormack and Breheny 1994),

---

[14] Zhang (2009) suggests that conjuncts, whether subwords, words, or phrases, have a uniform syntactic status in that they do not project further. She then builds a syntax for coordination on this uniformity, within the terms of Bare Phrase Structure (Chomsky 1995). It is not clear to us that this syntax can extend naturally to (79), though, or particularly to the contrast between (79) and (80).

[15] That is, it would be predicted if GPSG were to adopt a c-command-based theory of binding and NPI-licensing. However, c-command did not feature in GPSG research.

where the null initial conjunction is sufficient to remove any c-command relations between conjuncts.

(84)   (Progovac 1998b: 4)

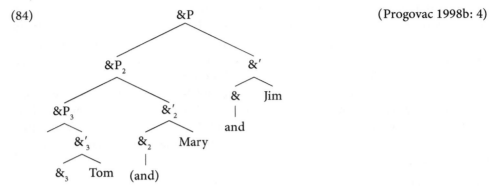

Neeleman and Tanaka (2020) achieve the same result by making use of the segment/category distinction introduced by May (1985).[16] They propose a structure in which conjuncts are mutually adjoined. The structure is based around the configuration in (85), where XP_1 and XP_3 form a multi-segment category, as do XP_2 and XP_3.[17]

(85)

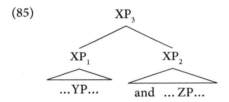

Neeleman and Tanaka adopt the definition of c-command in (86), which is standard in theories which make use of the segment/category distinction.

(86)   A category α c-commands a category β iff (i) no segment of α dominates β and no segment of β dominates α, and (ii) the first node that dominates α also dominates β.

In the structure in (85), this definition predicts that neither conjunct c-commands material properly contained within the other.[18] For instance, the first conjunct (corresponding to the category formed from segments XP_1 and XP_3) does not c-command ZP, within the second conjunct, because a segment of the first conjunct, namely XP_3, dominates ZP. For the same reason, mutatis mutandis, the second conjunct doesn't c-command YP. The same considerations imply that no conjunct c-commands another on the most straightforward extensions to multiple coordination structures, for example analyzing *Hobbs, Rhodes, and*

---

[16] Neeleman et al. (2021) develop Neeleman and Tanaka's analysis by embedding it in a general theory of phrase structure and selection.

[17] Precisely how *and* is integrated into this structure isn't important, so long as it doesn't change the category of XP. See Neeleman and Tanaka (2020) for discussion of the role of conjunctions in marking coordinate structures.

[18] We phrase it in this way because it is not actually clear to us what this approach predicts with respect to conjuncts c-commanding each other. It seems to us that the approach could be resolved either way (conjuncts c-commanding each other or not) depending on how the notions of 'category' and 'dominate' are defined.

Barnes as in (87). Because all conjuncts in (87) share NP$_5$ as a segment, no conjunct c-commands elements of any other.

(87)

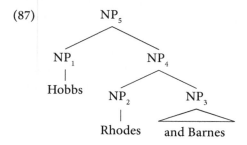

Neeleman and Tanaka therefore derive the same result as Progovac, in a different way. Progovac blocks c-command by disrupting sisterhood among conjuncts; Neeleman and Tanaka block c-command by disrupting the status of conjuncts as independent categories. Either approach has clear advantages over the alternative structures discussed for NP coordination. None of the conjuncts c-command each other, so the absence of the various binding effects discussed is automatically captured. At the same time, the structure is sufficiently flexible to respond to Borsley's challenges.

The structures proposed by Progovac and by Neeleman and Tanaka are symmetrical in all relevant syntactic respects, despite being quite distinct from the symmetrical GPSG structure discussed in Section 2.4.1. Importantly, no conjunct asymmetrically c-commands any other on either Progovac's or Neeleman and Tanaka's structure. This is noteworthy because it shows that there is no incompatibility between symmetrical coordinate structures and theories of phrase structure with a restriction to binary branching or an X'-theoretic approach to headedness.

Having said that, the evidence in favor of these symmetrical structures concerns specifically NP coordination, with no evidence for the structure from coordination of other categories. As we have seen, there is no reason to expect a strictly uniform crosscategorial syntax for coordination. It remains an open question whether the structures proposed by Progovac or by Neeleman and Tanaka are motivated for coordinate structures of all categories.

At present, it seems that there is no single clearly correct analysis of coordination, even within the GB/Minimalist tradition. This is an important choice point, which will have repercussions when we turn to extraction in the rest of this book.

Choice Point 1 What is the structure of coordination?

Option 1: Gazdar's symmetrical structure (all conjuncts c-command each other);
Option 2: Progovac's or Neeleman and Tanaka's symmetrical structure (no conjunct c-commands any other);
Option 3: Johannessen's and Zoerner's asymmetrical structure (specifier–head–complement);
Option 4: Munn's asymmetrical structure (all noninitial conjuncts adjoined to initial conjunct);
Option 5: Something else.

Different options may be appropriate for coordinate structures of different categories. We assume that Option 5 is required for at least word- or subword-level coordination. Progovac's evidence argues in favor of Option 2 for NP coordination. The agreement patterns described in van Koppen (2005) argue in favor of Option 3 or 4 for sentential coordination, but the arguments in Borsley (2005) weigh more heavily against Option 3. The key differences to bear in mind when considering extraction from coordinate structures are symmetry (Gazdar, Progovac, Neeleman and Tanaka) vs. asymmetry (Johannessen, Zoerner, Munn), and whether the coordinate structure is a projection of the initial conjunct (Munn) or not (Johannessen, Zoerner).

2.5 Summary

Despite the simplicity of our first-pass definitions of 'coordination' and 'coordinate structure', the impression that arises from the literature is of a heterogeneous group of structures that defies easy definition. Many coordinate structures can be analyzed semantically in terms of propositional conjunction and disjunction (generalized as in Partee and Rooth 1983), but 'group-forming' NP coordination cannot. A distinct semantics for NP coordination is therefore required, but other instances of NP coordination (those discussed in Section 2.4.2) must still be derived from sentential coordination.

From a morphosyntactic perspective, we must distinguish between binomial and iterating coordination, and allow for the possibility that different lexical items may signal coordination of different syntactic categories or semantic types, as discussed in Section 2.4.1.

In terms of the syntactic analysis of coordinate structures, all of the analyses surveyed in this chapter are conservative, in that the syntactic analysis of coordination stays close to the syntactic analysis of other constructions.[19] We saw a basic tension between the symmetrical structures discussed in Section 2.4.1 and the end of Section 2.4.3, and the asymmetrical structures discussed in the rest of Section 2.4.3. Even disregarding the fact that neither type of analysis extends straightforwardly to subword coordination of the type discussed by Artstein (2005), the evidence here is equivocal: it appears that Progovac (1998a,b) and Neeleman and Tanaka (2020) have successfully explained away Munn's (1993) binding-theoretic arguments in favor of an asymmetric structure, and, in fact, have shown that a symmetrical structure has empirical advantages with respect to binding and NPI-licensing. On the other hand, van Koppen's (2005) Dutch agreement data constitute evidence for an asymmetric structure. Although Borsley (2005) gives several telling arguments against the specific asymmetric analysis in Johannessen (1998) and Zoerner (1995), the arguments typically do not apply equally to the variant in Munn (1993).

This tension between symmetry and asymmetry will permeate the next couple of chapters. Coordinate structures are unusual with respect to locality theory in that the Across-The-Board phenomenon is a symmetrical extraction pattern, whereas a significant component of locality theory concerns asymmetries, between subject and object, argument

---

[19] Some analyses do ascribe distinctive properties to coordinate structures. For instance, in the analysis of Gazdar et al. (1985), coordinate structures have distinctive properties in terms of headedness. A further type of symmetrical structure, more clearly distinct from regular phrase structure, will be introduced in Section 4.5.5.

and adjunct, and so on. This could appear to support a symmetrical analysis of coordination. On the other hand, most of Chapter 3 is concerned with asymmetric patterns of extraction of a sort that constitute prima facie counterexamples to Ross's version of the facts. We will see in Chapter 4 that Munn's structure has properties that allow a straightforward syntactic explanation of some of these asymmetries. This could be taken as further evidence in favor of an asymmetric analysis of at least some coordinate structures. Clearly, these basic structural issues remain far from settled, even after sixty years of generative analysis.

3

Extraction from coordinate structures

3.1 Introduction

In this chapter, we introduce the main topic of this survey: patterns of extraction from coordinate structures. These patterns, and their implications for the syntax and semantics of coordination, have been taken since Ross (1967) to be one of the richest sources of information on the syntax and semantics of coordination, as well as the nature of extraction.

Section 3.2 describes the **Coordinate Structure Constraint** or CSC, introduced by Ross. The CSC, to put it simply, prohibits extraction out of coordinate structures. However, there are many classes of counterexample to this simple formulation. We discuss these in Section 3.3. Section 3.4 then sets out what is known about the generality of the CSC and its exceptions across conjunctions and across languages. Section 3.5 discusses the applicability of the CSC, and its exceptions, across several movement types beyond the A'-movement which preoccupied Ross and most subsequent most other researchers. Finally, Section 3.6 discusses the SLF construction, a case where the applicability of the CSC and the theoretical implications thereof require more subtle discussion.

After a brief summary in Section 3.7, we introduce our central puzzle. Over the course of this chapter, we accumulate a range of cases where the CSC apparently fails to apply. These counterexamples appear to have a basis that lies partially outside syntax, in the interpretation of coordinate structures. In Section 3.8, we are therefore led to ask: who calls the shots? Is extraction from coordinate structures regulated by syntactic conditions like the original CSC, or are discourse-semantic factors somehow conditioning the syntactic structures? The remainder of the volume will then take up this question.

3.2 The Coordinate Structure Constraint

The central topic in the study of extraction from coordinate structures is the Coordinate Structure Constraint, or **CSC** (Ross 1967), stated in (1).

(1) **Coordinate Structure Constraint**
In a coordinate structure, no conjunct may be moved, nor may any element contained in a conjunct be moved out of that conjunct. (Ross 1967: 161)

The CSC captures the fact that extraction out of a single conjunct in a coordinate structure is frequently degraded.

Coordination and the Syntax–Discourse Interface. Daniel Altshuler and Robert Truswell, Oxford University Press.
© Daniel Altshuler and Robert Truswell (2022). DOI: 10.1093/oso/9780198804239.003.0003

(2)   Henry [[plays the lute] and [sings madrigals]].
    a. *The lute [which Henry [[plays __] and [sings madrigals]]] is warped.
    b. *The madrigals [which Henry [[plays the lute] and [sings __]]] sound lousy.

(Ross 1967: 160)

However, simultaneous extraction from both conjuncts is possible. This is the **Across-The-Board**, or **ATB**, exception:[1]

(3)   The madrigals [which Henry [[writes __] and [sings __]]] are lousy.

The ATB exception applies only to extraction *from* a conjunct. Extraction *of* a single conjunct is completely ungrammatical in many languages (like English in (4)), but simultaneous extraction of multiple conjuncts is no better (see (5)). That is, there is no ATB extraction of conjuncts.

(4)   a. *What sofa will he put the chair between [[some table] and __]?
    b. *What table will he put the chair between [__ and [some sofa]]?

(Ross 1967: 158)

(5)   *What will he put the chair between [__ and __]?

As a first attempt to explain the impossibility of ATB extraction of conjuncts, Ross suggested a reduction of the Conjunct Constraint to the A-over-A principle of Chomsky (1964). The effect of that principle in this case is that movement cannot target individual XP conjuncts, and must instead target the whole conjoined XP. No such reduction is available for the Element Constraint, because the category of the extracted element does not always match the category of the conjuncts.

Because of differences like this between extraction from, and extraction of, a conjunct, some researchers (following Grosu 1972) distinguish two components of the CSC: the **Conjunct Constraint** prohibits extraction *of* conjuncts, while the **Element Constraint** prohibits extraction *from* conjuncts. We will adopt this terminology, and consider the ATB extraction pattern as an exception to the Element constraint only.

We will occasionally need to distinguish between the Conjunct Constraint, the Element Constraint, and the ATB exception. In most cases, however, we will be able to treat them together. For ease of readership, we will henceforth use 'CSC' to refer to the conjunction of these three generalizations (including the ATB exception), and refer directly to the three component parts when we need to. For now, we note that both the Conjunct Constraint and the Element Constraint have additional counterexamples beyond the ATB exception. We will discuss these counterexamples in Sections 3.3–3.6.

---

[1] See de Vries (2017) for a comprehensive survey of ATB phenomena. We have had to exclude many more complex cases of ATB dependencies from the scope of this survey.

3.3 Counterexamples to the CSC

3.3.1 Counterexamples to the Conjunct Constraint

Until recently, the Conjunct Constraint was widely believed to be a robust, absolute universal. This has now been challenged because counterexamples have been documented in a range of typologically unrelated languages. The main works of interest are Stjepanovic (2014), Oda (2017), and a string of works by Bošković (2019a,b,c, 2020). Here we give examples from Oda (2017). Japanese obeys the Element Constraint in canonical cases (we discuss counterexamples to the Element Constraint in the following subsection).

(6)   *Taro-o   John-wa   [Yamada-kyoozyu-ga [__   home] (&) [Hanako-o
      Taro-ACC   John-TOP   Yamada-Prof.-NOM   praise   Hanako-ACC
      shikitta] to]   itta.
      scolded   COMP said
      'John said that Prof. Yamada praised Taro and scolded Hanako.'   (Oda 2017)

However, extraction *of* a conjunct is better than extraction *from* a conjunct.

(7)   ?Kyoodai-to   kanojo-wa [__   Toodai]-ni   akogareteiru.
      Kyoto.University-and   she-TOP   Tokyo.University-DAT   admire
      'She admires Kyoto University and Tokyo University.'   (Oda 2017)

This means that Japanese violates the Conjunct Constraint more liberally than the Element Constraint. Oda reports the same pattern in Korean, Serbo-Croatian, Russian, and Polish, and also notes Conjunct Constraint violations in Old English and Latin. In each case, regardless of the basic word order of the language, only the first conjunct can extract. (8) illustrates the contrast in Serbo-Croatian.

(8)   a. ?Knjige je   Marko [__   i   filmove] kupio.
         books   is   Marko   and   movies   bought
         'Marko bought books and movies.'
      b. *Sobu   je   Ivan ušao   [[u   veliku __] i   [u   malu   kuhinju]].
         room   is   Ivan entered in   big   and   in   small kitchen
         'Ivan entered a big room and a small kitchen.'   (Oda 2017)

Zhang (2009) discusses a superficially similar pattern in Mandarin. She shows that apparent NP-coordination with *gen* admits several elements intervening between it and the first conjunct, including raising predicates like *hui* in (9a) and adverbials like *zai Riben* in (9b).

(9)   a. Huoche hui   gen   qiche xiangzhuang ma?
         train   might   gen   bus   collide   Q
         'Might the train collide with the bus?'   (Zhang 2009: 114)
      b. Akiu   zia   Riben gen   Baoyu jian-le   mian.
         Akiu   at   Japan gen   Baoyu meet-PFV face
         'Akiu and Baoyu met in Japan.'   (Zhang 2009: 115)

However, unlike Oda's examples, these elements can only intervene when the would-be coordinate structure is interpreted as what Zhang calls a 'comitative' coordinate structure. This arouses the suspicion that *gen* in (9) is, in fact, functioning as a comitative marker, rather than a true coordinator. Zhang gives four arguments that *gen* really is a coordinator, but none of them seem conclusive in the context of the more thorough discussion of the distinction between comitatives and coordination by Haspelmath (2007). Zhang also gives no evidence that the nonlocal relationship in (9) is derived by movement. Further research is therefore required to establish the strength of this putative counterexample, but it would be unsurprising if Mandarin does turn out to be a further instance of Oda's pattern.

Oda and Bošković develop an account of these Conjunct Constraint violations in which the clitic nature of the conjunction plays a major part. The crucial prediction is that Conjunct Constraint violations are possible if the conjunction is not realized in the head of &P, for instance because it has cliticized onto one of the conjuncts. While this may be a necessary condition for Conjunct Constraint violations, it probably isn't sufficient, because clitic conjunctions appear to be more widespread crosslinguistically than Conjunct Constraint violations. It is more striking, as Oda notes, that these languages are all article-less languages. Bošković (2008) has argued that only article-less languages allow left branch extraction, so a treatment of these Conjunct Constraint violations as similar to left branch extraction would seem promising (see also Stjepanovic 2014). This line of reasoning suggests grounds for optimism that the Conjunct Constraint, and its exceptions, will eventually be reduced to more general syntactic principles, although probably not to the A-over-A principle as Ross had proposed.

To our knowledge, only two other sets of counterexamples to the Conjunct Constraint have been proposed. The first concerns the alternation between 'simplex initials' and 'complex initials' in Afrikaans. Afrikaans allows an alternation between the two sentences in (10), where *sit* is an aspectual verb carrying durative entailments rather than entailments about posture. (10a), with a single verb in second position, is known as a simplex initial. (10b), with multiple coordinated verbs in second position, is a complex initial.

(10) a. Jan sit die boeke en   lees.
        Jan sit the books and read
        'Jan sits reading the books.'
     b. Jan sit en   lees die boeke.
        Jan sit and read the books
        'Jan sits reading the books.'   (de Vos 2005: 117)

As a V2 OV language, the base position of the verbs in (10) is clause-final, as indicated in (11).

(11) Jan sal   die boeke sit en   lees.
     Jan will the books sit and read
     'Jan will sit reading the books.'   (de Vos 2005: 117)

The verbs therefore reach second position by movement. In (10b), the entire coordinate structure *sit en lees* is moved. In contrast, only one of the conjuncts is moved in (10a), in apparent violation of the Conjunct Constraint. Although no analysis has been attempted to our knowledge, it would be natural to investigate the possibility that this pattern is a verbal analog of Oda's examples of extraction of NP conjuncts.

The other putative counterexample is more distant. It concerns elliptical answers like (12b), documented by Lawler (1974).

(12) a. Can linguists study negation?
     b. Not and stay sane, they can't.   (Lawler 1974: 370)

Lawler assumes that this pattern is a violation of the Conjunct Constraint, because he assumes that (12b) is derived from an underlying representation similar to that of (13) by operations of VP ellipsis, copying of the negative morpheme, and (crucially) movement of *(not) and stay sane* to a left-peripheral position.

(13) They can't study negation and stay sane.

Although this latter component of Lawler's analysis isn't strictly a violation of the Conjunct Constraint (it doesn't just move a conjunct), it is close.[2]

However, this is a complex construction, showing many restrictions (noted by Lawler) which do not follow directly from Lawler's analysis. The construction requires (among other things): (i) realization of negation in both conjuncts, without a double-negative interpretation as in (14), (ii) conjunction specifically of VPs as in (15), and (iii) what Lawler calls a 'conditional' interpretation of the coordinate structure.[3]

(14) a. *Not and stay sane, they can.
     b. *And stay sane, they can't.

(15) a. (i) Can Frank eat peas?
        (ii) *Not and carrots, he can't.
     b. (i) Can we go over the river?
        (ii) *Not and through the woods, we can't.
     c. (i) Can we say that Mary came to the party?
        (ii) *Not and that she enjoyed it, you can't.   (Lawler 1974: 370)

Examples like (12b) are only relevant to the Conjunct Constraint if we accept Lawler's movement-based derivation from (13). If it transpires that a base-generation analysis is better able to account for the complexities of the construction, then the whole construction will cease to be relevant to the Conjunct Constraint.

We assume that all of the counterexamples, if they are indeed counterexamples, will not ultimately invalidate the Conjunct Constraint. Rather, they will prove informative about the correct formulation thereof, and perhaps guide a reduction to other, more central, locality principles (for instance, the analysis in Oda 2017 is grounded in Bošković's conception of phase theory). In every case except perhaps Lawler's, the phenomenon at hand seems to be purely syntactic.

---

[2] Likewise, note that -*to* is piedpiped when the conjunct moves in Oda's example (7).
[3] We will see in what follows that many 'nonlogical' properties of coordinate structures are found only in VP-coordination. It may well be, then, that the restriction of this construction to VP coordination follows in some way from the semantic restrictions Lawler describes.

3.3.2 Counterexamples to the Element Constraint

The Element Constraint is less robust than the Conjunct Constraint, and more obviously conditioned by nonsyntactic factors. We have already encountered the ATB generalization, which describes a productive class of exceptions to the Element Constraint. This section is concerned with other, less well-understood exceptions, noted by Ross (1967), Schmerling (1975), Goldsmith (1985), Lakoff (1986), and many others. These are grammatical examples of extraction from a single conjunct, precisely the sort of thing that the Element Constraint is designed to exclude. Some of the examples that have recurred in the literature are gathered in (16).[4] As is common in the literature, they all involve VP conjunction with *and*—although our discussion will also focus on this configuration, we will discuss coordination of other categories, and other conjunctions, from time to time.

(16) a. Here's the whiskey which I [[went to the store] and [bought __]].
     b. Who did he [[pick up the phone] and [call __]]?
     c. How many lakes can we [[destroy __] and [not arouse public antipathy]]?
     d. How many counterexamples can the Coordinate Structure Constraint [[sustain __] and [still be considered empirically correct]]?   (Goldsmith 1985)
     e. Which dish is it that people always [[order __ here] and then [get sick]]?

These examples are particularly interesting because they appear to demonstrate conditioning of a syntactic phenomenon by discourse factors. Ross (1967) noted that such examples of extraction out of a single conjunct (unlike the ATB exception illustrated in (3)) involve 'asymmetrical' interpretations of *and*, distinct from symmetrical logical conjunction (recall Section 2.2). The sequence of events depicted in (16a) or (17a) is distinct from that in (17b), and situations can easily be imagined in which the most salient readings of (17a) would be considered true and (17b) false, or vice versa.

(17) a. I [[went to the store] and [bought the whiskey]].
     b. I [[bought the whiskey] and [went to the store]].

However, as Postal (1998) notes, it is not simply the case that any asymmetric interpretation allows asymmetric extraction, as demonstrated by the paradigm in (18). (18a) demonstrates the asymmetry of the interpretation, and (18b) demonstrates the unavailability of asymmetric extraction.[5]

---

[4] We will not be concerned with examples like (i) in this survey.

(i) What have you gone and done __ now?

Although it is tempting to assume that (i) involves coordination of VPs *gone* and *done* __ , with extraction from the latter, de Vos (2005) argues persuasively that they involve coordination of the heads *gone* and *done* instead. On that analysis, there is no violation of the CSC.

[5] Levine (2001: 157) offers the following counterexample to Postal's argument: *It was De Gaulle who Frank [[criticized __] and [in doing so criticized a Frenchman]].* We are unsure about whether there is a contrast with the examples reported in the text, but regardless, we believe that Postal's general claim is likely to be correct: it is likely not to be the case that just any semantic asymmetry licenses asymmetric extraction.

(18) a. (i) Frank [[criticized De Gaulle] and [hence criticized a Frenchman]].
      (ii) #Frank [[criticized a Frenchman] and [hence criticized De Gaulle]].
   b. (i) *It was De Gaulle who Frank [[criticized __] and [hence criticized a Frenchman]].
      (ii) *It was a Frenchman who Frank [[criticized De Gaulle] and [hence criticized __]].   (Postal 1998: 53)

We will focus, in this chapter and indeed throughout the book, on three different types of asymmetric interpretation, initially identified by Lakoff (1986). Below we review each type in turn, and describe the extraction patterns associated by Lakoff with each.

Type A

The first type of scenario that Lakoff considers is called **Type A,** involving a 'sequence of events [which] fits normal conventionalized expectations'. Depending on which theory of discourse one adopts, Type A scenarios are referred to as instances of OCCASION (Hobbs 1985, Kehler 2002) or NARRATION (Lascarides and Asher 1993, Asher and Lascarides 2003). We adopt a convention of writing the names of these interpretive relations in small caps, and will give more precise definitions of them in Chapters 5 and 6 respectively. We employ NARRATION rather than OCCASION in this chapter for reasons that will be clear in Chapter 6 (though nothing rides on this choice for now).

Type A scenarios can involve arbitrarily many conjuncts. Extraction occurs from the final conjunct, perhaps as well as other conjuncts. (16a) and (16b) are examples; two slightly more complex examples are in (19).

(19) a. What did he [[go to the store], [buy __], [load __ in his car], [drive home], and [unload __]]?
   b. Which courses did he [[take __ for credit], [work hard], and [feel satisfied with __]]?   (Lakoff 1986)

These examples have five and three conjuncts, respectively, unlike the binary conjunction we have considered so far. There is a gap in the final conjunct in each, but no other discernible pattern to the distribution of gaps. Lakoff suggests, with some reservations, a discourse-based analysis, in which there are gaps in all conjuncts except for those which describe background states or preparatory actions. The tendency to find a gap in the final conjunct would therefore reflect a discourse principle to the effect that background states and preparatory actions are infelicitous as final events within a narrative sequence.[6]

Type B

Type B scenarios involve narratives 'in which a conventionalized expectation is violated'— we will refer to them as instances of **VIOLATED EXPECTATION,** following the more worked-out classification provided by Hobbs (1985) and Kehler (2002).[7] In such cases, Lakoff showed that asymmetric extraction from the first conjunct is possible. (16c) and (16d) are

---

[6] We revisit this claim in Chapter 5.
[7] It's worth noting that some theories of discourse relations choose not to adopt VIOLATED EXPECTATION as a distinct relation, a point that we return to in Chapters 5 and 6.

commonly cited examples. (20) is a further example from Goldsmith (1985) that Lakoff uses: since drinking does not typically lead to sobriety, the question contains a narrative where expectations are violated.

(20)   How much can you [[drink __] and [still stay sober]]?

Lakoff in fact appears to assume a tighter relationship between extraction patterns and the Type A/Type B distinction. In (21a), he claims that a gap in the second conjunct forces an interpretation where eating herbs leads to not getting certain cancers, while in (21b), he claims that a gap in the first conjunct forces an interpretation where eating herbs is normally expected to lead to getting cancer.[8]

(21)   a. What forms of cancer can you [[eat herbs] and [not get __]]?   (Type A)
        b. What kinds of herbs can you [[eat __] and [not get cancer]]?   (Type B)

We will critically examine these claims in Section 5.4, but for the time being the descriptive puzzle is clear: Type A scenarios (instances of NARRATION) and Type B scenarios (instances of VIOLATED EXPECTATION) can license different extraction patterns, and this difference requires an explanation.

With this in mind, consider the following example:

(22)   How many courses can you [[take __ for credit], [still remain sane], and [get all A's in __]]?

In (22), the second conjunct violates an expectation relative to the first,[9] and sets up a conventionalized expectation with the third conjunct. This is what Lakoff calls an 'AB sequence', since it has an instance of VIOLATED EXPECTATION within an example of NARRATION. The first part of this sequence works like any other Type B relation, requiring extraction from the initial conjunct. The rest works like any other Type A relation, requiring extraction from the final conjunct. The result is extraction from initial and final conjuncts, but not the middle conjunct.

The analysis just given is suggestive of a hierarchical discourse structure, with the first two conjuncts (a Type B relation) jointly forming a preparatory action in a Type A relation. This implies that (22) decomposes into a Type B relation with a gap in the first conjunct, as in (23a), and a Type A relation with a gap in *each* conjunct, as in (23b).

(23)   a. [[take __ for credit] (&) [still remain sane]]
        b. [[take __ for credit (&) still remain sane] and [get all A's in __]]

---

[8] Lakoff's contrast in (21) is not very robust, and one of the authors cannot replicate the judgments. Partly, though, this appears to be an orthogonal, lexical matter. The contrast in (i), although less minimal, may be clearer.

(i)   a. What forms of cancer can you [[eat herbs] and [prevent __]]?
       b. What kinds of herbs can you [[eat __] and [still not get cancer]]?

[9] Of course, remaining sane does not violate an expectation generated by taking a single course for credit, but as the number of courses rises, the chances of remaining sane diminish. We will be more precise about this in Chapter 5.

We return to the interpretation of these 'mixed' examples of discourse relations when we develop a more precise hierarchical approach to discourse structure in Chapter 6.

Type C

Lakoff briefly considers a third pattern, which we will refer to as instantiating a relation of **CAUSE–EFFECT** or, using the terminology from Lascarides and Asher (1993) and Kehler (2002), **RESULT**. In Type C scenarios, extraction from just the first conjunct is possible, but the interpretation is that the eventuality described by the second conjunct is the result of the eventuality described by the first conjunct. Examples from Lakoff are in (24).

(24)   a.   That's the stuff that the guys in the Caucasus [[drink __] and [live to be a hundred]].

       b.   That's the kind of firecracker that I [[set __ off] and [scared the neighbors]].

Type C scenarios are problematic, primarily because it is hard (if not impossible) to come up with an example which purely exemplifies Type C and doesn't also exemplify Type A. It can therefore be hard to escape the impression that Type C exists in Lakoff's account purely to provide an alternative analysis of some problematic NARRATION scenarios which don't follow the Type A extraction pattern. However, we will keep Lakoff's descriptive terminology here and return to the task of constructing a more solid analysis of Type C in Chapter 5.

Further types

The three scenarios just discussed are the only three that Lakoff considers. However, at least two further combinations of asymmetric extraction and asymmetric interpretation have been documented. The first, illustrated in (25), was discovered by Schmerling (1975), who referred to it as a **Type D** scenario (see also discussion in Na and Huck 1992). The hallmark of this scenario is that the second conjunct explains in what respects Doc was following his coach's instructions.

(25)   Which baserunner was Doc [[following his coach's instructions] and [keeping __ close to first]]?   (Na and Huck 1992: 260)

The second additional scenario was first described by Culicover and Jackendoff (1997). We will refer to these examples for now as instances of a **conditional** interpretation.[10] Culicover and Jackendoff demonstrate that extraction from either conjunct is at least marginally possible with a conditional interpretation.

---

[10] Culicover and Jackendoff themselves used the term 'left-subordinating *and*'. However, for reasons that will become clear in Chapter 6, we believe that it is unhelpful to use the term 'subordination' for examples like this. We draw two independent interpretive distinctions:

1.   A coordinate structure is **symmetrical** iff *P and Q* ≡ *Q and P*; otherwise it is **asymmetrical**.
2.   A discourse structure is **coordinating** if it meets certain criteria to be discussed in Chapter 6; otherwise it is **subordinating**.

We will see in Chapter 6 that these conditional coordinate structures are asymmetrical but coordinating, according to these definitions.

(26)   a. ?This is the loot that [[you just identify __] and [we arrest the thief on the spot]].
       b. ?This is the thief that [[you just identify the loot] and [we arrest __ on the spot]].
                                                        (Culicover and Jackendoff 1997: 206)

Summary
The data discussed in this section raise the central architectural question for this survey: how is it possible for patterns of extraction to be sensitive to nonsyntactic phenomena like the different symmetrical and asymmetrical interpretations of *and*? Linguistic modularity is not meant to work this way! The central task of this survey is unpicking the patterns of interaction between syntax and discourse structure uncovered in the works just discussed.

3.3.3 Syntactic conditioning of asymmetric interpretations

Before we dive into the syntax of asymmetric extraction from coordinate structures, in this section we collate some observations about syntactic structures which block the asymmetric interpretations we have enumerated in the previous subsections. Roughly speaking, conjuncts allowing asymmetric interpretation and asymmetric extraction must be as small as possible. This is in contrast to symmetrical, ATB extraction, which is available for coordination of constituents of any size. An immediate consequence of this is that repetition of material across conjuncts often blocks an asymmetric interpretation.

The two main cases of this pattern that have been discussed in the literature are firstly that CP coordination blocks asymmetric interpretations, and secondly that repeated subjects in each conjunct appear to allow asymmetric interpretation, but still block asymmetric extraction.

CP coordination blocks asymmetric interpretations
Bjorkman (2013) notes a correlation between the size of the syntactic units in a coordinate structure and their interpretation, and argues that the availability of asymmetric interpretations is conditioned by syntactic structure. Consider the pair of sentences in (27):

(27)   a. The newspaper reported <u>that</u> [[a new government was elected] and [there was a riot]].
       b. The newspaper reported [[<u>that</u> a new government was elected] and [<u>that</u> there was a riot]].

In (27a), but not in (27b), there is an asymmetric (sequential) interpretation of the events reported. Bjorkman argues that the difference is due to the fact that in (27a) two TPs are coordinated (and introduced by a single complementizer *that*), while in (27b) two full CPs are coordinated by *and*. She concludes that TP coordination, at least in embedded contexts, gives rise to an asymmetric interpretation of *and*, whereas CP coordination has the symmetrical properties of logical *and*. These findings are reinforced by examples from a range of languages including Greek or Dutch, showing that the generalization is not specific to English.

In the context of the present survey, Bjorkman's example establishes an upper bound on the size of asymmetric coordination structures: CP coordination is interpreted symmetrically, while smaller coordinate structures at least allow asymmetric interpretations.[11] Asymmetric extraction from conjoined CPs is then expected to be impossible. The contrast between (28b) and (28c) suggests that this prediction is borne out, but we will see immediately below that the status of (28b) is in itself problematic.

(28) a.   This is the drink that I heard that people in the Caucasus [[drink __] and [live to be 100]].   (VP coordination)
      b.   ??This is the drink that I heard that [[people in the Caucasus drink __] and [they live to be 100]].   (TP coordination)
      c.   *This is the drink that I heard [[that people in the Caucasus drink __] and [that they live to be 100]].   (CP coordination)

Repeated subjects block asymmetric extraction
Ross (1967) already noted that (29), with a subject in the second conjunct, is noticeably worse than (16a).

(29) *Here's the whisky [sic] which [[I went to the store] and [Mike bought __]].
                                                                        (Ross 1967: 168)

This is unsurprising: it is much harder to construe the two event descriptions in (29) as a coherent narrative, and so the logical, symmetrical interpretation is the most salient. The ungrammaticality of asymmetrical extraction is therefore predicted.

More surprising, though, is that (30a) is equally ungrammatical. (30b) demonstrates that the asymmetrical, narrative interpretation is available here,[12] so the unavailability of asymmetrical extraction is in need of explanation.

(30) a.   *Here's the whisky which [[I went to the store] and [I bought __]].
      b.   [[I went to the store] and [I bought some whisky]].

The ungrammaticality of (30a) is plausibly related to a generalization from Bjorkman (2014), that TP coordination under a nonempty CP layer only allows a subject in each conjunct if the subjects are distinct. (31) shows that this effect is independent of any movement.

(31) The TSA asks that [[passengers remove their shoes] and [(*they) move quickly through security]].   (Bjorkman 2014: 492)

In light of Bjorkman's generalization, repetition of the subject in (30a) would be an indication of CP coordination, which then (according to Bjorkman) would require a symmetrical

---

[11] Bjorkman in fact claims that TP coordination *requires* an asymmetric interpretation. Coordination of matrix clauses is then treated as structurally ambiguous: symmetrical interpretations arise from CP coordination with a null complementizer, and asymmetric interpretations from TP coordination.

[12] Our judgment in this respect differs from that expressed in Schmerling (1975). There is of course something slightly unnatural about the repetition of the subject in (30a), but that does not prevent the two conjuncts from receiving a narrative interpretation. The interpretive contrast with (i) is clear.

(i)   [[I bought some whisky] and [I went to the store]].

interpretation. This, in turn, would block asymmetrical extraction from a single conjunct, accounting for the ungrammaticality of (30a).

Summary and other cases

Because of the two restrictions just discussed, asymmetric extraction from coordinate structures almost always involves VP coordination.[13] The work discussed in this section suggests that it may be possible to treat this fact as the result of a conspiracy of sorts: asymmetric extraction from CP coordination and many cases of TP coordination is blocked by a variety of orthogonal factors, while asymmetric extraction from other categories would require investigation in the light of Lakoff's demonstration that discourse structure conditions the availability of asymmetric extraction, as it is unlikely that the same range of discourse structures is available within, say, noun phrases as within clauses or suprasentential discourses. Accordingly, in what follows we will often focus without comment exclusively on VP coordination, and we take it that the predominance of VP coordination in asymmetric extraction data has some other explanation, outside the main concerns of this volume.

A plausible alternative take on this phenomenon would be to seek to reduce the effects discussed here to a constraint broadly like MaxElide (Takahashi and Fox 2005, Merchant 2008), which requires deletion of all recoverable material. There are, in fact, some other cases, like (32), where repeating omissible material blocks an asymmetric interpretation: (32a) describes a single complex desire, while (32b), with repeated *to*, describes two independent desires. The more general this effect is, the more natural it is to seek to formulate some kind of generalization relating repeatable material to symmetrical interpretations.

(32)   a. Sullivan wants the government to [[declare martial law] and [arrest labor activists]].
       b. Sullivan wants the government [[to declare martial law] and [to arrest labor activists]].   (Goldsmith 1985)

However, no such generalization has currently been formulated. Although there is a loose resemblance with MaxElide, the effect is not the same. (32b) is not ungrammatical; it just lacks the asymmetric interpretation of (32a). It is not clear what that restriction could follow from, and Bjorkman's stipulated correspondence between size of conjuncts and interpretation is one of the very few attempts at an account.

In the next three sections, we sketch out the scope of the CSC and of its exceptions. First, Section 3.4 asks to what extent the patterns reported in this section on the basis of English *and* can be generalized to other languages and other conjunctions. Then Section 3.5 tracks CSC effects, and the absence thereof, across different movement types, including overt and covert movement, head and phrasal movement, and A- and A'-movement. Section 3.6 discusses a particularly complex case, the German SLF construction, in more detail.

---

[13] The main exception to this statement consists of some examples of what superficially looks like asymmetric extraction from NP coordination, to be discussed in Section 3.6.

3.4 Generality of asymmetric extractions

Symmetrical extraction from coordinate structures is crosslinguistically widespread. Indeed, Haspelmath (2004) goes so far as to suggest that symmetrical extraction is a hallmark of coordination crosslinguistically, and that asymmetrical extraction patterns could indicate that a superficially coordinating structure is, in fact, subordinating. However, Section 3.3 has just demonstrated that structures which appear in all other respects to be regular coordinate structures can nevertheless permit asymmetric extraction. The aim of this section is to demonstrate that the patterns illustrated in Section 3.3 are not unique to English, or to *and*, but are in fact quite widespread across coordinate structures.

In the rest of Section 4, we briefly summarize what is known about the distribution of the asymmetric extraction patterns. In short, the availability of asymmetric A'-extractions is not completely restricted to conjunctions like *and*, but the interpretive requirements on asymmetric extraction are less commonly satisfied with other conjunctions. Those interpretive requirements, or at least rough equivalents, are found in many languages besides English, suggesting that the patterns described in the preceding sections on the basis of mainly English examples, despite some crosslinguistic variation, are not reflections of arbitrary facts about the grammar of a single language.

3.4.1 Generality across conjunctions

Symmetrical extraction can straightforwardly be replicated across a range of different conjunctions.[14]

(33) a. What do [[you enjoy __] and [I hate __]]?
   b. What did [[you buy __] or [I sell __]]?
   c. Which exam did [[I pass __] but [you fail __]]?

Although we omit a demonstration, similar facts hold across any number of conjuncts, and the range of A'-dependencies discussed in Section 3.5.1.

In contrast, it can initially appear that asymmetric extraction is restricted to structures with *and* or its translated equivalents. Simple-minded attempts to substitute other conjunctions often result in unacceptability:

(34) a. #Here's the whiskey which I [[went to the store] or [bought __].
   b. #Who did he [[pick up the phone] but [call __]]?

The reason for the unacceptability is straightforward: it is not possible, in the general case, to simply exchange one conjunction for another while maintaining the same discourse relation between conjuncts. With *and*, both of the examples in (34) would be interpreted as Type A scenarios, with NARRATION, but such an interpretation is not possible, in these cases, with *or* or *but*.

---

[14] At least, judgments like these are widely reported in the literature. For one of the authors, though, (33b) and (33c) are ungrammatical.

This could in principle motivate an analysis like that of Steedman (2011), where *and* is treated as lexically ambiguous. Steedman claimed that one lexical entry for *and* has a syntax and semantics based on ∧, while others have the non-Boolean interpretations which license asymmetric extraction.[15]

However, Kubota and Lee (2015) show that, when an appropriate discourse relation holds, it is possible to extract from coordinate structures with *or* and *but* as well as *and*, as in (35).

(35)   a. [He] regards the limitless abundance of language as its most important property,
            one that any theory of language must [[account for __] or [be discarded]].
        b. What did John [[go to the store] but [forget to buy __]]?

(Kubota and Lee 2015: 644)

Kubota and Lee also show that the same patterns hold in Japanese and Korean, despite substantial differences in the syntax of the relevant constructions. This suggests that the availability of asymmetric extraction is not an idiosyncratic lexical property of *and*.

A natural hypothesis, which we will develop in Chapter 6, is the following: if a coordinate structure containing a conjunction other than *and* can felicitously be interpreted in a way that is compatible with one of the scenarios permitting asymmetric extraction, then the relevant asymmetric extraction pattern should be possible. First, we note that (35b) is a minimal variant on Ross's (16a). In addition, (36a–b) show instances of Type B scenarios with *but*, and (36c) shows a Type C scenario, also with *but*. All of these are minimal variants on classic examples listed in (16). They show that VIOLATED EXPECTATION and RESULT are compatible with *but* as well as *and*.

(36)   a. How many lakes can we [[destroy __] but [not arouse public antipathy]]?
        b. How many counterexamples can the Coordinate Structure Constraint [[sustain
            __] but [still be considered empirically correct]]?
        c. Which dish is it that people always [[order __ here] but then [get sick]]?

As for *or*, Kubota and Lee's (35a) is an example of a construction which Culicover and Jackendoff (1997) refer to as 'threat-*or*'. This construction, illustrated in (37), couples an approximately conditional interpretation with a range of morphosyntactic restrictions documented by Culicover and Jackendoff.

(37)   a. [[You hide that loot right now] or [we're in big trouble]].
        b. [[Little Oscar makes himself scarce by midnight], or [we're in big trouble]].

(Culicover and Jackendoff 1997: 213)

We will be in a better position to understand the interpretation of 'threat-*or*' in Chapter 6, when we discuss recent work on the discourse semantics of conjunctions. For now, we can follow Culicover and Jackendoff (1997) in thinking of 'threat-*or*' as approximately equivalent to their conditional 'left-subordinating *and*', discussed in Section 3.3. This

---

[15] Mark Steedman (pers. comm.) has clarified that he intended the analysis to apply to all conjunctions, not just to *and*.

would again suggest that conjunctions other than *and* allow asymmetric extraction to the extent that they can be interpreted in an appropriate way.

These examples support the claim that patterns of extraction from coordinate structures are tightly conditioned by interpretation. However, it would be premature to conclude that interpretation alone determines extractability. Noncoordinate structures with similar interpretations but different syntax show different extraction patterns. Culicover and Jackendoff claim that *if*-conditionals do not show the same extraction patterns as left-subordinating *and* (but see Taylor 2006, Woodgate 2010 for dissenting views—the judgments reproduced below are Culicover and Jackendoff's).

(38)   ??This is the loot that [[if you identify __], [we will arrest the thief on the spot]].
(Culicover and Jackendoff 1997: 207)

Likewise, and probably less controversially, *unless*-conditionals do not allow asymmetric extraction to the same extent as threat-*or*.

(39)   ??This is the loot that [[unless you hide __ right now], [we're in big trouble]].
(Culicover and Jackendoff 2005: 215)

On the other hand, Culicover and Jackendoff (1999) demonstrate that extraction from either half of a comparative correlative (another noncoordinate structure with an asymmetric, conditional-like interpretation) is surprisingly acceptable.

(40)   a. [[The sooner you solve this problem], [the more easily you'll satisfy the folks up at corporate headquarters]].
   b. This is the sort of problem which [[the sooner you solve __], [the more easily you'll satisfy the folks up at corporate headquarters]].
   c. The folks up at corporate headquarters are the sort of people who [[the sooner you solve this problem], [the more easily you'll satisfy __]].
(Culicover and Jackendoff 1999: 564)

There is scope for further comparative research in this area. Crosslinguistically, it seems common for the lines between coordinate structures, conditionals, and correlatives to be somewhat blurred, with morphemes canonically associated with one structure yielding an interpretation associated with another (see many of the papers collected in Culicover and Jackendoff 2005, and for a crosslinguistic perspective Lipták 2009). To our knowledge, there is not yet any systematic study of how these different alignments of syntactic structure and interpretation condition extraction possibilities.

3.4.2 Generality across languages

Symmetrical extraction from coordinate structures is crosslinguistically widespread. For instance, Georgopoulos (1985) demonstrates that the Austronesian language Palauan obeys the CSC. (41) shows ungrammatical extraction from a single conjunct, while (42) shows grammatical Across-The-Board extraction.

(41) *a del-ak   [a uleker   er ngak [el kmo ng-ngera_i [a
       mother-1SG   REAL.PST.IPFV.ask P me   COMP CL-what

       sensei a milsk-ak   a buk] me [a se?el-ik   a
       teacher REAL.PST.PFV.give-1SG book and   friend-1SG

       ulter-ur   __i er ngak]]]
       REAL.PST.PFV.sell-3SG   P me
       'My mother asked me what the teacher gave me a book and my friend sold me.'

(42) a del-ak   a uleker   [el kmo ng-ngera_i [a l-ulter-ur
       mother-1SG   REAL.ask COMP CL-what   IRR.3SG-PFV.sell-3SG

       __i a Latii el   me   er ngak] me [a Tmerukl a   ulter-ur
           Latii LNK come P me   and   Tmerukl   REAL.PFV.sell-3SG

       __i el   mo er a Toiu]]
           LNK go P Toiu
       'My mother asked what Latii sold to me and Tmerukl sold to Toiu.'

                                                    (Georgopoulos 1985: 87)

Palauan has an alternation between gaps and resumptive pronouns at the foot of A'-chains,
conditioned by agreement morphology. The CSC applies equally to A'-chains with gaps,
with resumptive pronouns, and to mixed cases like (43) with a pronoun in the first conjunct
and gap in the second.

(43) [ng-ngera_i [mirruul   er ngii_i a Sie] e   [a ?o?od-al   a
       CL-what   REAL.IPFV.make P it   Sie and   sister-3SG

       me?er-ar   __i]]
       REAL.PFV.buy-3SG
       'What did Sie make and her sister buy?'   (Georgopoulos 1985: 88)

On Georgopoulos' analysis, the 'gaps' are in fact null resumptive pronouns. This suggests
that the CSC in Palauan could be reconstrued as a parallelism constraint on binding along
lines developed by Ruys (1992) and discussed in Section 3.5.2.[16]
  Likewise, Kubota and Lee (2015) give the following examples to demonstrate that the
CSC holds in Japanese and Korean to the same extent as in English.

(44) a. [kami-ga   __ kyodakusi(-te)] [ningen-ga __ kinsisi-ta] ai
         god-NOM   allow-TE/allow-I man-NOM   forbid-PST love
         'a form of love which the god approved and the men forbade'
      b. #[kami-ga iseiai-o   kyodakusi(-te)] [ningen-ga __ kinsisi-ta] ai
          god-NOM heterosexuality allow-TE/allow-I man-NOM   forbid-PST love
          'a form of love which the god approved heterosexuality and the men forbade'

---

[16] Georgopoulos actually argued that the CSC in Palauan reflected a constraint on binding at S-structure, not
LF, but for reasons bound up in the GB theory of the time.

(45) a. [pwumo-ka __ cohaha(-yess)-ko] [canye-ka __ an-cohaha-nun]
       parent-NOM   like(-PST)-KO   child-NOM   NEG-like-REL
       panchan
       dish
       'the side dishes that parents like(d) and children do not like'

   b. #[pwumo-ka __ cohaha(-yess)-ko] [canye-ka kimchi-lul
        parent-NOM   like(-PST)-KO   child-NOM kimchi-ACC
        an-cohaha-nun] panchan
        NEG-like-REL   dish
        'the side dishes that parents like(d) and children do not like kimchi'

                                            (Kubota and Lee 2015: 654)

Patterns of asymmetrical A' extraction across different types of coordinate structure can also be replicated in Japanese and Korean. For instance, Kubota and Lee (2015) give the following examples of asymmetric extraction with 'cause–effect' and 'stage-setting' conjunctions, in (46) and (47) respectively. These correspond roughly to Lakoff's Type C and Type A, respectively.[17]

(46) a. [__ syutuensi(-te)]   [kookaisi-ta] sakuhin
           appear-TE/appear-I   regret-PST   piece
       'the piece (movie) that he appeared in and regretted'

   b. [__ mek-ko] [paythal-i   na-n]   umsik
          eat-KO   stomach.ache-NOM happen-REL food
       'the food that (I) ate and got a stomach ache'

(47) a. [daigaku-o sotugyoosi(-te)]   [__ syuusyokusi-ta] kaisya
          college-ACC graduate-TE/graduate-I   get.employed-PST company
       'the company that he graduated from college and got employed at'

   b. [shyaweha-ko]   [__ palu-n]   patiloshyen
       take.a.shower-KO   apply-REL body.lotion
       'the body lotion that I took a shower and applied'

                                            (Kubota and Lee 2015: 654–5)

Kazenin and Testelets (2004) demonstrate the same pattern in the Daghestanian language Tsakhur.[18]

However, the asymmetric extraction patterns are not universal. Postal (1998) demonstrates that two of the three patterns that Lakoff (1986) documented for English are unavailable in French. The example in (48a) shows an ungrammatical case of extraction in a Type A scenario with NARRATION, while (48b) shows ungrammatical extraction from a Type B scenario with VIOLATED EXPECTATION.

---

[17] The English translation of (46a) might suggest an undiagnosed ATB extraction pattern. However, this is just an artifact of the translation. Aoi Kawakita (pers. comm.) suggests that *kookaisita* would be better translated as intransitive 'felt regret', and that the noncoordinated ??*kookaisita sakuhin* ('the movie that he felt regret') is marginal, presumably because the relative *kookaisita* does not contain a gap. This suggests that the structure indicated in (46a) is accurate.

[18] Their description of the semantic factors conditioning asymmetric extraction differs slightly from Lakoff's, but the examples they give all appear to be compatible with Lakoff's generalizations.

(48) a. *le   pain   que Jacques [[a   couru au   marché], [(a) acheté
          the bread that Jacques has run   to.the market   has bought
          __], [(a) foncé   chez   lui], et   [(a) mangé __]]
               has rushed house.of him and   has eaten
          'the bread which Jacques ran to the market, bought, rushed home, and ate'

          (Postal 1998: 75)

   b. (i) *Combien de calvados Arnaud peut-il [[boire __] et
          how.many of calvados Arnaud can-he   drink   and
          [rester   lucide]]?
          remain   lucid
          'How many calvados can Arnaud drink and remain clear-headed?'

      (ii) *Quels véhicules Arnaud peut-il [[boire onze   calvados] et
           which vehicles   Arnaud can-he   drink eleven calvados and
           [rester   capable de conduire __]]?
           remain   capable of drive.INF
           'Which vehicles can Arnaud drink eleven calvados and remain capable of
           driving?'   (Postal 1998: 87)

We return to crosslinguistic differences like this in Chapter 4. However, the analyses discussed there suggest that the range of crosslinguistic variation is constrained: languages
do not vary without limit in which patterns of extraction from coordinate structures they
allow.

3.5 Scope of the CSC

The CSC was originally formulated with an implicit focus on what Chomsky (1977) called
wh-movement, now commonly known as overt A'-movement: apparently unbounded leftward phrasal movement showing a characteristic profile of island effects. Most of Ross's
examples involve relative clauses or questions (canonical examples of A'-dependencies),
and we will see below that other types of A'-dependency show similar patterns.

However, Ross's formulation clearly implies that movement in general, overt or covert, of
whatever type of constituent, should be similarly constrained. And, in fact, some of the most
interesting hypotheses about the CSC have sprung from comparing overt A'-movement
with other types of movement where it may seem that the CSC doesn't hold.

In the following subsections, we discuss evidence concerning the CSC as it applies
across the range of A'-dependencies, then covert movement, overt A-movement, and head
movement. We then turn in Section 3.6 to a more focused discussion of the so-called SLF
construction, where the status of the CSC is particularly nuanced.

3.5.1 Generality across A'-dependencies

The canonical examples illustrating the CSC and its exceptions all involve questions and
relative clauses. Since Chomsky (1977), these have been acknowledged to be part of a family

of A'-dependencies. Other members of this family also show the same pattern. For instance, ATB topicalization out of multiple conjuncts is grammatical.

(49)   This book, I [[read __] and [enjoyed __]].

However, topicalization out of a single conjunct is often ungrammatical, as in (50a). The comparison with (50b) shows that the topicalization is to blame for the ungrammaticality.

(50)   a.   ??This book, I [[read __] but [enjoyed this trashy movie more]].
       b.   I [[read this book] but [enjoyed this trashy movie more]].

Extraction out of a single conjunct is possible as shown in (51), though, in examples with the characteristic asymmetric interpretations described in Section 3.3.2. Example (51a) corresponds to Lakoff's Type A scenario, (51b) corresponds to Lakoff's Type B, and (51c) corresponds to Type C.

(51)   a.   This book, I [[stood on a soapbox] and [read __ out loud]] for hours.
       b.   This much wine, I could [[drink __] and [still stay sober]].
       c.   This book, I [[read __] and [felt queasy afterwards]].

The same kind of pattern can be demonstrated with *tough*-movement, which has been understood since Chomsky (1981) to involve an A'-dependency. The examples (52)–(54) are parallel in all relevant respects to the topicalization pattern just demonstrated.

(52)   This book is tough to [[read __] and [really enjoy __]].

(53)   a.   ??This book is tough to [[read __] and [enjoy the trashy movie adaptation]].
       b.   It is tough to [[read this book] and [enjoy the trashy movie adaptation]].

(54)   a.   This book is tough to [[stand on a soapbox] and [read __ out loud]] for hours.
       b.   This book is tough to [[read __] and [not feel queasy]].
       c.   This book is easy to [[read __] and [impress your friends with your newly acquired knowledge]].

This confirms that overt A'-dependencies are in general subject to the CSC, as we would expect. In practice, though, naturally occurring examples of asymmetrical A'-extraction from coordinate structures are much more uniform. In her study of asymmetric extraction from coordinate structures in the Penn Treebank (Marcus et al. 1999), Page (2017) found that virtually all of the examples contained relative clauses. We do not fully understand Page's findings, but suspect that they relate to factors to be discussed in Chapter 6: despite their syntactic similarity, A'-dependencies are not all alike information-structurally, and relative clauses may be particularly congenial to asymmetric extraction for fundamentally nonsyntactic reasons.

Rightward movement
Rightward movement out of coordinate structures is constrained by the CSC, as expected.

(55)   a. I [[took __ from Paul] and [gave __ to Sharon]] a classic book on horticulture.
        b. *I [[took a DVD from Paul] and [gave __ to Sharon]] a classic book on horticulture.
        c. *I [[took __ from Paul] and [gave a DVD to Sharon]] a classic book on horticulture.

There is some debate about the availability of asymmetric rightward movement out of co-ordinate structures. Lakoff (1986) demonstrated that rightward movement is compatible with Type A scenarios:

(56)   I [[went to the toy store], [bought __], [came home], [wrapped __ up], and [put __ under the Christmas tree]] one of the nicest little laser death-ray kits I've ever seen.

However, Steedman (2011) notes that rightward extraction from initial conjuncts in Type C scenarios is ungrammatical:

(57)   *Those guys in the Caucasus [[drink __ every day] and [live to be a hundred]] a kind of fermented mare's milk.   (Steedman 2011: 95)

Although neither Lakoff nor Steedman discusses this, we note that the same is true for Type B scenarios:

(58)   *I [[drank __] and [still stayed sober]] a gallon of fermented mare's milk.

Steedman takes this ungrammaticality as evidence for the marginality of asymmetric extraction from coordinate structures, as opposed to the productive and generally available symmetric extraction pattern (see Section 3.4.1 for brief discussion of Steedman's analysis of this putative marginality). However, Lakoff's Type A example speaks against this conclusion. We will see repeatedly in what follows that Type A extraction obeys different constraints from Types B and C, although we are unaware of any hypothesis that links rightward movement to these differences.

3.5.2 Covert movement

Very soon after Ross enumerated his constraints on movement, it was claimed that the same constraints restrict scope inversion. Specifically with respect to the CSC, Lakoff (1970) gave a contrast between (59a) and (59b), while Rodman (1976) made essentially the same point using structurally slightly different examples such as (60).

(59)   a. Abdul believes that many men like baba ganouze.
        b. Abdul believes that [[many men] and [few women]] like baba ganouze.
                                                        (Lakoff 1970: 408)

(60)   Every woman loves [[a dog] or [a cat]].   (Rodman 1976: 171)

The sentence in (59a) is scopally ambiguous: *many men* can take scope under or over *believes*, yielding readings paraphrasable as in (61a) and (61b), respectively.

(61)   a. Abdul believes that the men who like baba ganouze are many.

      b. There are many men of whom Abdul believes that they like baba ganouze.

If the scope of *many men* and *few women* were independently determined in (59b), we might therefore expect that example to be at least four-ways ambiguous, as either quantifier could independently scope under or over *believes*. However, (59b) is only two-ways ambiguous, like (59a). This limited ambiguity is explained if scope inversion is constrained by the CSC, so that the entire coordinate structure can take inverse scope, but neither conjunct can independently scope out of the coordinate structure.

The examples just given illustrate the effect of the Conjunct Constraint on scope inversion. Ruys (1992) gives (62) as an illustration that the Element Constraint also constrains scope inversion.

(62)   [[Someone from every branch of science] and [a student who had won the sweep-stakes]] (all) had dinner together.   (Ruys 1992: 33)

The sentence in (62) is two-ways ambiguous, but a third reading is missing. On one of the available readings, two people had dinner: a student, and an implausible person who is from every branch of science. On the other, if there are n branches of science, then as many as $n + 1$ people may have had dinner together: one person per branch of science, plus a student. These two readings can be obtained by permuting the relative scope of *someone* and *every branch of science* within the first conjunct.

The missing reading requires *every branch of science* to scope out of the first conjunct and take scope over *a student who had won the sweepstakes*. In that reading, for every branch of science, someone from that branch and a possibly different student had dinner, so for n branches of science, there are $2n$ diners. The absence of that reading follows from the Element Constraint, if the CSC constrains scope inversion.

Lakoff took data like these as evidence corroborating the hypothesis that movement was involved in relating semantic and syntactic representations—for Generative Semanticists, this took the form of the lowering of quantifiers from their scope position into their surface position, but more modern versions of the idea, following May (1977), assume instead that quantifiers raise from their surface position to their scope position at the syntactic level of Logical Form. Quantifier Raising, as an instance of syntactic movement, should obey the same locality constraints as overt movement.

Regardless of the general merits of the Lakoff/May hypothesis that scope inversion is an instance of movement, interactions between covert movement and coordination have been particularly informative about the nature of the Coordinate Structure Constraint. Central to the discussion have been examples of *wh* in situ like (63), from Ruys (1992) (see also Muadz 1991):

(63)   a. *I wonder who [[took what from Mary] and [gave a book to Fred]].

      b. I wonder who [[took what from Mary] and [gave it to Fred]].   (Ruys 1992: 36)

The ungrammaticality of (63a) follows if *what* moves out of the first conjunct to Spec,CP at LF, violating the CSC. The puzzling grammaticality of (63b), then, suggests that *it* in the second conjunct is an A'-bound pronoun at LF, functionally equivalent to the trace in the first conjunct. At LF, (63b) would then look approximately as in (64).

(64)   I wonder [who$_i$ [what$_j$ [t$_i$ [[took t$_j$ from Mary] and [gave it$_j$ to Fred]]]]].

The same kind of analysis explains (65), already noted by Rodman, in which a pronoun in the second conjunct appears to allow a quantifier to scope out of the first conjunct, provided that that quantifier binds the pronoun.

(65)   A soldier [[found every student] and [shot him]].   (Rodman 1976: 172)

This ability of bound pronouns to be used in the place of gaps in these contexts[19] suggests that the CSC should be reconstrued not as a condition on movement, but on interpretation: an operator must be associated with a variable in each conjunct, regardless of whether that association is derived by movement or not.

Ruys's reconstrual of the CSC did not reduce it to any independently motivated property. However, Fox (2000) claimed that the requirement that an operator bind a variable in each conjunct can be thought of as a **parallelism** constraint on the logical form of coordinate structures.[20] Fox (building on Sag 1976, Williams 1977, Hirschbühler 1982, among others) gets a lot of empirical leverage from a requirement that conjuncts have parallel structures at LF in certain respects. For instance, (66a) is scopally ambiguous, as we have seen. However, the second conjunct in (66b) disambiguates the first conjunct in favor of the reading where the existential has wide scope (this explains the impossibility of *different* in (66b), if *different* is interpreted as entailing that the students covary with the professors).

(66)   a. A (different) student likes every professor.   ($\exists > \forall, \forall > \exists$)
        b. A (#different) student [[likes every professor] and [hates the dean]].
                                                ($\exists > \forall, *\forall > \exists$, Fox 2000: 52)

Fox's explanation of this comes in several stages. First, *A student hates the dean* is 'scopally uninformative' because it only contains one quantifier, so there is no interpretive difference corresponding to a difference in relative scope of *a student* and *the dean*. Second, scope inversion is ruled out in scopally uninformative sentences for reasons of economy (optional operations with no effect on interpretation are disallowed), so *a student* must take wide scope in the second conjunct. Finally, parallelism constraints require the same scope relations to hold in each conjunct. In this way, the scopally uninformative second conjunct, together with parallelism and economy constraints, force the indefinite to take wide scope in the first conjunct.

An important open question concerns the scope of applicability of parallelism at LF. Parallelism is clearly closely related to the notion of symmetry discussed in Section 2.2. We have seen in Section 3.3.2 that patterns of extraction from coordinate structures deviate from those predicted by the CSC when an asymmetrical interpretation of the two conjuncts obtains. One possible way of making sense of this difference is that the parallelism requirements explored by Ruys and Fox only hold of symmetrical interpretations of coordinate structures. We will return to this possibility in Chapters 5 and 6.

---

[19] They are not fully interchangeable, of course. In all examples that we are aware of, the bound pronouns occur in noninitial conjuncts, but this is hardly surprising given general facts about the grammar of pronouns.
    [20] Fox also showed how this parallelism constraint can be made to follow from a 'multiplanar' analysis of coordination, which we will discuss in Chapter 4.

The foregoing discussion suggests that the CSC holds at LF, but should be reconstrued as following from a parallelism constraint on the LF representation of coordinate structures. This raises the question of the status of covert ATB movement. We will not be able to address this question in full until Chapter 4, but we report here some evidence from Bošković and Franks (2000) which suggests that there is no covert analog of classically construed ATB movement. The crucial point concerns sentences like (67).[21]

(67)   (*)Who said [[that John bought what] and [that Bill bought what]]?

The interpretation of (67) is distinct from that of (68), where overt ATB movement has taken place.

(68)   What did Mary say [[that John bought __] and [that Bill sold __]]?

This suggests that the two *what*s in (67) cannot both move covertly to a single Spec,CP position at LF. This in turn implies that the classical construal of ATB movement, with movement of multiple elements to a single position, is unavailable at LF. However, anticipating the discussion in Chapter 4, we note, following Gazdar (1981), that this way of thinking about ATB movement has not been operationalizable in any case since more restrictive theories of *wh*-movement emerged in the 1970s (e.g. Chomsky 1977).

We return to this issue in Section 4.5.5, where we discuss recent approaches to ATB movement based on multidominance or sideward movement. Those approaches predict directly that there is no covert ATB movement, by rejecting the problematic premise that ATB movement involves distinct copies of the moved element in every conjunct.

3.5.3 A-movement

The debate on A-movement out of coordinate structures initially focused on a straightforward prediction of the CSC, namely that A-movement out of a single conjunct should be impossible. In the 1970s and early 1980s, this prediction was widely taken to be falsified by coordination of active and passive VPs, as in (69).

(69)   I [[sinned] and [was forgiven]].   (McNally 1992: 336)

On classical transformational approaches, there is no VP-internal trace of *I* in unergative *I sinned*, while passive *I was forgiven* is derived by A-movement of *I* from an internal argument position. When the active and passive VPs are conjoined in (69), this requires that *I* form a chain with a trace in only the second, passive VP, giving a representation like (70).[22]

---

[21] Bošković and Franks give (67) as ungrammatical. We cannot agree with this judgment, but agree that it doesn't have a reading akin to (68). We speculate that the reason for the discrepancy between our judgments and those reported by Bošković and Franks is a matter of accessibility of an elided representation of the second conjunct, like (i), which is compatible with our interpretation of (67).

(i)   [[Who said that John bought what] and [~~who said~~ that Bill bought what]]?

[22] This analysis also requires that the surface subject position is simultaneously a θ-position with respect to *sinned* and a non-θ-position with respect to *was forgiven*.

(70)   I [[sinned] and [was forgiven __]].

This challenge was pounced on by two main groups of researchers. On the one hand, researchers in lexicalist traditions (particularly GPSG, following Gazdar 1981) took this as evidence in favor of nontransformational approaches to the passive, as in Bresnan (1978). If passives are derived in the lexicon, then there is no trace in either conjunct, and (69) is a complete representation of the relevant aspects of the structure.

   On the other hand, researchers committed to a transformational analysis of passives took (69) as evidence for an analysis involving sentential coordination and conjunction reduction, deriving (69) from a representation with an elided subject *I* in the second conjunct, as in (71).

(71)   [[I sinned] and [I̶ was forgiven]].

This latter analysis was quickly shown to be empirically inadequate, because of the familiar problem with quantificational subjects and conjunction: (72a) and (72b) are not truth-conditionally equivalent, so a derivation of one from the other by ellipsis is unfeasible.

(72)   a. Few people [[sinned] and [were forgiven]].
       b. [[Few people sinned] and [few people were forgiven]].

The same conclusion is reached when we consider a variant proposed by van Valin (1986), in which the second conjunct has an empty category as subject, as in (73).[23]

(73)   [[Few people sinned] and [PRO/*pro* were forgiven]].

As discussed by van Valin and by Godard (1989), (74) is truth-conditionally distinct from (72a). If the null pronoun in (73) is interpreted similarly to the overt pronoun in (74), this would entail that (73) also cannot represent the structure of (72a).

(74)   [[Few people sinned] and [they were forgiven]].

This debate dissolved with the emergence of the VP-internal subject hypothesis (Fukui and Speas 1986, Koopman and Sportiche 1991). Under this hypothesis, Spec,IP is always a derived subject position (at least, in the relevant cases), to which noun phrases move from a θ-position within VP (later *v*P or VoiceP). As shown almost simultaneously by Burton and Grimshaw (1992) and McNally (1992), this hypothesis requires a trace within each conjunct, as in (75), in compliance with the CSC.

(75)   I [[__ sinned] and [was forgiven __]].

This advance essentially nullified the above debate because conjunction of active and passive sentences now had an analysis that conformed with the CSC, making them uninformative about the scope of the CSC, the domain of application of conjunction reduction, and the analysis of passive sentences.

---

[23] Van Valin demonstrated that none of the standard GB empty categories were in fact a good match for this environment.

This uninformativeness allowed Kyle Johnson, in a string of papers (2000, 2002, 2004, 2009, 2014; see also Lin 2001, 2002) to claim that the CSC does not, in fact, directly constrain A-movement.[24] His reasoning was grounded in Gapping examples like (76), originally discussed by Siegel (1987), Oehrle (1987), and McCawley (1993).

(76) a. [[Ward can't eat caviar] and [Mary eat beans]].
      b. [[Mrs. J can't live in Boston], or [Mr. J anywhere near LA]].
      c. [[No one$_i$'s duck was moist enough], or [his$_i$ mussels tender enough]].
      d. [[The duck is dry] and [mussels tough]].[25]

In principle, it would be possible to analyze such examples as derived from sentential coordinations like (77) by ellipsis (Johnson calls this the 'Large Conjuncts analysis').

(77) a. [[Ward can't eat caviar] and [Mary can't eat beans]].
      b. [[Mrs. J can't live in Boston] or [Mr. J can't live anywhere near LA]].
      c. [[No one's duck was moist enough] or [his mussels were tender enough]].

However, (76) and (77) have clear interpretive differences. For instance, (77a) could be represented as $(\neg P) \wedge (\neg Q)$, while (76a) appears instead to have the form $\neg(P \wedge Q)$ (for instance, in a scenario where both Ward and Mary can eat caviar, the former is interpreted as false while the latter may be true). Similarly, (76b) is interpreted as $\neg(P \vee Q)$, which is truth-conditionally identical (through De Morgan's law) to $(\neg P) \wedge (\neg Q)$. So a paraphrase with sentential coordination would have to be (78) and not (77b).

(78) [[Mrs. J can't live in Boston] and [Mr. J can't live anywhere near LA]].

Deriving (76b) from (78) is no longer a simple matter of ellipsis, though: a complete analysis would also have to explain how *and* in (78) has become *or* in (76b).

Finally, a comparison of (76c) and (77c) reveals a further problem: in (77c), *his* cannot be interpreted as bound by *no one*, but that binding relationship is in fact established in (76c). On standard assumptions, this indicates that *no one* c-commands *his* in (76c) but not in (77c).

Johnson takes these contrasts as evidence in favor of an alternative, 'Small Conjuncts', analysis (illustrated schematically in (79), following Lin 2002), in which elements smaller than clauses are conjoined, an apparent gap in the noninitial conjunct results from ATB head movement from both conjuncts, and Spec,IP is filled by a subject extracted from only the first conjunct.[26]

---

[24] Johnson (2004) is a manuscript originally circulated in approximately 1996, known under two different titles ('Bridging the gap' and 'In search of the English middle field'), and with the content apparently changing significantly over time. The comments made here are representative of the version publicly available on Johnson's personal homepage as of early 2019.

[25] This last example, with a determiner apparently shared across conjuncts to the exclusion of the rest of the subject, raises a range of issues that are ultimately orthogonal to those that we focus on. See McCawley (1993) and Johnson (2000).

[26] Lin chooses an asymmetric analysis of VP conjunction but notes that Johnson's analysis is equally compatible with a symmetrical *n*-ary branching structure.

(79)

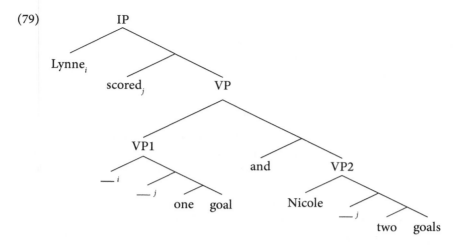

This Small Conjuncts analysis relies crucially on the VP-internal subject hypothesis also leveraged by McNally (1992) and Burton and Grimshaw (1992): the subject of the second conjunct remains in its VP-internal position, while the EPP is satisfied only by the subject of the first conjunct. This is only even conceivable, though, if A-movement out of a single conjunct is possible.

The facts seem to require an analysis along these lines, at least on orthodox assumptions about the relationship between syntactic structure and semantic scope. The more pertinent question for us is why asymmetric A-movement is possible. In fact, Johnson argues that there are two distinct cases in which asymmetric A-movement is possible, both building on Ruys's argument (see Section 3.5.2) that the CSC is a constraint on operator–variable relations at LF.

In the first case, the A-moved subject undergoes total reconstruction at LF. This means that the A-movement is essentially invisible at LF, yielding an LF representation like (80a), eventually translated into a semantic representation along the lines of (80b). In such a representation, the CSC has nothing to do at LF, because movement has been 'undone' and there is no variable binding across the boundary of the coordinate structure.

(80) a.

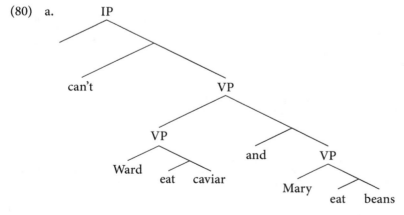

b. $\neg[\diamond[\text{eat}'\,(w, c) \wedge \text{eat}'\,(m, b)]]$

In the other case, *no one* is interpreted in its surface position, binding a variable in each conjunct and thereby satisfying the CSC at LF. As in Ruys's example (63), the variable in the first conjunct is the trace of A-movement, and the variable in the second conjunct is a pronoun. This allows a semantic representation for (77c) like (81).

(81) $\neg\exists x.[\text{person}(x) \wedge [\text{moist}(\text{duck-of}(x)) \vee \text{tender}(\text{mussels-of}(x))]]$

A structure like the one in (79) can account for such examples: *no one* must be high enough to establish an appropriate structural configuration for binding of the pronoun in the second conjunct,[27] but must undergo total reconstruction if it doesn't bind such a variable in each conjunct.

This approach renders the CSC almost inert with respect to A-movement, but not quite. Firstly, Johnson notes a difference with respect to variable binding in (82), which follows from the impossibility of raising *no boy* high enough to bind the pronoun in the *there*-insertion structure.[28]

(82)   a.   [[No boy$_i$ is in this room] and [his$_i$ mother in the other]].
       b.   *[[There is no boy$_i$ in this room] and [his$_i$ mother in the other]].

(Johnson 2004: 42)

In sum, it may be that the CSC does not constrain asymmetric A-movement to the same extent as asymmetric A'-movement. Rather, Ruys's approach to the CSC, as developed by Johnson, predicts that asymmetric A-movement out of coordinate structures is permitted under certain circumstances. That prediction is largely borne out, although extensive tests of the limits of asymmetric A-movement have not yet been developed.

3.5.4   Head movement

Although we do not have much to say about interactions between head movement and the CSC, the following example from Johnson suggests that head movement, too, is subject to the CSC.

---

[27] This structural configuration is often taken, slightly simplistically, to be c-command. *No one* does not in fact c-command *his* on the surface, so the validity of the c-command claim relies on assumptions about Quantifier Raising out of noun phrases, a debate which falls outside the scope of this book. All that matters for us is that, if NP c-commands *his*, then Spec,NP can bind *his*, as illustrated in (i).

(i)   [[*Every diner*]'s mussels] tested *his* jaw muscles.

This is the same configuration as in Johnson's analysis of (76c), in all relevant respects.

[28] A further place to look for predictions may be in examples like (i).

(i)   #[[No boy is in this room] and [my mother in the other]].

Unlike (82a), here there is no bound variable in the second conjunct, so the sentence is predicted to be unacceptable. Indeed, it is very odd, but this is plausibly unrelated to the CSC, because (ii) is still odd, despite being an instance of regular sentential conjunction with no extraction. We assume that this is because it is unclear what discourse relation holds between the conjuncts in (ii).

(ii)   #[[No boy is in this room] and [my mother is in the other]].

The conclusions for A-movement and the CSC are therefore unclear.

(83)   *What$_i$ has$_j$ [[Betsy __$_j$ purchased __$_i$] and [Sally will talk about __$_i$]]?

(Johnson 2002: 118)

The ungrammaticality of (83) is surprising if Ruys's LF-based approach to the CSC is combined with the common assumption (e.g. Chomsky 2001) that head movement is semantically vacuous. If the CSC is a constraint on operator–variable configurations at LF, and if head movement does not create such operator–variable relations, then one might reasonably expect head movement to be immune to the CSC. Of course, this may indicate either that Ruys's approach is problematic, that head movement is visible at LF (as for example in Lechner 2007), or that (83) is somehow not representative. For lack of a clearer understanding, we do not pursue the matter further here.

3.6 The SLF construction

This section discusses the **SLF** construction, which has been the focus of a large amount of research in the Germanic syntax–semantics community since Höhle (1983, 1990).[29] A German example of the construction is in (84); although it has a much more restricted distribution in English, (85) illustrates essentially the same phenomenon.

(84)   In den Wald ging der Jäger und fing einen Hasen.
        in the forest went the hunter and caught a hare
        'Into the forest went the hunter and caught a hare.'   (Wunderlich 1988: 289)

(85)   Down came the rain and washed the spider out.   (Bjorkman 2014)

In these examples, the subject of the first conjunct is also interpreted as the subject of the second conjunct. However, the subject is buried within the first conjunct, apparently in a position where it doesn't c-command any material in the second conjunct. Standard syntactic constraints on subject–predicate relations therefore apparently fail to obtain. Because of this, it may seem that these examples are derived from sentential coordination by deletion of a preverbal subject in the second conjunct—the *Subjektlücke*, or subject gap, referenced in Höhle's name for the construction.

On this analysis, SLF constructions would be examples of sentential coordination with ellipsis, and therefore largely unrevealing about our core topic of extraction from coordinate structures. However, there are grounds for preferring an alternative analysis, a variant of the Small Conjuncts analysis developed by Johnson (2002) and discussed in Section 3.5.3. According to this analysis, SLF constructions are instances of subsentential coordination (for instance, coordination of VP), allowing the subject in Spec,TP to c-command both conjuncts. This entails that the fronted presubject material has been asymmetrically extracted from the first conjunct.

---

[29] The naming of these constructions is shrouded in confusion. In Höhle's term 'SLF', the 'SL' stands for *Subjektlücke* 'subject gap'. The 'F' stands for 'finit' or 'frontal'. This was then translated by Wunderlich (1988) into English as 'subject gap in fronted finite verb coordination', or 'SGF-coordination' for short. We therefore have multiple acronyms, one of which has multiple expansions, for this construction. We will call it the 'SLF construction' and try not to think too deeply about why.

The construction is especially revealing about the syntax of asymmetric extraction, because German displays different word orders in main and embedded clauses. Neither conjunct in (84) displays the verb-final order associated with subordinate clauses, and in certain related examples this allows a more precise probe into the syntax of the relevant co-ordinate structures. Because of these differences in word order, it will turn out that German allows us to study asymmetric coordination, independently of asymmetric extraction.

At the same time, the lessons learned from the German construction only straightfor-wardly generalize to a proper subset of the mainly English data considered so far, because the asymmetric extraction in SLF constructions is always from the initial conjunct alone. For this reason, we treat the phenomenon separately here in depth, draw what we take to be the key lessons, and then refer back only sporadically in what follows.

In Section 3.6.1, we describe what is known about the crosslinguistic distribution of the SLF construction, before focusing on German for the rest of the section. Section 3.6.2 lays out some key empirical generalizations concerning the SLF construction, and Section 3.6.3 critically surveys current analyses of the construction.

3.6.1 Crosslinguistic distribution of the SLF construction

Most research on the SLF construction has been conducted on German, and the construc-tion is known to be widespread across Germanic languages. However, there are differences among Germanic languages in the degree of availability of the SLF construction. As shown below, in (86), Dutch only very marginally allows argument-initial SLF constructions, unlike German, while English allows SLF constructions only in a handful of inversion contexts like (87a), repeated from (85), and (87b).

(86) ??Dit voorstel   heeft de   commissie __ gevolgd en heeft een nieuwe
     this suggestion has   the committee   followed and has   a   new
     subcommissie gevormd.
     subcommittee set.up
     'The committee has followed this suggestion and has set up a new subcommittee.'
                                                     (Heycock and Kroch 1994: 273)

(87) a. Down came the rain and washed the spider out.
      b. 'You'll never see me again', said the assassin and rode into the sunset.

Although precise analyses do not appear to have been developed, it seems likely that these crosslinguistic differences reflect a combination of independent factors, including degree of acceptability of non-ATB movement (which Heycock and Kroch claim is lower in Dutch than in German), and availability of inversion (which is much more limited in English than Dutch or German because of its largely non-V2 grammar).

The distribution of SLF constructions beyond Germanic is largely unknown. At this point we can offer only a handful of data points, mainly summarizing the findings of Kus-mer (2018), whose main focus is an SLF-like construction in the Central Khoesan language, Khoekhoegowab. This construction is shown in (88)–(89). (88) exemplifies a standard VP-coordination structure, (89a) shows the characteristic SLF structure, and (89b) illustrates the ungrammaticality of a similar extraction from the second conjunct.

(88)   Dandagob   ge   [[amsa ǁnae] tsi   [ǂnaba ra   ǂna]].
       Dandagob   DECL   song sing and   dance IPFV dance
       'Dandagob is singing a song and dancing a dance.'

(89)   a. Amsa$_i$=b   ge   Dandagoba __$_i$ ǁnae tsi ǂnaba ra   ǂna.
           song-3SM DECL Dandagoba   sing and dance IPFV dance
       b. *ǂnaba$_i$=b ge Dandagoba amsa ǁnae tsi __$_i$ ra ǂna.   (Kusmer 2018: 1)

Kusmer's Khoekhoegowab data reveal several structural similarities with German and
Dutch, which in turn suggest hypotheses about the relationship between SLF constructions and more central word order phenomena. First, Khoekhoegowab is underlyingly
OV, as shown in (88)–(89). However, OV order is clearly not a necessary condition for
the emergence of SLF constructions, as demonstrated by the existence of such structures in
English and North Germanic. Kusmer demonstrates that it is also not a sufficient condition,
because Hindi does not allow SLF constructions.

(90)   a. Raam [[kuttoN-ko pasand kartaa hai]   aur   [billiyoN-se nafrat
           Raam   dogs-DAT   liking do   PRES and   cats-COM   hatred
           kartaa hai]].
           do   PRES
           'Raam likes dogs and hates cats.'
       b. *kuttoN-ko Raam pasand kartaa hai   aur   billiyoN-se nafrat
           dogs-DAT   Raam liking do   PRES and   cats-COM   hatred
           kartaa hai.
           do   PRES
           'As for dogs, Raam likes them and hates cats.'   (Kusmer 2018: 9)

Khoekhoegowab also exhibits second-position phenomena: clitics like *ge* in (88)–(89)
must be preceded by precisely one constituent, not necessarily the subject. It is possible that second-position phenomena are a necessary condition for the SLF construction:
even the examples in English come from the 'residual V2' parts of English syntax. However, Kusmer shows that second-position phenomena are not a sufficient condition for
SLF constructions. He cites Manetta (2006) as demonstrating that Kashmiri is a language
with second-position phenomena, and demonstrates that Kashmiri does not allow SLF
constructions.

(91)   a. Mohan [[chu film vuch-aan] ta   [chu su boz-aan]].
           Mohan AUX film see-PRT   and   AUX it hear-PRT
           'Mohan is seeing the film and hearing it.'
       b. *Film chu Mohan vuch-aan ta   chu su boz-aan.
           film AUX Mohan see-PRT   and   AUX it hear-PRT
           'Mohan is seeing the film and hearing it.'   (Kusmer 2018: 9)

The current state of knowledge of the crosslinguistic distribution remains quite preliminary, then: it is found across several Germanic languages, and at least one unrelated
language, but no factor has been identified which predicts its availability in a given
language. With that proviso, we focus in the following subsections on German.

3.6.2 Asymmetric coordination and SLF-coordination

Reich (2009) demonstrates that ATB extraction is dissociable from asymmetric extraction from coordinate structures: there are coordinate structures which permit only ATB extraction, only asymmetric extraction, or both extraction patterns. He goes on to define 'asymmetric coordination' as a coordinate structure allowing only asymmetric extraction, and then shows that instances of asymmetric coordination, in this sense, always show verb-fronting in noninitial conjuncts. That is, the verb always surfaces in first or second position, depending on whether the second conjunct contains an overt subject. This restriction is quite unsurprising in those cases where the first conjunct also shows V2 order, but remarkable in cases, such as conditionals with *wenn* 'if', where the initial conjunct is in a verb-final order. Examples are in (92).

(92) a. Wenn du   nach Hause kommst und siehst den Gerichtsvollzieher
         if   you to   house come   and see   the bailiff
         vor   der Tür   stehen ...
         before the door stand
         'If you come home and see the bailiff standing in front of the door ...'
                                                      (Büring and Hartmann 1998)

     b. Wenn du   nach Hause kommst und den Gerichtsvollzieher steht
         if   you to   house come   and the bailiff   stands
         vor   der Tür, ...
         before the door
         'If you come home and the bailiff is standing in front of the door, ...'

These asymmetric coordinations contrast with the symmetrical structure, with all conjuncts verb-final:

(93) Wenn du   [[nach Hause kommst] und [den Gerichtsvollzieher vor
       if   you to   house come   and the bailiff   before
       der   Tür   stehen siehst]], ...
       the   door stand   see
       'If you come home and see the bailiff standing in front of the door, ...'

SLF-coordination is just the matrix-clause counterpart of this structure. As expected of German matrix clauses, V2 word order is found in the first conjunct and V-final word order is not generally available. If the preverbal position in the first conjunct is filled by the subject, as in (94), the sentence is in principle ambiguous between a symmetrical C'-coordination structure, and an asymmetric structure in which verb fronting in the second conjunct reflects the correlation just described. In such cases, according to Reich, the sentence patterns with symmetrical coordination.

(94) Der Jäger   [[ging in   den Wald] und [fing   einen Hasen]].
       the hunter went into the forest and caught a   hare
       'The hunter went into the forest and caught a hare.'

When the preverbal material in the first conjunct is *not* a subject, it becomes clear that the structure is asymmetric.[30] The fronted material is associated with a gap only in the first conjunct, and it is not possible to associate it with a gap in both conjuncts simultaneously (as in (95b)) or in the second conjunct alone (as in (95c)).

(95) a. Die Briefmarken zeigt   Karl dem   Onkel und bietet sie   ihm
         the stamps   shows Karl the.DAT uncle and offers them him
         zum   Verkauf an.
         to.the sale   PRT
         'Karl shows the stamps to the uncle and offers them for sale.'   (Höhle 1983)

      b. *Die Briefmarken zeigt   Karl dem   Onkel und bietet __ ihm
         the stamps   shows Karl the.DAT uncle and offers   him
         zum   Verkauf an.
         to.the sale   PRT

      c. *Die Suppe wird der Peter sich hinlegen und essen __ .
         the soup   will   the Peter self down.lie   and eat
         'Peter will lie down and eat the soup.'   (Schwarz 1998: 210)

All of this is different if the second conjunct contains an overt subject: suddenly, symmetrical ATB extraction is required. From this, Reich concludes that the subject gap in (95) is an indicator of asymmetric coordination when the initial conjunct is a matrix V2 clause.

(96) Die Briefmarken [[zeigt Karl dem   Onkel] und [bietet er
      the stamps   shows Karl the.DAT uncle   and   offers he
      {__ / *sie} ihm zum   Verkauf an]].
                   them him to.the sale   PRT
      'Karl shows the stamps to the uncle and offers him them for sale.'

This is the most important property for our purposes: asymmetric coordination in Reich's sense, as diagnosed by the presence of a subject gap, only allow asymmetric extraction from the first conjunct, not ATB movement.

  The challenge posed by asymmetric coordination and the SLF construction is that in many respects, it is just like any other binary coordinate structure: there are two conjuncts, with a conjunction in between. Moreover, the material before the conjunction looks like a regular sentence of the language in question. However, the material after the conjunction looks neither like a subordinate clause (the verb is in the wrong place) nor like a main clause (there must be a subject gap, and the usual verb-second order is absent).

---

[30] There is some unclarity as to which nonsubjects are possible in SLF-coordination. Reich claims that the initial position can only be filled by the 'formal movement' of Frey (2005), and not by the kind of 'true A'-movement' that generates information-structurally nonneutral interpretations. This predicts that the structurally highest element in TP must be asymmetrically moved to Spec,CP in SLF-coordinations. This accounts for cases where the adverbial elements which fill Spec,CP arguably could scramble past the subject within TP to become the structurally most prominent element.

  However, examples of SLF constructions with apparent true A'-movement, like (i) or indeed (95a), are attested in the literature. These are incompatible with Reich's claim.

(i) Das   Gepäck ließ er   fallen und rannte zum   Hinterausgang.
     the.ACC luggage let   he   fall   and ran   to.the rear.exit
     'He dropped the luggage and ran to the rear exit.'   (Heycock and Kroch 1994: 258)

As we fill in the details of the SLF construction in the remainder of this subsection, we will not find a single analysis that accounts for all of the properties of the construction. However, we will see that the most promising analyses treat the construction as structurally very similar to certain analyses of regular coordination, particularly the adjunction analysis of Munn (1993). In this way, learning about the SLF construction is informative about the analysis of coordination in the general case.

Interpretation of the second conjunct subject
The subject in an SLF construction must be interpreted as scoping over the predicates denoted by the individual conjuncts. This can be demonstrated by comparing the data presented in the next examples. (97), with symmetrical conjunction, can be interpreted as true if two different women hold these two roles or if (less plausibly) the same woman holds both.

(97)   Eine Frau   [[ist in Amerika Außenministerin] und [bekleidet in
       a   woman   is in America foreign.minister   and holds   in
       Deutschland sogar das zeithöchste   Amt des   Staates]].
       Germany   even the second.highest office of.the country
       'A woman is foreign minister in America and even holds the second highest office
       of the country in Germany.'   (Büring and Hartmann 1998: 188)

(98) is an SLF-variant of (97), and the only reading which remains is one where the same woman holds both positions.

(98)   In Amerika ist eine Frau   Außenministerin und bekleidet in
       in America is a   woman   foreign.minister and holds   in
       Deutschland sogar das zweithöchste   Amt des   Staates.
       Germany   even the second.highest office of.the country
       'In America, a woman is foreign minister and even holds the second highest office
       in Germany.'   (Büring and Hartmann 1998: 187)

In principle, this interpretation of (98) could suggest that the subject of the second conjunct is a null pronominal, equivalent to overt *sie* 'she'. However, other examples show that this is not the case. (99) is interpreted with *jeder* scoping over both predicates, but an overt pronoun in the second conjunct blocks this interpretation.

(99)   Um drei Uhr   war jeder$_i$ angekommen und (*er$_i$) hatte seine$_i$
       at three o'clock was everyone   arrived   and he   had   his
       Freundin geküßt.
       girlfriend kissed
       'At three o'clock everyone had arrived and had kissed his girlfriend.'
                                                (Heycock and Kroch 1994: 269)

And (100) makes it clear that the SLF-variant in (100a) and the variant in (100b) differ with respect to the scope of negation.

(100) a. Katharina kam noch nie   nach Hause und war betrunken.
          Katharina came still never to   house and was drunk
          'Katharina never came home and was drunk.'

b. [[Katharina kam noch nie   nach Hause] und [sie war betrunken].
   Katharina came still   never to   house and she was drunk
   'Katharina never came home, and she was drunk.'

(Büring and Hartmann 1998)

The conclusion, exactly parallel to the facts discussed in Section 3.5.3, is that deletion analyses of the missing subject are not promising in the general case.

Binding from first to second conjunct

In addition to the anaphoric dependency between the subject roles of the two conjuncts, quantifiers in the first conjunct can bind variables in the second conjunct. This includes cases where there is no plausible surface c-command relationship between the quantifier in question and the pronoun interpreted as a bound variable.

(101) a. Im   Zirkus Krone steht   hinter jedem Löwen eine Dompteuse
          in.the circus Krone stands behind every lion a   tamer
          und krault   ihm den Rücken.
          and scratches him the back
          'In the Krone circus, a tamer stands behind every lion and scratches his back.'
       b. Im   Zirkus Krone serviert der Dompteur jedem Löwen eine
          in.the circus Krone serves   the tamer   every lion an
          Antilope und würzt   sie mit   Löwensenf.
          antelope and seasons it with lion.mustard
          'In the Krone circus, the tamer serves every lion an antelope and seasons it with lion mustard.'
          (Büring and Hartmann 1998)

Nonsubject gaps in SLF constructions

We have seen that the second conjunct in SLF constructions must contain a subject gap. Gaps associated with object roles are generally not permitted.

(102) *Den Hund hat keiner gefüttert und hat er geschlagen.
        the dog has no-one fed   and has he hit
        'No-one has fed the dog and he has hit (it).'   (Johnson 2002: 107)

Fortmann (2005) offers a more subtle generalization: the gap in the second conjunct must correspond to the structurally highest argument. If the main verb in the second predicate prefers non-subject-initial orders, then gaps corresponding to the initial argument are possible. For instance, *beschimpfte* in (103) prefers an object–subject order, and Fortmann claims that this drives the acceptability of the object gap in the second conjunct.

(103) %Gestern   beleidigte uns der Staatsanwalt und beschimpfte der
        Yesterday insulted   us the prosecutor   and cursed   the.NOM
        Schöffe.
        jury
        'Yesterday the prosecutor insulted us and the jury cursed (us).' (Reich 2009: 49)

Reich (2009) states that such examples are ungrammatical for him, and we are unaware of the status of Fortmann's claim. Regardless, it is uncontroversial that the gap in the second conjunct does not range freely over arguments, and almost always corresponds to the subject.

Interpretive relation between conjuncts

Asymmetric extraction from coordinate structures is commonly taken to require an asymmetric discourse relation between the two conjuncts. This is not true in the general case for asymmetric coordination in Reich's sense, and plausibly also not true for the special case of SLF-coordination. Although many researchers, following Heycock and Kroch (1994) among others, assume that 'Across-The-Board violations of this nature appear to be most acceptable when the actions referred to in the two conjuncts can be interpreted as occurring in sequence' (Heycock and Kroch 1994: 273), this is probably not a necessary condition. We summarize several pieces of evidence which suggest that SLF-coordination does not require such a sequential interpretation.

First, Mayr and Schmitt (2017) show that some instances of asymmetric coordination (as diagnosed by word order, including the subject gap in the second conjunct) are reversible.[31]

(104)   a. Leider   [[haben viele Kinder   Probleme mit dem Gewicht]
            unfortunately have   many   children problems with the   weight
            und [können nicht lesen]].
            and can   not   read
            'Unfortunately, many children have weight problems and are unable to read.'
        b. Leider   [[können viele Kinder   nicht lesen] und [haben
            unfortunately can   many   children not   read   and have
            Probleme mit   dem Gewicht]].
            problems with the weight
            'Unfortunately, many children are unable to read and have weight problems.'
                                                            (Mayr and Schmitt 2017: 7)

This kind of coordinate structure is even possible with disjunctions. This is in contrast to the examples of asymmetric extraction discussed in previous subsections, which are limited to conjunction.

(105)   Leider   [[können viele Kinder   nicht lesen] oder [haben
        unfortunately can   many   children not   read   or   have
        Probleme mit   dem Gewicht]].
        problems with the weight
        'Unfortunately, many children are unable to read or have weight problems.'
                                                            (Mayr and Schmitt 2017: 8)

Second, Reich (2009) shows that SLF-coordination is compatible, with overt signaling, with examples in which the iconic temporal order of events is reversed, as in (106).

---

[31] Although (104) shows a subject gap in the second conjunct, it is not an unambiguous instance of SLF-coordination because the initial adverb *leider* arguably scopes over both conjuncts, which would imply that it has not moved from within the first conjunct.

(106) Morgen   werde ich meine besten Freunde bekochen und bereite
      tomorrow will   I   my   best   friend   cook.for and prepare
      deswegen heute schon mal ein paar Sachen vor.
      therefore today already   a   few   things for
      'Tomorrow, I'll cook for my best friend, and therefore today I'm already preparing
      a few things.'   (Reich 2009: 105)

Finally, data from Schwarz (1998), to be discussed further in the following subsection, perhaps show asymmetric extraction from the first of two conjoined NPs, a kind of nominal analog of SLF-coordination. The only possible interpretation of this coordinate structure appears to be as an instantiation of the discourse relation PARALLEL.

(107) Äpfel ißt   der Hans [[drei   __] und [zwei Bananen]].
      apples eats the Hans three   and two bananas
      'Hans eats three apples and two bananas.'   (Schwarz 1998: 195)

Admittedly, none of these examples constitute watertight evidence that the SLF construction allows symmetrical interpretations. Ideally, we would see a case of genuine verbal SLF-coordination with PARALLEL holding between the two conjuncts. We haven't quite seen that: (104) has PARALLEL in an SLF-like surface string, but without the asymmetric extraction; (106) has an atypical, but still asymmetrical, discourse relation between the two conjuncts; and (107) with NP-coordination, is strictly speaking a separate construction, albeit one with clear formal similarities to SLF-coordination, because it involves extraction from noun phrases rather than clauses.

Having said that, the examples just examined jointly imply that any constraint requiring an asymmetric interpretation of SLF-coordination would be worryingly construction-specific. In particular, (104) shows that SLF-like asymmetric coordinate structures (with a subject gap in the noninitial conjunct) don't require an asymmetric interpretation, and (107) shows us that asymmetric extraction from coordinate structures doesn't require an asymmetrical interpretation. SLF-coordination is really just the combination of these two properties, so we do not expect that there should be any direct constraint on the discourse relation holding between conjuncts in SLF-structures.

3.6.3 Analyses

Ellipsis

The most conservative approach to the analysis of SLF-structures is to deny that asymmetric extraction is involved. Instead, SLF-coordination could be analyzed as a result of ellipsis applying to sentential coordination. This approach was popularized by Wilder (1994) and elaborated by Schwarz (1998). Schwarz offered a generalization which is probably the strongest piece of evidence in favor of this approach, namely that the initial conjunct must be a well-formed independent sentence, while the noninitial conjunct needn't be. For example, the well-formedness of (107), for Schwarz, is directly related to the well-formedness of the following two sentences, where ellipsis has applied to the second.

(108) a. Äpfel ißt der Hans drei.
    apples eats the Hans three
    'Hans eats three apples.'
  b. Der Hans ißt zwei Bananen.
    the Hans eats two bananas
    'Hans eats two bananas.'

However, the ellipsis analysis is no longer widely adopted, because of the facts reported in the previous section concerning the interpretation of the subject of the second conjunct. As shown above (see discussion of (99) and (100)), there is no unelided sentential equivalent of the interpretation of the second conjunct in an SLF-structure: when there is a quantifier or negation in the first conjunct, neither repeating the quantifier or inserting a pronoun in the subject position of the second conjunct gives the correct truth conditions. This suggests that the conjuncts in SLF constructions are smaller than full sentences, so material placed before the conjunction can scope over both conjuncts. This, in turn, implies that sentential coordination with ellipsis will not be able to provide the basis of an empirically adequate account of the SLF construction.

We note in passing that the same appears to be true of Schwarz's nominal 'odd coordination' construction in (107). Variants with quantified subjects exhibit readings which are not compatible with straightforward variants of the ellipsis approach. (109a) describes a single woman who eats five pieces of fruit, not one woman who eats three apples and another who eats two bananas. (109b) is quite degraded, plausibly because of an intervention effect caused by *keine Frau*, but to the extent it is interpretable, it is interpreted as saying that there is no woman who eats five pieces of fruit.

(109) a. Äpfel ißt eine Frau drei und zwei Bananen.
    apples eats a woman three and two bananas
    'A woman eats three apples and two bananas.'
  b. ??Äpfel ißt keine Frau drei und zwei Bananen.
    apples eats no woman three and two bananas
    'No woman eats three apples and two bananas.'

The fact that these interpretative effects mirror those observed in SLF constructions simultaneously strengthens the evidence that nominal 'odd coordination' is essentially the same kind of beast as the SLF construction, and that that construction cannot be derived by ellipsis from sentential coordination.

Direct coordination

The ellipsis account is the only current analysis of the SLF construction which does not involve asymmetric extraction from the first conjunct.[32] To the extent that the arguments just given against that analysis are valid, we can conclude that the SLF construction involves asymmetric extraction from coordinate structures. However, we can go further

---

[32] There is one other exception, namely the LFG account of Frank (2002). This analysis pairs symmetrical CP-coordination in c-structure with asymmetric projection of values for 'grammaticalized discourse functions' such as SUBJ or TOPIC from the initial conjunct at f-structure. We do not discuss Frank's account in detail because it is not fully developed, and we have doubts about its descriptive adequacy as it stands. In principle, though, this LFG-based approach could be a third alternative.

and learn about the internal syntax of the coordinate structures from which this asymmetric extraction takes place. In the next few paragraphs, we largely follow Heycock and Kroch (1994), before critiquing their analysis.

The first conjunct of an SLF construction is straightforwardly a CP, because it displays all the hallmarks of standard German verb-second. If we adopt the standard analysis of V2, involving verb movement to C and movement of some XP to Spec,CP, the initial conjunct must be a CP.

The second conjunct is at least a C', because the verb is not in final position. IP and VP in German are head-final, while CP is head-medial. The nonfinal position of the verb in the second conjunct of an SLF construction suggests that the verb in that conjunct is also in C.

However, the subject of the first conjunct (typically in Spec,IP, given that the initial conjunct shows non-subject-initial V2 orders) scopes over both conjuncts. This suggests that the second conjunct should be no larger than I', in order to allow the subject to c-command it.

Heycock and Kroch propose an ingenious solution to this apparent paradox. It revolves around the idea that in certain circumstances, the IP and CP projections can be 'collapsed' into a single CP/IP projection, essentially because all material in the IP layer moves on further to CP. This innovation allows Heycock and Kroch to analyze SLF constructions as coordination of an initial I' conjunct with a final C'/I' conjunct (see (110)), where the C' element accounts for the verb-initial order of the final conjunct, and the I' element accounts for the fact that it conjoins with an initial I'.

(110)

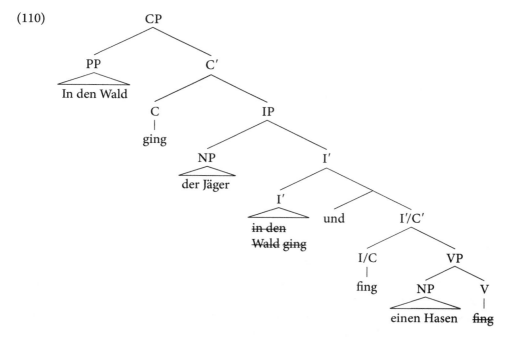

Johnson (2002) advocates another version of this Small Conjuncts approach, but involving conjunction of phrases slightly larger than VP, which Johnson calls FP. Because the second conjunct is smaller than CP for Johnson, he cannot adopt Heycock and Kroch's labeling-based approach to the word order of the second conjunct. Instead, he uses the existence of verb projection raising constructions like West Flemish (111) to argue that OV West Germanic languages sometimes allow verb movement to an initial projection below IP. FP is Johnson's label for that projection.

(111)   ... da   Jan   wilt   dienen   boek   kuopen.
         that Jan wants that   book   buy
         '... that Jan wants to buy that book.'   (Johnson 2002: 112)

This leads Johnson to propose the structure in (112) for SLF-coordination.

(112)

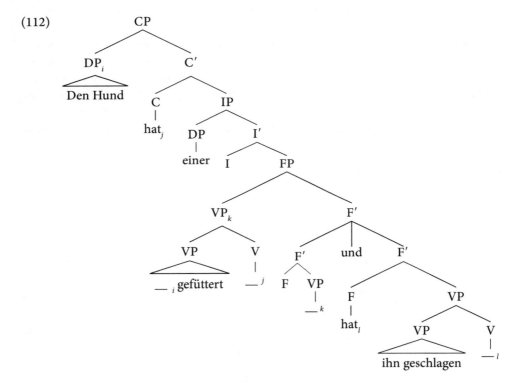

However, there are several challenges to Johnson's approach. One problem is that there is no independent evidence for verb projection raising in languages (including German) which nevertheless allow SLF-coordination. This does not mean that the approach is incorrect, but rather that it does not reduce the number of unanswered questions.

A more direct empirical problem for Johnson's approach is that there is evidence, from Mayr and Schmitt (2017), that the initial conjunct is larger than FP. In particular, (113a) shows that SLF coordination cannot be embedded in IP-coordination. The idea is that the first two conjuncts are an SLF construction, while the first and third conjuncts contain subjects and are therefore naturally analyzed as IP-coordination. On Johnson's analysis, this should be analyzable as a nested coordinate structure as in (113b), with the SLF-coordination, realized as conjoined FPs, embedded within conjoined IPs. The fact that this structure is ungrammatical is simply explained if Johnson's hypothesis is incorrect, and the SLF construction involves at least IP-coordination.

(113)   a. *Gestern   musste   [[[der Hans morgens   mit der Anna
            yesterday must.PST   the Hans in.morning with the Anna
            frühstücken] und [sollte   abends   mit der Maria
            have.breakfast and should.PST in.evening with the Maria
            ausgehen]] und [der Peter die Susi treffen]].
            go.out   and   the Peter the Susi meet
            'Yesterday, Hans had to have breakfast with Anna in the morning, and was
            supposed to go out with Maria in the evening, and Peter had to meet Susi.'
            (Mayr and Schmitt 2017: 10)

       b. $[_{IP} [_{IP_1} [_{FP}\ FP_1\ and\ FP_2]]\ and\ IP_3]$

A further challenge for both approaches comes from the fact that the order of conjuncts cannot be reversed (see also Kathol 1993). For Heycock and Kroch (similar concerns apply to Johnson, mutatis mutandis), it should be just as possible to have a C'/I' initial conjunct, and an I' final conjunct, but that leads to ungrammatical orders. Depending on various assumptions, this might be expected to generate sentences like (114), where the subject is in the initial Spec,IP/CP and *ging* is in I/C. Other more outlandish suggestions for ways in which Heycock and Kroch's analysis overgenerates are given in Schwarz (1998) and elsewhere.

(114)   *Der Jäger $[_{I'/C'}$ ~~der Jäger~~ ging in den Wald] und $[_{I'}$ einen Hasen
        the hunter   went in the forest and   a   hare
        fing].
        caught

Again, it is possible in principle that some independent factor will rule out this example and others like it. We just don't know what that factor is.

Adverbial analyses

All of the analyses considered so far assume that SLF constructions are coordinate structures, to be analyzed in broadly the same terms as any other coordinate structure. An alternative, first pursued by Büring and Hartmann (1998), treats noninitial conjuncts in SLF constructions as adverbials, with *und* as a kind of subordinating conjunction. For Büring and Hartmann, this variety of *und* adjoins to I', and selects a CP within which topic drop has taken place: a null operator corresponding to a topic moves to Spec,CP, as in (115).

(115)

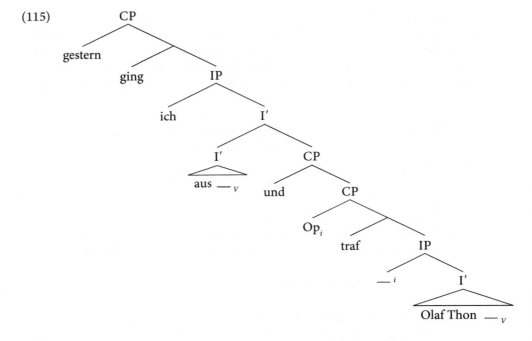

The major empirical challenge for this approach is explaining why the element undergoing topic drop must be a subject, as under normal circumstances topic drop is not restricted in this way.

Reich (2009) offers perhaps the most promising analysis in this vein. Simplifying many details concerning the precise attachment height and nature of the heads in the noninitial conjunct, the structure Reich proposes is approximately as in (116).

(116)

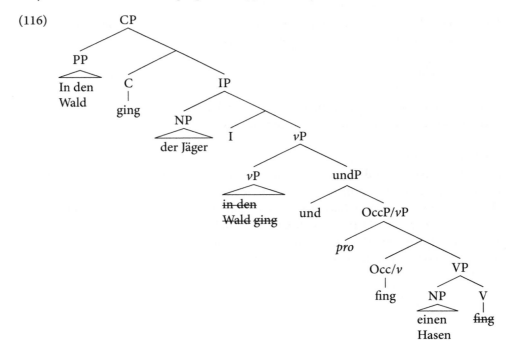

This structure is similar to Büring and Hartmann's: the second conjunct is an adverbial, headed by *und*, adjoined to the first. However, the internal structure of that second conjunct is smaller than a clause, so the problem with topic drop is avoided. All of the action is on the *v*P projection in that second conjunct: Reich postulates a feature, [OCC], which triggers the semantic effects Reich observes in asymmetric coordination and licenses verb movement as a marker of those effects (specifically, it requires the event described in the second conjunct to be part of the event described by the first conjunct). The system he develops then requires the subject of the noninitial conjunct to be realized as a *pro* in Spec,*v*P.

The primary empirical improvement of Reich's analysis over Büring and Hartmann (1998) is that it explains why the gap in noninitial conjuncts must be a subject. At the same time, it improves on Heycock and Kroch (1994) in that it hints at an explanation for why the subject gap must be in the noninitial conjunct. At the same time, though, questions remain. First, Reich's use of [OCC] essentially lumps together, by stipulation, all distinctive syntactic and semantic/pragmatic properties of SLF-coordination in a single head (indeed, Reich describes [OCC] as a grammatical reflex of a discourse-structuring strategy). Second, it is not clear that this approach addresses the challenge from Mayr and Schmitt (2017) concerning the impossibility of embedding an SLF-coordination within an IP-coordination. Finally, the status of Reich's *pro* requires further scrutiny, given that Heycock and Kroch (1994) demonstrate that the subject of the second conjunct is not interpreted like an overt pronominal (see Bjorkman 2014 and Mayr and Schmitt 2017 for alternative, multidominance-based approaches to the problem of the missing subject).

3.6.4 SLF-coordination: Summary

Although no fully satisfactory analysis has been developed, established properties of the SLF construction, and asymmetric coordination more broadly, impose several constraints on possible analyses. These constraints in turn imply several lessons for the analysis of coordinate structures.

In SLF-coordination, instances of binding from the first to the second conjunct, and interactions of the second conjunct subject position with quantifiers, indicate that the second conjunct attaches below the initial conjunct subject position. The second conjunct must be at least large enough to accommodate whatever triggers verb fronting, but the structure of the second conjunct must be 'truncated' relative to a main clause, to account for the fact that the usual range of V2-related phenomena is not found in the second conjunct. Some asymmetric syntactic dependency of the second conjunct on the first is required to account for the fact that this 'truncation' (including the subject gap) is located specifically in the noninitial conjunct.

Although Büring and Hartmann, and Reich, are at pains to distinguish the phrase structure of SLF-coordination from that of regular coordination, we observe, with Reich, that the phrase structure adopted in the adverbial analysis is very close to that proposed for coordination in general by Munn (1993), in which noninitial conjuncts are also treated as adjuncts. The main difference is that, while Munn's system requires coordination of likes, the adverbial analysis allows some divergence in the categories of the conjuncts (this divergence is very slight for Reich, and greater for Büring and Hartmann). However, we have already seen, in Section 2.4.1, the argument from Sag et al. (1985) that the categories which figure in coordinate structures may be nondistinct rather than literally identical (this being why it is possible to coordinate, for instance, an AP and an NP in certain contexts). It is possible that the categories employed by Büring and Hartmann, or Reich, count as nondistinct in that sense.

If we commit to an analysis along these lines, there are three important implications for our broader research questions. The first is that the SLF construction offers some indirect support for Munn's adjunction analysis of coordination. The second is that the construction allows asymmetric extraction from the first conjunct only. The third, following the discussion in Section 3.6.2, is that this extraction is available across many discourse relations, and does not appear to be restricted to the scenario types described by Lakoff (1986) and discussed in Section 3.3.2. This is an early indication that asymmetric extraction from initial conjuncts is not restricted in the way that Lakoff proposed, a theme that we will develop in Chapters 5 and 6.

3.7 Summary

It would be easy to get the impression that the CSC is a hallmark of coordinate structures, in that all coordinate structures obey the constraint (even coordinate structures which do not allow movement obey it vacuously). The CSC would then be a unique, and uniform, syntactic property, capable of diagnosing coordinate structures, unlike the properties discussed in the previous chapter. Whether or not this is actually the case is perhaps the major subject of empirical disagreement among researchers working on coordination, revolving around the status of asymmetric extraction patterns:

Choice Point 2 What is the relationship between symmetrical and asymmetric patterns of extraction from coordinate structures?

>   Option 1: The unmarked pattern of extraction is symmetrical ATB extraction; all asymmetric extraction patterns are marked in some way (e.g. Postal 1998, Haspelmath 2004, Steedman 2011).
>   Option 2: ATB extraction has no special status in the syntax vis-à-vis asymmetric extraction patterns (though it may have a special status in the semantics, for instance because of a parallelism constraint, e.g. Ruys 1992, Munn 1993).

Although we will entertain both options in what follows, our impression is that the evidence favors Option 2. We have seen the following cases of asymmetric extraction from coordinate structures—a list long enough to call the status of the CSC into question.

- Extraction of a whole conjunct (Section 3.3.1);
- Lakoff's three scenarios and their different asymmetric extraction patterns (Section 3.3.2);
- Other asymmetric patterns, including Schmerling's Type D, and Culicover and Jackendoff's coordinate structures interpreted as conditionals (Section 3.3.2);

- Covert *wh*-movement from a single conjunct (Section 3.5.2);[33]
- The SLF construction (Section 3.6) and related constructions discussed by Johnson and others (Section 3.5.3).

If one claimed that all coordinate structures obey the CSC, it would follow that none of the phenomena just listed could involve coordinate structures. And yet those phenomena look like coordinate structures, swim like coordinate structures, and quack like coordinate structures.

Moreover, interpretive factors occupy a prominent, but evanescent, place in this list. The classes of counterexamples from Lakoff, Schmerling, and Culicover and Jackendoff described in Section 3.3.2 are defined in terms of their asymmetric interpretation, whereas the covert *wh*-movement analyzed by Ruys (1992) is constrained by considerations of semantic parallelism among conjuncts. However, the SLF construction may permit both asymmetric and symmetrical interpretations, as discussed in Section 3.6.2, and there does not appear to be a semantic angle to research on extraction of whole conjuncts as described in Section 3.3.1.

In the light of these considerations, three broad approaches can be discerned.[34]

Choice Point 3   What do the CSC and its exceptions derive from?

Option 1: Coordination is syntactically unique; the CSC follows from the unique syntax of coordination, together with general syntactic locality principles; apparent exceptions to the CSC can also be explained in syntactic terms;

Option 2: Coordination is not syntactically unique; the CSC and its exceptions follow from general syntactic locality principles;

Option 3: Coordination is not syntactically unique; the CSC follows from a semantic parallelism constraint as in Ruys (1992), Fox (2000); exceptions to the CSC follow from nonsyntactic considerations of the sort sketched by Lakoff (1986).

The rest of this book is about the tension between these three approaches.

3.8 Who calls the shots?

Of the three options just enumerated in Choice Point 3, the first two are strictly syntactic, in that they approach the challenge of extraction from coordinate structures in purely syntactic terms, while the third is not, because of the explanatory role it affords to discourse structure in accounting for patterns of extraction from coordinate structures. The first option is syntactically maximalist, in that it allows construction-specific statements about the syntax of coordination. The other two options are syntactically minimalist, in

---

[33] This asymmetric movement pattern is explained by the Ruys/Fox reconstrual of the CSC as a constraint on binding patterns at LF, as discussed in Section 3.5.2. However, it seems unlikely that this account can capture any of the other asymmetric patterns listed here.

[34] There is also a fourth logical possibility: coordination is syntactically unique, but the CSC does not follow from its unique properties. While there is nothing incoherent about this position, it has not been seriously pursued, to our knowledge.

that they assume that there is nothing special about coordination syntactically. The simplest option, from a syntactic perspective, would be the second, if it were feasible, but this is also the option with the least scope for analyzing the diversity of extraction patterns listed in the previous section. There is therefore a tension concerning the degree to which the explanatory burden is placed on bespoke pieces of syntactic theory, as in Option 1, and extrasyntactic influence, as in Option 3. We will refer to these two approaches as **syntax calls the shots** and **discourse calls the shots**, respectively.[35]

The 'syntax calls the shots' approach typically involves postulating a syntactic analog of interpretive distinctions, to ensure that distinctions between symmetrical and asymmetrical *and* are syntactically visible and allow their different extraction patterns to be described in syntactic terms. This was the approach of Ross (1967): he claimed that the asymmetrical interpretation of (17a), reproduced as (117), reflected an underlying subordination structure along the lines of (118).

(117)   I went to the store and bought the whiskey.

(118)   I [went to the store [to buy the whiskey]].

Ross suggests that in (16a), repeated in (119), conversion of *to buy* to *and bought* occurs after relativization of *the whiskey*, so at the point at which relativization occurs, the syntactic representation does not contain a coordinate structure.

(119)   Here's the whiskey which I [[went to the store] and [bought __]].

Schmerling (1972) demonstrated that Ross's specific analysis was untenable: (117) is not semantically reducible to (118), because the former entails that I bought whiskey, while the latter doesn't. This leads to minimal pairs like the following.

(120)   a.   I [went to the store [to buy some whiskey]], but the sales clerk persuaded me to buy Ripple instead.
         b.   *I [[went to the store] and [bought some whiskey]], but the sales clerk persuaded me to buy Ripple instead.   (Schmerling 1972: 94)

Lakoff (1986) also argued against Ross's proposal. He demonstrated that in sentences that contain more than two conjuncts, like (121) below, extraction can take place from sets of conjuncts that look quite arbitrary from a syntactic perspective. There is no connective that can replace *and* in such examples.

(121)   a.   What did he [[go to the store], [buy __], [load __ in his car], [drive home], and [unload __]]?
         b.   This is the kind of brandy that you can [[sip __ after dinner], [watch TV for a while], [sip some more of __], [work a bit], [finish off __], [go to bed], and [still feel fine in the morning]].   (Lakoff 1986)

---

[35] Another possible approach is to deny that syntax and discourse are encapsulated from each other, but this is probably a nonstarter, because of the problem of scale: syntax is concerned with sentential phenomena, and discourse is not. There are only loose similarities between the intersentential structures of interest in discourse semantics, and the sentence structures of interest to syntacticians.

Ross's specific proposal therefore cannot be maintained. However, Ross's methodology remains viable, and has in fact been pursued in essence by Goldsmith (1985) and Postal (1998), among others: introduce a syntactic difference between symmetrical and asymmetric *and*, and build a purely syntactic locality theory which is sensitive to that difference.

Perhaps the most subtle analysis along these lines to date comes from Weisser (2015), which we will discuss as representative of both the potential of this approach, and the challenges facing it. Weisser proposes that instances of asymmetric coordination arise when a coordinate structure is derived transformationally from an underlyingly subordinate structure. The proposed structure is as in (122), where the structurally highest conjunct moves from within the other conjunct.[36] Although we omit the details, iterated conjunction structures such as those discussed by Lakoff are taken to be the result of nesting this kind of coordinate structure.

(122)   the whiskey...

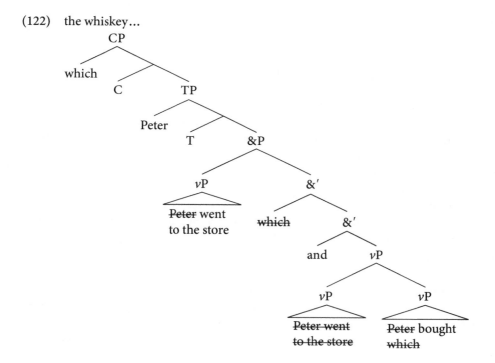

Weisser claims that asymmetric extraction is possible if the extractee moves *before* the coordinate structure is created. In the terms of the tree diagram in (122), the *v*P *Peter went to the store* is initially adjoined to the *v*P *Peter bought which*. Movement of *which* occurs at this point, and only afterwards is the coordinate structure created by movement of *Peter went to the store* to Spec,&P. This allows Weisser to build an analysis which creatively mixes subordinate and coordinate properties of asymmetric coordination, in just the way

---

[36] No tree diagram in Weisser (2015) represents all the details of Weisser's analysis simultaneously. In (122), we have extrapolated (we hope faithfully) from the partial diagrams he provides.

that Ross envisioned. He also avoids Schmerling's objection to Ross's original analysis, because nothing in his proposal entails a semantic identity between asymmetric coordination and a regular subordinating structure.

Nevertheless, there are serious concerns about Weisser's approach. On a basic analytical level, we don't have a semantics for his analysis of asymmetric coordination: it would appear that asymmetric *and* takes two arguments, one of which is underlyingly a proper part of the other. How this works compositionally is unclear.

A further concern arises from the derivation of asymmetric extraction. The conjunct which moves to Spec,&P must be the conjunct from which extraction *doesn't* take place (see Weisser for a generalization of this statement to cases with more than two conjuncts). If extraction takes place from the final conjunct, this entails a traditional Specifier–Head–Complement order.[37] However, if extraction takes place from the initial conjunct, the final conjunct must be in Spec,&P. This entails instead a mirror-image Complement–Head–Specifier order. This raises eyebrows in its own right, and also is incompatible with the correlations established by Johannessen (1998) (see Section 2.4) between basic word order and asymmetric inflectional patterns in coordination. For these reasons and others, we believe that Weisser's approach is not tenable in its current form, despite its clear advances over previous purely syntactic treatments.

The purest form of the alternative 'discourse calls the shots' approach denies that the CSC is a syntactic phenomenon at all: patterns of extraction from coordinate structures are claimed either to reduce to independent constraints, or to correspond to certain discourse-semantic or information-structural effects. The acceptability of the extractions then reflects conditions on those strictly nonsyntactic effects. Lakoff (1986), discussed in Section 3.3.2, is an example of this approach; we discuss other examples in Chapters 5 and 6.

A major problem for pure 'discourse calls the shots' approaches is that crosslinguistic differences in extraction patterns are a poor fit with the discourse-structural explanations which might be expected to be universal. In contrast, it is uncontroversial that languages differ syntactically, so crosslinguistic variation is less of a challenge for 'syntax calls the shots'.[38]

As noted at the outset, there are no clear grounds for preferring either approach a priori, and there are several conceivable intermediate positions, where the range of attested empirical phenomena arises from a combination of syntactic and extrasyntactic considerations (in fact, the approach that we will advocate in this survey is just such a hybrid approach). There is complexity inherent in the data, and the research question is how to distribute that complexity across components of a grammar. It is clear that empirical phenomena in this area do not come neatly labeled as syntax or discourse. The goal is for theories of syntax and discourse to interact well to predict the kinds of patterns described in this chapter.

---

[37] A similar problem arises in the adjunction-based approach of Cormack and Smith (2005).

[38] A more basic problem for 'discourse calls the shots' is that no discourse-based theory exists that engages with anything like the full range of extraction patterns that we have observed, whatever the other merits of the work that has been done in this broad approach. We will discuss this, and evaluate the prospects for developing such a theory, in Chapters 5 and 6.

In Chapter 4, we concentrate on the 'syntax calls the shots' approach. We will see that nuanced syntactic theories can capture some of the patterns described, including a surprisingly large proportion of the asymmetric cases, but these theories are no match for the semantic conditioning of asymmetric extraction described in Section 3.3. Notions like NARRATION or VIOLATED EXPECTATION simply are not plausible components of syntactic structures. Lakoff's claims are therefore the empirical focus of Chapter 5. We will see that there are grains of truth in Lakoff's claims, but also several notions that cannot be integrated into a full theory of discourse relations, and several empirical challenges which call into question the basis of Lakoff's account.

In short, by the end of Chapter 5, we will have established that both 'syntax calls the shots' and 'discourse calls the shots' have their merits, but neither is particularly promising on its own. This paves the way for a more exploratory discussion in Chapter 6 of other potential approaches, which move beyond the syntax–discourse dichotomy.

4

Syntax calls the shots

4.1 Introduction

This chapter surveys syntactic theories which attempt to explain patterns of extraction from coordinate structures in purely syntactic terms. This type of research has developed in response to a challenge left open by Ross (1967), namely how to make sense of the observed constraints on movement.

The chapter is structured as follows. In Section 4.2, we make some preliminary remarks about what a purely syntactic explanation would look like in this context, and then, in Section 4.3, we summarize key themes in locality theory, the branch of syntax inspired by Ross's challenge. Section 4.4 then demonstrates that the CSC is an outlier in narrowly Chomskyan approaches to locality theory, and in fact always has been.[1] In the context of the lack of fit between the CSC and the rest of narrowly Chomskyan locality theory, it is helpful to distinguish three broad types of syntactic account.

1. Approaches which reject narrowly Chomskyan locality theory and develop alternatives in which the CSC is not an outlier;
2. Approaches which superimpose a narrowly Chomskyan locality theory on a unique theory of the syntax of coordination;
3. Approaches which attempt a unification with narrowly Chomskyan locality theory by reducing coordinate structures to other syntactic structures (in particular, adjunction).

We survey these three approaches in the second half of this chapter. Section 4.5 discusses approaches to locality which diverge from the narrowly Chomskyan approach. Arguably, these theories are sometimes too successful in deriving the CSC: they integrate it into the core set of constraints on nonlocal syntactic dependencies, and therefore struggle to account for the exceptions to the CSC documented in the second half of Chapter 3. Much the same seems to be true of 'multiplanar' theories of coordinate structure, which exemplify the second approach listed just listed, although the details of these approaches are often less clear. We discuss multiplanar theories of coordination in Section 4.5.5.

---

[1] By 'narrowly Chomskyan', we mean the string of theories developed by Chomsky and colleagues since Ross's thesis, including the Extended Standard Theory and Revised Extended Standard Theory (e.g. Chomsky 1973, 1977), Government and Binding Theory and Principles and Parameters (Chomsky 1981), and the Minimalist Program (Chomsky 1995). We mean to exclude the broader class of generative syntactic theories, including Generalized Phrase Structure Grammar (Gazdar 1981) and Combinatory Categorial Grammar (Ades and Steedman 1982) among others, which have developed formally quite different locality theories, also discussed in this chapter, which give a more central place to the CSC.

Coordination and the Syntax–Discourse Interface. Daniel Altshuler and Robert Truswell, Oxford University Press.
© Daniel Altshuler and Robert Truswell (2022). DOI: 10.1093/oso/9780198804239.003.0004

As for the third approach, we will discuss reductions of adjunction to coordination, and vice versa. Takahashi (1994) reduces adjunction to coordination, and proposes a variant of narrowly Chomskyan locality theory which incorporates the CSC (see Section 4.5.4). This approach faces the same challenge as the approaches mentioned in the previous paragraph: it integrates the CSC so tightly into locality theory that it is hard to see how to account for exceptions.

We discuss attempts to reduce coordination to adjunction in Section 4.6. A key consideration here is the similarities and differences between ATB extraction and **parasitic gaps**, the other major class of multiple gap construction, in which adjuncts figure prominently. We believe that this approach holds real promise, particularly because adjunction is an asymmetric relation, and as such can be pressed into service to explain certain asymmetric extraction patterns. However, it is too weak to capture only the range of extraction patterns documented in Chapter 3 on its own. This understanding of what can, and what cannot, be explained by a reduction of coordination to adjunction will feed into our survey of 'discourse calls the shots' in Chapters 5 and 6.

4.2 Desiderata for a syntactic account

Before we turn to syntactic accounts of the CSC, a few brief words are in order about a distinction which can be hard to draw in practice, but which we believe is useful in navigating the syntactic literature in this area. This distinction is similar, but not identical, to the classic distinction between **descriptive** and **explanatory adequacy**, in the terms of Chomsky (1965).

For Chomsky, a descriptively adequate linguistic theory is one which 'makes a descriptively adequate grammar available for each natural language', where a descriptively adequate grammar is one which 'correctly describes the intrinsic competences of the idealized native speaker' (p. 24), and so can distinguish between well-formed and ungrammatical sentences, and assign an appropriate structural description to the well-formed ones. An explanatorily adequate theory is one which can map primary linguistic data to descriptively adequate grammars, and so account for relevant aspects of 'the innate predisposition of the child to develop a certain kind of theory to deal with the evidence presented to him' (p. 26).

There is a link between explanatory adequacy and formal universals, in Chomsky's sense, because some formal universals are surely consequences of the fact that infants, as language learners, are not blank slates. Rather, 'the child approaches the data with the presumption that they are drawn from a language of a certain antecedently well-defined type' (p. 27).

Many of the theories to be discussed in this chapter assume that the CSC is, or is derived from, a formal universal, and therefore that an explanatorily adequate theory of grammar should contain some statement or statements which entail the CSC.[2] We want to distinguish two ways in which this could be the case. On the one hand, it would be possible to take any theory of grammar which contained definitions of 'movement' and 'coordinate structure', and add the CSC as an additional stipulation constraining possible grammatical structures.

---

[2] However, as Mark Steedman (pers. comm.) points out, theories which reduce the CSC to universal properties of conjunctions, rather than strictly structural universals, instead reduce the CSC to a substantive universal. The Law of Coordination of Likes is one such candidate for a substantive universal. We will consider another in Chapter 6.

We will call this an **extrinsic** account, because there would be no great consequences for the heart of the theory of grammar if this stipulation were omitted. On the other hand, a researcher might develop a theory where the CSC follows as a consequence of more basic properties of grammar. We will call this an **intrinsic** account.

An example from a different empirical area may make the difference clearer. Imagine (contrary to fact—see Shieber 1985) that there are no cross-serial dependencies in any natural language. That is, imagine that languages may exhibit nested dependencies of the form in (1a), but they never exhibit crossing dependencies of the form in (1b).

(1)   a. $A_1B_1C_1 \ldots C_2B_2A_2$
      b. $A_1B_1C_1 \ldots A_2B_2C_2$

An extrinsic account of this generalization may consist of some very general statement about the nature of grammars (for example, that a Turing machine can be constructed that recognizes all and only grammatical sentences of any given language), supplemented by the following statement.

(2)   No grammar allows arbitrarily many crossing dependencies.

The statement in (2) guarantees that no grammar generates the pattern in (1b), but it does not follow from any more fundamental properties of a general characterization of grammars.

Alternatively, we could account for the putative absence of patterns like (1b) through a general hypothesis like the following.

(3)   A Context-Free Grammar can be constructed that recognizes all and only grammatical sentences of a given language.

The absence of cross-serial dependencies follows from (3): it is an intrinsic property of Context-Free Grammars that they do not allow arbitrarily many crossing dependencies. If (again, contrary to fact) there were no cross-serial dependencies in natural language, (3) would give us a chance of explaining why not.

Extrinsic constraints are often used in linguistic theories to rein in 'misuse' of an overly expressive formalism. Extrinsic statements may also exceptionally allow some structure which is banned in the general case, to describe some construction whose properties do not follow from a general theory of grammar. In contrast, intrinsically weak statements, aiming at explanatory adequacy, have the virtue of tying one's hands analytically: if you remove an extrinsic statement from a theory of grammar, nothing much else changes. The same is not true for intrinsic properties. For instance, the demonstration by Shieber (1985) of cross-serial dependencies like (4) in Swiss German is universally accepted as a demonstration that natural language syntax is not context-free, because there are no promising ways to argue against the conclusion. Falsification of a nontrivial hypothesis is rarely so cut and dried.

(4)   ... mer d' chind   em Hans   es   huus   lönd   hälfe   aastriiche.
         we_1 the children.ACC_2 Hans.DAT_3 the house.ACC let_1 $help_2$ $paint_3$
      '... we_1 let_1 the $children_2$ $help_2$ $Hans_3$ $paint_3$ the house.'   (Shieber 1985: 335)

In (4), three verbs come at the end, preceded by their respective arguments. The first subject is associated with the first verb, the second with the second verb, and so on—the cross-serial pattern from (1b), as opposed to the nested pattern in (1a). Moreover, the dative case on *em Hans* is governed by *lönd*, strongly suggesting that the dependencies are syntactic, rather than purely semantic, in nature.

Shieber's data argue equally strongly against an extrinsic formulation like (2), or an intrinsic one like (3). But the consequences that follow from falsification of the intrinsic formulation are more wide-ranging, precisely because (3) represents an attempt to hardwire a ban on cross-serial dependencies into the way grammar works. The demonstration that natural languages can contain cross-serial dependencies entails that the theory of grammar should be built on a formalism that is (slightly) more expressive than Context-Free Grammars (see, e.g., Weir 1988 for a description of such formalisms).

Ross (1967) stated the CSC extrinsically. In the grammatical architecture of the day, a grammar consisted of a context-free base component, augmented by cyclically ordered transformations, yielding a grammatical formalism of what was subsequently shown (Peters and Ritchie 1973) to be very high expressive power.[3] Ross's constraints extrinsically reduced the scope of the transformational component.

Since Chomsky (1973), a major focus of generative syntax has been on the development of syntactic formalisms that derive constraints like Ross's as direct consequences of intrinsic properties of the way syntax works.[4] A major thrust of Chomsky's research in the 1970s and beyond (Chomsky 1973, 1977, 1981, 1995) was a gradual integration into the core of syntactic theory of both the locality constraints themselves, and the transformational operations that they were intended to constrain: conditions like the Subjacency condition (Chomsky 1973) generalized over Ross's constraints, thereby reducing the number of extrinsic statements. The introduction of traces (Wasow 1972, Chomsky 1973, Fiengo 1974) paved the way for a unification of movement and anaphora, which in turn paved the way for replacement of individual transformations like passivization with very general statements of movement rules (Chomsky 1976, 1977, 1981). Finally, the copy theory of movement (Chomsky 1993, 1995) allowed the obliteration of the distinction between movement and basic syntactic structure-building (Internal and External Merge, Chomsky 2000), following a trend toward movement-free theories of syntax visible since at least Gazdar (1981) and Ades and Steedman (1982). By this point, not only had the extrinsic nature of Ross's locality constraints been eradicated to a large extent, but so had the exceptional nature of the transformations that they were intended to constrain.

This attempt to integrate locality constraints into the heart of syntactic structure-building presupposes that those constraints are syntactic. On Ross's original formulation, where locality constraints extrinsically restrict the power of the transformational component, it is less critical what the ultimate source of those constraints is, even though Ross himself clearly conceived of his constraints as syntactic, and stated them in syntactic terms. That leaves open the possibility that the ultimate explanation for the constraints is not

---

[3] Given that transformations were relatively poorly understood at the time, it is arguable that they themselves were extrinsic to the context-free core of the syntactic component.

[4] This presentation is influenced by comments from Mark Steedman about the motivation for the development of Combinatory Categorial Grammar (Ades and Steedman 1982, and many subsequent publications). Steedman claimed that Chomskyan theories of the 1970s and 1980s (though possibly not Chomskyan theories from Chomsky 1995 on) were content with extrinsic statements of constraints on transformations, in the terms used here.

syntactic—a possibility made more salient in this particular case because of the assumption, prevalent in the Generative Semantics of the time, that the underlying structures of syntactic representations were transparently related to semantic representations. Indeed, discourse-semantic reductions of Ross's locality constraints were sketched already by Morgan (1975) and Kuno (1976). Although we will save the details of these approaches for Chapter 6, the implication is already clear: to the extent that Ross's constraints are not really syntactic, a reduction of those constraints to intrinsically syntactic properties is misguided.

In this way, subtle empirical debates about questions and relative clauses quickly expand to imply distinctive hypotheses about the architecture of the grammar, and the empirical questions raised in Chapter 3, particularly Section 3.3.2, can potentially inform our understanding of the nature of the relationships between syntax, semantics, and discourse.

The different analyses of coordinate structures that we saw in Chapter 2 imply different explanations of the CSC. A major point of the GPSG theory of coordination, particularly as in Gazdar (1981), was to provide an intrinsic, explanatory account of the CSC, which we will discuss in Section 4.5.1. The same goes to an extent for the multiplanar theories of coordination in Section 4.5.5, and some of the other theories surveyed in this chapter. The challenge for these theories should already be clear: they make strong predictions, which means that they are particularly affected by apparent counterexamples in the form of asymmetric extraction patterns.

Other theories do not share this property. For some, like Pesetsky (1982), discussed in Section 4.5.2, the statements which derive the CSC are more or less extrinsic, and could be modified without affecting the heart of the syntactic theory. This is weaker, and therefore less affected by the challenges from asymmetric extraction. Particularly interesting are Munn (1993), Zoerner (1995), and Johannessen (1998), which reduce coordinate structures to other X'-theoretic structures. These theories intrinsically derive predictions which do not match the CSC, and so directly challenge the status of the CSC as a formal universal. Section 4.6 shows that the predictions which follow intrinsically from Johannessen's theory are a poor fit for the patterns observed in Chapter 3, but the intrinsic predictions of Munn's theory may hold empirical advantages over the CSC, relating to a comparison between extraction from coordinate structures and from adjuncts, which have not been widely acknowledged.

Before we reach these discussions, we demonstrate that mainstream Chomskyan locality theory does not make clear intrinsic empirical predictions about extraction from coordinate structures (unless a structure such as Munn's or Johannessen's is adopted), and in particular does not predict the CSC or provide a natural framework for making sense of the CSC. Section 4.3 briefly introduces key elements of that locality theory, and then Section 4.4 shows that the CSC is a poor fit for the theory.

4.3 The rest of locality theory

In this section, we describe major developments in Chomskyan locality theory from Ross (1967) to Rizzi (1990). We will initially only discuss Chomskyan locality theory, as it is among the best-known current approaches, and is useful as a point of comparison for other theories to be discussed here. We also initially restrict ourselves to the period 1967–90, because Ross (1967) is the catalyst for the development of locality theory, and Rizzi (1990) introduced the principle which underpins much of the more recent research on locality, within the Minimalist Program. Since more recent research has not coalesced around a single widely accepted set of principles, we have decided to stop at Rizzi (1990) as the last widely accepted development. We refer the reader to Boeckx (2012) and Rizzi (2013) for more up-to-date surveys of locality theory.

4.3.1 Ross's other constraints

The Coordinate Structure Constraint (CSC) was one of a family of constraints on syntactic dependencies formulated by Ross (1967). Two other constraints which featured prominently in Ross's work were the **Complex Noun Phrase Constraint** and **Sentential Subject Constraint**, reproduced in (5)–(6).

(5) **The Complex NP Constraint**
No element contained in a sentence dominated by a noun phrase with a lexical head noun may be moved out of that noun phrase by a transformation. (Ross 1967: 127)

(6) **The Sentential Subject Constraint**
No element dominated by an S may be moved out of that S if that node S is dominated by an NP which is itself immediately dominated by S.   (Ross 1967: 243)

These two constraints were intended to account for contrasts like those in (7) and (8), respectively. The minimal pair in (7) shows extraction from a PP within NP, which becomes degraded when the PP is further embedded in a relative clause (a 'sentence' in the terms of the theory within which the Complex NP Constraint was originally formulated).

(7) a. The man [who I read [$_{NP}$ a statement [$_{PP}$ about __]]] was sick.
     b. *The man [who I read [$_{NP}$ a statement [$_S$ which was [$_{PP}$ about __]]]] was sick.
                                                                          (Ross 1967: 119)

Meanwhile, (8) contrasts successful extraction from an extraposed clause associated with *it* in (8a), with degraded extraction from a minimally different sentence without extraposition in (8b). The contrast shows that the degradation has a phrase-structural basis, on the assumption that there is no relevant semantic difference between the two sentences in (8).

(8) a. The teacher [who [$_S$ it was expected by the reporters [$_S$ that the principal would fire __]]] is a crusty old battleax.
     b. *The teacher [who [$_S$ [$_S$ that the principal would fire __] was expected by the reporters]] is a crusty old battleax.   (Ross 1967: 241)

4.3.2 Subjacency

Although Ross formulated the Complex NP Constraint and Sentential Subject Constraint as independent constraints, there is a striking similarity between them: in each case, a certain configuration of NP and S nodes blocks movement. Ross himself produced the beginnings of an account of these similarities in his final chapter, developing a characterization of **islands** that went some way toward unifying these movement-blocking configurations, along with several other phenomena.

In these terms, the CSC was already an outlier: rather than 'S' and 'NP', the CSC is defined in terms of 'conjuncts'. This became more significant as syntacticians began to develop theories according to which the Complex NP Constraint and Sentential Subject Constraint followed from intrinsic properties of grammar. The first major step in this direction was the **Subjacency** constraint proposed by Chomsky (1973), given in (9).

(9)   No rule can involve X, Y, X superior to Y, if Y is not subjacent to X.

(Chomsky 1973: 247)

Chomsky's formulation of Subjacency is one of the hallmarks of the Extended Standard Theory (later Revised Extended Standard Theory), which improved on the syntactic theory described by Chomsky (1965), and was the immediate precursor to Government and Binding theory (Chomsky 1981). In what follows, we will refer to **EST locality theory** as an umbrella term for direct descendants of Chomsky (1973).

The idea underpinning the Subjacency constraint is quite simple. Tree diagrams represent two dimensions of syntactic structure, linear precedence and hierarchical dominance. The notion of adjacency, defined in terms of linear precedence, is straightforward. Subjacency is basically 'hierarchical adjacency'. It works by dividing a tree into domains, partially ordered by dominance. The Subjacency constraint says that you can move from one domain to the neighboring domain, but no further than that. This idea has remained a mainstay of Chomskyan locality theory, resurfacing since Chomsky (2000) as a core component of **phase theory**.

In Chomsky (1973), domains were defined by the **cyclic nodes** S and NP, though the characterization of the set of cyclic nodes was later considered as a point of potential parametric variation. In the configuration in (10), *who* can move no further than NP, the domain immediately above the domain in which it originates. If we now add the well-motivated stipulation that *wh*-movement targets the left periphery of clauses (S nodes, in the terms of Chomsky 1973), but not noun phrases, the Complex Noun Phrase Constraint is derived: there is no way of moving *who* to the higher S node without bypassing the cyclic domain defined by NP. This movement step therefore necessarily involves two nodes which are not subjacent.

(10)

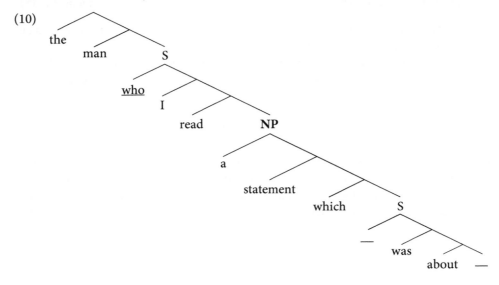

The same constraint can be pushed to do more. For instance, *wh*-islands like (11) can be subsumed under the same generalization.

(11)   *What do you wonder who bought __ ?

The nuance here is that *wh*-phrases do not move to a position within S, but to COMP (dominated by $\bar{\text{S}}$ in the terms of the era—S is now typically taken to be IP or TP, and $\bar{\text{S}}$ to be CP). In English, there is no overt multiple *wh*-movement: we can ask (12a) but not (12b).

(12)   a.   Who bought what?
       b.   *Who what bought?

This indicates that COMP is only filled by a single *wh*-phrase at S-structure. In (11), the embedded COMP position is occupied by *who*. As a consequence, if *what* is to reach the front of the sentence in (11), it must do so in one fell swoop. That violates Subjacency, as a whole domain (between the two S nodes in (13)) is skipped.

(13)

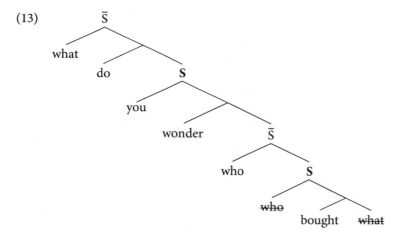

In other words, Subjacency forces **successive-cyclic movement**, or the reduction of apparently unbounded dependencies to a series of local steps. In more modern terms, a *wh*-phrase can only cross a large distance by moving to the nearest Spec,CP position, and then to the next, and so on. This predicts that a syntactic structure containing an unbounded dependency may contain information about that dependency, such as traces of movement, in places in between the head and foot of the dependency.

A number of phenomena attest to the accuracy of that prediction, the best-known of which is complementizer alternations in Irish. Irish complement clauses are typically introduced by a complementizer *go*, as in (14a), while relative clauses are introduced by *aL*, as in (14b).[5]

(14)   a. Deir   siad   [gur   ghoid   na   síogaí í].
          say   they   *go*.PST stole   the   fairies her
          'They say that the fairies stole her away.'

---

[5] The notation *aL* indicates that the complementizer itself is typically written as *a*, and has a leniting effect on the following consonant.

b. an   ghirseach [a   ghoid na   síogaí   __]
   the   girl   aL   stole the   fairies
   'the girl that the fairies stole away'   (McCloskey 2001: 67)

Remarkably, if an element is relativized across multiple embedded clauses, every complementizer on the path from gap to filler is a relative complementizer. For instance, in (15),
the most embedded clause is *dhéanfá*, which is a complement of *gheall*, but despite being a
complement clause, it is introduced by the relative complementizer *aL*. This can be taken to
indicate that information about an A'-dependency is present not only at the head and foot
of the A'-chain, but at some intermediate positions along the chain as well. This is precisely
what would be expected on a successive-cyclic approach to unbounded dependencies, such
as that pioneered by Chomsky (1973).

(15) rud   [__ a   gheall   tú   [__ a   dhéanfá   __]]
      thing   aL promised you   aL do.COND.2SG
      'something that you promised that you would do'   (McCloskey 2001: 68)

There is still some debate as to precisely how local *wh*-movement is (see Abels 2003 for a
summary): movement could proceed clause by clause, phase by phase, phrase by phrase,
or directly from daughter to mother. It is wise to see phenomena like those illustrated in
(15) as establishing an upper bound on the distance covered by a single movement step;[6]
the question of whether information about such dependencies is encoded on every node
between the head and foot of the dependency (**uniform paths**, in Abels' terms), or on some
nonempty proper subset thereof (**punctuated paths**) is still up for grabs (see Section 4.5.1
for an influential approach utilizing uniform paths). The material in this volume directly
informs this debate, but we will not explore the consequences particularly thoroughly as
they are tangential to our core concerns.

Subjacency is often formalized as a constraint on movement operations, rather than on
the representations created by those movement operations. This allows for the possibility
that base-generated configurations which mimic A'-movement in certain respects could be
immune to Subjacency. This was investigated by Chomsky (1982) in the context of an analysis of parasitic gaps in which a base-generated empty category was nonsubjacently bound
by an operator in an A'-position (see further Section 4.6). The implication of this analysis is that there are two types of A'-dependency, one created by movement and subject
to Subjacency, and one base-generated. The latter option is more restricted than Subjacency because of properties of the empty category in question. A series of works in the
1980s and 1990s (Chomsky 1982, Kroch 1989, Rizzi 1990, Cinque 1990, Postal 1998) proposed increasingly precise versions of the hypothesis that the empty category in question
must be a referential NP ('A'-bound *pro*', in Cinque's analysis). This predicts correctly that
referential NPs can 'escape' Subjacency violations more easily than phrases of other categories or nonreferential NPs (compare (16a) with (16b) and (16c)), where we differentiate
between traces of movement, notated with subscripted *t*, and base-generated, A'-bound
empty categories, notated with subscripted Ø symbols).

---

[6] But see Adger and Ramchand (2005) for a movement-free analysis of similar phenomena in Gaelic.

(16)   a.   [CP [Which problem]ᵢ were [IP you wondering [CP whether [IP to tackle Øᵢ]]]]?
       b.   *[CP Howᵢ were [IP you wondering [CP whether [IP to tackle the problem tᵢ]]]]?
       c.   *[CP [How many kilos]ᵢ were [IP you wondering [CP whether [IP the obstacle weighed tᵢ]]]]?

The contrast is explained if *whether* occupies Spec,CP and thereby prevents successive-cyclic movement, and only *which problem* doesn't need to move successive-cyclically. If Spec,CP is available, long movement of *how* or *how many kilos*, as in (17), is fully grammatical.

(17)   a.   [CP Howᵢ did [IP you say [CP t'ᵢ that [IP you would tackle the problem tᵢ]]]]?
       b.   [CP [How many kilos]ᵢ did [IP you say [CP t'ᵢ that [IP the obstacle weighed tᵢ]]]]?

We will return to this contrast between movement and A'-binding in Section 4.3.5, and discuss potential implications for extraction from coordinate structures in Section 4.6.

4.3.3   The Empty Category Principle

Chomsky (1981) noted an asymmetry between subjects and objects which appears to be irreducible to Subjacency. In many cases, extraction of subjects of finite clauses is more restricted than extraction of objects. A well-known example of this is the **that–trace** effect (Perlmutter 1968, Chomsky and Lasnik 1977): long-distance *wh*-movement of an object across complementizer *that* is possible, as in (18), but the corresponding pattern of subject movement is impossible, as in (19a). Omitting *that*, as in (19b), renders the sentence grammatical.

(18)   a.   Who do you think [__ that [I saw __]]?
       b.   Who do you think [__ Ø [I saw __]]?

(19)   a.   *Who do you think [__ that [__ saw me]]?
       b.   Who do you think [__ Ø [__ saw me]]?

The analysis of this effect in Chomsky (1981) has two main components. The first is the **Empty Category Principle** or ECP, reproduced in (20) (where [α e] is a trace, the empty category in question). The second is a set of statements characterizing the notion of 'proper government' referenced in (20).

(20)   ECP: [α e] must be properly governed.   (Chomsky 1981: 250)

Proper government was redefined several times in the course of the 1980s, prior to its abandonment by Chomsky (1993). Rather than tracking the history of the notion (see, among others, Chomsky 1981, Kayne 1981a, Huang 1982, Lasnik and Saito 1984, Chomsky 1986, Aoun et al. 1987, and Rizzi 1990), we will focus on what it was meant to capture.

    In broad strokes, the main consequence of the ECP, at least in Chomsky's initial formulation, was that movement of objects is robust, in that it is relatively immune to intervention of elements like *that*, while movement of finite subjects is fragile, in that certain intervening elements (like *that* in (19)) can lead to ungrammaticality. This is despite the fact that subjects, in Spec,IP, asymmetrically c-command objects within VP, so movement of a subject to Spec,CP or beyond covers less distance than movement of an object. This suggests a strong prima facie argument that the ECP is distinct from Subjacency, which penalizes longer movements and has nothing to say about short movements such as movement of a subject to Spec,CP.

The implementation of the ECP's guiding intuition, in outline, is as follows. First, proper government is a special case of government, the major structural relation in Chomsky (1981). Government can be thought of as minimal c-command by a head. The object position is governed by V, while the finite subject position is governed by INFL, or AGR.

One type of proper government is **theta-government**, or government by a theta-assigner such as V. Object traces are always properly governed, because they are governed by V, and therefore satisfy the ECP. Government by INFL or AGR is not 'proper' in this sense, because those heads do not assign θ-roles. As a result, subject traces do not automatically satisfy the ECP.

A second type of proper government is called **antecedent government**. The insight behind antecedent government, implemented in different ways by different authors, is that the contrast between (19a) and (19b) reflects the relationship between the intermediate trace in embedded Spec,CP, and the trace in subject position. In (19b), the trace in subject position is properly governed by the intermediate trace, which in turn is properly governed either by the matrix verb or by *who* in its surface position. In (19a), in contrast, *that* somehow blocks this chain of proper government relations, for instance by affecting the structural relation between the two traces, or by making it impossible to establish an agreement-like relation between the two.

This core insight was developed in a range of surprising ways over the course of the 1980s. For instance, Kayne (1981b) used it to explain the distribution of the French NPI *personne*, translatable as 'no one' or 'anyone' depending on context. *Personne* associates with the negative morpheme *ne*, which marks the scope of *personne*. Kayne operationalizes this as covert movement of *personne* to a position local to *ne*. The interest of this for the ECP is that *personne* in embedded object position can associate with matrix *ne*, as in (21a), but (21b) shows that the same doesn't hold for *personne* in embedded subject position. (21c) shows that there is no general prohibition against *personne* as a subject, but the instance of *ne* that licenses it must be in the same clause.

(21) a. Je   n'   ai   exigé   qu'   ils   arrêtent   personne.
          I   NEG   have   demanded   that   they   arrest.SBJV *personne*
          'I didn't demand that they arrest anyone.'

      b. *Je   n'   ai   exigé   que   personne   soit   arrêté.
          I   NEG   have   demanded   that   *personne* be.SBJV   arrested
          'I didn't demand that anyone be arrested.'

      c. J'   ai   exigé   que   personne   ne   soit   arrêté.
          I   have   demanded   that   *personne* NEG   be.SBJV   arrested
          'I demanded that no-one be arrested.'

Precisely this pattern is predicted if we assume that covert movement of *personne* leaves a trace which is subject to the ECP.

This conclusion, that the ECP applies at LF, allowed Huang (1982) to give a persuasive empirical argument that Subjacency cannot be reduced to the ECP (contra Kayne 1981a) or vice versa. Huang demonstrated that 'covert *wh*-movement' in Mandarin (that is, the process that associates an in situ interrogative phrase with its scope, construed as a form of movement taking place between S-structure and LF) does not obey Subjacency. In other words, in situ interrogative phrases in Mandarin can occur inside complex noun phrases, sentential subjects, etc., while taking scope outside those domains, as in (22).

(22)   a. Ni   mai-le   [$_{NP}$ [$_S$ shei xie]   de   shu]?
          you buy-ASP   who   write DE   book
          'Who is the *x* such that you bought books that *x* wrote?'   (Huang 1982: 493)

       b. [$_S$ Lisi da-le   shei] shi   ni   hen   bugaoxing?
             Lisi hit-ASP who   make you very unhappy
          'Who is the *x* such that the fact that Lisi hit *x* made you very unhappy?'
                                                                                (Huang 1982: 496)

Huang also expanded the empirical scope of the ECP into a general complement/noncomplement asymmetry (see also Lasnik and Saito 1984). Movement of complements is more robust than movement not only of subjects, but also of adjuncts. The core Mandarin data motivating this conclusion are more complex than we can do justice to here (see Huang 1982: 525–34), but a flavor of the contrast can be seen in (23).

(23)   a.   What did you give ___ to whom?
       b.   *What did you buy ___ why?   (Huang 1982: 557)

Assume that the in situ *wh*-phrases in (23) move covertly to COMP at LF, yielding LF representations like (24).

(24)   a.   [$_{CP}$ who$_j$ what$_i$ [$_{IP}$ you [$_{VP}$ give t_i [$_{PP}$ to t_j]]]]
       b.   *[$_{CP}$ why$_j$ what$_i$ [$_{IP}$ you give [$_{VP}$ [$_{VP}$ buy t_i] t_j]]]

Assume also that these covertly moved phrases do not antecedent-govern their traces. The contrast in (24) (or (23)) then reduces to proper government. In (24a), t_j is properly governed by the preposition *to*, while there is no θ-assigner in an appropriate structural configuration to properly govern t_j, because adjuncts are structurally more remote from heads than complements are.

4.3.4 CED effects

A second type of complement/noncomplement asymmetry is that extraction from within complements is also more robust than extraction from within subjects or adjuncts (see Chomsky 1973: 250 for extraction from subjects, and Cattell 1976 for extraction from adjuncts). (25) gives representative contrasts.

(25)   a.   Who did John think [that Mary kissed ___]?
       b.   *Who did [that Mary kissed ___] upset John?
       c.   *Who did John cry [because Mary kissed ___]?

Kayne (1981a) and Huang (1982) realized that the notion of proper government, central to the ECP, could be pressed into service to explain the contrast in (25). Kayne proposed that

(25) in fact followed from a reformulation of the ECP. However, Huang resisted a full con-flation of the contrast in (25) with the core ECP complement/noncomplement asymmetry. His reason is that covert *wh*-movement out of subjects and adjuncts, at LF, is possible both in Mandarin and in English multiple *wh*-questions. (26a–b) give examples of Mandarin *wh* in situ (in Huang's terms, covert *wh*-movement) in subjects and adjuncts, respectively, while (27a–b) do the same for English.[7]

(26) a. [$_S$ [$_S$ Lisi da-le   shei] shi   ni   hen   bugaoxing]?
           Lisi hit-ASP who   make you very unhappy
       'Who is the *x* such that the fact that Lisi hit *x* made you very unhappy?'

(Huang 1982: 495)

   b. [$_S$ Zhejian shi   [$_{\bar{S}}$ gen   [$_S$ shei mei lai]]   you   guan]?
        this   matter   with   who   not come have relation
    'Who is the *x* such that this matter has something to do with *x*'s not coming?'

(Huang 1982: 497)

(27) a. Who thinks that [[pictures of who] would please John?
   b. Who came back [before I had a chance to talk to whom]?   (Huang 1982: 497)

We have already seen in the previous subsection that the ECP does constrain covert move-ment, including in Mandarin. The demonstration that covert movement out of adjuncts and subjects is possible therefore constitutes a strong argument that restrictions on *overt* movement out of adjuncts and subjects should not be reduced to the ECP.

Instead, Huang proposed the **Condition on Extraction Domain**, or CED, given in (28), and it is now common for contrasts between movement out of complements vs. impossible movement out of noncomplements to be referred to as **CED effects**. Unlike the ECP, but like Subjacency, the CED does not apply at LF.

(28) **Condition on Extraction Domain**
    A phrase *A* may be extracted out of a domain *B* only if *B* is properly governed.

(Huang 1982: 505)

This precise formulation did not fare well, not least because it was subsequently noted by Chomsky (1986) that VP in English is not properly governed, so the CED had the unintended effect of blocking movement out of VP. Later reformulations in the Minimal-ist Program (Uriagereka 1999, Nunes and Uriagereka 2000, Johnson 2003, Zwart 2009) reduced this complement/noncomplement asymmetry instead to an approximately equiv-alent phrase-structural configuration: extraction from specifiers (including subjects) and adjuncts is barred as a consequence of the fact that only specifiers and adjuncts are nonpro-jecting phrases whose sisters are phrases. The different Minimalist accounts give different reasons for the impossibility of extraction in this configuration, but the move away from proper government toward phrase structure in the analysis of CED effects is common

---

[7] Example (26b) is offered by Huang as an example of covert *wh*-movement out of an adjunct. From the trans-lation of the example, it is somewhat surprising that *gen shei mei lai* is treated as an adjunct. However, we have not investigated this further, and Huang's generalization has been widely accepted regardless of the pertinence of this particular example.

to all. Although this generalization has been significantly finessed or even attacked since (Stepanov 2007, Truswell 2011), it is at least approximately correct.

There is a well-known class of apparent counterexamples to the CED, in the form of **parasitic gap** constructions, as in (29), in which a gap within a subject or adjunct is coindexed with a gap in a complement.

(29)   a.   Which books did you file *t* [before reading *p.g.*]?
       b.   Which book did [everyone who read *p.g.*] enjoy *t*?

Parasitic gaps are of particular interest to us because they are the other main example (other than ATB movement) of a configuration in which multiple gaps are apparently paired with a single overt filler. We will discuss them in detail in Section 4.6. For now, we note that the consensus (following Chomsky 1982, Kayne 1983, Chomsky 1986) is that they are only apparent counterexamples to the CED, and that in fact the parasitic gap is a variant on the Subjacency-avoidance strategy, discussed in Section 4.3.2, of binding of a base-generated empty category.

4.3.5 Minimality effects

Rizzi (1990) proposed a very powerful locality condition on movement chains, namely that only the closest potential governor can govern a trace. That is, in the configuration in (30), X cannot govern Y if Z is a closer potential governor of Y.

(30)   ... X ... Z ... Y ...   (Rizzi 1990: 1)

This constraint is known as **Relativized Minimality**, in contrast to the earlier, 'rigid' Minimality constraint of Chomsky (1986). It is 'relativized' in that the class of potential governors for a trace depends on the status of the trace. Heads intervene in head movement (as in (31), deriving the Head Movement Constraint of Travis 1984), A-specifiers (typically subjects) intervene in A-movement, prohibiting the hyperraising pattern in (32), and A'-specifiers (canonically moved *wh*-phrases, but also various operators such as negation) intervene in A'-movement, as in (33).[8]

(31)   a.   Could$_i$ they t_i have left?
       b.   *Have$_i$ they **could** t_i left?   (Rizzi 1990: 11)

(32)   a.   It seems that [John$_i$ is likely [t_i to win]].
       b.   *John$_i$ seems that [**it** is likely [t_i to win]].   (Rizzi 1990: 10)

(33)   *[How$_i$ do you wonder [[which problem]$_j$ to solve t_j t_i]]?   (Rizzi 1990: 8)

Rizzi intended Relativized Minimality as a constraint on the government relations that feature in the ECP. He reconstrued the ECP as a conjunctive set of principles stating that a trace needs to be licensed and identified (the latter in the sense that it is possible to identify the antecedent of a trace). Local antecedent government relations are one way of identifying a trace.

---

[8] In the following sets of examples, interveners are indicated in boldface.

There is a second mechanism available for identification of a trace. This mechanism can only apply in the case of A'-movement of a referential NP, discussed at the end of Section 4.3.2.[9] Rizzi observed that (34a) is ambiguous (with possible answers *apples* or *200lbs*), but (34b) is not, with the only possible answer being a referential NP like *apples*.

(34)   a. What does John weigh?
       b. What does John wonder **how** to weigh __ ?   (Rizzi 1990: 78)

The absolute impossibility of *200lbs* as an answer to (34b) suggests that the ECP is implicated, rather than Subjacency, which from Chomsky (1986) onward has been taken to yield only mild unacceptability in some cases when violated. Rizzi accounted for this by replacing the 'theta-government' option in Chomsky (1981) original formulation of the ECP (see Section 4.3.3) with a similar condition allowing identification of NPs bearing 'referential' θ-roles through their referential indices (see Kroch 1989, Cinque 1990, Postal 1998 for further refinement of this idea). This also captures the contrast between (35) and the ungrammatical (33): in (35), as in (33), it is impossible for a well-formed chain of antecedent government links to respect Relativized Minimality, because *how* will always intervene between two links of the *which problem* chain. However, in (35), unlike (33), no such chain is necessary, because the relationship between *which problem* and its trace can be determined through their shared referential index.

(35)   [[Which problem]$_j$ do you wonder [how$_i$ to solve t_j t_i]]?

The result of this is that, although Relativized Minimality applies equally to chains of A'-, A-, and head movement in carefully controlled cases, more care is needed with A'-movement to see clear Relativized Minimality effects, because the effect of referentiality needs to be controlled for.

Ironically, although Rizzi (1990) was probably the clearest and most satisfying statement of the ECP in the decade since Chomsky (1981), it also paved the way for the abandonment of the ECP in Chomsky (1993, 1995). Relativized Minimality, for Rizzi, was a constraint on the government relations which the ECP refers to. However, its success was such that it became possible to pursue a program which places minimality and intervention at the heart of locality theory, with no reference to government. Government could then be abandoned, and with it the ECP, as a theoretical device.

This abandonment of government is one of the main properties distinguishing the Minimalist Program from Government and Binding theory. From a conceptual perspective, it was natural to reformulate the heart of Relativized Minimality in terms of Minimalist conditions such as Shortest Move (Chomsky 1993), or the Attract Closest condition of Chomsky (1995).

The empirical challenge then revolves around those cases, particularly of A'-movement, which do not reduce naturally to Relativized Minimality. Regardless of its clear empirical attractions, it is not obvious that a purely minimality-based approach to locality has the same empirical coverage that the GB locality theory did, because the terms of the two theories are so different.

---

[9] In fact, although Chomsky first raised the possibility of base-generating A'-dependencies as a way of avoiding Subjacency effects in particular, in fact most discussion of this option has focused on interactions with the ECP and Relativized Minimality.

Analysts have responded to these challenges in different ways, exploring the hypothesis that the cluster of phenomena singled out by the classical ECP do not really cluster. For instance, the argument–adjunct asymmetries first discussed by Huang (1982) may now plausibly be subsumed under the referentiality-based analysis of Rizzi (1990). On the other hand, subject–nonsubject asymmetries such as the *that*–trace effect, central to the initial development of the ECP, clearly do not reduce to Relativized Minimality, because the subject, the structurally higher argument, enjoys less freedom of movement than objects. An influential approach to subject–nonsubject asymmetries, developed by Pesetsky and Torrego (2001), marks a clean break with the ECP, building instead on the special status of TP as the complement of C, and the relationship between T and the subject reflected in verbal agreement and nominative case.

There is a lot more to say about Chomskyan locality theory since Rizzi (1990) (see Boeckx 2012, Rizzi 2013 for surveys), but we believe that it is fair to say that the works surveyed in this section set the direction of travel. We turn now to the status of the CSC in relation to this theoretical approach.

4.4 The CSC doesn't fit

The elements of EST locality theory just sketched do not extend to cover the CSC as described by Ross. Specifically, although we saw in Section 3.3.1 that there are hints that the Conjunct Constraint bears some similarity to constraints on left branch extraction, the Element Constraint and the ATB exception are unlike anything else in this approach to locality.

A hallmark of the EST locality theory is that certain classes of objects (e.g. cyclic nodes, interveners, or whichever domains trigger CED effects) interfere with unbounded dependencies. If an unbounded dependency crosses such an object, the result is a degraded sentence. As a consequence, more instances of movement just generate more potential for violating a locality condition, and often, longer movements are more prone to violating a locality constraint than shorter movements. Crossing more material may or may not make an unbounded dependency construction less acceptable, but it will not make it more acceptable.[10] Unbounded dependencies can be penalized, but they cannot be rewarded.

All of this is squarely at odds with the CSC (see discussion in Gazdar 1981 and Pesetsky 1982). There are at least two reasons. First, the CSC is a prohibition against movement out of coordinate structures *of any size*: it is just as ungrammatical (says the CSC) to move out of coordinated VPs like (36a) as out of coordinated sentences like (36b), for instance. This suggests that the CSC is distinct from constraints on extraction domains, such as Subjacency or the CED.

(36) a. *What did John [[buy __] and [eat tomatoes]]?
      b. *What did [[John buy __] and [Bill eat tomatoes]]?

---

[10] These statements need qualification in several respects. For instance, we have seen in our discussion of ECP effects that movement of complements is often more acceptable than movement of noncomplements, despite covering more ground. Moreover, there is a class of exceptions to this statement, namely the 'antilocality' patterns described by Grohmann (2003) and Abels (2003), but they only apply in specific contexts quite remote from matters relating to coordination.

Secondly, the CSC is a prohibition against movement out of coordinate structures *from any position*. It does not include any kind of complement/noncomplement or argument/adjunct asymmetry. In fact, Williams (1978) demonstrated that in many cases, gaps must appear in the same position in different conjuncts: examples like (37), mixing subject and object gaps, are degraded. In other words, if one conjunct contains a subject gap, they all must. This is unlike the way that the ECP works.

(37)   *I know a man who [[Bill saw __] and [__ likes Mary]].   (Williams 1978: 34)

Thirdly, the CSC does not appear to be a Minimality-style intervention effect. There is only one *wh*-phrase in the core examples of extraction from coordinate structures, with no other obvious intervening A'-operator. It is of course possible, given sufficient ingenuity, to attempt to develop analyses of the CSC along the lines of any of these constraints (we will discuss some attempts presently), but the CSC is distinct at first blush from all of these other constraints.

Finally, and most critically, the ATB exception is unique in that it describes a case in which a single instance of movement out of one conjunct is ungrammatical, while multiple instances of movement out of multiple conjuncts is grammatical. The rest of Chomskyan locality theory (with the exception of parasitic gaps, noted repeatedly in Section 4.3 and discussed further in Section 4.6) simply doesn't look like this, so the CSC is more or less on its own.

There are also claims based on crosslinguistic comparisons that the CSC should be treated separately from the rest of locality theory. One of the most persuasive comes from the analysis of Palauan A'-dependencies in Georgopoulos (1985). Georgopoulos shows that Palauan allows violation of other island constraints, including the Sentential Subject Constraint in (38a) and the Complex NP Constraint in (38b).

(38)   a. a Mary$_i$ [a kltukl   [el kmo   ng-oltoir   er   a   John __$_i$]]
          Mary   R-clear COMP   R.3SG-IPFV.love P   John
          'Mary, it's clear that __ loves John.'[11]

       b. a buk$_i$ [a ku-dengel-ii   [a redil   [el   uldurukl-ii
          book   IR.1SG-PFV.know-3SG   woman   COMP   R.PFV.send-3SG
          __$_i$ [el   mo   er   a   del-ak]]]]
                 COMP   go   P   mother-3SG
          'The book, I know the woman who sent __ to my mother.'
                                                          (Georgopoulos 1985: 73)

However, Palauan does obey the CSC, as mentioned in Section 3.4.2. This leads Georgopoulos (p. 88) to claim that 'the CSC is a constraint different *in kind* from those that are analyzed in terms of Bounding Theory (i.e. in terms of subjacency)'.

There are at least three types of responses to the challenge posed by the distinctness of the CSC, even within the confines of narrow syntactic theory. First, the distinctness of the CSC could motivate a rethink of locality theory from the ground up, as for instance in Gazdar (1981). Or one could argue that EST locality theory is fundamentally sound, but that the structural analysis of coordination needs to be modified, in a way which makes the CSC

---

[11] This translation is taken verbatim from Georgopoulos (1985). We assume that 'Mary, [that __ loves John] is clear' would reflect the sentential subject more clearly.

look more natural. This approach is represented, for instance, by the novel multiplanar analysis of coordinate structures in Williams (1978). We discuss these approaches, and others with similar properties, in Section 4.5.

Another possibility is that a closer look at the syntax of extraction from coordinate structures could reveal that extraction from coordinate structures is not so distinct from other extraction patterns as it appears on Ross's formulation. There is a natural synergy between this possibility and the data discussed in Chapter 3, illustrating that the original formulation of the CSC has several systematic groups of exceptions—exceptions which are often problematic for attempts (such as Gazdar's) to integrate the CSC into the core of locality theory. The discourse-calls-the-shots approach to be discussed in Chapter 5 is a radical version of this approach, which claims that there is no CSC, so the question of goodness of fit with the rest of locality theory does not arise. We will not discuss such an approach in this chapter, but we are interested in claims that the effects of the CSC partially reduce to other locality constraints. In Section 4.6, we discuss the attempt by Williams (1990) to unify ATB movement with parasitic gap constructions, as well as Postal's (1998) demonstration of similarities between extraction from coordinate structures and extraction from adjuncts. These latter approaches turn out to offer new insights into patterns of extraction from coordinate structures.

4.5 Making the CSC fit

4.5.1 The GPSG account

The new approach to coordination in Gazdar (1981) was part of a wide-ranging program aimed at demonstrating the inaccuracy of Chomsky's (1956) claim that natural languages could not be recognized by Context-Free Grammars. That program stimulated a remarkable burst of research in the late 1970s and early 1980s, culminating in Gazdar et al. (1985). Gazdar's theory is known as **Generalized Phrase Structure Grammar**, where 'phrase structure' is a near-synonym for 'context-free'.[12] One of Chomsky's arguments concerned the nonlocality of various relations, including movement. Context-free rewrite rules are not sensitive to the internal structure of the constituents they manipulate, so the complementarity between the moved phrase and the in situ phrase in (39), which persists over arbitrary depth of embedding (see (40)), was posed as a challenge for Context-Free Grammars: the rule that combines *who* with the *(did) John see* (of category S) in (39b) would have to 'know' that there was a gap inside that S, while there must not be a gap inside the

---

[12] Chomsky offered a proof that natural languages, construed as potentially infinite stringsets, could not be recognized by Finite State Automata. He offered a plausibility argument suggesting that they also could not be recognized by Context-Free Grammars, but no proof. The Swiss German data from Shieber (1985) discussed in Section 4.2 confirmed Chomsky's suggestion and is largely taken to have directly falsified the guiding hypothesis of GPSG, but on grounds only distantly related to those originally put forward by Chomsky. Meanwhile, by the time of Gazdar et al. (1985), GPSG had evolved in its own right to the point where it was no longer using conventional context-free rewrite rules, but a system of constraints in which statements about immediate dominance and linear precedence were dissociated—this is the reason why we state that *phrase structure* is only a near-synonym of *context-free*.

The falsification of the hypothesis that natural language grammars are context-free led to a renewed interest in the expressive power of natural language grammar and a convergence on the **Mildly Context-Sensitive** class of grammar formalisms (Joshi 1985), while many specific GPSG analyses have been directly adopted in Head-driven Phrase Structure Grammar (Pollard and Sag 1994) and other frameworks.

S in (39a), or the sentence would be incomplete. Failure to match *who* with a gap leads to ungrammaticality, as in (39c–d).

(39)   a. John saw someone.
      b. Who did John see __ ?
      c. *Who did John see someone?
      d. *John saw __ .

(40)   a. Who did John think that Mary said that Bill saw (*someone)?
      b. John thought that Mary said that Bill saw *(someone).

Gazdar developed a context-free analysis of these patterns, that works by enriching the set of syntactic categories in such a way as to ensure that the relevant information (presence or absence of a gap) is passed locally up the tree, from daughter to mother, and so is visible to context-free phrase structure rules. Although the analysis developed substantially between Gazdar (1981) and Gazdar et al. (1985), the details of this development are largely orthogonal to this survey, so we describe the simpler (1981) system.

The key ingredient in Gazdar's theory is a set of **derived categories** (later variants were known as **slash categories** or **slash features**, though Gazdar was at pains to point out that his use of the slash symbol was distinct from that of categorial grammarians). If α and β represent regular syntactic categories such as S or NP, then α/β is a derived category. This statement is not recursive in the Gazdar (1981) formulation: α and β cannot themselves be derived categories.

In parallel, a set of **derived rules** (built from basic rules) refer to derived categories. The algorithm for constructing derived rules guarantees that if (41) is a set of basic rules, then (42) is a set of corresponding derived rules.[13]

(41)   a. $S \rightarrow NP\,VP$
      b. $VP \rightarrow V\,NP$

(42)   a. $S/NP \rightarrow NP\,VP/NP$
      b. $VP/NP \rightarrow V\,NP/NP$

Nodes of the form α/α have a special status: rather than dominating a regular constituent of category α, they dominate traces (conceived of as null 'dummy elements'), resumptive pronouns, or $\emptyset$: elements appropriate for the foot of an unbounded dependency. These elements do not enter the derivation otherwise, so the set of derived categories is directly related to the set of constituents containing the foot of an unbounded dependency.

Because derived rules are the major class of rules that make reference to derived categories, and derived rules relate constituents that belong to derived categories, information about movement dependencies is passed locally up the tree, from daughter to mother. In the terms of Abels (2003), introduced in Section 4.3.2, this means that GPSG generates **uniform paths**: every node which dominates the gap and is c-commanded by the filler has an explicit indication that it is in the middle of a filler–gap dependency. This contrasts with the **punctuated paths** described in Chomsky (1973) and in subsequent work, which do not have this property.

---

[13] Other derived rules may be formed from (41) by using derived categories in other positions.

At the 'top' of a dependency, a rule licenses a derived category as daughter but not as mother. For instance, Gazdar (1981) has the following (simplified) rule for one type of relative clause (*R* is the symbol dominating relative clauses):

(43) $R \rightarrow NP\ S/NP$

These three ingredients, concerning the foot, middle, and head of a movement dependency (respectively: the statements about categories of the form α/α, the rules for percolation of derived categories, and the rules for resolving dependencies) combine to generate structures like (44).

(44)   (Gazdar 1981: 163)

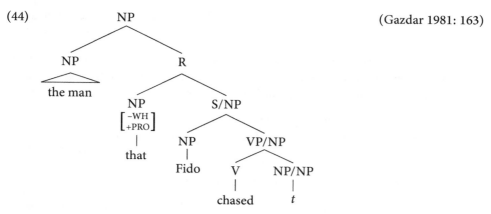

This approach offers competing analyses of many of the phenomena covered by Chomsky (1973). For instance, *wh*-islands follow from the stipulation that derived categories contain a single slash, or a single gap. On this assumption, there is no way to derive sentences like (11), repeated below.

(45)   *What do you wonder who she gave __ to __ ?

The crucial point in the derivation is in (46). There are two traces, but the derived category VP/NP can only register the presence of a single gap, so there is no way to track two independent *wh*-dependencies.[14]

(46)

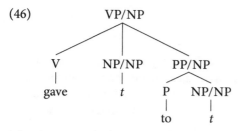

Most importantly for us, Gazdar's analysis captures the CSC intrinsically. This is a direct consequence of the fact that Gazdar's 'movement' paths are uniform, while Chomsky's are punctuated, and more specifically of the fact that nodes on 'movement' paths belong to

---

[14] This point relies solely on the GPSG category structure, and is independent of any assumptions about the syntax of ditransitives. The same point would apply if one were to somehow transplant a shell-based analysis of ditransitives (Larson 1988) into GPSG, because at some point in the structure, a VP/NP node would still dominate two independent traces.

different categories. It is commonly stipulated that coordination is restricted to like categories. For Gazdar, VP and VP/NP are distinct categories and so cannot be coordinated. However, VP/NP can be coordinated with another VP/NP. This derives both the Element Constraint of the CSC and the ATB exception: a gap in some, but not all, conjuncts entails that the categories are distinct, which blocks coordination, but a gap in all conjuncts creates like categories. For instance, the contrast in (47) follows directly from the categories of the conjuncts.

(47) a. The man [who [$_{S/NP}$[$_{S/NP}$ Mary loves __] and [$_{S/NP}$ Sally hates __]] computed my tax.
      b. The man [who [$_{???}$[$_{S/NP}$ Mary loves __] and [$_S$ Sally hates George]] computed my tax.   (Gazdar 1981: 173)

The majority of cases which fall under the Conjunct Constraint can be captured by a second natural condition on coordination, namely that conjunctions must conjoin at least two conjuncts. This rules out (4) and (5) from Chapter 3, repeated below.

(48) a. *What sofa will he put the chair between [[some table] and __]?
      b. *What table will he put the chair between [__ and [some sofa]]?
                                                                                (Ross 1967: 158)

(49) *What will he put the chair between [__ and __]?

Sag (1982) derived this condition from a constraint, an indirect descendant of the A-over-A principle, which prohibits the configuration *[$_{\alpha/\alpha}$ ... [$_{\alpha/\alpha}$ t] ...]. (49) instantiates this prohibited configuration, because the coordinate structure would look as in (50). The trace licenses a node of category NP/NP, which itself is immediately dominated by another NP/NP node, the offending configuration.

(50)

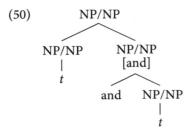

GPSG makes these predictions intrinsically, because of its theory of unbounded dependencies based on uniform paths and percolation of derived categories. Perhaps unsurprisingly, analyses which share many properties of this approach have been adopted into a range of grammatical formalisms, such as HPSG (Pollard and Sag 1994), which maintain the assumption of uniform paths.

4.5.2 Pesetsky (1982): The Path Containment Condition

The GPSG approach to extraction from coordinate structures ties the CSC to a particular theory of syntactic categories. It is essential to GPSG that information about no more than one unbounded dependency is captured in the set of derived categories.

Pesetsky (1982) argued, though, that the GPSG theory of syntactic categories does not make the right information available on intermediate nodes between the head and foot of the dependency. It works perfectly for the case in which there is a single filler linked to a single gap in each conjunct, but, Pesetsky argues, it fails to generalize to other, more complex configurations of fillers and gaps. To follow Pesetsky's argument, we need to first go through some background on Pesetsky's own locality theory.

Pesetsky's starting point is a set of constructions with multiple overlapping filler–gap relations. Although speakers may vary in how acceptable they find (51a), it is clearly much better than (51b). It seems reasonable to assume that (51b) is ungrammatical, while any degradation of (51a) is due to extragrammatical factors, perhaps related to the complexity of the sentence.

(51)   a.   What subject$_i$ do you know who$_j$ to talk to __$_j$ about __$_i$?
       b.   *Who$_j$ do you know what subject$_i$ to talk to __$_j$ about __$_i$?

(Pesetsky 1982: 267)

Pesetsky's generalization is as follows (see also Kuno and Robinson 1972, Frazier and Fodor 1978): when there are multiple filler–gap dependencies, the paths must not cross, though they can nest. More precisely, Pesetsky defined the notion of **path** as in (52), and then the **Path Containment Condition** as in (53).[15]

(52)   Suppose t is an empty category locally Ā-bound by b. Then
       (i)   for α the first maximal projection dominating t
       (ii)   for β the first maximal projection dominating b
       (iii) the **path between** t **and** b is the set of nodes P such that $P = \{x | (x = \alpha) \vee (x = \beta) \vee (x \text{ dom. } \alpha \, \& \, \neg x \text{ dom. } \beta)\}$.   (Pesetsky 1982: 289)

(53)   a.   Two paths **overlap** iff their intersection is non-null and non-singleton.
       b.   **Path Containment Condition:**
            If two paths overlap, one must contain the other.   (Pesetsky 1982: 309)

The contrast in (51) is then captured: the *who*-dependency in (51a) is properly contained within the *what subject*-dependency, so the PCC is respected. In (51b), though, the paths overlap (they have more than one node in common) but neither contains the other. The PCC is violated, and the ungrammaticality of the sentence is captured.

Although the definition of paths in (52) seems tailor-made for movement dependencies, Pesetsky's conception of paths is significantly broader, in ways that will become directly relevant to the CSC. For instance, Pesetsky assumed a path between INFL and COMP (in present terms, I^0 and C^0) in every finite clause.[16] This path intersects with nonlocal movement of finite subjects to capture *that*–trace effects such as (54).

(54)   a.   Who do you think __ came?
       b.   *Who do you think that __ came?

---

[15] These initial definitions were refined over the course of Pesetsky's thesis, but the subsequent complexities are largely irrelevant to the points made here.

[16] We will not go into the motivation for these nonmovement paths here. The distribution of nonmovement paths is not stipulated, but the conditions on their distribution are complex and largely orthogonal to our concerns.

Given a structure like (55), we have three, or potentially four paths to consider: two paths between INFL and COMP, one in each clause (the paths in (56a,b)), plus the paths generated by movement of *who*, either successively via COMP2 (the two paths in (56c,d)), or in one fell swoop (the long path in (56e)).[17]

(55)

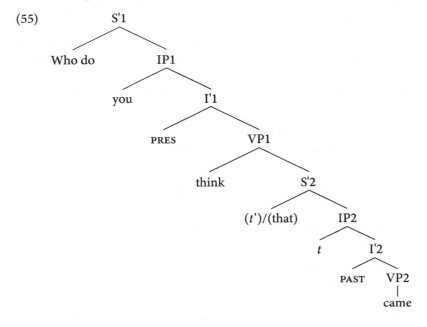

(56) a. {I'2, IP2, S'2   }
      b. {   I'1, IP1, S'1}
      c. {   IP2, S'2,   }
      d. {   S'2, VP1, I'1, IP1, S'1}
      e. {   IP2, S'2, VP1, I'1, IP1, S'1}

The combination of (56a–d) (with successive-cyclic movement of *who* from *t* to *t'*, and on to the surface position) satisfies the PCC: (56a) contains (56c), (56d) contains (56b), and no other paths overlap. However, the combination of (56a,b,e) (with long-distance movement of *who* skipping *t'*) violates the PCC: (56a) and (56e) overlap (they share IP2 and S'2) but neither contains the other. The PCC, with the extra assumption of nonmovement paths from INFL to COMP, can force successive-cyclic movement of subjects in this way. If we make the further assumption that *that* blocks successive-cyclic movement (for example by filling the intermediate COMP position), the PCC derives *that*–trace effects.

The same approach rules out extraction from (rather than of) subjects. For instance, (57) is ruled out because the path created by *wh*-movement in (59a) does not contain the path linking INFL and COMP in (59b).

(57)   *a person who [close friends of __] admire me

---

[17] Pesetsky's theory of clause structure had three projections dominating VP, namely INFL', S, and S'. We use the terms I', IP, and S' in the rest of this section, in a partial modernization. It is important for the precise details of the theory developed in Pesetsky (1982) that S' is not split into a more modern C' and CP.

(58)

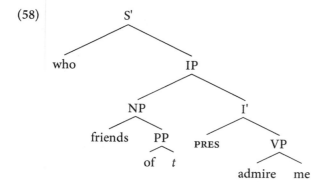

(59) a. {PP, NP, IP, S'}
      b. {   I', IP, S'}

However, this becomes licit in a **parasitic gap** construction like (60).

(60) a person who [close friends of ___] admire ___   (Pesetsky 1982: 358)

Pesetsky takes this as evidence that there is a single path linking *who* to both gaps, rather than two independent paths: the addition of a second gap makes the *who*-path in (62a) larger, and so able to contain the INFL-to-COMP path in (62b).

(61)

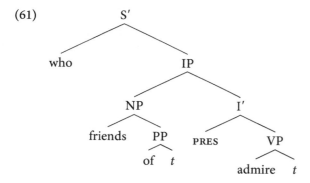

(62) a. {PP, NP, VP, I', IP, S'}
      b. {   I', IP, S'}

This pattern is striking: more movement can create larger paths, which can affect satisfaction of the PCC both positively, as in this example, and negatively, as in (55). It is a direct consequence of Pesetsky's fundamental innovation in reconstruing locality effects as products of interactions between paths, rather than phrase-structural constraints on a single movement dependency.

To capture the ATB pattern, Pesetsky extends this analysis by adding a nonmovement path between a coordinate structure and the individual conjuncts. The ungrammaticality of a CSC-violating example like (63), with a structure like (64), is then analyzed as a violation of the PCC, because the movement path in (65a) doesn't nest with the coordination path in (65b).[18]

---

[18] We omit the path from INFL to COMP, which is contained in the movement path and does not overlap with the coordination path.

(63)   *the lute which Henry [bought __] and [sold a cello to Casals]

(64)
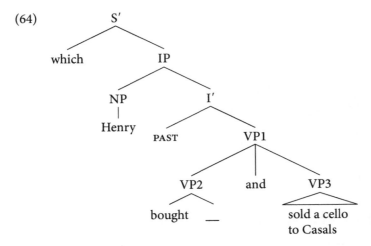

(65)   a. {   VP2, VP1, I', IP, S'}
       b. {VP3, VP2, VP1   }

However, movement out of all conjuncts (as in (66), with the structure in (67)) allows the movement path to contain the coordination path, as demonstrated in (68).

(66)   the lute which Henry [bought __] and [sold __ to Segovia]   (Pesetsky 1982: 445)

(67)
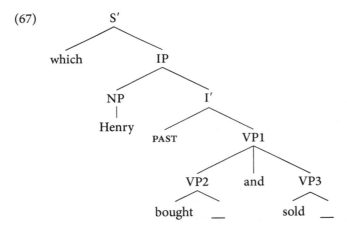

(68)   a. {VP3, VP2, VP1, I', IP, S'}
       b. {VP3, VP2, VP1   }

Pesetsky goes on to argue that this approach to extraction from coordinate structures is superior to Gazdar's. In brief, the argument revolves around a distinction between tracking the distribution of gaps (Gazdar) and tracking the geometry of paths (Pesetsky). The argument concerns contrasts like (69) vs. (70):

(69)   a book Ø$_i$ that I know who$_j$ to persuade __$_j$ to buy __$_i$

(70)   *a book $\emptyset_i$ that I know who$_j$ to [$_{VP1}$ [$_{VP2}$ talk to __$_j$] and [$_{VP3}$ buy __$_i$]]

(Pesetsky 1982: 556)

(69) is a construction with multiple nested gaps, conforming to the PCC. In contrast, (70) violates the PCC: neither the path headed by $\emptyset_i$ nor that headed by who$_j$ contains the path relating VP1 to VP2 or VP3. However, in the terms of Gazdar's syntax, there should be no difference between the two. *Talk to __* and *buy __* are both of category VP/NP, so there is no syntactic obstacle to coordination. Gazdar's syntax doesn't capture the fact that different NPs are extracted from the two conjuncts, which is the root of the ungrammaticality.

To our knowledge, Pesetsky's argument is unanswered in the GPSG literature (although Sag et al. 1985 do detail other areas in which Pesetsky's theory of coordination is either inexplicit or incomplete). However, Mark Steedman (pers. comm.) has detailed several flaws in Pesetsky's criticisms. Most importantly, the Gazdar (1981) syntax for coordination, coupled with the crosscategorial semantics for coordination in Gazdar (1980), simply couldn't generate example (70), because the semantics would force the gaps in the two conjoined VPs to be bound by the same operator. This means that the structure in (70) simply couldn't be generated in the first place, on a GPSG analysis.

4.5.3 Coordination in CCG

Pesetsky's theory of unbounded dependencies is a hybrid: it requires a nonlocal, successive-cyclic movement operation (see discussion around (55) and (56)), as opposed to a strictly local treatment of unbounded dependencies like Gazdar's. The PCC, as a condition on paths formulated in strictly local terms, is superimposed, as an extrinsic constraint, on this nonlocal theory of movement.

Pesetsky's theory is important from the perspective of the CSC, because it is the first account to integrate an analysis of extraction from coordinate structures within a theory which addresses the major weakness of Gazdar (1981), namely the restriction to a single gap. However, the empirical adequacy of the PCC is itself called into question by the existence of crossing dependencies in natural language grammar (see Section 4.2).

Steedman (1985) was the first to develop an account of extraction and coordination within a framework, Combinatory Categorial Grammar, which is expressive enough to allow both nested and crossing dependencies. As noted in Section 2.2, CCG embeds the strong hypothesis that all strings which can be coordinated are constituents. This requires a nonstandard theory of constituent structure, which works in outline as follows—for a full presentation, see Steedman (1996).

In common with standard categorial grammar, CCG treats many lexical items as functions. An English intransitive verb is of category S\NP, a function from noun phrases to sentences.[19] An intransitive verb may then combine with a noun phrase, by Function Application, yielding a sentence. Diagrammatically, this can be represented as follows (the < symbol represents the fact that *they* and *smiled* combined by Function Application, with the argument on the left).

---

[19] CCG now distinguishes between categories S\ NP, a functor looking for an NP to the left, and S/NP, a functor looking for an NP to the right, and similarly for all other functional categories. Steedman (1985) does not actually include this distinction.

(71) **They   smiled**

$$\frac{\qquad}{NP} \quad \frac{\qquad}{S\backslash NP}$$

$$\frac{\qquad\qquad\qquad}{S} {<}$$

Taking this one step further, an English transitive verb is of category $(S\backslash NP)/NP$, a function from noun phrases to intransitive verbs. Combining with two NPs, in the appropriate places, again yields a sentence (the > symbol indicates Function Application with the argument on the right).

(72) **They   saw   it**

$$\frac{\qquad}{NP} \quad \frac{\qquad\qquad}{(S\backslash NP)/NP} \quad \frac{\qquad}{NP}$$

$$\frac{\qquad\qquad\qquad\qquad}{S\backslash NP} {>}$$

$$\frac{\qquad\qquad\qquad\qquad\qquad\qquad}{S} {<}$$

In fact, noun phrases in CCG do not typically appear in derivations with category NP. Rather, they use a series of type-raised categories, according to their role in the sentence. For instance, a subject noun phrase is analyzed as a function from intransitive verbs to sentences, category $S/(S\backslash NP)$. An object noun phrase is a function from transitive verbs to intransitive verbs, category $(S\backslash NP)\backslash((S\backslash NP)/NP)$. This allows a derivation similar to (72), but with functor and argument switched at each step.

(73)   **They   saw   it**

$$\frac{\qquad\qquad}{S/(S\backslash NP)} \quad \frac{\qquad\qquad}{(S\backslash NP)/NP} \quad \frac{\qquad\qquad\qquad\qquad}{(S\backslash NP)\backslash((S\backslash NP)/NP)}$$

$$\frac{\qquad\qquad\qquad\qquad\qquad\qquad\qquad}{S\backslash NP} {<}$$

$$\frac{\qquad\qquad\qquad\qquad\qquad\qquad\qquad\qquad\qquad}{S} {>}$$

Function Application to the left and to the right are two **combinators**, general purpose functions for combining expressions. In their general form, the two Function Application combinators can be written as follows.

(74)   a. $X/Y + X \rightarrow Y$ (Forward application, >)
          b. $X + X\backslash Y \rightarrow Y$ (Backward application, <)

The distinctive properties of CCG stem from its use of other combinators besides Function Application. The most important of these other combinators is Function Composition, notated as > **B** (for forward composition) or < **B** (for backward composition) and defined as follows.

(75)   a. $X/Y + Y/Z \rightarrow X/Z$ (Forward composition, > **B**)
          b. $Y\backslash Z + X\backslash Y \rightarrow X\backslash Z$ (Backward composition, < **B**)

Function composition allows for alternative derivations of many sentences, with different constituent structures. For instance, a subject can combine with a transitive verb, and the output subsequently combine with an object. This gives a nonstandard constituent structure in which subject and verb form a constituent to the exclusion of the object.[20]

(76)

They	saw	it
$S/(S\backslash NP)$	$(S\backslash NP)/NP$	NP

$$\underline{\qquad\qquad\qquad}{>}\mathbf{B}$$
$$S/NP$$
$$\underline{\qquad\qquad\qquad\qquad\qquad}{>}$$
$$S$$

The Law of Coordination of Likes then automatically generates Right Node Raising structures, which have to be analyzed as instances of rightward movement in a theory with more standard constituent structure.[21]

(77)

They	saw	and	you	ignored	the	problem
$S/(S\backslash NP)$	$(S\backslash NP)/NP$	$((S/NP)\backslash(S/NP))/(S/NP)$	$S/(S\backslash NP)$	$(S\backslash NP)/NP$	NP/N	N

$$S/NP \quad {>}\mathbf{B} \qquad\qquad S/NP \quad {>}\mathbf{B} \qquad NP \quad {>}$$
$$(S/NP)\backslash(S/NP) \quad {>}$$
$$S/NP \quad {<}$$
$$S \quad {>}$$

The same mechanism automatically generates Across-The-Board leftward movement, while ruling out CSC violations. Relative *that* can be analyzed as being of category $(N\backslash N)/(S/NP)$, a function from clauses with a missing NP argument to noun modifiers. It can combine with coordinated subject–verb constituents generated just as in (77), to generate the equivalent of ATB-moved structures.

(78) the problem ...

that	they	saw	and	you	ignored
$(N\backslash N)/(S/NP)$	$S/(S\backslash NP)$	$(S\backslash NP)/NP$	$((S/NP)\backslash(S/NP))/(S/NP)$	$S/(S\backslash NP)$	$(S\backslash NP)/NP$

$$S/NP \quad {>}\mathbf{B} \qquad\qquad S/NP \quad {>}\mathbf{B}$$
$$(S/NP)\backslash(S/NP) \quad {>}$$
$$S/NP \quad {<}$$
$$N\backslash N \quad {>}$$

Steedman (1985) uses generalizations of these combinatory operations to analyze the interplay between coordination and crossing dependencies of the sort introduced in Section 4.2. The Dutch examples that he focuses on are of the following form.

(79) ... omdat   ik   Cecilia   Henk   de   nijlpaarden   zag   helpen   voeren.
          that   I   Cecilia   Henk   the hippos   saw   help   feed
      '... because I saw Cecilia help Henk feed the hippos.'   (Steedman 1985: 524)

---

[20] We represent the category of the object in (76) simply as NP. In a fuller treatment, it would have a raised category, but this is irrelevant to the discussion of Function Composition.

[21] *And*, on this treatment, must be associated with multiple categories of the form $(X\backslash X)/X$, where X ranges over conjoinable categories.

Steedman argues on the basis of extraction patterns that such examples have a structure in which the major constituents are the verbal group, and the group of preverbal NPs. Such a constituent structure is quite unusual on a more conventional theory of phrase structure. However, Steedman provides an analysis in terms of a generalization of the Function Composition operation just described (see Steedman 1985 for the details).

The relevance of this structure for our purposes is that it makes predictions about the set of strings which can be coordinated. These predictions are in general borne out. Any string of verbs within the verbal group can be coordinated ((80) illustrates one of these possibilities).

(80) ... omdat   ik   Henk   de   kinderen [hoorde leren   en   zag   helpen]
           because I   Henk   the   children   heard   teach   and   saw   help
      zwemmen.
      swim
      '... because I heard Henk teach, and saw Henk help, the children to swim.'

                                                                 (Steedman 1985: 559)

Likewise, any string of NPs can be coordinated (again, (81) illustrates just one possibility).

(81) ... dat   [Jan Marie   en   Cecilia Henk]   de   kinderen zag   helpen
           that Jan   Marie   and   Cecilia Henk   the   children saw   help
      zwemmen.
      swim
      '... that Jan saw Marie, and Cecilia saw Henk, help the children swim.'

                                                                 (Steedman 1985: 559)

Finally, the entire verbal group can be coordinated with any rightmost string of NPs.

(82) ... dat   ik   [Cecilia de   nijlpaarden zag   voeren   en   Henk   de
           that I   Cecilia   the   hippos   saw   feed   and   Henk   the
      olifanten   hoorde   wassen].
      elephants   heard   wash
      '... that I saw Cecilia feed the hippos and heard Henk wash the elephants.'

                                                                 (Steedman 1985: 561)

To generate equivalent results from a theory of grammar with more standard constituent structure would surely require a large amount of movement and/or ellipsis operations. However, all of these predictions fall out for free from Steedman's strictly local, surface-compositional theory of grammar, because of the more flexible constituent structure that it allows.

It is worth emphasizing the virtues of this analysis: it is intrinsic, in that the basic combinatorial operations directly predict which strings can be coordinated, and the CSC falls out as a special case of those predictions. It is also expressive enough to handle nested and crossing dependencies, without being too expressive. In these respects, Steedman (1985) represents the first unequivocal step beyond Gazdar (1981) in the analysis of coordinate structures: it maintains the virtues of Gazdar's approach (intrinsic, local), while removing the limitation in terms of expressive power.

4.5.4 Takahashi (1994)

Daiko Takahashi's (1994) dissertation was an attempt to develop a general theory of locality on the basis of the Shortest Move Condition (SMC) proposed by Chomsky and Lasnik (1993). Takahashi also attempts to subsume the CSC within this general theory, one of the relatively few Minimalist attempts to make the CSC fit with the rest of locality theory, while still making fairly conservative assumptions about the syntax of coordination. In this respect, Takahashi (1994) contrasts with the works just discussed, which largely rejected Chomskyan locality theory in their attempts to integrate the CSC.[22] We will not reproduce the whole theory here, but will sketch the elements which are relevant to the integration of the CSC with other locality constraints.

The SMC has the effect of enforcing very local movement, with A'-movement often proceeding via adjunction to every, or almost every, maximal projection between the head and the foot of the movement dependency. Takahashi's major innovation is to force the SMC to interact with a condition (the Uniformity Corollary on Adjunction, or UCA), given in (83).

(83)   Adjunction is impossible to a proper subpart of a uniform group, where a uniform
         group is a nontrivial chain or a coordination.   (Takahashi 1994: 26)

(83) entails a novel hypothesized link between the CSC and the effects covered by Huang's (1982) Condition on Extraction Domain, which blocks extraction from subjects and adjuncts. We will illustrate this first with extraction from subjects. Takahashi adopts the VP-internal subject hypothesis, according to which subjects originate in Spec,VP,[23] and subsequently move to Spec,IP. This movement forms a nontrivial chain, in the terms of (83), consisting of NP_i and t_i in (84a).

(84)   a.

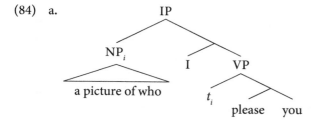

         b. *Who did a picture of ___ please you?

Now, to extract *who* from the subject in (84a) and form the question in (85b), there are two options. One would be to move directly from within NP to Spec,CP. This, however, would violate the Shortest Move Condition, because it skips potential intermediate landing sites.

The alternative is to adjoin *who* to NP_i (and perhaps to other intermediate landing sites en route). This, however, violates the UCA, because *who* adjoins to one member of the

---

[22] Zoerner (1995) made a similar attempt to reduce the CSC to the Minimal Link Condition, on the basis of the asymmetric, specifier–head–complement structure discussed in Section 2.4.3. We do not discuss Zoerner's theory in detail because we do not fully understand his account of the Element Constraint, but it shares the property of accepting the CSC as an empirical generalization, while trying to eliminate it as a theoretical primitive. More recent work has addressed the topic of locality and coordination within a Minimalist framework, such as te Velde (2006), Zhang (2009), and the recent string of papers by Bošković (2019a,b,c, 2020). However, these works tend to reject, or at least modify, the original CSC as an empirical generalization. Other work, such as Citko (2005), accepts the CSC but makes more radical assumptions about the syntax of coordination.

[23] Or Spec,vP. We disregard matters relating to functional structure in the lower part of the clause, and also Agr-projections, as orthogonal to our interests.

chain $\langle NP_i, t_i \rangle$, but not the other. The SMC and UCA interact to block movement out of moved phrases in this way, and the ban on extraction from subjects follows as a special case.

Although it instantiates a different phrase-structural configuration, the ban on non-ATB extraction from coordinate structures follows a similar logic. To derive (85), one would either have to skip adjunction to *photographs of __* , violating the SMC, or adjoin to one conjunct but not the other, violating the UCA.

(85)   *Who did you see [[portraits of John] and [photographs of __]]?

On the other hand, ATB extraction as in (86) has a derivation compatible with both the SMC and the UCA.

(86)   Who did you see [[portraits of __] and [photographs of __]]?

Who must adjoin to both conjuncts, as required by the SMC. This is unproblematic, though, as this pattern of adjunction is compatible with the UCA: the 'uniform group' of conjuncts have all been adjoined to.

It is clear that the UCA is central to Takahashi's unification of the CSC with other aspects of locality theory. However, the unification is not fully successful, because the UCA itself is disjunctive: adjunction is impossible to a nontrivial chain *or* a coordination. Although this disjunction is not unnatural, it means that the CSC is not yet fully integrated with the rest of locality theory.

4.5.5 Multiplanar coordinate structures

The final class of attempts to derive the CSC works by enriching the set of possible phrase structures so as to allow a 'parallel' representation of a set of conjuncts. Different authors have developed this idea in different ways, but the recurring theme is that conjuncts are not related by classical hierarchical relations such as sisterhood, dominance, c-command, or any more complex relation defined in terms of these.[24] We will call these 'multiplanar' representations, a term first used to our knowledge by Muadz (1991). It is also common to hear the terms 'three-dimensional' or 'multidimensional' used in relation to this family of approaches, and we will see that there is also a link to recent theories of phrase structure incorporating a notion of multidominance.

The appeal of multiplanar approaches to the CSC is that they allow the analyst to state conditions requiring that all conjuncts obey some structural constraint, either that they bear some structural similarity to each other or that they each stand in some appropriate structural relation to the rest of the sentence in which the coordinate structure is embedded. This section describes several variations on this theme.

Williams (1978) was the first to propose that the distinctive behavior of coordinate structures with respect to locality reflects a multiplanar structure. Williams suggested that the

---

[24] There are also theories which have a multiplanar element in a level of representation other than phrase structure. Winter (1995) models conjuncts as members of a tuple in the compositional semantics, while Kaplan and Maxwell (1988) and Peterson (2004) model coordination in terms of sets of f-structures in LFG. The LFG model shares many of the strengths and weaknesses we describe in the main text, while Winter's semantic model is not directly concerned with matters related to extraction.

ATB generalization reflects a 'parallel' syntactic representation of the two conjuncts, as in (87).[25]

(87)   Who did $\begin{bmatrix} [\text{John see } \emptyset]_S \\ [\text{Bill hit } \quad \emptyset]_S \end{bmatrix}_S$ and

His approach relies on a constraint on factorization of a sentence to meet the structural description for a transformation, essentially stating that all conjuncts must be factorized in the same way.[26] If a factor is then moved, the corresponding factor must be moved in each conjunct, and the principle of Recoverability of Deletion then forces the material moved from each conjunct to be the same (p. 36). This causes no problems in (87), which would be derived from an underlying structure like (88) (factorization indicated by vertical bars).

(88)   COMP $\begin{bmatrix} [\text{John saw} & \text{who}]_S \\ [\text{Bill hit} & \text{who}]_S \end{bmatrix}$ and $\Big]_S$ (Williams 1978: 32)
         1   2   3   4

However, it blocks asymmetric cases of extraction from a single conjunct (e.g. *Who did John see Mary and Bill hit*), where *who* in one conjunct corresponds to *Mary* in another, violating the enforced parallelism across conjuncts. Although other factorizations are possible, none allows the moved element to appear in the same factor in each conjunct.

(89)   COMP $\begin{bmatrix} [\text{John saw} & \text{Mary}]_S \\ [\text{Bill hit} & \text{who}]_S \end{bmatrix}$ and $\Big]_S$
         1   2   3   4

Williams's constraint also blocks cases like (90), where there is a gap in a different position in each conjunct. Williams shows that there is no way of factorizing such examples which respects the parallelism constraints sketched out in this section. For instance, (90b) is ruled out because factor 3 contains the left bracket of the clause *who likes Mary*, but not the clause *Bill likes who*.

(90)   a. *I know a man who [Bill saw ___] and [___ likes Mary].

         b. COMP $\begin{bmatrix} [\text{Bill saw} & \text{who}]_S \\ & [\text{who} & \text{likes Mary}]_S \end{bmatrix}$ and $\Big]_S$
               1   2   3   4   5

Despite its empirical advances, Williams's approach raises questions because of its introduction of new formal devices of unknown expressive power (see the debate in Williams 1981 and Gazdar et al. 1982). In addition, a direct empirical challenge came from Pesetsky (1982: 526), who noted that the interaction with parasitic gaps entailed that different conjuncts could contain different amounts of movement.

---

[25] Interestingly, Chomsky (2004), building on ideas in Lebeaux (1988), suggested that adjunction structures involved a separate representational 'dimension' in a way not far removed from Williams's proposal. For some Minimalists, then, it would be possible to claim that conjunction and adjunction form a natural class with distinctive locality properties related to their distinctively 'parallel' phrase-structural properties.
[26] The precise phrase-structural definition of 'the same way' is on p. 32 of Williams (1978).

(91)   I know who [[[close friends of __] admire __] and [Mary hates __]].

It is not immediately clear how any factorization could enforce parallel movements in the two conjuncts, when there are more instances of movement in the first conjunct than in the second.[27]

Williams's basic insight was developed by Goodall (1987), using the notion of 'reduced phrase marker' from Lasnik and Kupin (1977). Reduced phrase markers capture information about precedence and constituency in a similar way to trees, but without the extra assumption that the constituents identified can be assembled into a tree (in particular, for any two nodes in a tree diagram, either one precedes the other or one dominates the other, but this does not necessarily hold of reduced phrase markers). Instead, a reduced phrase marker is a set of 'monostrings', each of which consists of the terminal string, with precisely one substring replaced by a nonterminal node. A phrase marker for a noncoordinate sentence like (92a) could then be as in (92b).[28] Implicit in these monostrings is the information that, for instance, *eat butter* is a VP.

(92)   a. I eat butter.

$$\left\{ \begin{array}{c} \text{S,} \\ \text{NP eat butter,} \\ \text{I VP,} \\ \text{I V butter,} \\ \text{I eat NP} \end{array} \right\}$$

b.

The monostrings in (92b) imply a regular tree structure. However, this is not always the case, meaning that reduced phrase markers are more flexible in some respects than regular phrase markers. Goodall leveraged this extra flexibility to describe coordinate structures as the union of noncoordinate phrase markers, as in (93) (see Muadz 1991 for a broadly similar approach, which instead base-generates multiplanar structures).

(93)   a. I eat butter and shun margarine.

$$\left\{ \begin{array}{c} \text{S,} \\ \text{NP eat butter,} \\ \text{NP shun margarine,} \\ \text{I VP,} \\ \text{I V butter,} \\ \text{I V margarine,} \\ \text{I eat NP,} \\ \text{I shun NP} \end{array} \right\}$$

b.

The heart of Goodall's and Muadz's approach to the CSC is a ban on vacuous quantification, taken to apply plane-by-plane (an approach reminiscent of the parallelism-based approach to the CSC developed by Ruys 1992 and Fox 2000, and discussed in Section 3.5.2). A CSC-violating sentence such as (94) has at least one plane in which the *wh*-phrase does not bind a variable; that plane violates the prohibition on vacuous quantification.

---

[27] The reader should be able to verify, on the basis of the information in Section 4.5.2, that this example does not pose any problems for the analysis in Pesetsky (1982).
[28] We ignore extraneous details here, in particular relating to unary-branching nodes.

Moltmann (1992) identifies several problems with this approach, which in fact apply equally to all multiplanar theories previous to hers. Among the most serious, the first is that wellformedness conditions on coordinate structures are taken to reduce to wellformedness conditions on the individual phrase markers. This is particularly problematic in the case of group-forming coordination: the wellformedness of (94a) cannot be reduced to the set of ungrammatical basic sentences in (94b).

(94)   a. Mary and Sue met.
       b. {*Mary met, *Sue met}

The second is that conjunctions are nowhere to be seen in Goodall's phrase markers. The basis of distributional differences between, for instance, *and* and *but*, and the representation of the scope of a conjunction, are therefore obscure on this approach.

Moltmann developed a new analysis which avoids these specific difficulties, and which allows for base-generation of multiplanar structures composed of two different varieties of plane, which she calls 'formal' and 'meaningful' planes. This descriptively very rich approach opens up several new topics in the syntax and semantics of coordination and comparatives, based on the interactions among multiple multiplanar sentence structures.

We cannot give Moltmann's theory the space that it deserves here, because the complexity of her system defies easy summarization. To our mind, the concerns about expressive power we have expressed apply to a greater extent in Moltmann's case, because wellformedness for Moltmann is a function of the relation between two multiplanar representations. We are sure that an empirically adequate system can be built out of so many moving parts. However, any theorist with an interest in representational parsimony must surely be biased against such a system.[29]

Two further analyses, bearing some similarity to multiplanar approaches, emerged in the mid-2000s. One, due to de Vries (2005), treats coordinate structures as a product of a distinct kind of Merge, that he labels 'b-merge'. De Vries's idea is that regular Merge ('d-merge' in his terms) establishes dominance relations between the domain and range of the operation, while b-merge establishes a different relation, 'behindance'. Because dominance is part of the definition of c-command, and because behindance is by definition not dominance, b-merged constituents do not c-command each other. In this way, de Vries derives the claim from Progovac (1998a,b) that there is no evidence that any conjunct c-commands another (see discussion in Section 2.4.3). However, it does so essentially by stipulation: the distinction between d-merge and b-merge amounts to a diacritic indicating that c-command relations do not reach into certain constituents.[30]

---

[29] Very late in the process of writing this book, we became aware of Lyskawa (2021), which argues for a multiplanar structure for coordination in the context of an analysis of agreement with coordinate structures. We have not been able to fully consider this work. However, it is interesting in that it applies the multiplanar structure to a new empirical area.

[30] Away from coordinate structures, this relation of behindance has been a major research focus for de Vries and colleagues, with analyses of parentheticals, appositives, and various dislocation structures developing this kind of approach. Many of these constructions loosely resemble coordination in their interpretation. However, their behavior with respect to extraction is quite distinct, so we do not discuss them further here.

De Vries does not intend to use b-merge to derive the CSC.[31] Rather, the generalization that he proposes is that noninitial conjuncts are 'invisible' to external syntactic relations. He gives evidence that it is possible to extract asymmetrically from initial conjuncts in English and Dutch such as (95) ((95a) is repeated from (20) in Chapter 3), and he claims it as a virtue of his system that it can capture this pattern as well as ATB movement, while prohibiting asymmetric extraction from noninitial conjuncts.

(95) a. How much can you [[drink __] and [still stay sober]]?
      b. Hoeveel   chocola   denk je   dat je   kunt [[__ eten] en   [toch
          how.much   chocolate think you that you   can   eat   and still
          niet   misselijk   worden]]?
          not   sick   get
          'How much chocolate do you think you can eat and still not get sick?'

                                                                  (de Vries 2005: 97)

Of course, the discussion in Chapter 3 has shown that the pattern de Vries describes is not universal, in that there are languages, such as English, which also allow asymmetric extraction from noninitial conjuncts. The crucial examples include (16a) from Chapter 3 (repeated here):

(96) Here's the whiskey which I [[went to the store] and [bought __]].

It is possible that an extension of de Vries's approach would be compatible with these data, treating (96) as binding of a null pronominal along the lines discussed in Section 4.3 (see also Section 4.6). However, the diacritic nature of b-merge means that we should prefer a priori a theory without b-merge (after all, once we've allowed one diacritic to specify exceptional behavior, why not more?). Again, then, concerns of expressivity militate against this approach, particularly once it transpires that the data do not straightforwardly match the predictions of the theory.

The second recent approach with some similarity to multiplanar analyses comes from Citko (2005). Citko's theory is perhaps unique in arguing for a 'parallel' syntactic representation of coordination, of a sort which cannot reduce to a canonical phrase-structure tree diagram, and arguing at the same time that these representations derive from regular application of the basic structure-building operation Merge. The concerns which we have raised in this section about additions to basic compositional syntactic machinery therefore do not apply to Citko.

The starting point for Citko's theory is the shift from a conceptualization of displacement phenomena based on copying, as in Chomsky (1995), to one based on repeated Merge of a single constituent, as in Chomsky (2001) or Starke (2001). The important conceptual distinction here is between multiple instances of a single unit, each Merged once with a single sister and single mother, as in the classical copy theory, and a single instance of a single unit, Merged repeatedly with multiple sisters and multiple mothers, yielding so-called **multidominance** structures, as in (97).

---

[31] In this respect, his analysis does not fit with the others discussed in Section 4.5. We discuss it here purely because of its conceptual similarity to other multiplanar approaches.

(97) α (Citko 2005: 476)

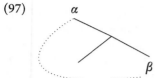

In most cases of movement, like (97), the multiple mothers of a single moved constituent stand in a relation of dominance (this is extensionally equivalent to the classical generalization that a moved phrase c-commands its trace). If a constituent has multiple mothers which *don't* stand in a dominance relation, a structure like (98) arises.

(98) x^{max} y^{max} (Citko 2005: 478)

(98) poses problems for linearization. Assume a condition of the form 'If A precedes B, then every overt unit that A dominates precedes every overt unit that B dominates.'[32] In (98), x^{max} precedes y^{max}. Moreover, x^{max} and y^{max} both dominate z^{max}. The constraint just sketched then entails that z^{max} precedes itself.

This problem disappears if z^{max} is not pronounced in (98), for instance because it moves. This means that (99) is an unexceptional structure for ATB movement, on a multidominance approach.

(99) C^{max} (Citko 2005: 483)

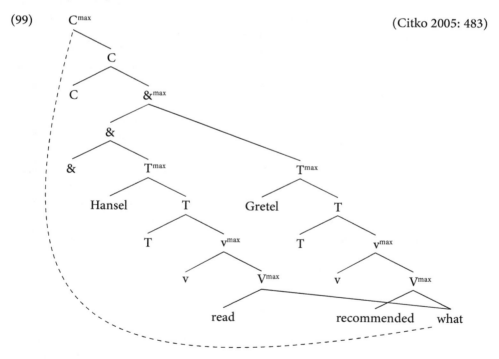

---

[32] Citko derives this constraint from the LCA of Kayne (1994). However, it is also a natural consequence of many linearization algorithms less rigid than Kayne's.

The strongest evidence in favor of Citko's approach comes from the comparison by Bošković and Franks (2000) of *wh*-questions in coordinate structures in languages with *wh*-movement, and with *wh* in situ (see Section 3.5.2). Bošković and Franks demonstrated that there is no covert ATB movement, in the sense that there is no covert movement of multiple *wh*-phrases to a single specifier position. This means that (100a) cannot mean the same as (100b): the former asks two distinct questions about two possibly distinct people, while the latter asks a single complex question about a single person (see (67) and (68) in Chapter 3 for a similar contrast in English).

(100) a. [[Zhangsan xihuan shenme ren]   [Lisi   taoyan shenme ren]]?
           Zhangsan like   which   person Lisi   hate   which   person
           'Which person does Zhangsan like and which person does Lisi hate?'
       b. 'Which person does [[Zhangsan like __] and [Lisi hate __]]?'
                                                        (Citko 2005: 489)

This is as predicted for Citko, because in her ATB structure, there is a single *wh*-phrase, which does not unambiguously belong to either conjunct. This is only possible when the *wh*-phrase in question moves, because of the problems relating to in situ linearization just discussed. This implies that there should be no direct equivalent of ATB constructions in languages with *wh* in situ.

Citko's theory does justice to the original intuition from Williams (1978) that ATB extraction reflects a non-context-free base structure, in a way which does not require novel primitives or relations, and answers the challenge from Gazdar (1981) about the operations which apparently permit movement of a single constituent from multiple base positions. However, we will see in Section 4.6 that it does not make essential use of multidominance structures. The 'sidewards movement' approach developed by Hornstein and Nunes (2002), Nunes (2005) derives the same prediction within a more conventional phrase structure.

In sum, the analysis of coordinate structures and the CSC has been the spur for a diverse range of analytical approaches which propose to enrich the basic structure-building mechanisms included in syntactic theory. Some of these approaches straightforwardly derive the CSC, possibly (as for Williams 1978, Citko 2005) along with some further locality patterns which could reasonably be grouped under the heading 'parallelism'. Others (such as de Vries 2005) aimed to capture other empirical generalizations, but not with notable success. However, despite their intuitive appeal and obvious potential, after four decades, the field has not yet converged on a widely used formalization of these enriched phrase-structural representations, or a core set of facts which motivate their use.

4.5.6 Summary

Across a range of theoretical approaches (GPSG, CCG, HPSG, GB, Minimalism, and surely others), it is clearly possible to develop unified theories of locality which either intrinsically predict the CSC (as in Gazdar 1981) or are amenable to natural extensions which derive the CSC (as in Pesetsky 1982 or Takahashi 1994). It is notable that almost all of these approaches, other than the multiplanar structures just discussed, depend on uniform paths to derive their accounts of the CSC. There are few if any locality theories which are built on punctuated paths, in the tradition of Chomsky (1973); and which offer an account of the CSC which is integrated with the rest of locality theory and with standard models of phrase structure. Takahashi (1994) is arguably an attempt to build such a theory. However, even Takahashi's approach relies on what Abels calls 'quasi-uniform paths', with movement proceeding successive-cyclically through every maximal projection (a consequence of the Shortest Move Condition), as opposed to the less local 'punctuated paths' of classical EST locality theory.

This is indicative of a theoretical schism of sorts. On the one hand, we have theories like Chomsky's with punctuated paths, which do not straightforwardly extend to CSC effects unless they are enriched with the kind of phrase structures discussed in Section 4.5.5, but which have probably the most fully developed account of other locality phenomena. On the other hand, we have uniform theories like those discussed in this section, which naturally integrate the CSC with the rest of locality theory.

Extraction from coordinate structures is therefore a particularly informative phenomenon for the purpose of comparing theories. We *can* integrate the CSC with the rest of locality theory, even if standard versions of Chomskyan locality theory, with punctuated paths, don't (the works discussed in this section demonstrate that). The question is, *should* we?

To begin to address this question, in Section 4.6 we discuss another class of approaches to the syntax of extraction and coordination. In these approaches, the CSC, as a property specifically of coordinate structures, is rejected, and patterns of extraction from coordinate structures are compared to other constructions which potentially contain multiple gaps.

4.6 Parasitic gaps and ATB extraction

4.6.1 Introduction

Section 4.5 has shown that it is possible to develop a theory of locality which derives the CSC, at varying degrees of remove from the classical EST locality theory. However, the catalog of counterexamples to the CSC in Chapter 3 constitutes a good reason to doubt whether a theory of locality *should* derive the CSC. There is no real doubt about the existence of such counterexamples; the question is whether the counterexamples are in any way exceptional. If a theory of locality derives the CSC, the implicit claim is that the counterexamples must be exceptional.

In this section, we piece together an analysis which rejects the CSC and incorporates the CSC's counterexamples into the core empirical base of locality theory. We are certainly not the first to do this, and the extent to which we are standing on the shoulders of giants will soon become clear. The purpose of this analysis, in the context of the survey, is to allow a more even-handed evaluation of the approaches to the CSC in Section 4.5.

In fact, theories which seek to reject the CSC have a natural starting point. A distinctive property of ATB extraction is the association of a single moved element with multiple distinct gaps, none of which c-commands any of the others. There is only one other major class of movement phenomena with this property, namely the **parasitic gap** construction discussed in Section 4.3 and illustrated in (101).

(101)   a. This is a document that you need to [[burn __] [after reading __]].
         b. This is a book that [[people who read __] [never enjoy __]].

Accordingly, in this section we will start from parasitic gap constructions and work toward extraction from coordinate structures.

4.6.2 Basic properties of parasitic gaps

A parasitic gap construction contains one gap inside a CED island (a subject or an adjunct), and one gap in a regular gap site, such as complement-of-V. The former gap is the parasitic gap; the latter gap is sometimes called the 'real' gap.

The real gap doesn't need the parasitic gap: examples like (102) are just as grammatical as (101).

(102)   a. This is a document that you need to [burn __ [after receiving instructions from on high]].
         b. This is a book that [[people who read trashy horror novels] never enjoy __].

However, the parasitic gap does need the real gap: extracting just from the subject or adjunct violates the CED.[33]

(103)   a. *This is a document that you need to [burn your house down [after reading __]].
         b. *This is a book that [[people who read __] enjoy sushi].

In the best-known analysis of parasitic gaps, along the lines of Kayne (1983) and Chomsky (1986), the parasitic gap is derived by movement of a null operator to the left periphery of the subject or adjunct. In this position, the null operator can be licensed by A'-movement of (for example) a *wh*-phrase from the real gap position. This leads to a configuration in which the movement path with the parasitic gap at its foot is **connected**, in the sense of Kayne (1983), to the movement path with the real gap at its foot (see also Pesetsky 1982, Steedman 1996): the PP dominating the head of the 'parasitic' movement path is the immediate daughter of a node on the 'real' movement path. The structure of (101a) is taken to be approximately as in (104), with irrelevant details omitted.

---

[33] It will become important later in this section that neither subjects nor adjuncts are completely robust as islands, as already discussed in Section 4.3.4. See Stepanov (2007) and Chomsky (2008) for discussion of some cases of grammatical extraction from subjects, and Chomsky (1982), Postal (1998), and Truswell (2011) for discussion of grammatical extraction from adjuncts. However, extraction from subjects and adjuncts is clearly not as free as extraction from complements—that is, the CED is approximately, but not completely, correct—and it is reasonable to blame the contrast between (101) and (103) on whatever derives the restrictions on extraction from subjects and adjuncts.

(104)

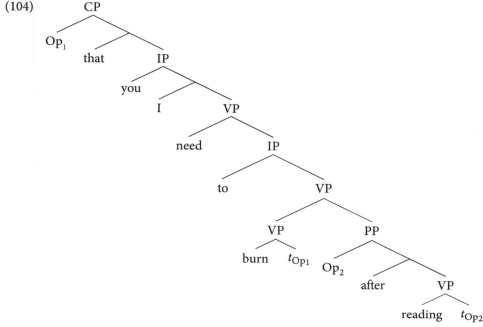

This analysis makes several largely accurate predictions about the distribution of parasitic gaps. These include:

- Anti-c-command: the real gap must not c-command the parasitic gap, or vice versa.

  (105)   a.   the person who [[friends of *p.g.*] are fond of *t*]

          b.   *the person who [*p.g.* is fond of *t*]

                         (intended interpretation: the person *x* s.t. *x* is fond of *x*)

- Locality within the CED domain: movement from the parasitic gap site to the edge of the subject or adjunct must not violate any locality conditions.

  (106)   a.   *a book that [[people that discover [[the first chapter of *p.g.*] missing]] usually end up disliking *t*]

          b.   *the person who [you admire *t* [because [friends of *p.g.*] became famous]]

                                             (Kayne 1983: 231–2)

- Reconstruction asymmetries: the moved phrase can show connectivity effects with the real gap site, but not the parasitic gap site.

  (107)   a.   Which books about himself did John [[file *t*] [before Mary read *p.g.*]]?

          b.   *Which books about herself did John [[file *t*] [before Mary read *p.g.*]]?

                               (attributed by Chomsky 1986 to Kearney 1983)

However, it is fair to say that the proper analysis of parasitic gap constructions is far from settled, and reviewing more recent theories would require a survey of its own.[34] To give one indication of the challenges faced by Chomsky's account, Levine and Sag (2003)

[34] For more recent work, see Nissenbaum (2000), and the papers collected in Culicover and Postal (2001).

demonstrate that the reconstruction asymmetries illustrated in (107) do not always obtain (compare (108), where reconstruction is apparently possible into either gap site).

(108) a. There were pictures of herself which, [once Mary finally decided she liked *p.g.*], John would have to put *t* into circulation.
       b. There were pictures of himself which, [once Mary finally decided she liked *p.g.*], John would have to put *t* into circulation.   (Levine and Sag 2003: 240)

This surely casts doubt on the general validity of Chomsky's reconstruction asymmetry. However, a possible confound remains, in that English -*self*-anaphors have logophor-like unbound uses not shared by more 'pure' reflexives in many other languages (see Büring 2005 for discussion of the implications of this for analysis of apparent reconstruction effects).

Perhaps more challenging, Levine and Sag also document the existence of **symbiotic gaps**: two gaps within CED domains, each of which apparently requires the presence of the other (compare (109a–b) with (109c)).

(109) a. ??What kinds of books do authors of malicious pamphlets argue about royalties [after writing __]?
       b. *What kinds of books do [authors of __] argue about royalties after writing malicious pamphlets?
       c. What kinds of books do [authors of __] argue about royalties [after writing __]?

(Levine and Sag 2003: 242)

These empirical challenges share a common theme: the relationship between the two gaps is not as asymmetrical as it should be, on Chomsky's analysis.

4.6.3 Parasitic gaps and coordinate structures

Parasitic gaps are relevant to extraction from coordinate structures because it has frequently been proposed (e.g. Haïk 1985, Williams 1990, Takahashi 1994) that parasitic gaps can be thought of as a special case of ATB extraction. This requires thinking of adjunction structures such as (110a) and subject–predicate relations like (110b) as types of coordinate structure, as reflected in the distribution of Williams's COORD operator in these representations.[35]

(110) a. Who would you [[warn *t*] COORD [before striking *p.g.*]]?
                                                              (Williams 1990: 265)
       b. Which stars do [[pictures of *p.g.*] COORD [annoy *t*]]?   (Williams 1990: 270)

One obvious difference between ATB extraction and parasitic gaps is that ATB extraction is symmetrical (in that a gap in either conjunct requires a gap in the other conjunct), while

---

[35] The representations in (110) differ from those given by Williams, partly for consistency with the rest of this survey and partly to correct some apparent minor errors in Williams's own representations. We maintain a representational distinction between 'real' gaps (marked by *t*) and parasitic gaps (marked by *p.g.*). If Williams's proposal was adopted, this distinction would not reflect an actual difference in the status of the two gaps, which would both be traces of ATB movement.

parasitic gap constructions are asymmetrical, in that only one of the gaps is parasitic on the other (the empirical challenges from the previous subsection notwithstanding). In other words, examples like (111) are just as grammatical as examples like (110).

(111)   a.   Who would you [[warn __] [before striking a wall]]?
        b.   Which stars do [[pictures of kittens] [annoy __]]?

Given Williams's proposal to model (110) as coordinate structures, the implication is that the examples in (111) are not coordinate structures—otherwise, ATB extraction would be required and (111) would be ungrammatical. In other words, structures as diverse as *before*-adjuncts and even subject–predicate articulations are systematically structurally ambiguous for Williams, allowing both a coordinate structure like (110) and a noncoordinate structure like (111). Only the distribution of gaps disambiguates between the two structures.

A reduction in the opposite direction was proposed by Munn (1992, 1993, 2001). On Munn's analysis, noninitial conjuncts are adjoined to initial conjuncts. This means that a regular case of ATB movement out of a coordinate structure is a parasitic gap construction: the 'real' gap is in the initial conjunct and the noninitial conjuncts contain parasitic gaps.

Munn gives several arguments in support of this reduction. The first is that reconstruction asymmetries parallel to (107) exist in ATB movement.

(112)   Which pictures of himself/*herself did [[John buy __] and [Mary paint __]]?
                                                                    (Munn 1993: 52)

Secondly, Weak Crossover effects show up in only the initial conjunct, and not in other conjuncts. On Munn's analysis, this follows from the observation in Lasnik and Stowell (1991) that parasitic gaps are among the constructions which do not show WCO effects.

(113)   a.   Which man$_i$ did [[you hire __], [his$_i$ boss fire __], and [his$_i$ sister vouch for __]]?
        b.   *Which man$_i$ did [[his$_i$ boss fire __] and [you hire __]?   (Munn 2001)

Thirdly, ATB constructions in Hebrew show the same pattern as parasitic gap constructions: if the initial conjunct contains a gap then noninitial conjuncts may contain resumptive pronouns, but the initial conjunct must not contain a resumptive pronoun if a noninitial conjunct contains a gap.

(114)   kol   profesor   še   Dani roce   lehazmin (*ʔoto) ʔaval lo   maarix
        every   professor that   Dani wants to-invite him   but   not   esteems
        (ʔoto)   maspik
        him   enough
        'every professor that Dani wants to invite but doesn't esteem enough'
                                                                    (Munn 2001)

Likewise, Zhang (2009) gives (115) as evidence for an asymmetry between gap sites.[36]

---

[36] Zhang (2009) does not adopt Munn's adjunction structure, but nevertheless proposes an analysis of ATB movement in which the base position of the *wh*-phrase is in the first conjunct only, with corresponding positions in other conjuncts filled by null pronominals.

(115)   Himself$_{i/*j}$, [[John$_i$ likes __] and [Bill$_j$ hates __]].   (Zhang 2009)

The force of this argument depends in part on the analysis of (108), from Levine and Sag (2003). In light of that example, it is not completely clear that the asymmetry demonstrated in (112) and (115) actually is also found in parasitic gap constructions. Clearly, further careful empirical work is needed in this area.

Munn's analysis is also open to the criticism just described with respect to Williams (1990): ATB movement does not look like a parasitic gap construction, because every gap in an instance of ATB movement requires the others, while the 'real' gap is not dependent on the parasitic gap. To address this, Munn supplements his syntactic analysis with a semantic parallelism requirement, which he relates to the Law of Coordination of Likes. This is of course congenial to the claims in Lakoff (1986) that interpretation determines patterns of extraction from coordinate structures. However, Munn only considers symmetrical coordination. In Section 4.6.5, we will investigate how Munn's analysis may be extended to Lakoff's crucial cases of asymmetric coordination.

4.6.4 Differences between ATB movement and parasitic gap constructions

Postal (1993) demonstrates that ATB movement and parasitic gap constructions are not as similar as Munn's analysis would appear to predict. Postal claims that parasitic gaps display similar properties to extraction from weak islands ('selective islands' in Postal's terms). Postal adopts a variant of the analysis of weak islands described in Sections 4.3.2 and 4.3.5, according to which they block regular A'-movement, but allow construal with a fronted null resumptive pronoun within the island. Extending this analysis to parasitic gaps predicts that parasitic gaps must correspond to referential NPs, while there is no such restriction on ATB gaps. This additional restriction on parasitic gaps drives contrasts like (116) and (117).[37,38]

(116)   a.   *How sick did John look t [without actually feeling $p.g.$]?
         b.   How sick did John [[look __] and [say he actually felt __]]?

(Postal 1993: 736)

---

[37] Reich (2007) notes a more basic way in which parasitic gaps are more restricted than ATB movement: some languages, like German, have the latter but not the former.

[38] Levine (2001), building on Kroch (1989) and Pollard and Sag (1994), documents several cases where Postal's reliance on null resumptive pronouns makes incorrect predictions. In (ia), the filler is an adverb, and therefore not of an appropriate category for pronominal resumption (there are no resumptive pro-adverbs—compare (ib)). Nevertheless, the A'-dependency into a weak island is grammatical (in this case, the weak island is the embedded *wh*-question).

(i)   a.   That rudely, I wonder [why anyone would word a letter __].
       b.   *I worded the letter it.   (Levine 2001: 154)

However, such examples do not challenge the relationship Postal establishes between parasitic gaps and weak islands. It only challenges the analysis of these constructions in terms of null pronominals. It is worth noting that Abrusán (2014), citing similar data from Kuno and Takami (1997) via Fox and Hackl (2007), builds a semantic analysis of weak islands in which the extraction of a nonreferential phrase as in (ia) triggers a presupposition failure, except in the presence of further quantifiers or modals like *would* in (ia). We do not know whether such alternatives can be extended to parasitic gap constructions.

(117)   a. *It was that color that [everyone who painted their house *p.g.*] wanted to paint
their car *t*.

b. The color that they [[chose __ yesterday] and [will paint their barn __
tomorrow]] is red.   (Postal 1993: 744)

There have been two responses to Postal's challenge, in the reductionist spirit of this section.
Both involve postulating two derivations for ATB movement, one of which is restricted
to referential NPs and is shared with parasitic gaps, while the other does not share this
categorial restriction but is only available for ATB movement.

The first of these responses is from Munn (2001). In short, Munn claims that the restrictions on parasitic gaps, at least in adjuncts, follow not from the nature of the gap itself, but
from other operators contained within the adjunct.

Munn argues that adjuncts which contain parasitic gaps also contain a null operator
in their left periphery. This includes negation in (118a) and temporal operators in adjuncts like (118b) (see Larson 1990—the idea is that (118b) is ambiguous as to whether the
speaker saw Mary after the time of swearing or the time of putative leaving, and movement
of a null operator is implicated in deriving that ambiguity).

(118)   a. John left [without anyone hearing].
b. I saw Mary in New York [after [she swore [that she had left]]].

To create a parasitic gap construction, a null operator has to move across these other operators. Munn claims that this is the source of the restrictions on parasitic gaps, following
the logic outlined in Section 4.3.5.

In contrast, in a coordinate structure, as analyzed by Munn, noninitial conjuncts are
adjuncts headed by a coordinating conjunction. Those conjunctions are not operators in
the same sense, and so do not create intervention effects. Accordingly, they do not induce
categorial restrictions on the gaps contained within these noninitial conjuncts.

A second response to Postal's challenge comes from Hornstein and Nunes (2002), Nunes
(2005). These authors develop an account of parasitic gaps in terms of sideward movement
between the two gap sites, and claim that the extra constraints on parasitic gaps stem from
constraints on when sideward movement is licensed. More specifically, they claim that parasitic gaps must be formed by last-resort sideward movement into an argument position,
while ATB gaps *can* be formed like this, but can also be licensed by parallelism requirements of the type associated with Ruys (1992) and Fox (2000) (see Section 3.5.2). So long
as an approach like Munn's or Hornstein and Nunes's is tenable, Postal's demonstration that
ATB movement has different properties from parasitic gap constructions need not stand as
an impediment to building unified theories of the two types of construction.

4.6.5 Parasitic gaps, weak islands, and asymmetric extraction
from coordinate structures

Postal has established that parasitic gaps obey several restrictions which do not constrain
regular ATB movement, and a plausible interpretation of those facts is that the formation
of parasitic gap constructions involves the same mechanisms as extraction from a weak island, while ATB movement does not. These conclusions become more subtle, though, when

asymmetric extraction from coordinate structures is considered. Postal (1998) investigates these patterns. The full set of facts which emerge from that study can be subsumed under the generalizations below, where by 'weak island-like restrictions', we mean the restrictions documented in Sections 4.3.2 and 4.6.4 on the nature of the extracted category.[39]

- ATB extraction is not subject to weak island-like restrictions.
- Asymmetric extraction from an initial conjunct is not subject to weak island-like restrictions.
- Asymmetric extraction from noninitial conjuncts *is* subject to weak island-like restrictions.
- Parasitic gap constructions *are* subject to weak island-like restrictions.

These generalizations relate to Lakoff's three scenarios as follows.[40] In Lakoff's Type A scenarios (narrations, in which extraction is required from all nonbackgrounded conjuncts), extraction from the initial conjunct alone is impossible.

(119)   ?*Which store did he [[go to __] and [buy groceries]]?   (Postal 1998: 66)

Extracting from other conjuncts yields the characteristic pattern of extraction only of referential NPs. Note that in the following examples, extraction is fully grammatical until the Type A scenario conjunction is introduced.[41]

(120)   a. What color did she (*fly to Vancouver and) dye her hair __ ?
        b. How much thought did they (*get drunk, drive home, and) give those proposals
           __ ?   (Postal 1998: 67)

In Type B scenarios, on the other hand, where a violation of expectation is detected, extraction is typically from initial conjuncts.

(121)   the courses which Bob can [[take __ for credit] and [still stay sane]]
                                                                      (Postal 1998: 78)

Extraction from the initial conjunct is clearly not subject to weak islandhood constraints—in fact, the canonical Type B scenario examples involve extraction of a nonreferential *wh*-phrase. Examples like (16c) and (16d) from Chapter 3, repeated in (122), demonstrate this.

---

[39] These generalizations diverge significantly from those described by Postal, who presented his findings in terms of the different scenarios licensing asymmetric extraction that Lakoff identified. The generalizations presented by Postal (1998) in fact represent a radical syntacticization of the different patterns that Lakoff noted: Postal seems to imply that each of Lakoff's three scenarios is coupled with a different set of syntactic properties, such as coordination vs. subordination, and which conjuncts are strong or weak islands. These correlations between syntax and interpretation, as presented by Postal, appear to be arbitrary, and therefore necessarily stipulated. Moreover, they were strongly criticized by Levine (2001). The alternative set of generalizations presented here is equally compatible with the facts that Postal uncovers, and appears to us to hold greater potential for explanation of the correlations between syntax and interpretation.

[40] We continue to present Lakoff's generalizations uncritically for now. In Chapter 5, however, we will find that the bulleted list of generalizations just presented represents a significant empirical improvement over Lakoff's original generalizations in terms of Type A, Type B, and Type C scenarios.

[41] Levine (2001: 157–8) notes that not all cases of extraction from noninitial conjuncts in Type A scenarios involve referential NPs, giving counterexamples like (i).

(i)   That rudely, I can't imagine anyone [[sitting down] and [wording a letter to an old friend __]].

However, as he notes, this is still parallel to the behavior of other weak islands. His final assessment is that '[these] conjuncts are weak islands to about the same degree that *wh* islands are' (p. 158).

(122)   a. How many lakes can we [[destroy __] and [not arouse public antipathy]]?
        b. How many counterexamples can the Coordinate Structure Constraint [[sustain __] and [still be considered empirically correct]]?   (Goldsmith 1985)

In fact, Postal, contrary to Lakoff, claims that Type B scenarios also allow asymmetric extraction from noninitial conjuncts. We will return to this claim in Chapter 5, when we sharpen the description of the semantics of these scenarios, but regardless, (123) demonstrates that any such extractions show the usual properties of weak islands.

(123)   a. Who did Mike [[remain celibate] and yet [still date __]]?
        b. What color did Mike [[paint his ears __] and [still make it seem he was normal]]?
        c. *What color did Mike [[go colorblind] and [still paint his ears __]]?
                                                              (Postal 1998: 79, 80)

Although Postal does not discuss Type C scenarios (where a causal relation holds between the conjuncts) in comparable detail, it would appear that the same initial/noninitial contrast holds there too.[42] Compare nonreferential adjunct extraction from the first conjunct in (124a) and from the second conjunct in (124b).

(124)   a. For how long have the guys in the Caucasus [[eaten that stuff __] and [lived to be 100]]?
        b. *How rapidly do the guys in the Caucasus [[eat snails] and [recover from that disease __]]?   (Postal 1998: 90)

These generalizations align very well with the structure for coordination proposed by Munn (1993), as described in Section 4.6.3.[43] Munn's syntactic analysis predicts that initial conjuncts are not islands, while extraction from noninitial conjuncts is subject to the same weak island-like restrictions as parasitic gaps. The ATB pattern is imposed by a semantic parallelism constraint. A natural synthesis of Munn's analysis with Postal's findings would be to claim that, when there is no semantic parallelism, there is no restriction to ATB movement, but there may be other, Lakovian discourse-semantic constraints on which conjuncts permit extraction.

A further potential point of synthesis of Munn and Postal concerns the island status of adjuncts. As discussed in Section 4.3.4, adjuncts are frequently considered to be strong islands for extraction, following Cattell (1976) and Huang (1982), and indeed many classes of adjuncts disallow any extraction. However, Postal (1998) claims instead that some nonfinite adjuncts, at least in English, pattern with weak islands (see also Chomsky 1982, Truswell 2011, and many others).[44] Extraction from those classes of adjuncts is subject to the same restrictions as discussed for parasitic gaps. For instance, adjuncts cannot contain gaps in antipronominal contexts.

---

[42] Postal also attempts a demonstration that Type B and Type C scenario coordination is not true coordination, which is perhaps one reason for his focus on Type A scenarios. Like Levine (2001), though, we find Postal's notion of 'true coordination' too obscure for constructive discussion.

[43] To be clear, what follows is not Munn's analysis of extraction from coordinate structures. We are pointing out that it may be fruitful to use Munn's analysis of the syntax of coordination to ground Postal's observations about extraction from coordinate structures.

[44] We have not explored in any detail the consequences of this claim for the analysis of parasitic gaps.

(125) a. (i) *How much money did John drive Mary crazy [spending __]?

   (ii) *What color did John drive Mary crazy [painting the door __]?

   b. (i) *How much money did you decorate your room [without spending __]?

   (ii) *What color did you redecorate your house [without painting your room __]?

This in turn predicts several other patterns of extraction from coordinate structures, although it is currently an open question how well these patterns match attested facts. First, extraction from adjuncts appears to be unavailable in many, or perhaps even most languages. Postal (1998) shows that it is impossible in French, and Truswell (2008) states that the same is true for most Romance, West Germanic, and Insular North Germanic languages, as well as Russian and Greek. Examples of ungrammatical extraction from adjuncts in French and Icelandic are given below.

(126) *le   directeur qu' elle y   est allée en avion [pour confronter   __]
       the   director that she   there is   gone   in plane for   confront.INF
       'the director that she flew there to confront'   (Postal 1998: 76)

(127) *Hvað kom   Jón   [flautandi __]?
       what came John   whistling
       'What did John arrive whistling?'   (Truswell 2008: 154)

Likewise, Postal demonstrates that asymmetric extraction from noninitial conjuncts is ungrammatical in French.

(128) *le   pain   que Jacques [[a   couru au   marché], [(a)   acheté   __],
       the   bread that Jacques has   run   to.the market   has   bought
       [(a) foncé chez   lui],   et   [(a) mangé __]]
       has   rushed to.home.of him   and has   eaten
       'the bread that Jacques ran to the market, bought, rushed home, and ate'
                                                                   (Postal 1998: 75)

Initial crosslinguistic evidence suggests that our reformulation of Postal's account makes correct predictions in these respects at both a fine and a coarse grain.[45] At a coarse grain, the account predicts an implicational relationship: in some languages, extraction from initial conjuncts (for instance in Type B and Type C scenarios) should be possible but extraction from noninitial conjuncts should be impossible, while the converse should not be found. This prediction is derived from the hypothesis that extraction from noninitial conjuncts is subject to the same crosslinguistic variation as extraction from adjuncts, while initial conjuncts are not islands. (128) shows that French is an example of a language which only allows extraction from initial conjuncts. Dutch, in (129), is another. In contrast, we have not come across any languages which only allow extraction from noninitial conjuncts.

---

[45] Thanks to Nairan Wu for discussion of these patterns, and to Nils Franzén, Lisa Gotthard, Dag Haug, Jet Hoek, Andreas Stokke, and Hans Wilke for examples and judgments.

(129) a. Wat had [[Joopje nog niet ___ gekregen] of [hij begon ermee   te
          what had Joopje   not yet   got   or he   started therewith to
          gooien]]?
          throw
          'What did Joopje just receive and he already started demolishing it?'
       b. *Wat was [[Joop nog niet vertrokken] of [Jaap heeft ___ gekocht]]?
          what was Joop still not left   and Jaap has   bought
          'What had Joop still not left before Jaap bought?'   (de Vries 2005: 97–8)

A broader, but often overlooked, class of examples of extraction from solely initial conjuncts is the SLF construction discussed in detail in Section 3.6 (a representative example
is repeated in (130)).

(130) In den Wald ging der Jäger   und fing   einen Hasen.
       in the forest went the hunter and caught a   hare
       'Into the forest went the hunter and caught a hare.'   (Wunderlich 1988: 289)

In Section 3.6, we reproduced arguments that the SLF construction should be given what
Johnson (2002) calls a Small Conjuncts approach, rather than the approach of Wilder
(1994), based on clausal conjuncts and ellipsis. Assuming that conclusion, the important
points about the SLF construction are that it involves asymmetric extraction from the initial conjunct, without restrictions on the category of the extracted element or the discourse
relation holding between the conjuncts.[46]

At a finer grain, the account predicts extraction from noninitial conjuncts in only those
languages which allow extraction from adjuncts. Postal offers the contrast between English
and French as an example of this correlation. Other languages which allow both types of extraction include the Mainland North Germanic languages, represented by Danish in (131).
Dutch, in contrast, disallows extraction from adjuncts, as in (132), as well as from noninitial
conjuncts.

(131) a. Hvad gik   du   ned   i   butikken og   købte   ___?
          what went you down in store-DEF and bought
          'What did you go to the store and buy?'
       b. Hvor meget kan du [[drikke ___] og   [forblive ædru]]?
          how   much   can you   drink   and remain   sober
          'How much can you drink and stay sober?'
       c. Det tog   jeg ned   til Køge [for at lære ___].
          that went I   down to   Køge for to learn
          'I went down to Køge in order to learn this.'   (Müller 2019: 66)

---

[46] This latter claim appears to contradict Reich (2009). Reich claims that the SLF construction is paired with an
asymmetric semantics for coordination, but as far as we can see, the details of the semantics that Reich proposes
are permissive enough to be compatible with many apparently symmetrical discourse relations such as PARALLEL.
Regardless, the existence of SLF-like constructions with relations like PARALLEL is empirically well-supported, as
discussed in Section 3.6.

(132)   *Wat   is   Jan   [__   fluitend]   gearriveerd?
      what   is   John   whistling   arrived
      'What did John arrive whistling?'   (Truswell 2008)

The initial signs are encouraging, then. At this point, however, Postal's patterns, and their relationship to patterns of extraction from adjuncts, have not been tested on a more reliable crosslinguistic sample, particularly beyond Romance and Germanic.

A second connection between asymmetric extraction from coordinate structures and extraction from adjuncts is that both are subject to what we might call 'size constraints'. We have seen in Section 3.3.2 that asymmetric interpretations of coordinate structures require the conjuncts to be as small as possible. However, asymmetric *extraction* from coordinate structures tends to be specifically from coordinated VPs. For Type A scenarios with extraction from noninitial conjuncts, Neeleman and Tanaka (2020) relate this directly to patterns of extraction from adjuncts: they build on an account of extraction from adjuncts in Borgonovo and Neeleman (2000) which entails that the adjunct must be adjoined to an unaccusative or reflexive VP, for reasons grounded in the syntax of θ-role assignment (see also Cormack and Breheny 1994, Cormack and Smith 2005 for a related account). Similarly, Truswell (2011) argues that extraction from adjuncts requires that the adjunct is smaller than a full finite clause, on the basis of contrasts like (133). On Truswell's account, this follows from a requirement that the adjunct contain an event variable which hasn't been existentially quantified.[47]

(133)   a.   Who did John get upset [after talking to __]?
      b.   *Who did John go home [after he talked to __]?   (Truswell 2011: 129, 176)

However, a significant challenge for extending this account to a general account of asymmetric extraction from coordinate structures is that asymmetric extraction tends to require VP coordination, regardless of which conjunct is extracted from. Neeleman and Tanaka's account can only be extended to cover extraction from initial conjuncts, as far as we can see, if we accept their claim that *all* conjuncts are adjuncts (that is, that coordination is a mutual adjunction structure). That claim appears to be incompatible with Postal's account, discussed in this section, of asymmetries between extraction from initial and from noninitial conjuncts.

In sum, it seems plausible that the patterns of asymmetric extraction documented by Postal could follow from an analysis along the following lines. Coordinate structures which allow asymmetric extraction are based on the structure in Munn (1993), where noninitial conjuncts are adjuncts. Adjuncts are weak islands, so extraction from noninitial conjuncts is subject to the same constraints as extraction from weak islands. The initial conjunct is not an island, so is not subject to any such constraint. A possible extension, based on Neeleman and Tanaka (2020), would have it that *all* conjuncts are adjuncts. This extension is potentially able to explain the restriction of asymmetric extraction to VP coordinate structures, but loses the ability to account for Postal's asymmetries between initial and noninitial conjuncts.

---

[47] Cormack and Smith (2005) and Reich (2009) made similar claims about event variables in their analyses of asymmetric coordination. However, their assumptions about event structure are very different from Truswell's, and not obviously compatible.

This synthesis of Munn and Postal makes a rich set of empirical predictions, and our preliminary investigation suggests that some of those predictions may be remarkably accurate. This approach clearly deserves close study in further research, and we will continue to bear it in mind in subsequent chapters, as in our opinion the most promising alternative to the classical CSC, with scope for incorporating Lakoff's discourse-semantic generalizations without losing Postal's and Munn's important, and purely syntactic, empirical observations.

4.7 Summary

The last two sections have introduced a range of theories pulling in opposite directions, in response to the challenge outlined in the introduction to this chapter. On the one hand, the CSC fits poorly with the core of Chomskyan locality theory, as discussed in Sections 4.3 and 4.4. On the other hand, following the discussion in Chapter 3, it is not clear whether the CSC actually represents the full range of attested patterns of extraction from coordinate structures, or whether those patterns should even be captured by a narrowly syntactic locality theory. The question of how to square this circle is another major choice point.

Choice Point 4 What is the relationship between the CSC and Chomskyan locality theory?

Option 1: Chomskyan locality theory should be rejected in favor of alternatives in which the CSC is not an outlier (e.g. Gazdar 1981, Pesetsky 1982).

Option 2: The CSC can be integrated into Chomskyan locality theory (e.g. Takahashi 1994). This may require a novel, multiplanar syntax of coordination (e.g. Williams 1978).

Option 3: The CSC should be rejected as a syntactic constraint, although it may be reinterpreted as a semantic parallelism constraint. Syntactic locality theory may make other predictions about extraction from coordinate structures (e.g. the adjunction theory of Munn 1993 implies that extraction from an initial conjunct is syntactically unmarked).

This choice point is closely related to Choice Point 3 in Chapter 3, the question of the source of the CSC and its exceptions. In particular, Options 1 and 2 here, like Options 1 and 2 in Choice Point 3, entail that a syntactic CSC should be maintained. Option 3 here, and Option 3 in Choice Point 3, reject that assumption.

Choice Point 4 is also related to Choice Point 2, the question of whether the symmetrical ATB extraction has a special status as the only unmarked pattern of extraction from coordinate structures. If that is the case, then on a syntax-calls-the-shots approach, syntactic theory should explain that special status. Options 1 and 2 aim to do just that, while Option 3 requires a semantic account of any special status of ATB extraction.

Section 4.5 was concerned with theories pursuing Options 1 and 2, which normalize the CSC but struggle to capture the asymmetric extraction patterns. In contrast, Section 4.6 was concerned with theories of coordinate structures which have the scope to offer a nuanced account of patterns of asymmetric extraction, but diverge from the basic CSC to such an extent that they predict that extraction from initial conjuncts is essentially unconstrained. Both of these types of approach address the challenge articulated in Sections 4.3 and 4.4, namely that the CSC does not appear at first sight to fit with the rest of Chomskyan locality theory, but they do so in very different ways.

A particular challenge for the synthesis of Munn (1993) and Postal (1998) developed in Section 4.6 concerns the handling of ATB movement, and particularly the fact that ATB movement is less restricted than parasitic gap constructions (see Section 4.6.4). One approach to this discrepancy is already available to us, proposed by Hornstein and Nunes (2002) and Nunes (2005). Their claim, also discussed in Section 4.6.4, is that there are two mechanisms for licensing multiple gap constructions (whether parasitic gaps or ATB movement). One is restricted to argumental (or referential) NPs, with no further discourse-semantic constraints. One imposes a parallelism constraint on the interpretation of the coordinate structure, but does not impose any further syntactic constraint on the category of the extracted element. The former condition fits naturally within a purely syntactic approach to the CSC, while the latter has a striking flavor of 'discourse calls the shots'.

In order to evaluate the tension between the approaches discussed in this chapter, in Chapters 5 and 6 we develop a theoretical understanding of the discourse semantics of coordinate structures and extraction from coordinate structures. This will put us in a better position to evaluate claims about the division of labor between syntax and discourse.

5
Discourse calls the shots

5.1 Introduction

Chapter 3 described two main types of extraction from coordinate structures. First, there is ATB extraction, the best-known pattern. Second, there is a range of less well-described asymmetric extraction patterns.

These extraction types are provocative because ATB extraction is unlike the extraction patterns described in the rest of locality theory and the asymmetric extraction patterns are poorly understood. Chapters 3 and 4 documented three types of response to that provocation. These are summarized below, with representative references.

1. Develop a form of locality theory which derives the CSC; treat asymmetric extraction as marginal (Williams 1978, Gazdar 1981, Steedman 1985);
2. Assimilate coordinate structures to adjunction structures and/or ATB extraction to parasitic gap constructions (Williams 1990, Munn 1993, Postal 1998);
3. Deny that there are specific syntactic constraints on extraction from coordinate structures, and aim to reduce the observed limits on extraction to discourse-structural considerations (Lakoff 1986).

There are grounds to reject the third approach, because there are crosslinguistic differences in extraction from coordinate structures which do not plausibly have discourse-structural reflexes (consider Sections 3.6 and 4.6 in particular). In Section 4.6, we also tentatively suggested that the second approach has certain empirical virtues apparently out of reach of the mainstream, ATB-centric first approach, in that the adjunction approach gives us some traction on the crosslinguistic distribution of asymmetric extraction. Postal (1998) suggested that extraction from noninitial conjuncts (in the Type A scenarios of Lakoff 1986) is crosslinguistically restricted in the same way as extraction from adjuncts, while extraction from initial conjuncts (in Lakoff's Type B and C scenarios) apparently is not. The adjunction analysis, with noninitial conjuncts adjoined to initial conjuncts, explains that contrast for free.

However, it is important to appreciate that a syntactic analysis is incomplete on any of these three approaches, and must be supplemented with an account of interpretive factors in order to give a complete picture of these extraction patterns. This goes without saying for the first approach (where asymmetric extraction patterns are outside the scope of the ATB-based syntactic analysis) and the third approach (which has as its raison d'être the elimination of syntactic constraints on extraction from coordinate structures). On the adjunction approach, the point is only slightly more subtle. No syntactic factor explains Lakoff's correlations between: (i) Type B/C scenarios and extraction from initial

Coordination and the Syntax–Discourse Interface. Daniel Altshuler and Robert Truswell, Oxford University Press.
© Daniel Altshuler and Robert Truswell (2022). DOI: 10.1093/oso/9780198804239.003.0005

conjuncts, and (ii) Type A scenarios and extraction from final (and possibly other) con-juncts. Moreover, one of the best-known examples of the adjunction approach, Munn (1993), requires that the adjunction-based syntax of coordination be supplemented with a semantic parallelism constraint (see also Ruys 1992, Fox 2000) to explain ATB extraction patterns.

In this chapter, we investigate Lakoff's observations about interpretation and extraction on their own terms, as an example of the discourse-calls-the-shots strategy outlined at the end of Chapter 3. We do not expect this approach to provide answers to all of the outstand-ing questions about extraction from coordinate structures, for the reasons just given. The reason for doing this is rather that we are interested in the division of labor, and interac-tions, between syntax and discourse, and the best way to approach that question is through a fuller statement of what 'discourse calls the shots' *can* account for.

Lakoff's own account is brief, and incomplete in several respects. It does not give us clear definitions of his three scenario types, or clearly applicable criteria for distinguish-ing them. We need to move beyond the suggestive correlations that he identifies between interpretation and extraction, and to do that, we need to reconstruct his claims within a general and formal theory of discourse relations. In this respect, this chapter is in the spirit of Kehler's (2002) development of Lakoff's insights. However, our conclusions differ signif-icantly from Kehler's as well as Lakoff's, about both the empirical fact of the matter and the proper framework for making sense of the data. Accordingly, this chapter does not iden-tify choice points in the way that Chapters 2–4 did. Rather, it highlights the weaknesses, as well as the virtues, of the Lakoff/Kehler approach, as a prelude to an exploration of another discourse-based approach, which we think is more promising, in Chapter 6.

In Section 5.2, we outline the principles underpinning taxonomies of discourse relations, based on the seminal work by Hobbs (1979, 1985, 1990) that Kehler (2002, 2019) builds on. Section 5.3 then develops formal definitions of some well-studied discourse relations that are particularly relevant to Lakoff's analysis, namely OCCASION, VIOLATED EXPECTATION, and RESULT, as well as PARALLEL, which is often invoked in the analysis of ATB movement.[1]

Next, Section 5.4 evaluates the fit between the independently motivated definitions of these discourse relations, and observed patterns of extraction from coordinate structures. We will conclude that there is no real possibility for analyzing discourse relations as di-rect causal factors accounting for the different extraction patterns that Lakoff identifies. Specifically, once we have explicit and reasonable definitions of the discourse relations just mentioned, it becomes apparent that these relations do not stand in opposition to each other. Rather, they stand in entailment relations. In particular, RESULT is a special case of OCCASION. This all but eliminates the scope for explaining Lakoff's patterns in these terms: if RESULT is a special case of OCCASION, how are we to explain Lakoff's empirical claim that RESULT (a key component of Lakoff's Type C scenarios) doesn't allow the same ex-traction patterns as OCCASION (as featured in his Type A scenarios)? This puzzle sets up Chapter 6, which explores the idea, first articulated by Deane (1991) and Kehler (2002), that the extraction patterns are linked to discourse relations indirectly, via the mediation of information structure.

---

[1] As noted in Chapter 3, NARRATION is used by some discourse coherence theoreticians instead of OCCASION, most notably by those working within Segmented Discourse Representation Theory (Asher 1993, Asher and Lascarides 2003). The difference between these two terms will not matter until Chapter 6.

5.2 Discourse Coherence Theory

Consider the following discourses from Hobbs (1979):

(1)   John took a train from Paris to Istanbul. He has family there.

(2)   #John took a train from Paris to Istanbul. He likes spinach.

There is a clear contrast between (1) and (2). While the former is a perfectly accept-able discourse, the latter sounds strange. Why is this? To answer this question, note that (1) does not merely list two random facts about John. Rather, a hearer normally un-derstands (1) as conveying that John took a train from Paris to Istanbul *because* he has family there. Understanding that there is this explanatory connection between these two pieces of discourse—often called **discourse units**[2]—is necessary for fully understanding the speaker's contribution in (1). In contrast, the failure to carry out this interpretive task by establishing a coherent connection between the two sentences in (2) results in infelicity. In-terlocutors are left with the feeling that they have not fully comprehended the contribution of the speaker. Without further context, they are left searching for an explanatory connec-tion: is Istanbul famous for its spinach? Or do they serve spinach on trains to Istanbul? Or does Paris have bad spinach? As noted by Hobbs (1979) (cited by Kehler 2002):

> ... the very fact that one is driven to such explanations indicates that some desire for coher-ence is operating, which is deeper than the notion of a discourse just being 'about' some set of entities.   (p. 67)

In order to explain what this desire for coherence amounts to, Hobbs cites David Hume's proposal that our ideas are associated according to three fundamental principles:

> Though it be too obvious to escape observation that different ideas are connected together, I do not find that any philosopher has attempted to enumerate or class all the principles of association—a subject, however, that seems worthy of curiosity. To me there appear to be only three principles of connection among ideas, namely Resemblance, Contiguity in time or place, and Cause or Effect.   (Hume 1748/1999)

Hume's project was quite general. He was interested in human cognition, broadly speak-ing, seeking to explain why our view of reality does not always line up with our assumed metaphysics, especially as it pertains to causality. Hobbs's main contribution was to apply the three Humean principles (Resemblance, Contiguity, and Cause/Effect) to natural lan-guage discourse. He introduced the notion of a **discourse relation**[3] to define a **coherent discourse**: a discourse is coherent if and only if the units that make up the discourse are re-lated by at least one discourse relation. Following Hume's insight, Hobbs proposed that the associated principles underlying the establishment of discourse relations are psychological in nature:[4]

---

[2] We will define this term in Chapter 6. For now, we can assume that a discourse unit is an eventuality description (Afantenos et al. 2012), i.e. a description of an event or a state (Bach 1986).
[3] Hobbs actually used the term *coherence relation*; see also the related term, *rhetorical relation*.
[4] For alternative views of discourse relations, see, e.g., Longacre (1983), Mann and Thompson (1986), Martin (1992), Sanders et al. (1992).

It is tempting to speculate that these [discourse] relations are instantiations in discourse comprehension of more general principles of coherence that we apply in attempting to make sense out of the world we find ourselves in, principles that rest ultimately on some notion of cognitive economy. [...] Recognizing [discourse] relations may thus be just one way of using very general principles for simplifying our view of the world. (Hobbs 1990)

Discourse relations correspond to **cue-phrases** in natural language. For example, *because* is often used as a cue-phrase for the discourse relation EXPLANATION, which Kehler (2002) proposes to be a Humean Cause/Effect relation. Observe that, without further context, it is incredibly difficult (if not impossible) to interpret (1) as *not* conveying exactly what (3) conveys.[5]

(3)   John took a train from Paris to Istanbul because he has family there.

The kind of information that justifies establishing a particular discourse relation (as opposed to others) is the subject of formal pragmatics research which we discuss in the next section. We preview this discussion here by considering Kehler's (2002) response to the following oft-asked question: how many discourse relations are there?[6]

Kehler proposes that there are four discourse relations in the Humean Cause/Effect category, six in the Humean Resemblance category and just one in the Humean Contiguity category. Below are some illustrative examples of Humean Cause/Effect relations, beginning with the just-noted EXPLANATION:

(4)   *Humean Cause/Effect relations* (examples from Kehler 2019)
       a. I hope it snows this weekend. I love building snowmen.   (EXPLANATION)
       b. I love building snowmen. I hope it snows this weekend.   (RESULT)
       c. I love building snowmen, but I hope it does not snow this weekend.
                                                                    (VIOLATED EXPECTATION)
       d. I hope it does not snow this weekend, even though I love building snowmen.
                                                                    (DENIAL OF PREVENTER)

According to Kehler, the relations **EXPLANATION** and **RESULT** are mirror images, with the data in (4a) and (4b) illustrating this idea: the causal relationships are understood to be the same, regardless of the order in which the eventualities are described. As we have seen, *because* is a common cue-phrase for EXPLANATION, while *so* and *as a result* are common cue-phrases for RESULT.

Analogously, **VIOLATED EXPECTATION** and **DENIAL OF PREVENTER** are mirror images, according to Kehler, with the former being a negated version of RESULT and the latter

---

[5] The same can be said about the incoherent discourse in (2), which does not improve when we add *because*:

(i) #John took a train from Paris to Istanbul because he likes spinach.

We understand that EXPLANATION holds in (i) despite the oddity.

[6] Theories of discourse coherence differ to a great extent in how they approach this question. It is not uncommon to find theories which adopt a long list of discourse relations, while others adopt a relatively short list. The reason that we choose to survey Kehler's (2002) list is that it contains discourse relations that match Lakoff's descriptions of frame-semantic 'scenarios', and indeed we are following Kehler's lead in this respect. In Chapter 6, however, we will adopt the set of discourse relations proposed by Asher and Lascarides (2003). For more discussion of the various approaches to discourse coherence, see Kehler (2002: Ch. 1) and references therein.

being a negated version of EXPLANATION. (4c) and (4d) have the cue-phrases *but* and *even though*. Unlike other Humean Cause/Effect relations, VIOLATED EXPECTATION and DENIAL OF PREVENTER typically require cue-phrases. To wit, the discourses below are incoherent.

(5) #I love building snowmen. I hope it does not snow this weekend.

(6) #I hope it does not snow this weekend. I love building snowmen.

Here are some illustrative examples of Humean Resemblance relations:

(7) *Humean Resemblance relations* (examples from Kehler 2019)
    a. Jill built a snowman, and Sue made snow angels.   (PARALLEL)
    b. Jill likes building snowmen, but Sue prefers making snow angels.   (CONTRAST)
    c. Today, Jill built a snowman. She piled three snowballs on top of one another, and decorated it with button eyes, a carrot nose, a pipe, and a scarf.   (ELABORATION)
    d. Children love to play in the snow after the storm. Today, Jill built a snowman.
                                                                         (EXEMPLIFICATION)
    e. Today, Jill built a snowman. Children love to play in the snow after the storm.
                                                                         (GENERALIZATION)
    f. Children love to play in the snow after a storm. But today Jill stayed inside.
                                                                         (EXCEPTION)

Kehler follows Hobbs (1985, 1990) in viewing the relation **PARALLEL** as establishing a relationship of similarity between two discourse units; negating this similarity leads to **CONTRAST**. We will have more to say about similarity (and lack thereof) in the next section and in Chapter 6. For now, note that *and* is often used with PARALLEL (as in (7a)), as well as the presuppositional marker *too* in VP ellipsis constructions (Hobbs and Kehler 1997):

(8) Jill built a snowman. Sue did too.

The quintessential cue-phrase for CONTRAST is *but*. Recall that *but* also cued VIOLATED EXPECTATION and that without this cue, (4c) was odd. As shown below, the same is not true with CONTRAST, which generally does not require a cue-phrase, though it is often cued by particular intonation patterns.[7]

(9) Jill likes building snowmen. Sue prefers making snow angels.

(10) Jill built a snowman. Sue did not.

Let us now consider the discourse relation **ELABORATION**. Following Hobbs, Kehler proposes that it is the most extreme case of similarity between two discourse segments—namely one of identity. For example, in (7c), the second sentence describes the subevents that constitute the event described by the first. Typical cue-phrases for ELABORATION include *in particular*, *specifically*, and *namely*. Punctuation such as ':' may also signal this relation.

---

[7] Sporleder and Lascarides (2008) considered 200 discourses from a corpus that use *but* to mark CONTRAST, finding that 30% of these discourses became incoherent when *but* was removed. See Andersson and Spenader (2014) for more general discussion about the role of explicit versus implicit cues of discourse relations.

As for **EXEMPLIFICATION** and **GENERALIZATION**, the similarity can be thought of in terms of subset and superset relationships respectively. The data in (7d) and (7e) illustrate how these relations are mirror images and can (though need not) be cued by phrases like *for example* and *therefore*, respectively. Finally, **EXCEPTION** is the negated version of EX-EMPLIFICATION. As was the case with VIOLATED EXPECTATION, this relation often requires a cue-phrase. The discourse in (7f) is slightly degraded without *but*:

(11)   Children love to play in the snow after a storm. Today Jill stayed inside.

To our ears, this discourse sounds less degraded than (5) and (6), raising the question of sources of gradience in discourse structure. We will revisit this question in Chapter 6.

Finally, here is an illustrative example of the lone Humean Contiguity relation:

(12)   *Humean Contiguity relation* (example from Kehler 2019)
         A huge storm hit Scranton this weekend. Many children were seen out playing in
         the snow.   (OCCASION)

Questions of gradience are especially pervasive when we consider this relation, which is especially important for our purposes since it is the backbone of narrative discourse (Hobbs 1990, Altshuler 2016, Cumming 2021). Consider (13) and its two possible continuations in (13a) and (13b):

(13)   Arash came over to see Akna.
         a. ... He drank a glass of water.
         b. ... They had lunch.

Both continuations justify an interlocutor inferring a sequence of eventualities whereby the former described event (Arash coming over to see Akna) sets up the occasion for the latter described event (drinking a glass of water and having lunch, respectively). The continuation in (13a) is a bit odder than (13b), however. It feels like a story is being set up without being 'cashed out'. The reader may question why Arash would merely drink a glass of water if his intention was to see Akna (cf. having lunch, which feels more appropriate).

So far, we have seen a relatively short list of discourse relations and some intuitive descriptions about how they relate to Humean principles of association of ideas. Before developing more precise definitions of some of these relations in the next section, we briefly demonstrate that the evidence for their linguistic reality is overwhelming. In particular, they have played a vital role in analyses of diverse linguistic phenomena at the semantics/pragmatics interface. The phenomenon which has received the most attention in the discourse coherence literature is the resolution of third-person pronouns. For example, consider the following influential discourse:

(14)   a. Phil tickled Stanley.
         b. Liz poked him.   (Smyth 1994)

One can understand (14) as comparing two events that happened to Stanley: Phil played with poor Stanley by tickling him, while Liz played with Stanley by poking him. Another truth-conditionally distinct interpretation is also possible: (14) can describe what happened as a result of the event described by the first sentence: Phil's tickling Stanley prompted Liz to play hero and poke Phil so that he would stop. Notice that on the 'Liz is the hero' interpretation, we infer RESULT analogous to (4b), and on the 'poor Stanley' interpretation, we infer PARALLEL analogous to (7a). Crucially, the choice of discourse relation is correlated with the resolution of the pronoun *him* (Hobbs 1979, Kehler et al. 2008). In particular, if (14) is understood as harboring PARALLEL, *him* is interpreted as picking out Stanley, and if it is understood as harboring RESULT, *him* is understood as picking out Phil.[8] In what follows, we will often talk of a discourse as **harboring** a relation or relations (Stojnić 2017).

These and related observations about discourses like (14) motivate the Mutually Constraining Tasks (MCT) Hypothesis, which has opened a new field of psycholinguistic research.[9]

(15)   **Mutually Constraining Tasks Hypothesis**:
        The resolution of pronouns and the establishment of discourse relations are correlated and mutually constraining tasks.[10]   (Stojnić 2016, Stojnić et al. 2017)

In light of this hypothesis, Altshuler (2016) observes that the choice of discourse relation is also correlated with the resolution of the past tense in (16b):[11]

(16)   a. Stanley screamed with pain in his eyes.
        b. Liz poked him.

If (16) is understood as harboring EXPLANATION, the prominent time in (16b) is understood to be *prior* to Stanley's scream. In other words, on the EXPLANATION reading, (16b) asserts what led Stanley to scream. If, however, (16) is understood as harboring RESULT, then the prominent time in (16b) is understood to be *after* Stanley's scream. In other words, on the RESULT reading, (16b) asserts how Liz responded to Stanley's scream.

The discourse in (16) suggests that the hypothesis in (15) may be generalized to context-sensitive expressions more generally. This position was proposed by Una Stojnić, who considered the role that discourse relations play in modal anaphora (Stojnić et al. 2013, Stojnić 2016, 2017). Other phenomena in which discourse relations have played a key role include: VP ellipsis (Hobbs and Kehler 1997, Kehler 2002), open questions (Schlöder 2018), attitude reports (Hunter 2016), aspect (Grønn 2003, Altshuler 2012, Kamp 2013), adverbs (Vieu et al. 2005, Altshuler and Stojnić 2015, Carter and Altshuler 2017, Stojnić and Altshuler 2021), demonstration and gesture (Lascarides and Stone 2009, Stone and Stojnić 2015), intonation (Schlöder and Lascarides 2015), focus (Schlöder and Lascarides 2020), cataphora (Asher et al. 2007, Trnavac and Taboada 2016, Altshuler and Haug 2017), garden path effects in discourse (Altshuler and Haug under contract), presupposition (Asher and Lascarides 1998b), and bridging (Asher and Lascarides 1998a), as well as broader questions about causal inferences and the definitional adequacy of discourse relations (Altshuler and Varasdi 2015, Altshuler 2016, 2021, Schlöder 2018, Altshuler and Schlöder 2021b), the meaning of dialogue (Lascarides and Asher 2009, Stone and Lascarides 2010, Schlöder

---

[8] Prosody plays an important role in disambiguating between the interpretive possibilities. See recent discussion by Schlöder and Lascarides (2020) for how prosody cues discourse relations.

[9] See, e.g., Wolf et al. (2004), Kertz et al. (2006), Kehler et al. (2008), Kaiser (2011), Rohde and Horton (2014), Kaiser and Cherqaoui (2016), Grütera et al. (2018).

[10] This hypothesis can be traced to work by Hobbs (1979), though to the best of our knowledge, Stojnić (2016) was the first to put it explicitly in this way.

[11] The idea that the interpretation of tense is correlated with the establishment of discourse relations goes back to Webber (1988) (see also Lascarides and Asher 1993, Kehler 2002, Kamp et al. 2011, Kamp 2013, Bittner 2014). This research builds on Partee (1973) idea that tenses are context-sensitive expressions on a par with pronouns (see also Kratzer 1998).

et al. 2016), argumentation (Pavese forthcoming), and narratives (Hobbs 1990, Altshuler 2016, Cumming 2021, Anand and Toosarvandani forthcoming), including sequential art (Maier and Bimpikou 2019, Altshuler and Schlöder 2021a, Altshuler and Schlöder 2021b), film (Cumming et al. 2017), and ballet mime (Newton-Haynes and Altshuler 2019).

It is noteworthy that this list runs the gamut from grammatically conditioned phenomena like VP ellipsis and focus, to artistic phenomena which are not even linguistic in a narrow sense. This raises the question of what kind of objects discourse relations are: are they grammatical formatives, visible in grammatical representations of phenomena like VP ellipsis, or are they, as Hobbs suggested in the quote reproduced on page 142, domain-general, 'just one way of using very general principles for simplifying our view of the world'? Both views have their adherents, though this will not be consequential for the purposes of this chapter which they are. However, in Chapter 6, we will explore the use of discourse relations in Segmented Discourse Representation Theory (SDRT, Asher 1993, Asher and Lascarides 2003), where discourse relations are linguistic objects, explicitly represented in logical form.[12] This view of discourse relations as discrete objects visible in logical form has clear implications for the questions concerning gradience raised earlier in this section. We will spell these out when we introduce SDRT in Chapter 6.

5.3 Defining discourse relations

In the rest of this chapter, we will mainly be concerned with a small set of discourse relations, which formed the basis of Kehler's (2002) reinterpretation of Lakoff's observations about extraction from coordinate structures. Kehler drew the following correlations between extraction patterns and discourse relations:

- ATB movement: PARALLEL

  (17) What did you [[eat __] and [drink __]]?

- Type A: OCCASION

  (18) What did you [[go to the store] and [buy __]]?

- Type B: VIOLATED EXPECTATION

  (19) How much can you [[drink __] and [still stay sober]]?

- Type C: RESULT

  (20) What do people always [[eat __ here] and [then get sick]]?

It should already be clear from Chapter 3 that extraction from coordinate structures is not, in fact, limited to these four relations, and we will return to other extraction patterns later in this chapter and in Chapter 6, but Kehler's correlations stand as a simple and plausible reformulation of Lakoff's generalizations within the terms of current approaches to discourse coherence. Of course, attaching these labels to the different scenarios does not explain why we find these specific correlations, rather than for instance the Type A pattern with PARALLEL or Type C with OCCASION. We will discuss aspects of Kehler's claims about these correlations as we proceed, over the course of this chapter and the next.

---

[12] This is also approximately the view of Stojnić and collaborators, the originators of the MCT hypothesis. A key difference between Asher and Lascarides and Stojnić is whether indeterminacy of a discourse relation is handled in terms of underspecification (Asher and Lascarides) or ambiguity (Stojnić). For more discussion, see Stojnić and Altshuler (2021: §2).

In this section, we develop and compare definitions of the four discourse relations we have listed. As noted by Kehler (2002: Ch. 2), many characterizations have been kept at an intuitive level, with the usual associated hazards of imprecision and conflicting interpretations. In Section 5.3.1 we introduce and critique Kehler's definitions of these relations. These definitions achieve a higher level of precision than many of their predecessors, but still fall short of the predictive and explanatory power we need. In particular, the definitions of RESULT and OCCASION don't allow us to classify examples in a way which predicts their extraction behavior.

In response to the problems identified in applying Kehler's definitions, in Section 5.3.2 we outline new definitions of OCCASION and RESULT developed by Altshuler and Varasdi (2015), and then discuss the prospects for extending these definitions to VIOLATED EXPECTATION. On Altshuler and Varasdi's definitions, RESULT asymmetrically entails, or is a special case of, OCCASION. This is a very different perspective on this system of relations from that assumed by Kehler, where these relations stand in opposition to each other. We critically revisit Lakoff's extraction patterns from this new perspective in Section 5.4.

5.3.1 Kehler's definitions, and some challenges

Parallel

Arguably the most difficult discourse relation to define is PARALLEL, briefly discussed in the previous section in connection to Humean Resemblance. It is historically related to the notion of **parallelism** that is widely employed by psychologists, linguists (see Section 3.5.2), and even writing teachers. Consider the following definition provided by the Evergreen Writing Center (https://www.evergreen.edu):

> Parallel structure (also called parallelism) is the repetition of a chosen grammatical form within a sentence. By making each compared item or idea in your sentence follow the same grammatical pattern, you create a parallel construction.

The goal of the Evergreen Writing Center is to 'increase the readability of [one's] writing by creating word patterns readers can follow easily'. From a psycholinguistic standpoint, achieving parallelism is a good way of satisfying this goal. Several studies have shown that in conjoined structures, parallelism is helpful to the processor (Frazier et al. 1984, Black et al. 1985, Henstra 1996, Frazier et al. 2000, Carlson 2001, Knoeferle and Crocker 2009). As summed up by Carlson (2001), 'the second conjunct is easier to process if it is parallel to the first in some way'. The works just cited verify the psychological reality of parallelism effects through experiments that manipulate grammatical factors such as voice, animacy of the object DP, thematic role assignment, and VP ellipsis. The focus of most of this research is on parallelism in coordinate structures. However, Dubey et al. (2005) and Sturt et al. (2010) demonstrate that similar parallelism effects hold between the subjects of a main clause and a subordinate clause (that is, between independent, noncoordinated noun phrases). Sturt et al. propose that parallelism is, in fact, an instance of structural priming, a pervasive effect where structurally similar forms tend to persist in sentence production, and repetition of structurally similar forms facilitates sentence processing.

There have also been many linguistic analyses of diverse and unrelated phenomena at the syntax–semantics interface that adopt the notion of parallelism. Here is one example, repeated from (66) in Chapter 3.

(21)   a. A (different) student likes every professor.
       b. A (??different) student [[likes every professor] and [hates the dean]].

(Fox 2000: 52)

Fox observes that whereas *a student* can have narrow scope in (21a) (where insertion of *different* disambiguates in favor of narrow scope), this is not possible in (21b). To explain the contrast, Fox proposes that it is not possible for *a student* to take scope under *the dean* in (22) for reasons of economy: scope inversion is only possible when it would lead to a different interpretation, and this is not the case in (22). Fox then argues that scope inversion is blocked for both conjuncts in (21b) because it is blocked by economy in the second conjunct, and a parallelism constraint requires the first conjunct to have parallel scope relations to the second.

(22)   A student hates the dean.

Fox does not define what he means by 'parallel', but implicitly assumes that there is some working definition of this notion in terms of aspects of LF representations. This is a common assumption, going back to seminal work by Sag (1976) and Williams (1977). However, as is well known from research on VP ellipsis (Dalrymple et al. 1991, Hardt 1992, 1993, Kehler 1993, Hardt 1999), things are much more complex. To the extent that there is such a thing as syntactic parallelism, Hobbs and Kehler (1997) and Kehler (2002) argue that it cannot be divorced from the semantic relation of PARALLEL.[13] To get a sense of how this view has been motivated, consider the contrast in (23)–(24), slightly altered from Kehler (2002: 5). Kehler notes that 'analyses that operate at the level of syntax, which generally require parallel syntactic structure between the antecedent and elided verb phrases, predict the unacceptability of examples like [(23)], in which the antecedent clause has been passivized ... Analyses that operate at a purely semantic level of representation do not predict this unacceptability. Examples like [(24)] are in fact acceptable, however, as predicted by semantic, but not syntactic, analyses.'

(23)   ??This problem was looked into by Teia, and Ava did too. ⟨look into this problem⟩

(24)   Teia asked for this problem to be looked into, and so, Ava did. ⟨look into this problem⟩

Kehler observes that what is different between (23) and (24) is that the former is understood as harboring PARALLEL (triggered by *too*), while (24) is understood as harboring RESULT (triggered by *so*). This difference, according to Kehler, is key in explaining the contrast.

---

[13] We note in passing that parallelism does not figure in the Minimalist theories of syntactic structure that Fox assumes. It is therefore likely that Fox also intended his parallelism constraint as a semantic, or at least an interface, relation.

Kehler offers the following definition of PARALLEL.[14]

(25)   PARALLEL(π_1, π_2): Infer $p(a_1, a_2, ...)$ from the assertion of discourse unit π_1 and $p(b_1, b_2, ...)$ from the assertion of discourse unit π_2, where for some property vector q, $q_i(a_i)$ and $q_i(b_i)$ for all i.

This definition makes essential reference to predicate–argument relations, in that it requires: (i) a common predicate p (which is inferred from the assertion of both discourse units), and (ii) corresponding arguments of p to be similar in some way, i.e. to have some property q_i in common. As an illustration of this definition, Kehler (2002: 16) considers the example in (26) and proposes the representation in (27), which satisfies PARALLEL.

(26)   Dick Gephardt organized rallies for Gore, and Tom Daschle distributed pamphlets for him.

(27)   a. do.something.to.support (Gephardt, Gore)
        b. do.something.to.support (Daschle, x)

According to Kehler, the common predicate p that generalizes over the denotations of the two predicates in (26) is, roughly, do.something.to.support. The first corresponding arguments denote Dick Gephardt and Tom Daschle, who are presumably known by the discourse participants to share the property q_i of being high-ranking Democrats. As for the second corresponding arguments, they trivially share a property if the pronoun is resolved to Gore.

This example also serves as an illustration of the MCT hypothesis discussed in the previous section. (26) can only be understood as harboring PARALLEL if *him* is resolved to *Gore*. If *him* is resolved instead to *Dick Gephardt*, PARALLEL cannot be inferred, and we derive instead a curious interpretation similar to the following oft-cited example, discussed by Kehler et al. (2008):

(28)   Margaret Thatcher admires Ronald Reagan, and George W. Bush absolutely worships her.

According to Kehler et al. speakers often judge (28) as being infelicitous—as if the speaker used *her* to refer to Reagan (with a gender mismatch), despite the fact that there is an available referent, Thatcher, that is introduced in the typically preferred subject position. This infelicity follows if (28) is interpreted as harboring PARALLEL, comparing Thatcher's and Bush's attitudes to Reagan, and if PARALLEL requires that the pronoun in object position be resolved to an antecedent introduced by the DP in object position.[15] The fact that many speakers initially leap to the infelicitous resolution of *her* to Reagan is an indication of the strength of parallelism effects.[16]

---

[14] This definition, like many of Kehler's definitions, is basically that of Hobbs (1985, 1990), with slight differences in notation.

[15] Again, intonation patterns do a lot of work in cueing this structure: other discourse relations and other patterns of anaphora resolution may become more salient if the intonation is altered.

[16] The strengths of these effects have been utilized by linguists to illustrate garden-path phenomena, often resulting in comedic effects, for example:

(i) Time flies like an arrow; fruit flies like a banana.

Although this effect on anaphora resolution provides powerful motivation for the grammatical reality of PARALLEL, it immediately becomes clear that it cannot account, on this definition, for all of the parallelism effects we have seen. There does not appear to be any purely semantic construal of PARALLEL which is flexible enough to assign (26) the parallel representations in (27), but inflexible enough to prevent the two sentences in (29) ((29b) is repeated from (23)) from being assigned the same representation, as in (30), where the two conjuncts satisfy the definition of PARALLEL.

(29) a.   Teia looked into this problem and Ava did too. ⟨look into this problem⟩
      b.   ??This problem was looked into by Teia, and Ava did too. ⟨look into this problem⟩

(30) look.into (teia,this.problem) ∧ look.into (ava,this.problem)

In fact, we can see from (31) that such active–passive pairs can be interpreted as harboring PARALLEL, as cued by *too*.[17] The contrast between (29b) and (31) poses a challenge to Kehler's attempt to reduce constraints on VPE to PARALLEL as defined in (25).

(31)   This problem was looked into by Teia, and Ava looked into the problem too.

Kehler (2002: §3.3) addresses this challenge by positing the following two constraints.

- **VP-Level Constraint**: the source and target VPs must be parallel.
- **Sub-VP Constraint**: recover parallel elements below the VP level.

Once these constraints are assumed to be operative, it becomes quite easy to account for the contrast in (29), since these two constraints force the recovered material to be identical to the source VP. Kehler reasons:

> [R]econstruction of the passive VP at the active VP site in the target would fail, thus eliminating that clause as a possible source for the ellipsis. In light of the need to establish coherence, the speaker should not have elided the VP with this choice of antecedent, since the signals the ellipsis sends to the hearer regarding parallelism in this context are not met.   (Kehler 2002: 51)

It seems that Kehler intends the VP-level and Sub-VP constraints as special cases of PARALLEL. However, this sense of 'parallel' appears to be stricter than in the definition of the discourse relation, PARALLEL, in that it requires the two conjuncts to have the same form, as well as parallel semantic representations. We assume, apparently diverging from Kehler, that these stricter constraints are specific to constructions such as VPE, rather than following directly from the discourse relation PARALLEL as Kehler defines it.

Clearly, the VP-level and Sub-VP Constraints drive Kehler's analysis of VP ellipsis to a greater extent than his definition of PARALLEL in (25). Given that these constraints directly refer to syntactic constituents, his purely semantic definition of PARALLEL arguably brings redundancy into the analysis. The VP-level constraint and Sub-VP constraint are indispensable if we want to explain the constraints on VP ellipsis, and they cannot follow from

---

[17] We agree with the judgment of Kehler (2002: 20) that (31) has 'diminished coherence', compared to (29a), but the clear contrast in acceptability between (31) and (29b) suggests that we cannot hold this diminished coherence responsible for the unacceptability of (29b).

PARALLEL itself, if PARALLEL allows formal discrepancies between discourse units to the extent seen in (26). Until we know what these two constraints follow from, we don't know to what extent the constraints on VPE follow from PARALLEL, and to what extent they follow from whatever derives the VP-level constraint and Sub-VP constraint.

We end our discussion of PARALLEL by coming full circle and considering the challenges inherent in coming up with a satisfactory definition of this relation. Without a theory of how we determine a common predicate p and a common property vector q, the definition in (25) is unexplanatory. If what we are after is to make sense of Humean Resemblance, then we cannot define a discourse relation which relies on the notion of similarity without an algorithm for determining similarity. Recall that in (26), it was assumed that Dick Gephardt and Tom Daschle share the property of being people who are presumably known by the discourse participants to be high-ranking Democrats. But what if this knowledge is not available? For example, we may not know anything about properties that Phil or Liz share, and yet PARALLEL can be (and often is) inferred in (14), repeated below.

(14)   a. Phil tickled Stanley.
       b. Liz poked him.

Asking what Phil and Liz have in common is different—and much harder—than asking what the proper names *Phil* and *Liz* have in common; the proper names are, for example, both subjects. Following Hobbs (1985, 1990), as Kehler does, we could assume that Phil and Liz share the property of being human, which suffices as long as the common property is independent of the common predicate (which in this case could be annoy). However, if such general properties license PARALLEL, then this definition is quite weak and has minimal predictive power. For instance, Kehler's definition of PARALLEL could not rule out the discourse in (32) from being interpreted as harboring this relation, vis-à-vis the representation in (33). However, it is hard, if not impossible, to understand this discourse as harboring PARALLEL, as shown by the infelicity of the cue-phrase *too*.

(32)   Ava walked in. She sat down (#too).

(33)   a. do.something.to.move(Ava)
       b. do.something.to.move(x)

In sum, the understanding of PARALLEL that derives from Kehler (2002) is a bit of a mess. We have clear evidence of its linguistic relevance from patterns of anaphora resolution, but the definition in (25) is lacking in predictive teeth, and is also apparently not well-suited to one of the main jobs Kehler intended it to do, namely derive constraints on VP ellipsis. In Chapter 6, we will revisit the definition of PARALLEL, this time within SDRT, which addresses some of the shortcomings just noted. For the purposes of this chapter, the definition of PARALLEL presented here will suffice, for all its limitations.

RESULT, VIOLATED EXPECTATION, *and* OCCASION

We now turn to the three other relations implicated in Kehler's discussion of extraction. As we discuss these relations, we will keep a critical eye on the semantic relationships between them, which we believe are not adequately captured in Kehler's framework.

We begin with RESULT, which is defined by Kehler as in (34).

(34)   RESULT(π_1, π_2): Infer P from the assertion of discourse unit π_1 and Q from the assertion of discourse unit π_2, where normally $P \to Q$.

Kehler uses '$\to$' to represent a looser relation than material implication, which he glosses as 'could plausibly follow from'. Applying this definition above to the discourse in (35), we would say that it is normally the case that if Wonder Woman chokes a Nazi (P) then it could plausibly follow that the Nazi dies (Q).

(35)   a. Wonder Woman choked a Nazi.
        b. The Nazi died.

Kehler's definition of VIOLATED EXPECTATION, in (36), is the same, except that the consequent is negated.

(36)   VIOLATED EXPECTATION(π_1, π_2): Infer P from the assertion of discourse unit π_1 and Q from the assertion of discourse unit π_2, where normally $P \to \neg Q$.

This formal similarity reflects Kehler's proposal, following Hobbs (1979, 1985, 1990), that VIOLATED EXPECTATION is a Humean Cause/Effect relation like RESULT.[18] Hence, (37) exemplifies VIOLATED EXPECTATION because normally, if Wonder Woman pushes an old Nazi, it could plausibly follow that he will fall (or at least, move).

(37)   Wonder Woman pushed an old, frail Nazi. The Nazi barely budged.

We will return briefly to the relationship between RESULT and VIOLATED EXPECTATION in Section 5.3.2. However, we can already identify one weakness in Kehler's definitions. Intuitively, one might expect RESULT and VIOLATED EXPECTATION to be opposites, such that RESULT(π_1, π_2) and VIOLATED EXPECTATION(π_1, π_2) never both hold of the same discourse units. However, it is straightforward to imagine scenarios in which both RESULT and VIOLATED EXPECTATION, as defined by Kehler, are applicable.

For instance, if a toddler pushes a tower of blocks, the tower may collapse, or it may wobble a little and stay upright. Accordingly, on Kehler's definitions, (38) should be construable as an instance of RESULT (because a proposition inferred from (38b) normally could plausibly follow from a proposition inferred from (38a)) or as an instance of VIOLATED EXPECTATION (because the negation of a proposition inferred from (38b) normally could plausibly follow from a proposition inferred from (38a)).

(38)   a. The toddler pushed the tower of blocks.
        b. It wobbled a little and stayed upright.

We will discuss ways of addressing this apparent shortcoming in Section 5.3.2, but first, we will identify a more serious concern, regarding the relationship between RESULT and OCCASION.

---

[18] This proposal is far from uncontroversial, as we shall see. For example, Ducrot (1984) proposed that there are two different types of CONTRAST relations, with VIOLATED EXPECTATION being equivalent to one of them (we will return to a related proposal from Asher and Lascarides 2003 in Chapter 6). This is significant because it conflicts with Kehler's claim that CONTRAST is a Humean Resemblance relation while VIOLATED EXPECTATION is a Cause/Effect relation.

Kehler's definition of OCCASION, the lone discourse relation in the Humean Contiguity class, is as follows:[19]

(39)   OCCASION(π_1, π_2) iff a or b hold.

   a. A change of state can be inferred from the assertion of π_1, whose final state can be inferred from π_2.

   b. A change of state can be inferred from the assertion of π_2, whose initial state can be inferred from π_1.

Kehler claims (p. 22) that our perception of OCCASION is 'based on knowledge gained from human experience about how eventualities can enable (or otherwise set the stage for) other eventualities in the world', and in our opinion this claim is more revealing than the definition in (39) (which he presents with several hedges). Kehler illustrates his intentions with OCCASION using the notion of **script** (Schank and Abelson 1977), a notion which is itself closely related to the frame-semantic notion of 'natural course of events' that Lakoff (1986) adopts in his discussion of Type A scenarios. For instance, Kehler discusses the following example:

(40)   Larry went into a restaurant. The baked salmon sounded good and he ordered it.

                                                                (Kehler 2002: 22)

The point is that, to make sense of this discourse, an interlocutor must activate a large amount of background knowledge (which baked salmon? How did it sound good? Who did he order it from?), which is part of our restaurant 'script'.

With that in mind, we think that the notion of **enablement**, introduced by Kehler in the passage just mentioned, is central to OCCASION. This notion relates to scripts in that being in a restaurant enables finding out about food served in that restaurant, and ordering it. The mention of 'change of state', 'initial state', and 'final state' in (39) is apparently intended as an approximation of this complex and multifaceted notion. The notion of 'final state' is particularly closely related to enablement. For instance, Moens and Steedman (1988) characterize final states as 'those consequences that the speaker *views* as contingently related to other events that are under discussion' (p. 16, emphasis original).[20] In many cases, this contingent relationship corresponds to enablement.

The definition of OCCASION, whether as stated in (39) or reformulated in terms of enablement, clearly cannot be stated in purely propositional terms, because of the essential reference to nonpropositional notions like 'final state' or enablement. As an example, consider (41).

(41)   a. John went into the shop.

       b. He bought a Coke.

This example can most straightforwardly be construed as compatible with the first of the two characterizations of OCCASION in (39). Sentence (41a), corresponding to π_1 in the

---

[19] Kehler's definition of OCCASION, like the alternative that we consider in Section 5.3.2, is binary. This is in contrast to the discussion of Type A scenarios in Lakoff (1986), where much is made of the compatibility of Type A scenarios with coordination of arbitrarily many conjuncts. Assume for now that *n*-ary conjunction with OCCASION (*n* > 2) can be modeled as recursively applied, binary conjunction, with a coordinate structure serving as one of the coordinates related by OCCASION. We discuss the issue more carefully in Chapter 6.

[20] Moens and Steedman actually use the term 'consequent state', but as far as we can see the only difference is terminology.

definition of OCCASION, describes a change of state, where the linguistically relevant final state is that John is in the shop. This can be inferred from (41b) (π_2 in the definition of OCCASION). In particular, we understand that John was in the shop (as was the Coke) when he bought the Coke, and that being in the shop enabled John to buy the Coke.

Example (41) is typical of instances of OCCASION in discourse, in that the initial or final state is not directly described by either of the discourse units (both discourse units in (41) describe events, not states). Rather, the final state is *inferred* from π_2, precisely because being in a shop enables buying a Coke.

However, there is a problem concerning the relationship between causation and enablement, and therefore the relationship between RESULT and OCCASION. The problem is that causes enable their effects.[21] It therefore transpires that RESULT(π_1, π_2) entails OCCASION(π_1, π_2) because the causal reasoning that underlies RESULT entails the reasoning that underlies OCCASION, whether that is ultimately cashed out in terms of contiguity or enablement.

For related reasons, Hobbs (1985, 1990) proposed (unlike Kehler) that RESULT and OCCASION are subsumed by a single discourse relation. Such a unification is unhelpful for our present purposes, though, because the two relations allow different extraction patterns according to Kehler's formalization of Lakoff (1986). In what follows, we will provide some data that, on the one hand, motivate Kehler's proposal to distinguish OCCASION from RESULT, but, on the other hand, cast further doubt on the precise way in which Kehler distinguishes the two discourse relations.

To illustrate the problem, we begin by demonstrating the asymmetric entailment relation between RESULT and OCCASION. According to Kehler's definition, (35), discussed with reference to RESULT, is interpreted as follows.

(42)   Wonder Woman choked a Nazi (π_1), the Nazi died (π_2), and π_1 could plausibly follow from π_2.

Provided that at least one of π_1 and π_2 describes a change of state, such an interpretation will always entail one or other case of OCCASION. For instance, (42) entails (43), on any reasonable definition of causation and enablement.

(43)   Wonder Woman choked a Nazi (π_1), the Nazi died (π_2), and a final state can be inferred from π_1 which constitutes an enabling condition for π_2.

Such a paraphrase is not only available when RESULT is inferred. For example, we can paraphrase (41) as in (44):

(44)   John went into the shop (π_1), he bought a Coke (π_2), and a final state can be inferred from π_1 which constitutes an enabling condition for π_2.

However, (41) clearly does not describe a causal relation like RESULT: going into the shop cannot reasonably be said to *cause* John to buy a Coke. This is the essence of the asymmetric entailment relation between RESULT and OCCASION.

---

[21] This is at least true for the canonical cases of eventive causation (where RESULT might be inferred), if not of all causal relations in natural language. See Copley and Martin (2014) for more discussion.

This entailment relation poses a challenge in accounting for the extraction data discussed in Chapters 3 and 4, because on Lakoff's account, Type C scenarios, with RESULT, only allow extraction from initial conjuncts, while Type A scenarios, with OCCASION, allow extraction from noninitial conjuncts. But if RESULT entails OCCASION, every Type C scenario should also be a Type A scenario, and therefore allow extraction from noninitial conjuncts. There should therefore be no such thing as a 'pure' example of a Type C scenario, which only allows extraction from the initial conjunct. We return to this prediction in Section 5.4, and tentatively suggest that it is inaccurate—that is, that there are instances of Type C scenarios which only allow extraction from initial conjuncts.

Before that, we turn to a more basic question: how do we even derive this entailment relation between RESULT and OCCASION from the formal definitions in (34) and (39)? This requires additional assumptions beyond those definitions, because RESULT is defined in purely propositional terms, while OCCASION is defined in terms of more fine-grained eventuality structures. As we shall see in Section 5.3.2, we can address this concern by defining RESULT in terms of eventuality structures as well. Because it eliminates the distinct formalisms employed in Kehler's different relations, this move is a step toward understanding the logical connections between the discourse relations across the Humean classes. However, it is a significant departure from the spirit of Kehler's proposal, in that it undermines the idea that each class of Humean relations is defined over a different class of objects.

One major challenge in defining discourse relations in terms of relations like enablement is that there is a threat of the discourse relations being trivially satisfiable in almost every case (Altshuler and Varasdi 2015). For example, John's buying a Coke requires that John exists, and John's being in the shop entails that John exists, so the linguistically relevant final state of (41a), i.e. that John is in the shop, trivially enables, or entails a precondition of, (41b). This pattern is quite general. In Section 5.3.2, we will outline some steps taken by Altshuler and Varasdi (2015) to address this shortcoming. In addition, we will see working definitions of RESULT and OCCASION that allow us to derive an asymmetric entailment relation between these two relations. With this in place, we can then ascertain how these relations are logically related to VIOLATED EXPECTATION. This discussion will be of paramount importance to a better understanding of Lakoff's extraction data.

5.3.2 Toward formal precision

Our aim in this section is to discuss alternative definitions of the discourse relations we have been considering, which avoid some of the challenges that arise with Kehler's definitions. These challenges include the following:

- Parallelism constraints on VP ellipsis do not appear to be derivable from the discourse relation PARALLEL, which renders the nature of PARALLEL obscure.

- There is good reason to think that RESULT asymmetrically entails OCCASION, but the formal discrepancies between Kehler's definitions of these relations do not allow us to derive this entailment pattern.

- Kehler's definition of OCCASION appears to be a poor fit for his intuitive understanding in terms of scripts, or Lakoff's characterization in terms of the 'natural course of events'.

We will defer the first of these problems until Chapter 6. In this section, we focus on the latter two challenges. We will approach them by discussing the broader question of the relationship between RESULT and OCCASION.

We begin by considering Definition 5.1 below, proposed by Altshuler and Varasdi (2015).[22] This definition, and those that follow in this subsection, have the following format: a set S of background propositions determined by a discourse $\pi_1; \pi_2$ (that consists of two discourse units π_1 and π_2), taken together with a set of relevant laws and regularities L, *entails* a particular formula that differs for every discourse relation. An advantage of this format is that it dissociates the background knowledge, laws, and regularities, which are essential to a full theory of natural language understanding but rarely amenable to linguistic analysis, from the distinctive semantic content of a particular discourse relation, which is embedded in the entailed formula.

In the following definition, the formula that is entailed is: $\mathbf{occ(s^{\text{i}}(\pi_1))} \Rightarrow \mathbf{occ(\tilde{s}(\pi_2))}$. This should be read as follows: if the final state $\mathbf{s^{\text{i}}}$ inferable from the assertion of π_1 occurs, then the initial state $\mathbf{\tilde{s}}$ inferable from the assertion of π_2 occurs.[23]

Definition 5.1 (OCCASION)

$$\text{OCCASION}(\pi_1, \pi_2) \overset{\text{def}}{\Longleftrightarrow} S(\pi_1; \pi_2) \cup L \vDash \mathbf{occ(s^{\text{i}}(\pi_1))} \Rightarrow \mathbf{occ(\tilde{s}(\pi_2))}$$

In describing the definition above, we relied on the notion of entailment: a set of background propositions and a set of relevant laws *entails* a particular formula (viz. the use of the turnstile, $\vDash$). By entailment, Altshuler and Varasdi do not mean 'there is no possible world in which the premise is true and the conclusion is false'; it has a more flexible meaning (cf. the use of 'inference' in (39)). Altshuler and Varasdi write:

> Proposition ϕ is said to **enthymematically entail** proposition ψ if there is a nonempty [restricted] set of propositions Φ such that $\Phi \cup \{\phi\}$ logically entails ψ. Thus, while being in the shop does not entail in a deductively valid way the conclusion that a nontrivial precondition of buying a Coke holds, it may entail it if an appropriate set of background propositions Φ is also taken into account ... These propositions may come from a wide variety of sources. For example, they may come from knowledge about how a normal shop is run: normally, the staff is at the counter and not on strike, normally, a shop sells a variety of common goods, and so on. Other propositions may come from the discourse itself: for example, we can infer from [(41)] that the shop mentioned in the discourse sells, among other things, Coke, and we can add to our stock of propositions this fact and whatever else it involves.[24] Also, it is asserted that John *bought* and not *stole* the Coke which, again,

---

[22] Following Lascarides and Asher (1993), Altshuler and Varasdi call this discourse relation NARRATION.

[23] Altshuler and Varasdi assume the Support Theory of conditionals, which is an unlikely candidate for a general theory of natural language conditionals. One major problem has to do with identifying the propositions that are co-tenable with the antecedent of a counterfactual conditional (Goodman 1947, Bennett 2003). Nevertheless, Altshuler and Varasdi show that it is fruitful to apply the theory in a tightly controlled way to derive particular constraints.

[24] Adding this information may not appear to amount to much. However, Altshuler and Varasdi consider a shop in which John buys a considerable amount of pesticide for his farm. Such shops are run very differently from a plain grocery store.

allows us to add certain propositions to our set of (hidden) premises (e.g. that John gave some money to the clerk, John legally came into the possession of a drink, etc.).[25]

The difficult task, of course, is to offer an algorithm that would separate trivial and non-trivial preconditions in the way described. This is not something that Altshuler and Varasdi offer. However, they do characterize the difference informally by saying that preconditions that belong to many different types of events count as more trivial than conditions that belong to a small and specific set.[26]

Building on these ideas, Altshuler and Varasdi propose that RESULT (like OCCASION) needs to be defined in terms of an event structure and in terms of enthymematic entailment. As previewed in the previous subsection, the reason for this is that $\text{RESULT}(\pi_1, \pi_2)$ asymmetrically entails $\text{OCCASION}(\pi_1, \pi_2)$ and we would like to have definitions that make this entailment apparent. To that end, consider the definition of RESULT below.

Definition 5.2 (RESULT)

$$\text{RESULT}(\pi_1, \pi_2) \overset{\text{def}}{\Longleftrightarrow} \mathcal{S}(\pi_1; \pi_2) \cup L \vDash \mathbf{occ}(\mathbf{c}(\pi_1)) \;\Rightarrow\; \mathbf{occ}(\mathbf{c}(\pi_2))$$

According to Definition 5.2, the discourse relation between π_1 and π_2 is RESULT just in case the proposition that the change of state (**c**) inferable from the assertion that π_1 occurs—taken together with the set of background propositions $\mathcal{S}(\pi_1; \pi_2)$ and the set of relevant laws and regularities L—entails the proposition that the change of state (**c**) inferable from the assertion of π_2 occurs. In other words, Altshuler and Varasdi propose that RESULT holds between two discourse units iff the occurrence of a change of state inferable from the first discourse unit enthymematically entails a change of state inferable from the second. For example, in (35a), repeated below, we infer that the Nazi's neck went from being unconstrained to being constrained. Given the elided premise that Wonder Woman exerted extreme force from her immense strength, we get the entailment that the Nazi went from being alive to being dead, i.e. the proposition asserted by (35b).

(35)   a. Wonder Woman choked a Nazi.
       b. The Nazi died.

Moreover, with some standard assumptions about event structure, Altshuler and Varasdi show that it follows from the definitions given that by virtue of inferring $\text{RESULT}(\pi_1, \pi_2)$, one thereby infers $\text{OCCASION}(\pi_1, \pi_2)$.[27] That is, when the occurrence of a change of state inferable from π_1 enthymematically entails the occurrence of a change of state inferable

---

[25] For more discussion of enthymematic reasoning, see Schlöder et al. (2016), Schlöder (2018), Breitholtz (2021) and references therein.

[26] As noted by Altshuler (2016), citing Andy Kehler (pers. comm.), this idea is inspired by AI research, which often appeals to initial states to account for indirect speech act recognition, e.g. one interprets the question *Do you know the time?* as a request rather than a yes–no question by way of an inference from an enabling precondition to the event itself (see, e.g., Perrault and Allen 1980). Moreover, initial states have been used to explain particular cases of pragmatic enrichment, e.g. why from *John went to the store and bought milk* one gets the enrichment that the milk was bought at the store, whereas the inference is not required as an answer to the question *What did John do today?*

[27] See Altshuler and Varasdi (2015: §3) for an abductive argument that this entailment holds.

from π_2, then also the occurrence of a post-state inferable from π_1 enthymematically entails the occurrence of a pre-state of π_2.[28] However, inferring OCCASION(π_1, π_2) does not thereby guarantee RESULT(π_1, π_2). For example, the occurrence of a change of state of the going-into-the-shop event described by (41a), repeated below, *does not* enthymematically entail a change of state of a buying-a-coke event that is described by (41b)—rather, it enthymematically entails that the initial state of a buying-a-coke event occurs.[29]

(41)   a. John went into the shop.
       b. He bought a Coke.

This asymmetric relation between RESULT and OCCASION will be especially important in Section 5.4, where it will fuel our argument that Lakoff's opposition between Type A examples (involving OCCASION) and Type C examples (involving RESULT) cannot be based directly on discourse relations.

Now that we have more precise definitions of RESULT and OCCASION, we need to ask about the status of VIOLATED EXPECTATION. To recap, the core of Kehler's definition of VIOLATED EXPECTATION in (36) was the phrase 'normally $P \rightarrow \neg Q$', where '$\rightarrow$' is glossed as 'could plausibly follow from'. As with the discussion of RESULT, though, we will look to replace this formulation of the semantics of $\rightarrow$ with a semantics based on the more precise notion of entailment. The most straightforward possibility is to follow Kehler's approach in defining VIOLATED EXPECTATION as a variant of RESULT, where the consequent is negated. On the basis of the definition of RESULT given (Definition 5.2), this would yield the following:

Definition 5.3 (VIOLATED EXPECTATION, first pass)

$$\text{VIOLATED EXPECTATION}(\pi_1, \pi_2) \stackrel{\text{def}}{\Longleftrightarrow} \mathcal{S}(\pi_1; \pi_2) \cup L \vDash \textbf{occ}(\textbf{c}(\pi_1)) \implies \neg\textbf{occ}(\textbf{c}(\pi_2))$$

However, this definition cannot work. The consequent of the conditional in this definition states that it is not the case that a change of state inferable from π_2 occurs. But if we revisit our example of VIOLATED EXPECTATION in (37), repeated below, we see that there is no change of state inferable from π_2 (*The Nazi barely budged*).

(37)   Wonder Woman pushed an old, frail Nazi. The Nazi barely budged.

We could address this problem by altering the scope of negation, as in Definition 5.4.

Definition 5.4 (VIOLATED EXPECTATION, second pass)

$$\text{VIOLATED EXPECTATION}(\pi_1, \pi_2) \stackrel{\text{def}}{\Longleftrightarrow} \mathcal{S}(\pi_1; \pi_2) \cup L \vDash \textbf{occ}(\textbf{c}(\pi_1)) \implies \textbf{occ}(\textbf{c}(\neg(\pi_2)))$$

This revised definition states that a change of state inferable from π_1 enthymematically entails a change of state inferable from the negation of π_2 (in this case, Wonder Woman

---

[28] This is intuitive in (35), where the occurrence of a post-state of Wonder Woman choking a Nazi enthymematically entails the occurrence of a pre-state of the Nazi dying.

[29] Here we assume that the same background propositions, laws, and regularities hold. If we change those, (41) could satisfy RESULT.

pushing the Nazi enthymematically entails that the Nazi budges). In this case, the fact that the Nazi does not budge allows us to infer that at least one of the set of background propositions Φ referenced in the definition of enthymematic entailment is false.

This modification takes us further from the spirit of Kehler's original definition. For instance, Kehler's distinction between Contiguity and Cause/Effect relations is not reflected in the definitions we have proposed here. This is an important point, which we have already touched on as we increase the precision and empirical adequacy of the definitions of these three relations, we cannot maintain the structure that Kehler sought to impose on the set of discourse relations.

A further virtue of this reformulation is that it affords some insight into a core case of VIOLATED EXPECTATION: in force-dynamic terms (Talmy 1988, Copley and Harley 2015), it seems that VIOLATED EXPECTATION typically involves maintenance of a state, where external forces would normally cause a change of state. We develop this insight further in Section 5.4.1.

5.4 Lakoff revisited

In this section, we return to Lakoff (1986) influential argument that there is no syntactic Coordinate Structure Constraint. Lakoff provided a series of examples, building on Goldsmith (1985) and a tradition going back to Ross (1967), illustrating that '[i]n purely syntactic terms, just about any kind of extraction pattern is possible with VP conjunctions.' He concluded that the CSC is not a syntactic phenomenon and further suggested that Fillmore's frame semantics (Fillmore 1975, 1976), rather than truth-conditional semantics, is the only framework in which the data in question could be insightfully analyzed. He developed an analysis in which predication principles constrain extraction possibilities and are directly visible to the syntax. Hence, for Lakoff, the interface between syntax and discourse was direct, without any intermediary of truth-conditional semantics—and discourse calls the shots!

At the start of this chapter, we gave two reasons to reject this approach in its purest form: there are crosslinguistic differences in extraction patterns, and the apparent differences between the syntactic properties of possible extractees from initial and from noninitial conjuncts make sense on an adjunction analysis of coordination. There does not seem to be a purely discourse-based account of either of these patterns, so we do not endorse Lakoff's architectural claims. However, his data—as we have already seen—have driven a multitude of analyses, employing a diverse set of frameworks and theoretical assumptions. This makes it worthwhile to identify the strengths and limitations of a discourse-calls-the-shots approach, as a step toward exploration of the division of labor between syntax and discourse.

In Sections 5.4.1–5.4.3, we discuss Lakoff's three scenarios in the order Type B–Type C–Type A. In terms of Kehler's reanalysis of Lakoff's data, these correspond to VIOLATED EXPECTATION, RESULT, and OCCASION, respectively. We subsequently discuss patterns not covered by Lakoff, including a discourse-based approach to ATB movement and several asymmetric patterns which are not covered by Lakoff's three scenarios.

The decision to discuss Lakoff's scenarios in this order is motivated by two factors: first, we want to separate the complexities regarding VIOLATED EXPECTATION laid out in Section

5.3.2 from the question of the relationship between RESULT and OCCASION. Second, the data in Section 4.6 suggest that extraction from initial conjuncts is subject to fewer constraints than extraction from noninitial conjuncts, a claim which will be further motivated in this section. Types B and C are the scenarios which (according to Lakoff) allow extraction from the initial conjunct only, so we will consider these first before turning to the syntactically more restricted case of extraction from noninitial conjuncts.

As we proceed, we have to contend with the fact that there has been little thorough empirical investigation of this area, and analyses (even those of Lakoff and Kehler) are often kept at an informal level. We will endeavor to do justice to these different analyses, while simultaneously filling in gaps in the empirical base, and noting challenges which arise as previous analyses are made more precise.

5.4.1 Type B scenarios and extraction

We begin with Lakoff's Type B scenario, 'in which a conventionalized expectation is violated' (p. 152). Here are some examples, repeated from Chapter 4, that match this description:

(45)   a. How many lakes can we [[destroy __] and [not arouse public antipathy]]?
       b. How many counterexamples can the Coordinate Structure Constraint [[sustain __] and [still be considered empirically correct]]?
       c. How much can you [[drink __] and [still stay sober]]?

We suggested in Section 5.3.2 that the interpretation of such examples involves maintenance of a state in the face of external forces which would normally cause a change of state. Typically, when one destroys a lake, it *would* arouse public antipathy, unlike the situation described in (45a); when one provides counterexamples to an empirical generalization, the generalization is no longer considered empirically correct, unlike the situation described in (45b); when one drinks alcohol, one does not stay sober, unlike the situation described in (45c).

For Lakoff, Type B scenarios were construed in opposition to those of Type A. Type A, as we will see in Section 5.4.3, involves a 'natural course of events' which 'fits normal conventionalized expectations' (p. 152). Type B is the opposite. Kehler (2002) proposed that Type B scenarios were those that harbored VIOLATED EXPECTATION, which obscures any opposition between Types A (built around the Contiguity relation OCCASION) and B (built around the Cause/Effect relation VIOLATED EXPECTATION). We will discuss the relationship between Types A and B in more depth in Section 5.4.3.

All of the examples in (45) have two conjuncts, with extraction from the initial conjunct only. Lakoff proposed the following generalization to reflect this.[30]

(46)   **Final Conjunct Constraint (Version 1)**: Only scenarios of Type B permit there to be no extraction from the final conjunct.   (Lakoff 1986: 154)

---

[30] Lakoff also suggests (pp. 158–9) that principles of predication might ultimately account for this generalization, in that only Type B scenarios allow for a well-formed propositional function consisting of a coordinate structure with no bound variable in the final conjunct. His concrete proposal in this respect is essentially a restatement of the purported facts, though.

Lakoff argues that this constraint also accounts for the contrast below:

(47)   a. *How big a meal did he [[eat __] and [feel satisfied]]?
       b. How small a meal can you [[eat __] and [feel satisfied]]?   (Lakoff 1986: 154)

In (47a), extraction from the first conjunct alone leads to an ill-formed question, according to Lakoff. Lakoff attributes the ill-formedness to (47a) exemplifying the natural course of events (so not a Type B scenario). The Final Conjunct Constraint therefore requires extraction from the final conjunct, unlike what is found in (47a). In contrast, (47b) is a Type B scenario, so extraction from just the first conjunct satisfies the Final Conjunct Constraint and derives a well-formed question.

The constraint is also intended to account for the following contrast:

(48)   a. What kinds of herbs can you [[eat __] and [not get cancer]]?
       b. What forms of cancer can you [[eat herbs] and [not get __]]?

(Lakoff 1986: 154)

In (48a), the extraction is from the first conjunct and (according to Lakoff) the question implies that eating herbs would lead to cancer, so not getting cancer is against the natural course of events. Lakoff claims that such is the case because the Final Conjunct Constraint entails that (48a) must be construed as a Type B scenario, running counter to the natural course of events. In contrast, (48b) exemplifies extraction from the second conjunct and implies that eating herbs can lead to not getting cancer. This is Lakoff's quintessential Type A scenario (see Section 5.4.3); it 'fits normal conventionalized expectations'.

However, this does not follow from the Final Conjunct Constraint. The Final Conjunct Constraint states that Type B scenarios *permit* there to be no gap in the final conjunct. The constraint does not *require* there to be no gap in the final conjunct, though. It is not hard to find cases of Type B scenarios with asymmetric extraction from the final conjunct. (49) is one example.

(49)   This is an argument that you can [[get blind drunk] and [still understand __]].

Accordingly, it seems that both extraction patterns in (48) are compatible with Type B scenarios, and any interpretive difference (which one of the authors of this book cannot perceive in any case) cannot follow directly from the different extraction patterns.

For completeness, we note that ATB extraction is also compatible with Type B scenarios, as in (50).

(50)   This is the kind of meal that you know you're going to [[pay too much for __] but [still enjoy __]].

At least in terms of distribution of gaps across conjuncts in binary coordinate structures, then, anything goes with Type B scenarios.

However, extraction from Type B coordinate structures does follow some recurring patterns. Lakoff noted that 'B-scenarios seem on the whole to be better at structuring hypothetical rather than realized situations' (p. 155), giving the following contrast.

(51)   a. How much can he [[drink __] and [still stay sober]]?
       b. *How much did he [[drink __] and [still stay sober]]?   (Lakoff 1986: 155)

We think that this perceptive comment paves the way for a new analysis of extraction from initial conjuncts in Type B scenarios, which preserves Lakoff's insight about an opposition with the 'natural course of events', and also builds on our observation about maintenance of a state, but does not directly invoke VIOLATED EXPECTATION. This alternative analysis also accounts for the striking uniformity of the canonical Type B examples collected in (45), which goes beyond the use of modals to describe hypothetical situations.

The examples in (45) all involve not just a modal, but specifically *can*, interpreted as a marker of ability. Moreover, as noted by Goldsmith (1985), the moved *wh*-phrase is typically a measure phrase of some variety, rather than a referential noun phrase, even though referential noun phrases are typically subject to fewer constraints on A'-movement (see Pesetsky 1987, Kroch 1989, Rizzi 1990, Cinque 1990, Postal 1998, and discussion in Chapter 4). This uniformity is not predicted by an analysis built on distinctions between discourse relations, because for the most part, this kind of subsentential structure does not feature in theories of discourse relations.[31] The generalizations made in this paragraph have exceptions, but they are robust enough to persuade us that alternative accounts of Lakoff's Type B extraction pattern should be sought: postulating VIOLATED EXPECTATION does not promise to account for all the special properties of Type B.

The alternative we propose is inspired by the semantics of *wh*-moved measure phrases developed by Szabolcsi and Zwarts (1993). Szabolcsi and Zwarts argue that phrases like *how many lakes* have several readings, including one which ranges over individuals (including plural individuals), and one which ranges over amounts. The most salient reading of a question like (52a) is one which asks for a measure of an amount (as in (52b)) as a response.

(52)   a. How much milk did you drink ___ ?   (Szabolcsi and Zwarts 1993: 242)
       b. Two pints.

(52b) describes the maximal amount of milk that the individual in question drank. Amount-readings of questions are ungrammatical when there is no such maximum. This explains the ungrammaticality of (53) on its most salient reading: if the addressee didn't drink three pints, then it follows that she also didn't drink four pints, or five pints.[32]

(53)   *How much milk didn't you drink ___ ?   (Szabolcsi and Zwarts 1993: 242)

This interacts in an interesting way with the modality expressed by *can*. It is logically possible that the addressee drinks any amount of milk. That is, there is no intrinsic maximal amount of milk that the addressee can drink: for any amount of milk, there is some possible world in which the addressee drinks that amount of milk. In the absence of such a maximum, we might expect (54) to be as ill-formed as (53).

(54)   How much milk can you drink ___ ?

---

[31] For notable exceptions, see Hobbs (2010) and Kehler (2019: §20.4).
[32] There is a reading on which (53) is well-formed. This is a **D-linked** reading in the sense of Pesetsky (1987). Imagine that the only contextually salient milk is a gallon jug, which was full before the addressee drank from it. If the addressee drank two pints, then the answer to (53) is *Six pints*. For Szabolcsi and Zwarts, this is an exception that proves the rule, because *Six pints* is not a measure phrase, but rather describes the individual consisting of six pints of milk in a gallon jug which was left undrunk by the addressee.

The fact that (54) isn't ill-formed tells us that the covert parameters associated with *can* (that is, the modal base and ordering source in the sense of Kratzer 1981, 1991) supply a 'threshold', which in turn implies a maximal amount of milk. This threshold is what makes (54) well-formed: we interpret the question as asking how much milk the addressee can drink before she feels full, or loses interest, or throws up, or whatever else lies behind the relevant interpretation of *can*.

The second conjunct in Type B scenarios makes this threshold explicit. For instance, in (55a) we understand that the relevant threshold is related to whether the addressee feels OK. Conjunction can do this, but other syntactic structures are equally able to perform this function. These alternatives are syntactically unremarkable because they do not involve extraction from anything which looks remotely like an island.

(55) a. How much milk can you [[drink __] and [still feel OK]]?
      b. How much milk can you drink __ if you want to still feel OK?
      c. How much milk can you drink __ before you stop feeling OK?

Examples like (55a) work to specify a threshold because there is a quantitative tension between the eventualities described in the two conjuncts: beyond a certain point, drinking more milk will make you feel less OK. Accordingly, (56b) is more surprising than (56a) for most people (people on a dairy- or lactose-free diet will find that the same holds of many other beverages). As the addressee in (55a) drinks more milk, she will approach and then cross the threshold: she will stop feeling OK.

(56) a. I drank half a pint of milk and felt OK.
      b. I drank two gallons of milk and felt OK.

This, we claim, is the source of the perceived discourse relation, VIOLATED EXPECTATION: the examples in (45) all ask about actions that, if performed in sufficiently large amount, lead us to expect the opposite of the effect described in the second conjunct.

We can now refine our understanding of Lakoff's Type B contrast, repeated as in (47).

(47) a. *How big a meal did he [[eat __] and [feel satisfied]]?
      b. How small a meal can you [[eat __] and [feel satisfied]]?

The question in (47b) is well-formed because we expect smallness of a meal to correlate with dissatisfaction. Accordingly, the smaller the meal, the greater the violation of our expectation of satisfaction. This is asking about a lower bound, unlike the previous examples of upper bounds, but the logic is otherwise just the same. (47a), in contrast, does not allow such an interpretation, because *feel satisfied* does not specify a threshold which will be crossed as the meals increase in size.

These considerations invite us to probe whether violation of expectation, or deviation from the natural course of events, is ever central to this extraction pattern. In fact, we believe that it isn't. To see this, consider the following.

(57) a. How much can you [[drink __] and [still stay sober]]?
      b. (i) I'm usually OK after a gallon of pure ethanol, but I go downhill quickly after
             that.
         (ii) Not much. Just a beer.

Both answers in (57b) are equally valid in response to the question in (57a), but only one of the answers violates our expectations. Most adults would stay sober after one beer, so the implicit full answer corresponding to (57bii) (*I can drink a beer and still stay sober*) cannot be taken to violate expectations (that is, in Kehler's terms, it is not the case that drinking a beer is expected to lead to not staying sober, or getting drunk). (57bi) does violate expectations, but it is no more felicitous as an answer for that.

In sum, although Lakoff's Type B scenario clearly identifies a distinct pattern of asymmetric extraction from coordinate structures, we are reluctant to see any special role for the relation of VIOLATED EXPECTATION in the theoretical description of that pattern. We believe that the analysis outlined here in terms of Szabolcsi and Zwarts's semantics of *wh*-measure phrases is faithful to Lakoff's original insight about 'the natural course of events', but is an empirically better fit with respect to the recurring use of measure phrases and *can* in Type B examples.

However, the notion of 'coordinate structure' does not figure at all in the analysis that we propose of extraction from Type B coordinate structures. This is unproblematic if we pursue an analysis according to which extraction from initial conjuncts is syntactically unrestricted. This is as predicted on Option 3 in Choice Point 4 (see Section 4.6 for discussion). If we pursue that option, we could say that the pattern has its roots partly in syntax (the amount-denoting *wh*-phrase extracts from the first conjunct only, consistent with the notion discussed in Chapter 4 that initial conjuncts are not weak islands), and partly in the interaction between the formal semantics of amount questions and of the modal *can*.

5.4.2 Type C scenarios and extraction

The Final Conjunct Constraint in (46) predicts a direct correlation between Type B scenarios (whether understood in terms of the 'natural course of events', VIOLATED EXPECTATION, or the monotonicity-based alternative developed in the previous subsection) and asymmetric extraction from the initial conjunct only. But now consider (58), discussed briefly in Chapter 3. This example involves asymmetric extraction of a referential noun phrase from the first of two conjuncts, as opposed to extraction of measure phrases as discussed in Section 5.4.1.[33]

(58)   That's the stuff that the guys in the Caucasus [[drink __] and [live to be a hundred]].
(Lakoff 1986: 156)

We can also expand on Lakoff's contrast in (47). Although (59a), repeated from (47a), is clearly degraded, the minimal variants in (59b) are quite acceptable and don't appear to harbor VIOLATED EXPECTATION.

(59)   a. *How big a meal did he [[eat __] and [feel satisfied]]?
       b. (i)   What did you [[eat __] and [feel satisfied]]?
            (ii) This is the meal that I [[ate __] and [felt satisfied]].

---

[33] It is notable that the examples of Type C scenarios which have circulated in the literature are typically generic, like (58). We don't know what to make of this. If this really is a characteristic of Type C scenarios, it would suggest, as with the discussion of Type B, that the discourse relation RESULT is not a primary factor in explaining this pattern. Further research is clearly needed.

Again, we see the crucial role of amount readings and circumstantial modals in biasing interlocutors toward a Type B interpretation. In the absence of those cues, the same extraction pattern is possible, but without the 'threshold' reading discussed in the previous subsection. (59bi) is simply asking the addressee to describe a meal, and the infelicity of (59a) presumably follows from the fact that *how big a meal* is a suboptimal way to convey that request.

According to Lakoff, these examples do not exemplify Type B scenarios, but a different scenario type, characterized by a 'cause–result' relationship rather than the 'natural course of events' (Kehler 2002 characterizes this scenario type as harboring RESULT). Lakoff calls this scenario type **Type C**, and states that the constraint in (46) needs to be revised (perhaps to the form in (60)) in order to explain examples of the (58) variety.

(60) **Final Conjunct Constraint (Version 2)**: Only scenarios of Type B and Type C permit there to be no extraction from the final conjunct.

For both Lakoff and Kehler, the interpretation of Type C scenarios is also clearly distinct from Type A scenarios, which (as we shall see in Section 5.4.3) Kehler takes to involve OCCASION. Lakoff (p. 156) writes: 'There is, of course, a difference between a natural course of events and a cause together with its result. Thus, going to the store and buying something is a natural course of events, but the buying is not *caused* by going to the store' (emphasis original). However, Lakoff does not provide evidence of a double dissociation: he shows OCCASION without RESULT, but not RESULT without OCCASION. We believe, as discussed in Section 5.3.2, that this is because it is not possible to do so: RESULT is a special case of OCCASION, as illustrated by Altshuler and Varasdi (2015).

In this respect, we follow Na and Huck (1992), who note that both Types A and C involve a 'natural flow of events'. Na and Huck suggest that 'the main difference between the two [scenarios] (beyond the fact that only Type C depicts a cause–effect connection) is that in a Type A scenario, the first conjunct is looked upon as a prelude to the primary (second) conjunct, whereas in a Type C scenario the second conjunct is regarded as an aftermath of the primary (first) conjunct' (Na and Huck 1992: 257). In other words, Na and Huck claim that Types A and C can be dissociated, but in terms of the relative prominence of the two conjuncts, rather than the truth conditions of RESULT and OCCASION (both of which involve a 'natural flow of events'): Type A obtains when the cause is a 'prelude' to the effect; Type C obtains when the effect is an 'aftermath' of the cause. We develop information-structural insights such as this in Chapter 6.

The Final Conjunct Constraint is incomplete as a description of extraction patterns with Type C scenarios, just as it was with Type A scenarios, because it does not tell us what other patterns are possible with these scenario types. However, it is slightly more challenging to investigate extraction patterns with Type C because we have to control for the possibility that, for instance, an example of asymmetric extraction from the final conjunct is actually a Type A reading, because of the entailment relationship between Types A and C noted by Na and Huck (1992) and in Section 5.3.2. There are two approaches that we are aware of for disambiguating in favor of a Type C reading, with RESULT, and excluding a Type A reading, with OCCASION. Both involve cue-phrases: *then* is a cue-phrase for OCCASION, while *as a result* is a cue-phrase for RESULT. Including the appropriate cue-phrase excludes the other discourse relation.

We use this approach in (61) and (62). The examples in (61a) and (62a) show that ATB movement is possible in Type C scenarios. However, unlike Type B, (61b) and (62b) suggest that extraction solely from the final conjunct is not possible in Type C scenarios. We return to this puzzling gap repeatedly in this chapter and Chapter 6.[34]

(61) a.   ?What can you [[swallow __] and, as a result, [feel instant euphoria from __]]?
      b.   ??Who did Kharms [[swallow a pill] and, as a result, [feel instant euphoria toward __]]?

(62) a.   ?What did you [[hear __] and, as a result, [think of __]]?
      b.   ??Who did Kharms [[hear a news story] and, as result, [think of __]]?

The major downside of using *as a result* is that it is somewhat clunky when combined with any extraction pattern.[35] Nevertheless, we think that the above contrast is real. The (a) examples are no worse than the canonical Type C example with *as a result* added, in (63), while the (b) examples are more degraded.

(63) ?That's the stuff that the guys in the Caucasus [[drink __] and, as a result, [live to be a hundred]].

Nevertheless, a cleaner test is desirable. In some cases, a second approach to cue-phrases may yield this cleaner test. In this approach, we proceed in two steps. First, we apply the cue-phrases *then* and *as a result*, one at a time, to check whether OCCASION and RESULT are compatible in a given example. If we select examples where RESULT, but not OCCASION, is possible, then we can omit the cue-phrase and check the acceptability of the different extraction patterns without this confound.

Here is an example of this method in action. Our baseline sentence is in (64a). Comparison with (64b–c) suggests that this example is more naturally construed as RESULT than as OCCASION: (64b) is not impossible but suggests that the loss of a tooth is not related to the candy, while (64c) makes the relationship clear.[36]

(64) a.   He ate too much candy and lost a tooth.
      b.   ?He ate too much candy and then lost a tooth.
      c.   He ate too much candy and lost a tooth as a result.

---

[34] Thanks to Ezra Keshet (pers. comm.) for providing the example in (62b).

[35] This may be related to the observation that discourses in which RESULT is inferred do not typically contain cue-phrases. Andersson and Spenader (2014) considered 1,014 examples of RESULT discourses in Penn Discourse Tree Bank, observing that only 21% had explicit cue-phrases. Andersson and Spenader also note that the use of explicit cues may be correlated with genre and register.

[36] We might wonder how this is possible, given the claim that RESULT entails OCCASION. There are several possible answers to this question. One is that the relative unacceptability of *then* in (64a) is due not to the truth conditions of OCCASION and RESULT, but rather to the kind of information-structural concerns that Na and Huck (1992) mentioned. Another possibility is related to an observation in footnote 33 concerning genericity in Type C: it may be that *then* is degraded as an indicator of a relation between a generic or habitual action and a one-off consequence of that action, and that the best-known Type C examples involve just such a relation. Finally, another possibility noted by Julian Schlöder (pers. comm.) is that (64b) is odd because the cue is not strong enough. In particular, the discourse units in (64b) harbor RESULT, so using a cue for a logically weaker OCCASION (namely *then*) comes off as being cagey. We don't pursue these possible analyses here, though we note that the one just mentioned would have to explain why (64b) is odd, while the previously mentioned (i) below is OK:

(i)   What do people always [[eat __ here] and [then get sick]]?

We can therefore investigate asymmetric extraction using the following paradigm, taking (64) as evidence that this really is a Type C scenario.

(65) a.   This is the candy that he [[ate __] and [lost a tooth]].
       b. ??This is the tooth that he [[ate too much candy] and [lost __]].

We believe that asymmetric extraction from the final conjunct is degraded. However, the judgments are subtle, and would merit more controlled study. We will proceed in this book on the assumption that asymmetric extraction with RESULT is only possible from the initial conjunct, but keep an eye on the consequences if this assumption turns out to be incorrect.

5.4.3 Type A scenarios and extraction

As noted in Section 5.4.1, the heart of Lakoff's account is the opposition between Type A scenarios (which follow 'the natural course of events') and Type B scenarios (which do the opposite). This correlates with a difference in extraction behavior: the Final Conjunct Constraint forces extraction from Type A coordinate structures to include a gap in the final conjunct, but does not impose such a requirement on Type B. A couple of examples of extraction from Type A coordinate structures are in (66). (66a) is taken from Lakoff (1986: 153). (66b) is modified slightly to create a 'pure' example of a Type A scenario—we return presently to Lakoff's deliberately 'impure' version.

(66) a. What did he [[go to the store], [buy __], [load __ in his car], [drive home], and [unload __]]?
       b. This is the kind of brandy that you can [[sip __ after dinner], [watch tv for a while], [sip some more of __], [work a bit], [finish __ off], [go to bed], and [enjoy __ again the following evening]].

In fact, though, the opposition between Types A and B is less neat than this might suggest. A significant distinction between Types A and B is that Type B scenarios appear to involve strictly binary coordination, whereas Type A scenarios can involve arbitrarily many conjuncts. (66a) contains five conjuncts, with extraction from the second, third, and fifth; (66b) contains seven conjuncts, with extraction from the first, third, fifth, and seventh. Lakoff's claim is that, at least in syntactic terms, so long as there is a gap in the final conjunct, anything goes. This means that we can find instances of ATB extraction with a Type A interpretation, like (67), where *then* cues OCCASION.

(67)   What did Ava [[write __ all night] and then [discuss __ with Teia]]?

Examples (66b) and (67) show that there is no ban on extraction from initial conjuncts in Type A scenarios: the effect of the Final Conjunct Constraint is that extraction from the initial conjunct is possible, so long as other conjuncts (including the final conjunct) are also extracted from. This means that the Final Conjunct Constraint can derive contrasts like (68), or the same effect with more than two conjuncts in (69).

(68) a.   What do you [[go to the store] and [buy __]]?
       b. ??What did you [[buy __] and [make a meal]]?

(69)   a.   What did you [[talk about __ all night], [take a short nap], and then [have to
            lecture on __ at your 8 a.m. class]]?   (adapted from Deane 1991)
       b.   ??What did you [[talk about __ all night], [have to lecture on __ at your 8 a.m.
            class], and then [take a short nap]]?
       c.   What do you [[go to the store], [look around], [pay the cashier], and [buy __]]?

Deane (1991) proposed a useful classification of the gapless conjuncts in Type A scenarios.
His description of these conjuncts is that 'instead of describing the main narrative sequence
they provide explanations and background' (p. 23). Deane divided these background conjuncts into four categories. The initial conjunct in (68a) is an example of a **preparatory
action**, while (66b) and (69a) contain **incidental events**. The other two categories are
scene-setters, as in (70), and **internal causes** like (71).

(70)   a.   Sam is not the sort of guy you can just [[sit there] and [listen to __]].
       b.   Who did you [[stand in the parlor] and [tell jokes about __]]?

(71)   a.   Which problem did he [[get bored] and [give up on __]]?
       b.   Who did he [[go berserk] and [start shooting at __]]?   (Deane 1991: 24)

We return to scene-setters in Section 5.4.4. In short, though, preparatory actions, scene-
setters, and internal causes behave in the same way with respect to extraction: they form
pairs with a following conjunct, from which extraction occurs. Incidental events are different: they occur between two conjuncts and do not form part of the narrative that
those other conjuncts develop. This means that incidental events, unlike the other three
categories, cannot be initial conjuncts.

The effect of all of these distinctions is to add some internal structure to the flat n-ary
coordinations that Lakoff discussed. All of Deane's categories of background conjunct, except for incidental events, form binary structures with the following conjunct. This implies
that the internal structure of even Type A coordinations is largely binary, a possibility
which fits well with the binary definitions of OCCASION proposed by Kehler and refined in
Section 5.3.2. It also promises to derive the Final Conjunct Constraint: if extraction in Type
A scenarios involves extraction from all conjuncts which form what Deane calls the 'main
narrative sequence' (that is, all conjuncts except those that describe preparatory actions,
scene-setters, internal causes, and incidental events), and if the structures which introduce
background conjuncts all feature a final conjunct which forms part of the main narrative
sequence, then Type A coordinations will always involve extraction from the final conjunct, and the Final Conjunct Constraint follows. All of this substantially sharpens Lakoff's
description of Type A.

All of these refinements of our understanding of Type A scenarios only reduce the similarity between Types A and B which was central to Lakoff's proposals. A further difference
between Type A and Type B, which follows from our previous considerations, concerns
the nature of the extracted element. We have seen that extraction from Type B coordinate
structures typically involves an extracted measure phrase and the modal *can*. Neither of
these restrictions applies to Type A. In fact, because many examples of asymmetric extraction from Type A coordinate structures (including all examples with only two conjuncts)
involve extraction from noninitial conjuncts only, there are many cases in which the kind

of measure phrase typically extracted in Type B examples *cannot* be extracted in Type A examples. This is the point of Postal's (1998) example in (72), repeated from (120) in Chapter 4.

(72)   How much thought did they (*get drunk, drive home, and) give those proposals __ ?
(Postal 1998: 67)

As discussed in Section 4.6, Postal argues that noninitial conjuncts in Type A scenarios are weak (or selective) islands, and therefore don't allow extraction of measure phrases like (72).

Because of all these differences, we do not follow Lakoff in trying to establish a neat opposition between Type A and Type B. There is a cluster of differences here: different interpretations, different constraints on number of conjuncts, different distributions of gaps, and different constraints on the nature of the extracted element.

Lakoff also discusses examples involving mixtures of Type A and Type B coordination, such as (73) (the original version of (66b)).

(73)   This is the kind of brandy that you can [[sip __ after dinner], [watch TV for a while], [sip some more of __], [work a bit], [finish __ off], [go to bed], and [feel fine in the morning]].   (Lakoff 1986: 153)

This whole string of conjuncts plausibly describes a 'natural course of events', except the last, if sipping so much brandy would normally prevent you from feeling fine in the morning. This is an example of Lakoff's 'AB-scenario', which could be construed as a relation of VIOLATED EXPECTATION holding between the final conjunct and a complex discourse unit consisting of the first six conjuncts, which themselves constitute a Type A scenario. In other words, an example like (73) hints at a Type A scenario nested within a Type B scenario, an example of a coordinate structure corresponding to a hierarchically structured discourse. We will see more of this kind of structure in Chapter 6. For now, we note only that the example behaves almost exactly as Lakoff would predict: no gap in the final conjunct (which is related to the rest by VIOLATED EXPECTATION), and gaps in several conjuncts within the Type A scenario.[37]

Kehler's (2002) approach to Type A scenarios differs from Lakoff's in that it makes no attempt to set up a direct opposition between Types A and B. We have seen that Kehler analyzes Type B scenarios as instances of VIOLATED EXPECTATION, and Type C scenarios as instances of RESULT, both Cause/Effect relations. In contrast, Type A scenarios are, for Kehler, instances of OCCASION, the sole Contiguity relation. As discussed in Section 5.3.1, there is no clear opposition between OCCASION and VIOLATED EXPECTATION in Kehler's theory, because they belong to these different families of Humean discourse relations. These different families might be thought to underpin the similar syntactic behavior of Types B and C (binary coordination, no gap required in the final conjunct) and the different behavior of Type A (*n*-ary coordination, gap required in the final conjunct).

---

[37] The only possible surprise in (73) is that the final conjunct of the Type A sequence of conjuncts is *go to bed*, which does not contain a gap, in violation of Lakoff's Final Conjunct Constraint. We do not dwell on this, because we provide more clearcut counterexamples to this constraint in what follows.

However, Cormack and Smith (2005), Brown (2017), and Neeleman and Tanaka (2020) have challenged this empirical picture. Brown presents (74), and Neeleman and Tanaka present (75a), as well-formed English questions exemplifying Type A scenarios without a gap in the final conjunct. This not only undermines the Final Conjunct Constraint in (60), but also Type A as a unified natural class.

(74) a. Which steak did Lizzie [[take a knife] and [hack __ to pieces]]?
      b. Which knife did Lizzie [[take __] and [hack the steak to pieces]]?
      c. Which knife did Lizzie [[take __] and [hack the steak to pieces with __]]?
                                                              (Brown 2017: 21)

(75) Mary went to NYC in order to buy a modernist painting.
      a. What city did Mary [[go to __] and [buy a modernist painting]]?
      b. What modernist painting did Mary [[go to NYC] and [buy __]]?
                                                   (Neeleman and Tanaka 2020: 16)

Example (75a) is unlike (68b) and (69b) in that the first conjunct is headed by an unaccusative motion verb. Examples where the first conjunct is not headed by a motion verb are often degraded (although Brown's (74b) demonstrates that this is not always the case).

(76) ?Mary presented her credit card in order to buy a modernist painting.
      a. ?What credit card did Mary [[present __] and [buy a modernist painting]]?
      b. ?What modernist painting did Mary [[present her credit card] and [buy __]]?
                                                   (Neeleman and Tanaka 2020: 17)

For Neeleman and Tanaka (2020: 18–19) this is significant. They conclude that 'extraction from type A coordination is sensitive to verb class in the same way as extraction from adjuncts,' drawing on a generalization from Borgonovo and Neeleman (2000) that extraction from adjuncts modifying unaccusatives is more acceptable than extraction from external argument-oriented adjuncts. More specifically, Neeleman and Tanaka compare felicitous cases of Type A extractions to felicitous cases of extraction from *in order* clauses. This comparison makes sense if, as seems likely, the semantics of *in order* is closely related to the semantics of OCCASION given in Section 5.3.2. And of course, any close similarity between Type A extractions and a class of VP adjuncts supports the hypothesis discussed in Section 4.6, namely that patterns of extraction from coordinate structures relate to patterns of extraction from adjunction structures.

Here are some further examples that are acceptable because they follow Neeleman and Tanaka's (2020) script for success: the nonextracted version is OK with *in order to* and the initial conjunct is headed by a motion verb.

(77) [Teia ran home in order to call the police].
      a. Where did Teia [[run __] and [call the police]]?
      b. Who did Teia [[run home] and [call __]]?

(78) [Ava skied down Mt. Kazbek in order to save Teia].
      a. What mountain did Ava [[ski down __] and [save Teia]]?
      b. Who did Ava [[ski down Mt. Kazbek] and [save __]]?

Neeleman and Tanaka's empirical findings open up new horizons in the study of coordinate structures harboring OCCASION, because the conditions on use of *in order to* are not statable over discourse units, but rather involve sentence- or VP-level notions of agency and aspectual class (see Truswell 2011 for discussion). The challenges of relating these two semantic systems have been a recurring theme in research on coordinate structures since Ross (1967) and Schmerling (1972) (see the discussion in Section 3.8), and addressing those challenges is likely to be a complex and empirically rich direction for future research in this area. At this stage, the only clear implications are that Type A may not be a unified class characterized solely by OCCASION, and that the Final Conjunct Constraint does not uniformly hold in Type A scenarios.

5.4.4 Type A patterns without OCCASION

A further issue for both Lakoff's construal of Type A as involving the 'natural course of events', and Kehler's formulation involving OCCASION, concerns cases like (79), which are like Type A scenarios in that they require a gap in the final conjunct.

(79)   Who did you [[stand in the hallway] and [scream at __]]?

In fact, Lakoff considers such examples to be regular examples of a Type A scenario, and Kehler likewise aims to subsume them under OCCASION. However, both of these moves are dubious. It is not clear in what sense (79) could describe a natural course of events, and the example fails a heuristic test for OCCASION: the sense changes drastically if the cue-phrase *then* is inserted, as in (80).

(80)   Who did you [[stand in the hallway] and then [scream at __]]?

The obvious reason for this is that (79) does not describe a sequence of events, but rather two overlapping eventualities. Unlike Kehler (2002), most theories of discourse coherence reserve a distinct label for this configuration, namely BACKGROUND (Lascarides and Asher 1993). In order to properly consider these examples, we digress briefly to discuss this new type of discourse relation.

Motivating two BACKGROUNDS

The precursor to BACKGROUND was a discourse relation that Hobbs (1985, 1990) called **GROUND–FIGURE**. This relation was inspired by work in Gestalt psychology, which holds that ground–figure organization is vital for visual perception: what it means to perceive writing on a printed page is to perceive the writing as the figure against the ground, namely the printed page.[38]

Hobbs extends this idea to discourse semantics by proposing the definition in (81). In the context of Kehler's ideas about different families of discourse relations, it should be noted

---

[38] In fact, there is a similarity of sorts between the Gestalt slogan 'perception is organization' (e.g. Koffka 1935) and the founding idea of formal theories of discourse that discourse interpretation is driven by a search for a coherent interpretation of an utterance.

that GROUND–FIGURE, with its essential reference to 'a system of entities and relations', must operate over something more fine-grained than unstructured propositions.

(81)   GROUND–FIGURE(π_1, π_2): Infer from the first discourse unit π_1 a description of a system of entities and relations, and infer from discourse unit π_2 that some entity is placed or moves against that system as a background.

Here is an example of a discourse that satisfies this definition:

(82)   Ava walked outside. It was cold.

We infer that there was a walking-outside event, whose agent is Ava. Take this event and participant to be the figure, which is placed against the ground, namely the state of being cold. The GROUND–FIGURE relation implies that the described event spatiotemporally overlaps the described state.

While it is an open (and surprisingly difficult) question whether GROUND–FIGURE can be exemplified when two states are understood to overlap in time and place,[39] it does not seem possible to infer GROUND–FIGURE when we have two event descriptions. While it is certainly possible to describe two overlapping events, there is no concomitant inference about one of the events (and its participants) being the ground. For example, one natural interpretation in (83) is that the described events are overlapping, though we don't understand the kazoo-playing to be the ground against which John plays the piano (or vice versa). Rather, both are understood to be constitutive of a musical performance.[40]

(83)   John played the piano. Mary played the kazoo.   (Webber 1988)

Therefore, it seems that the ground must be described by a stative predicate.

Unfortunately, however, this observation does not follow from the definition of GROUND–FIGURE just given. One possibility, which we will not pursue here, is to link the observation to a generalization going back to at least Jespersen (1924), namely that there is a strong tendency for eventive descriptions (often expressed with the perfective aspect) to move the narrative forward and for stative descriptions (often expressed with the imperfective aspect) to halt the narrative. Many analyses of temporality in narrative discourse have relied on this generalization (Kamp and Rohrer 1983, Partee 1984, Kamp and Reyle 1993, de Swart 1998, Bary 2009, Bittner 2014, Altshuler 2016), though there is some debate about whether this generalization reveals something about the grammar or pragmatic reasoning (Dowty 1986; see also Altshuler and Schlöder 2021a, Altshuler 2021 for recent discussion).

Another problem for the definition of GROUND–FIGURE above is the requirement that the first argument describe the figure and the second argument describe the ground. Example

[39] Below is an example from Alex Lascarides (pers. comm.) which she takes to be a kind of GROUND–FIGURE, with two stative descriptions.

(i)   Max lay on a couch. It was upholstered in tartan fabric.

However, (i) arguably also exemplifies ELABORATION. The question is whether (i) exemplifies ELABORATION in addition to or instead of GROUND–FIGURE. We don't pursue this question here.

[40] Given everything we have said thus far, (83) seems to exemplify PARALLEL. However, note that triggers like *too* and *also* are not possible here. This may be because (83) involves CONTINUATION—a core discourse relation in SDRT, to be introduced in Chapter 6, that is similar to PARALLEL is in several respects (Asher and Lascarides 2003).

(82) follows this pattern. However, compare this to (84). Here, the stative description serves as the ground for the event described in the second sentence.

(84)   Max lay on a couch. Mary turned to look at him.

In fact, a common technique in story-telling, often called **scene setting**, involves a structure in which the discourse opens with a stative description (or a series of stative descriptions) which serves as the ground for an event that is later described. Below are two naturally occurring examples, where the first instance of an eventive description (of the figure) appears in bold, after quite a few stative descriptions (some in the pluperfect) have set the scene. Collectively, the statives describe the ground for the figure to come.[41]

(85)   I was in great perplexity; I had to start on an urgent journey; a seriously ill patient was waiting for me in a village ten miles off; a thick blizzard of snow filled all the wide spaces between him and me; I had a gigi, a light gig with big wheels, exactly right for our country roads; muffled in furs, my bag of instruments in my hand, I was in the courtyard all ready for the journey; but there was no horse to be had, no horse. My horse had died in the night, worn out by the fatigues of this icy winter; a servant girl was now running around the village trying to borrow a horse; but it was hopeless, I knew it, and I stood there forlornly, with the snow gathering more and more thickly upon me, more and more unable to move. **In the gateway the girl appeared alone, and waved the lantern ...**   (*A country doctor*, Franz Kafka)

(86)   He had a job as a waiter in the international dining car of a German fast train. His name was Aleksey Lvovich Luzhin. He had left Russia five years before, in 1919, and since then, as he made his way from city to city, had tried a good amount of trades and occupations: he had worked as a farm laborer in Turkey, a messenger in Vienna, a housepainter, a sales clerk, and so forth. Now, on either side of the diner, the meadows, the hills overgrown with heather, **the pine groves flowed on and on, and the bouillon steamed and splashed in the thick cups on the tray that he nimbly carried along the narrow aisle between the window tables.**
(*A matter of chance*, Vladimir Nabokov)

While the Kafka story in (85) has first-person narration, opening with a first-person pronoun, the Nabokov story in (86) has third-person narration, opening with a third-person pronoun. It's not until the subsequent sentence that we learn that the third-person pronoun picks out 'Aleksey Lvovich Luzhin'. This is a case of **pronominal cataphora**. According to Asher et al. (2007), stative–eventive descriptions of this kind are cases of **temporal cataphora**. Applying this idea to (86), we would say the following: just as a processor builds expectations to resolve *he* in the first sentence of the discourse to some individual later described in the discourse (in this case Aleksey Lvovich Luzhin), a processor builds expectations to resolve the temporal extent of the described states to the temporal extent of some event later described in the discourse (in this case, Aleksey carrying a tray in the diner). While Asher et al. (2007) do not provide processing evidence for this hypothesis,

---

[41] There are much more extreme examples of this. For example, in *Modern Love* by Constance DeJong, Part Two and Part Three, spanning six pages, constitute solely stative descriptions. Part Four then opens with a series of eventive descriptions.

in what follows we shall adopt their terminology (see also Asher et al. 1996): we will use ⇒BACKGROUND (read as: 'forward-looking BACKGROUND') to describe stative–eventive or stative–stative sequences that first describe the ground and then the figure; we will use ⇐BACKGROUND (read as: 'backward-looking BACKGROUND') to describe eventive–stative or stative–stative sequences that first describe the figure and then the ground. We adopt these terms because they correlate with the process of resolving cataphors (looking forward) and anaphors (looking backward) respectively.[42] Finally, we will use BACKGROUND (with no arrow) to generalize over both instances.

Interestingly, some languages of the world have constructions, called 'bridging', which require ⇒BACKGROUND. According to Guérin (2019), these constructions consist of two clauses: 'a reference clause and a bridging clause. Across languages, bridging clauses can be subordinated clauses, reduced main clauses, or main clauses with continuation prosody.'

Here we briefly consider data of bridging constructions in two genetically unrelated languages, A'ingae[43] and Daakaka,[44] which feature a construction that disallows event–event sequences for narrative progression. Instead, one sees event–state–event sequences, where the state–event subsequence is a case of ⇒BACKGROUND. For example, a discourse such as 'John went into the shop. He bought a Coke.' would have to be expressed as 'John went into the shop. Having gone into the shop, he bought a Coke.' The discourses in (87) and (88) show naturally occurring examples of ⇒BACKGROUND in A'ingae (AnderBois and Silva 2018, AnderBois 2021), while (89) and (90) show naturally occurring examples of ⇒BACKGROUND in Daakaka (von Prince 2013):

(87) a. Tseninde   pûi   kuragandekhû   pa'fa'nijan   muen'jen'fa.
         Tse=ni=nde   pûi   kuraga-ndekhû   pa-'fa-'ni=jan   muen-'jen-'fa.
         ANA=LOC=RPT   all   shaman-HUM.PL   die-PLS=LOC=CNTR   send-IPFV-PLS
         'There, if all the shamans die, they send them.'
      b. Tsunsite   tseni   thesive   dapa   kanse'fa
         Tsun-si=te   tse=ni   thesi=ve   da-pa   kanse'-fa
         do-DS=RPT   ANA=LOC   jaguar=ACC2   become-ss   live-PLS
         'Them having done so, the shaman becomes a jaguar and stays that way.'

(88) a. Kuragandekhûtate   yajema   injan'tshe   kû'ipa
         kuraga-ndekhû=ta=te   yaje=ma   injan'tshe   kûi-pa
         shaman-HUM.PL=TOP=RPT   ayahusasca=ACC   much   drink-ss
         usha'chu   tsampini   kansekhesûve   di'shafa
         usha'chu   tsampi=ni   kanse-khesû=ve   di'sha-fa
         everything   forest=LOC   live-HAB=ACC2   transform-PLS
         'When the shamans drink a lot of yaje, they turn them into anything in the forest.'

<hr>

[42] The terms 'BACKGROUND$_1$' and 'BACKGROUND$_2$' are also used (Asher and Lascarides 2003).

[43] A'ingae is the language of the Kofán people, an indigenous group native to the province of Sucumbíos in northeast Ecuador and southern Colombia.

[44] Daakaka is the language of Ambrym, Vanuatu. It is spoken by about one thousand speakers in the southwestern corner of the island.

b. Tsa'kaen   di'shapate   pa'ta   tsesûveyi
tas-'ka-en   disha-pa=te   pa='ta   tse-sû=ve=yi
ANA-SIMIL-ADV   transform-SS=RPT   die=TOP   ANA.ATTR=ACC2=EXCL
di'shapa   tsangae   tsampini   kanseye   ja'fa
di'sha-pa   tsa=ngae   tsampi=ni   kanse-ye   ja'-fa
transform-SS   ANA=MANN   forest=LOC   live-INF   go-PLS
'Having transformed like that, if they die, then since they transformed into just that kind of thing, they go to live in the forest in that way.'

c. Tsa'kaen   japate   tsangae   kanse'fa
Tsa'-ka-en   ja-pa=te   tsa=ngae   kanse'-fa
ANA=SIMIL-ADV   go-SS=RPT   ANA=MANN   live-PLS
'Having gone like that, they keep living in that way.'

(89) ... te   ya=m   du   ngapngap te   ya=m   du   en.
         then 3PL=REAL stay rest   then 3PL=REAL stay eat
Ya=m   en   mo   nok   te   du   ngapngap, te   Yokon wuk
3PL=REAL   eat   REAL finish then stay rest   then Yokon already
mwe   tavya   te   vyan yen door
REAL   get.up   then go   in   bush
'They were resting and they were eating. Having eaten/They had finished eating and were [still] resting, and then Yokon got up first and went to the bush.'

(90) te   vyan te   op   yen myaek, te   op   mo   nok   te   tilya
         then go   cut firewood in   night   then cut REAL finish then take
op   nyoo ente
firewood 3PL   these
'He went to cut firewood at night, having cut the wood, he took these logs ...'

As we have noted, there is a strong tendency for eventive descriptions (often expressed with the perfective aspect) to move the narrative forward and for stative descriptions (often expressed with the imperfective aspect) to halt the narrative. Hence, it is interesting that the grammars of Daakaka and A'ingae require a stative description in these constructions in order for the next event description to move the narrative forward.[45] Another way of describing this observation is that instead of establishing OCCASION directly, the grammar of these constructions enforces ⇒BACKGROUND in order to make prominent the final state of the previously described event that is required by OCCASION. In the terms of Section 5.3.2, it may be that there is a close, and precisely statable, link between OCCASION and ⇒BACKGROUND: if OCCASION(π_1, π_2) then ⇒BACKGROUND($s'(\pi_1), \pi_2$) (that is, the post-state of the change of state described by π_1 is the background for π_2). The common ground between OCCASION and ⇒BACKGROUND is that the former relation implies the latter relation, and the special property of bridging constructions is that they make ⇒BACKGROUND overt.

---

[45] There are, however, other constructions in these languages which allow narrative progression with event–event sequences.

This suggestion is opposed to the approach taken by Kehler (2002), who considers BACK-GROUND to be a special case of OCCASION (Kehler 2002: 30). There are several reasons why Kehler's choice is problematic. One reason, discussed in Chapter 6, is that ⇐BACKGROUND (but not ⇒BACKGROUND) has a different discourse-structural property from OCCASION. Another is that while OCCASION entails narrative progression, BACKGROUND entails temporal overlap. As a simple illustration, note that (32) and (41), repeated below, exemplify OCCASION and the events are understood to have occurred in the order in which they are described.

(32) a. Ava walked in.
      b. She sat down.

(41) a. John went into the shop.
      b. He bought a Coke.

On the other hand, all the examples of BACKGROUND that we have seen in this subsection describe overlapping eventualities. Finally, recall that a pair of discourse units harbors BACKGROUND only when one of the discourse units is stative (i.e. does not describe an event). No such aspectual constraint is found with OCCASION.[46]

BACKGROUND *in coordinate structures, and extraction from* BACKGROUND*-conjuncts*
We return now to (79), repeated below. This was the example which prompted our introduction of BACKGROUND.

(79)   Who did you [[stand in the hallway] and [scream at ___]]?

Example (79) shows that ⇒BACKGROUND can be expressed by VP coordination structures and allows asymmetric extraction from noninitial conjuncts, the pattern described in Section 5.4.3. In fact, as illustrated below, ⇒BACKGROUND also allows extraction from solely the first conjunct (see (91)) and it allows ATB extraction (see (92)):

(91)   Where did Ava [[stand ___] and [scream at Teia]]?

(92)   Who does Anna [[live with ___] and [read *Grumpy Monkey* to ___]]?

Interestingly, we cannot simply reverse the predicates in (79) and (91) to get felicitous examples of ⇐BACKGROUND in coordinate structures. (93b) is not naturally interpreted as describing the same figure–ground relation, with temporal overlap, as (93a).

(93) a. Anna [[stood in the hallway] and [screamed at Teia]].
      b. #Anna [[screamed at Teia] and [stood in the hallway]].

Rather, (93b) is more naturally interpreted (to the extent that it is naturally interpretable) as expressing a sequence of events (as with OCCASION) or perhaps two overlapping events, neither of which is interpreted as figure or ground (perhaps a very weakly supported PARALLEL). These two interpretations can be cued by adding appropriate adverbs, as in (94).

---

[46] This is not to say that OCCASION is free of aspectual constraints. See Altshuler (2016: Ch. 3) and Cumming (2021) for more discussion.

(94)   Anna [[screamed at Teia] and then/also [stood in the hallway]].

This gives us an initial indication that there are constraints on the use of VP coordination to express ⇐BACKGROUND. It is therefore unsurprising that examples of extraction from VP coordination with ⇐BACKGROUND are degraded:

(95)   ??Who did you [[scream at __] and [stand in the hallway]]?

(96)   ??Where did Ava [[scream at Teia] and [stand __]]?

(97)   ??Who did Ava [[scream at __] and [stand next to __]]?

We return to the contrast between ⇒BACKGROUND and ⇐BACKGROUND in Section 6.4.[47]

In sum, this subsection has demonstrated that the ⇒BACKGROUND and OCCASION allow the same patterns of extraction from VP coordinate structures, and suggested that this similarity may follow from the semantic relationship between these two discourse relations. The same is not true, however, of ⇐BACKGROUND, which appears to be incompatible with *and*, let alone extraction from coordinate structures with *and*.

5.4.5   Patterns not discussed by Lakoff

Despite the real insight of Lakoff's three scenarios, it is important to remember that they do not exhaust the range of patterns of extraction from coordinate structures. In this section, we briefly recap the other patterns mentioned in Chapter 3, which Lakoff did not discuss.

The first pattern not discussed by Lakoff is ATB extraction, which has been the focus of most research on extraction from coordinate structures since Ross (1967). Here is an example:

(98)   What did you [[buy __] and [read __]]?

Kehler (2002) incorporated ATB extraction into a post-Lakoff theory by relating ATB extraction to PARALLEL. Kehler endorses a discussion of symmetrical conjunction (harboring relations such as PARALLEL) from Lakoff (1971), cited below.

> [A]t least one set of paired constituents must be reducible to partial or complete identity, in one of these ways, for a conjunction to be appropriate. This is essentially what is meant by *common topic*, and further implied by this name is the notion that, if only one pair is identical, this cannot be just a random pair, but, in some sense, the identity must involve that pair of constituents in the two conjuncts that are *what the sentence is particularly about*.   (Lakoff 1971: 122, cited in Kehler 2002: 123)

---

[47] Anticipating this discussion, we note that the contrast in (93) disappears when we replace *and* with *while*, as in (i). Not surprisingly, extraction is possible (at least from the host VP), as in (ii). This suggests that *and* is allergic to ⇐BACKGROUND in a way that *while* is not. A core part of Chapter 6 is an exploration of the basis of this allergy.

(i)   a. Anna stood in the hallway while screaming at Teia.
       b. Anna screamed at Teia while standing in the hallway.

(ii)   Who did you scream at __ while standing in the hallway?

Kehler's idea is that this common topic is the element that is targeted by ATB movement from coordinate structures with PARALLEL. This kind of information-structural explanation is our focus in Chapter 6. In the context of the current chapter, this can be seen as similar in spirit to Lakoff's analysis, in that semantic properties of the coordinate structure directly dictate extraction patterns, but different in the details, in that there is no reliance on frames, the 'natural course of events', causal relations, or any such notions.

Also omitted by Lakoff is the 'Type D' pattern described by Schmerling (1975) and Na and Huck (1992), as in (99), repeated from (25) in Chapter 3.

(99) Which baserunner was Doc [[following his coach's instructions] and [keeping __ close to first]]?   (Na and Huck 1992: 260)

At first glance, the best fit for Type D scenarios in Kehler's typology may seem to be ELAB-ORATION: the second conjunct in (99) elaborates on how Doc was following his coach's instructions. In fact, though, this claim will sit uneasily with the approach that we develop in Chapter 6, and we will return to the question of the interpretation of (99) in that chapter.

Next, there are two types of extraction discussed by Culicover and Jackendoff (1997), which are not discussed by Lakoff and do not fit neatly into Kehler's typology of discourse relations. The first is the conditional-like interpretation in (100), repeated from Section 3.3.2 (26).

(100) a. ?This is the loot that [[you just identify __] and [we arrest the thief on the spot]].
       b. ?This is the thief that [[you just identify the loot] and [we arrest __ on the spot]]   (Culicover and Jackendoff 1997: 206)

This demonstrates that asymmetric extraction from either conjunct is possible, per-haps slightly more naturally from the initial conjunct than from the final conjunct. ATB extraction is also possible, as in (101).

(101) This is the thief that [[you just identify __] and [we arrest __]].

In the context of Kehler's inventory of discourse relations, it would be most natural to con-sider these conditional examples as harboring a form of RESULT where neither the initial nor the final conjunct is asserted to occur in the actual world. However, the extraction from the final conjunct in (100b) is in contrast to the apparent behavior of Type C extractions. In Chapter 6, we suggest that these examples instead involve the standard SDRT relation for conditionals called CONSEQUENCE.

The other pattern from Culicover and Jackendoff is the so-called 'threat-*or*' interpreta-tion in (102) (discussed in Chapter 3).

(102) a. This is the loot that [[you hide __ right now] or [we're in big trouble]].
       b. Which kind of candy do [[you spit __ right out] or [you get real sick]]?
                                                        (Culicover and Jackendoff 1997: 215)

Although it would be natural to think of these examples as a close variant of CONSEQUENCE (where CONSEQUENCE would somehow hold between the negation of the first conjunct, and the second conjunct), Asher (2004) argues that *or* always ranges over alternatives (normally what he calls 'epistemic alternatives', but in the case of these examples, deontic alternatives). Asher calls this relation ALTERNATION. We will discuss it further in Chapter 6.

A final class of cases not considered by Lakoff is the SLF construction discussed in Section 3.6. It is important to repeat two conclusions from Section 3.6. First, although the analysis of this construction is controversial, we are persuaded that it involves asymmetric extraction from the initial conjunct. Second, although many examples, like (103) (repeated from (130) in Section 3.6), involve an interpretation with OCCASION, the extraction pattern does not match Lakoff's Type A.

(103)   In   den   Wald   ging   der   Jäger   und   fing   einen   Hasen.
        in   the   forest   went   the   hunter   and   caught   a   hare
        'Into the forest went the hunter and caught a hare.'   (Wunderlich 1988: 289)

Moreover, there are SLF constructions and related structures, as in (104) (also repeated from (106)–(107) in Section 3.6), which clearly do not harbor OCCASION.

(104)   a.   Morgen   werde   ich   meine   besten   Freunde   bekochen   und
             tomorrow   will   I   my   best   friend   cook.for   and
             bereite   deswegen   heute   schon   mal   ein   paar   Sachen   vor.
             prepare   therefore   today   already   a   few   things   for
             'Tomorrow, I'll cook for my best friend, and therefore today I'm already
             preparing a few things.'   (Reich 2009: 105)
        b.   Äpfel   ißt   der   Hans   [[drei   __]   und   [zwei   Bananen]].
             apples   eats   the   Hans   three   and   two   bananas
             'Hans eats three apples and two bananas.'   (Schwarz 1998: 195)

There is a useful cautionary tale implied by these extra scenarios: it is probably not surprising that the list of correlations established by Lakoff is incomplete, precisely because it is a list, and lists can be open-ended. The patterns discussed in this section suggest that, at the least, several more scenario types would be required to fully capture the range of patterns of extraction from coordinate structures. However, as the list grows, it becomes harder to ignore the question of why the list is the way it is. In Chapter 6, we consider a hypothesis about principles underpinning such a list.

5.5 Summary

We end this chapter by summarizing the main empirical patterns, as an evaluation of Lakoff's and Kehler's predictions concerning extraction from coordinate structures. We have shown, starting from the more explicit definitions of discourse relations in Section 5.3.2, that for all the insight yielded by Lakoff's three scenarios, it is not possible to account for those scenarios, and their associated extraction patterns, in terms of discourse relations. We have seen almost every combination of scenario type and extraction pattern, as shown in Table 5.1. The only exception is that we have not seen Type C scenarios with asymmetric extraction from the final conjunct.

This is not to say that there is no link between Lakoff's scenarios and extraction. But rather than robust correlations between scenario type and extraction patterns, what

Table 5.1 Distribution of gap sites in binary coordinate structures in Lakoff's different scenarios

	Initial conjunct	Final conjunct	ATB
Type A	(75a)	(68a)	(67)
Type B	(45)	(49)	(50)
Type C	(58)	—	(61a)

we have seen is that these scenarios characterize recurring, possibly violable, tendencies involving extraction patterns. They are as follows:

- **Type A** scenarios were analyzed by Kehler as involving OCCASION, but may also involve ⇒BACKGROUND (if the speculations in Section 5.4.4 are accurate, they actually always involve ⇒BACKGROUND). They are *n*-ary coordinate structures, and typically involve extraction of referential noun phrases from a set of conjuncts including the final conjunct. Examples from Brown (2017) and Neeleman and Tanaka (2020), such as (75a), have recently been identified as a cohesive class of exceptions to this typical pattern.

- **Type B** scenarios involve VIOLATED EXPECTATION in binary coordinate structures. They typically involve a 'threshold' reading, with extraction of an amount-denoting phrase from the first conjunct, which also typically contains *can*. Many variations on this theme, and examples with extraction from only the final conjunct, have also been attested.

- **Type C** scenarios involve RESULT in binary coordinate structures. They typically involve extraction of a referential noun phrase from only the initial conjunct, although ATB extraction is also possible. No clearly acceptable examples of extraction from only the final conjunct have been identified.

A particularly acute challenge for the project of relating the extraction behavior of the three scenarios to discourse relations comes from the claim in Section 5.3.2 that in terms of truth-conditional content, RESULT(π_1, π_2) entails OCCASION(π_1, π_2). In other words, every instance of RESULT can also be construed, in truth-conditional terms, as an instance of OCCASION. However, the Type A extraction pattern associated with OCCASION is apparently not available to coordinate structures harboring RESULT. We do not see a way to avoid this problem in the terms explored in this chapter.

Moreover, this relationship between RESULT and OCCASION challenges the Final Conjunct Constraint, the generalization that is at the heart of Lakoff's empirical predictions about extraction. Because RESULT entails OCCASION, it should not come as a surprise that there are Type A scenarios with asymmetric extraction from the initial conjunct, contrary to Lakoff's Final Conjunct Constraint. After all, this pattern is well-attested for Type C scenarios, with RESULT, which could therefore also be construed as instances of OCCASION. Any double dissociation between RESULT and OCCASION cannot therefore be stated in terms of the truth conditions of the two relations.

To put it another way, we could state (105), which follows from Lakoff's Final Conjunct Constraint in (46).

(105) **Initial Conjunct Extraction Generalization (Version 1)**: There are cases with two conjuncts related by RESULT and extraction from solely the initial conjunct.

However if RESULT(π_1, π_2) entails OCCASION(π_1, π_2), we can revise (105) as follows:

(106) **Initial Conjunct Extraction Generalization (Version 2):** There are cases with two conjuncts related by RESULT and OCCASION, and extraction from solely the initial conjunct.

In the light of this generalization, the existence of examples like (75a), with OCCASION and extraction from only the initial conjunct, is unremarkable. However, this is exactly what Lakoff's Final Conjunct Constraint denies!

A further problem for Lakoff's scenarios is that extraction from coordinate structures is not limited to the three scenarios that he identifies. Below, we provide the key data for each discourse relation that we think can be found in extraction from coordinate structures. This goes beyond Lakoff's scenarios in that we also consider ⇒BACKGROUND, PARALLEL, CONSEQUENCE, and ALTERNATION. We organize the data by: extraction from solely the first conjunct (a-examples), extraction from solely the second conjunct (b-examples), and ATB movement (c-examples).

The patterns that emerge are as follows: discourse relations can be grouped into three classes according to the extraction patterns that they allow.[48] Some discourse relations allow only ATB extraction. These include PARALLEL, illustrated in (107), and CONTRAST, a Resemblance relation cued by *but* that we have not yet discussed in detail. It behaves much like PARALLEL with respect to extraction, as illustrated in (108).

(107) **PARALLEL: ??solely 1st; ??solely 2nd; ATB**
  a. ??What book did John [[buy __] and [read a magazine]]?
  b. ??What magazine did John [[buy a book] and [read __]]?
  c. What book did [[John buy __] and [Bill read __]]?

(108) **CONTRAST: ??solely 1st; ??solely 2nd; ATB**
  a. ??Which drink did [[Mike like __] but [Kate hate schnapps]]?
  b. ??Which drink did [[Mike like kefir] but [Kate hate __]]?
  c. Which drink did [[Mike like __] but [Kate hate __]]?

The second class of discourse relations is best exemplified by RESULT, but we believe that ALTERNATION (the SDRT label for the relation instantiated by what Culicover and Jackendoff 1997 call '*threat*-or') shows the same pattern. The 'threshold' pattern of Type B extractions discussed in Section 5.4.1 may also fit here. These relations allow asymmetric extraction from the first conjunct, and ATB extraction, but not asymmetric extraction from noninitial conjuncts.

(109) **RESULT: solely 1st; ??solely 2nd; ATB**
  a. What's the stuff the guys in the Caucasus [[drink __] and, as a result, [live to be 100]]?
  b. ??Who did Kharms [[hear a news story] and, as result, [think of __]]?
  c. What did you [[hear __] and, as a result, [think of __]]?

---

[48] Of course, examples of the extraction patterns that a given relation allows may be unacceptable for orthogonal reasons, so the patterns described here are a kind of upper bound on acceptable extraction patterns.

(110)   ALTERNATION: solely 1st; ??solely 2nd; ATB

    a.   This is the loot that [[you hide __ right now] or [we're in big trouble]].

    b. ??This is the loot that [[you tell us what you know] or [you never see __ again]].

    c.   This is the loot that [[you hide __ from the thieves] or [we never see again]].

The final class, containing OCCASION and ⇒BACKGROUND among others, is the most permissive in that they allow all three extraction patterns.

(111)   OCCASION: solely 1st; solely 2nd; ATB

    a. What city did Mary [[go to __] and [buy a modernist painting]]?

    b. What modernist painting did Mary [[go to NYC] and [buy __]]?

    c. What did Ava [[write __ all night] and then [discuss __ with Teia]]?

(112)   ⇒BACKGROUND: solely 1st; solely 2nd; ATB

    a. Where did Ava [[stand __] and [scream at Teia]]?

    b. Who did you [[stand in the hallway] and [scream at __]]?

    c. Who does Anna [[live with __] and [read *Grumpy Monkey* to __]]?

Following the discussion in Section 5.4.5 of the 'left-subordinating *and*' identified by Culicover and Jackendoff (1997), it seems that the relation CONSEQUENCE also follows this pattern.

(113)   CONSEQUENCE: solely 1st; solely 2nd; ATB

    a. ?This is the loot that [[you just identify __] and [we arrest the thief on the spot]].

    b. ?This is the thief that [[you just identify the loot] and [we arrest __ on the spot]].   (Culicover and Jackendoff 1997: 206)

    c. This is the thief that [[you just identify __] and [we arrest __]].

There is also a fourth class of discourse relations, namely those that are simply inexpressible by coordinate structures. The relation of ⇐BACKGROUND discussed in Section 5.4.4 is an example of this class, but there are many others. EXPLANATION and DENIAL OF PREVENTER, the two Cause/Effect relations that Kehler (2002) identified other than RESULT and VIOLATED EXPECTATION, cannot be expressed by coordinate structures. The same goes for Kehler's four other Resemblance relations not discussed so far in this section (ELABORATION, EXEMPLIFICATION, GENERALIZATION, and EXCEPTION). The relevant examples can be constructed by inserting *and* between the sentences given in (4) (for Cause/Effect relations) and (7) (for Resemblance relations).[49] That *and* is incompatible with many discourse relations is something that none of the approaches surveyed so far have anything to say about.

The aim of the next chapter is to make sense of these four classes. We explore a different approach, where the lexical semantics of specific conjunctions may be compatible with only a limited set of discourse relations, and where the effect of discourse relations on extraction is indirect, and stated in terms of the constraints that different relations place on discourse structure and information structure.

---

[49] We focus on *and* as the conjunction which is a priori the most likely to be able to express these relations. Needless to say, it is also impossible to express any of these relations using *or* or *but*.

6

Discourse structure, information structure, coordination, and extraction

6.1 Introduction

The conclusion of Chapters 4 and 5 is a vexing one. Syntactic structure can potentially explain some facts about extraction from coordinate structures, such as an asymmetry between extraction from initial and noninitial conjuncts, but it leaves many observations from Lakoff (1986), Deane (1991), and Kehler (2002) untouched. Those three authors have demonstrated beyond reasonable doubt that discourse factors influence patterns of extraction from coordinate structures. So syntax doesn't call all the shots. However, the project of Chapter 5, namely to draw direct links between extraction patterns and discourse relations (as the best-theorized analog of Lakoff's 'scenarios') proved largely unsuccessful: there were few clear correlations between discourse relations and extraction patterns, and no clear basis for understanding the correlations that were identified. So we still don't know how discourse calls the shots, to the extent that it does.

In this chapter, we explore an alternative approach to discourse interpretation, namely **Segmented Discourse Representation Theory** (SDRT, Asher 1993, Lascarides and Asher 1993, Asher et al. 1997, Asher and Lascarides 1998a,b, Asher 1999, Asher and Lascarides 2003, Asher and Vieu 2005, Lascarides and Asher 2007, Asher et al. 2007, Lascarides and Asher 2009, Hunter et al. 2018, inter alia). SDRT is distinct from Hobbs's and Kehler's approaches to discourse relations for several reasons. First, the taxonomy of discourse relations that SDRT employs is not grounded in a domain-general, Humean taxonomy of principles of association of ideas. Second, SDRT separates *how* to assign a discourse relation from *what* the relation means. Third, SDRT is a more clearly hierarchical, rather than simply associative, theory of discourse structure. As a consequence, the precise label attached to a relation between two discourse units is less important in many respects than the structural properties of that relation. Finally, the SDRT notion of discourse structure is more fully integrated with and motivated by research on well-studied semantic phenomena such as structural constraints on anaphora resolution and identification of topics. These properties of SDRT give us new tools to describe the effect of discourse structure on patterns of extraction, and to address the question of the interactions, and division of labor, between syntax and discourse.

Our starting point, in Section 6.2, is an idea presented most clearly by Kehler (2002), that information-structural factors mediate the relationship between discourse structure and extraction from coordinate structures. Kehler relates Lakoff's patterns to a claim from Kuno (1976, 1987) that extracted elements correspond to topics. He does so by demonstrating that different discourse relations entail different distributions of topical material. This approach has held real intrigue since the mid-1970s because of the potential that it

Coordination and the Syntax–Discourse Interface. Daniel Altshuler and Robert Truswell, Oxford University Press.
© Daniel Altshuler and Robert Truswell (2022). DOI: 10.1093/oso/9780198804239.003.0006

holds for reducing Ross's islands to extrasyntactic factors. However, Section 6.2.4 lists several problems with adopting such a 'pure' topic-based approach to the analysis of extraction from coordinate structures. One of the tasks of this chapter is to find a way to make use of Kehler's insight, while avoiding these challenges.

Section 6.3 provides some background to our review of the SDRT treatment of topics and the related notion of **common theme**. We first spell out the graph-theoretic basics that underlie SDRT's analysis of discourse structure, including SDRT's innovative distinction between **subordinating** and **coordinating** discourse relations.[1]

Section 6.4 introduces proposals about the lexical semantics of English *and*, *or*, and *but*. Most of the attention is on *and*, and particularly on Txurruka's (2003) proposal that *and* requires a coordinating relation between its conjuncts, because of the way in which such relations contribute to the construction of topics. This innovation offers a response to the question raised in Chapter 5, namely why certain discourse relations never occur in coordinate structures.

Subsequently, in Section 6.5, we consider how logical forms of discourses are constructed according to SDRT. We will cover how discourse relations factor into the construction of topics, and how some discourse relations make reference to shared content among discourse units, or a 'common theme'. The particular interest of SDRT in this context is that these notions of topic and common theme are not global organizational principles. For some discourse relations, the discourse topic is what guarantees the coherence of the discourse, but for others, the coherence comes from a common theme, or from other organizational schemas, such as causal relations. In short, for SDRT, a discourse must be coherent, but different discourse relations have different means of ensuring coherence. This means that topics and common themes are only sporadically important in the SDRT theory of discourse structure.

With these ingredients in place, in Section 6.6 we return to the data summarized at the end of Chapter 5 and consider the prospects of working out an analysis of extraction from coordinate structures based on the SDRT theory of discourse relations and topics, in tandem with the constraints on discourse structure encoded by different coordinating conjunctions. The analysis we explore is a hybrid, motivated by the demonstration in Section 6.2.4 that topicality alone cannot explain all the observed extraction patterns. Returning to Choice Point 4 from Chapter 4, we consider the possibility of supplementing Munn's (1993) adjunction-based syntax for coordinate structures with an SDRT-based theory of the discourse structure of coordination. As described in Section 4.6, Munn's analysis predicts differences between asymmetric extraction from initial and noninitial conjuncts. We will also suggest in Section 6.2 that topical material has a special status in being extractable from weak islands. This leads to a new set of predictions: the different ways in which different discourse relations relate to topics can influence extraction from noninitial conjuncts only. Because initial conjuncts are not islands on Munn's syntax, there is nothing syntactically ill-formed in extracting from them, but there may be discourse-based constraints on extraction. This combination of syntactic, information-structural, and discourse-structural factors is a natural way to join the dots between key works on extraction from coordinate

---

[1] This distinction was first proposed by Hobbs (1985), and it has been applied to coordinate structures by Deane (1991) and Culicover and Jackendoff (1997). However, as we shall see, the SDRT conception of this distinction is different in several respects that turn out to be central in analyzing extraction from coordinate structures.

structures in different research traditions, like Munn's (1993) and Kehler (2002), but it has not been explicitly proposed before. We think that it is worthy of further investigation in future, as a potential source of insight which may help in discriminating between the various options in the choice points that we have identified.

The role of common themes in this approach to extraction is to enforce ATB movement with relations like PARALLEL and CONTRAST. The idea is essentially that of Kehler (2002): a gap in one conjunct requires a gap in all conjuncts for purely discourse-structural reasons. This implies an interesting set of syntax–discourse interactions: common themes rein in the syntactic analysis, by ruling out asymmetric extraction from the initial conjunct in those cases where ATB extraction is required, while topics expand the range of the syntactic analysis, by delimiting a class of constituents which can extract from weak islands. The predictions of the theory are captured by the following descriptive statement.

(1) **Extraction from coordinate structures**
     Match at least one of the following configurations:
     a. gaps in parallel positions in each conjunct;
     b. a gap in the initial conjunct;
     c. the extracted constituent corresponds to a topical element.

We emphasize that this is exploratory work, aimed at developing the hints in the published literature, surveyed in Chapter 5 and Section 6.2, in a way that is responsive to current research on discourse structure. We believe that the approach is promising enough to be presented as a prompt to further research, and as a foil to the syntactocentric approaches surveyed in Chapter 4. Nevertheless, we think that it is appropriate to warn the reader that the current chapter is less surveylike and more preliminary than the rest of the monograph.

6.2 Discourse relations, topichood, and extraction

In this section, we consider proposals to link discourse relations to extraction indirectly, namely via the mediation of information structure. Our focus is on Kehler's (2002) proposal, building on earlier work by Erteschik-Shir (1973), Morgan (1975), Kuno (1976), and Erteschik-Shir and Lappin (1979), that **topicality** acts as the intermediary which allows discourse relations to indirectly influence extraction patterns. This claim breaks down into two main components. The first is the so-called **Topichood Condition for Extraction**, given in (2) as originally formulated by Kuno (1976, 1987).

(2) **Topichood Condition for Extraction**
     Only those constituents in a sentence that qualify as the topic of the sentence can undergo extraction processes (i.e., *WH*-Q Movement, *Wh*-Relative Movement, Topicalization, and *It*-Clefting).   (Kuno 1987: 23)

This condition has been explored at length since Kuno's original formulation. It has even repeatedly been deployed to explain counterexamples to the CSC. We give a brief summary of this research, with special reference to coordinate structures, in Section 6.2.1.

The originality of Kehler's proposal comes from the combination of the Topichood Condition for Extraction with a second component: the observation that different discourse relations condition the distribution of topical material, in coordinate structures and elsewhere. The interaction of these two components gives Kehler's analysis a level of predicative detail that surpasses its predecessors. We summarize Kehler's proposal in Section 6.2.2, and suggest some refinements and extensions in Section 6.2.3. However, for all the attraction of Kehler's proposal, it leaves several unanswered questions with respect to coordination, extraction, and discourse. Moreover, we do not see easy fixes for these problems within Kehler's theory of discourse relations. We describe these problems in Section 6.2.4. This motivates the material in the rest of this chapter, which constitutes a sketch of Kehler's insight reconstructed in a different theory of discourse relations and discourse structure, namely Segmented Discourse Representation Theory, which we think has potential to avoid these problems.

6.2.1 Topichood, semantic dominance, and extraction

Kehler's (2002) project of relating patterns of topicality to patterns of extraction from coordinate structures builds on several investigations in the 1970s into topicality and extraction. The idea is primarily associated with a string of publications by Kuno (1973, 1976, 1987). Related notions were developed by Erteschik-Shir (1973) and Morgan (1975).

Kuno's ideas were founded on the observation that noun phrases can be relativized in Japanese only if they can be topic-marked with the suffix -*wa* (Kuno 1973). In (3) and (4), the (a) example is a baseline without *wa*-marking; the (b) example has *wa*-marking of an NP; and the (c) example relativizes the same example. As we see, the acceptability of relativization tracks the acceptability of topic-marking with -*wa*.

(3) a. [Sono hito ga sinda noni]   dare mo kanasimanakatta.
         the   man   died   although   nobody   was-saddened
         'Although the man died, nobody was saddened.'

     b. Sono hito wa [Ø sinda noni]   dare mo kanasimanakatta.
         the   man   died   although   nobody   was-saddened
         'That man, although (he) died, nobody was saddened.'

     c. [[Ø sinda noni]   dare mo kanasimanakatta]   hito ...
             died   although   nobody   was-saddened   person
         'the man who (lit.) although (he) died, nobody was saddened'

(4) a. [Sono hito ga dekinakereba]   watakusi ga yaru.
         the   man   if-cannot   I   do
         'If that man cannot do it, I will do it.'

     b. *Sono hito wa [Ø dekinakereba]   watakusi ga yaru.
          the   man   if-cannot   I   do
          'That man, if (he) cannot do it, I will do it.'

     c. *[[Ø dekinakereba]   watakusi ga yaru]   hito   ...
              if-cannot   I   do   person
          'the person who if (he) cannot do it, I will do it'   (Kuno 1987: 14–15)

A broadly similar observation (we will come back to some differences shortly) was made by Erteschik-Shir (1973), namely that the utterance in (5a) can be used to convey either of the two messages in (5b).

(5) a. I believe that Mary is a fool.
     b. (i)   Mary is a fool (at least, that's what I believe).
         (ii) My attitude toward the proposition that Mary is a fool is one of belief.

The same is not true of the factive statement in (6a), which can convey something along the lines of (6bii), but not (6bi).

(6) a. I rejoice that Mary is a saint.
     b. (i)   #Mary is a saint (at least, I rejoice because of that).
         (ii) My attitude toward the proposition that Mary is a saint is one of rejoicing.

Erteschik-Shir takes the syntactic structure of (5a) and (6a) to be the same.[2] She takes the difference between (5) and (6) instead to be rooted in an information-structural notion of **semantic dominance**. In (5), either clause can be semantically dominant: in (5bi) the syntactically subordinate clause is semantically dominant, while in (5bii) the syntactically superordinate clause is semantically dominant. In contrast, in (6), only the superordinate clause can be semantically dominant.

One indicator of semantic dominance is the discourse contexts in which an utterance is appropriate. (7a) is a discussion of Mary, not of Francine's beliefs, while in (7b), Francine's contribution focuses on her beliefs. Francine's utterance is appropriate in either context.

(7) a. Otto: I saw Mary today. What do you think of her?
         Francine: I believe that Mary is a fool.
     b. Otto: Mary is such a fool—I saw her acting up again today.
         Francine: I *believe* that Mary is a fool, but why do you have to harp on it?

(Erteschik-Shir 1973: 8–9)

In contrast, (8a), with *rejoice*, is odd in the context of a discussion of Mary. This indicates that the proposition that Mary is a saint cannot be dominant in Francine's utterance.

(8) a. Otto: I saw Mary today. What do you think of her?
         Francine: #I rejoice that Mary is a saint.
     b. Otto: Mary is a saint—I saw her doing good deeds again today.
         Francine: I *rejoice* that Mary is a saint, but even so, you talk about her too much.

Erteschik-Shir offers several tests for semantic dominance. The first is embedding a sentence S in the frame *Tom said 'S', which is a lie*. The linking hypothesis is that the property of being a lie is ascribed to the semantically dominant material, but not to the semantically subordinate material. (9) shows that either the matrix or the embedded clause can

---

[2] There is a tradition, starting with Kiparsky and Kiparsky (1970), of postulating syntactic differences between factive and nonfactive complement clauses. We do not discuss that tradition in detail here because the approach does not generalize to the other locality effects that motivated this line of research.

be semantically dominant with the matrix predicate *think*, while (10) shows that only the matrix predicate can be dominant with *rejoice*.

(9)   Tom said: 'Bill thinks that they're gonna win.'
   a.   ..., which is a lie—he doesn't.
   b.   ..., which is a lie—they're not.   (Erteschik-Shir 1973: 12)

(10)   Tom said: 'John rejoices that they came to the party.'
   a.   ..., which is a lie—he doesn't.
   b.   #..., which is a lie—they didn't.   (Erteschik-Shir 1973: 13)

A second, similar, test involves tag questions. Tag questions are again taken to relate to dominant material. This leads to contrasts like that between (11), where either the matrix or embedded clause can be dominant, and (12), where only the embedded clause can be dominant.

(11)   a.   I think they're going to win, don't I?
   b.   I think they're going to win, aren't they?

(12)   a.   I rejoice that they're going to win, don't I?
   b.   *I rejoice that they're going to win, aren't they?

A final test along the same lines involves the interjection *ah*. (13) can express surprise at Kissinger's vegetarianism, or at *Newsweek*'s reporting on Kissinger's vegetarianism. (14) can only have the latter reading.

(13)   Ah, it is reported by *Newsweek* that Kissinger is a vegetarian.

(14)   Ah, it is editorialized in today's *Times* that Kissinger is a vegetarian.
                                                            (Erteschik-Shir 1973: 15)

These tests for semantic dominance permit Erteschik-Shir (p. 27) to formulate the hypothesis that 'Extraction can occur only out of clauses or phrases which can be considered dominant in some context.' The hypothesis predicts contrasts like those in (15).

(15)   a.   Who do you think that they beat __ ?
   b.   *Who do you rejoice that they beat __ ?

(16)   a.   Who did the *Times* report that they beat __ ?
   b.   *Who did the *Times* editorialize that they beat __ ?

This subsumes Kiparsky and Kiparsky's (1970) observation that factive clauses are islands for extraction, and generalizes to other classes of complement clause, like the complement of *editorialize* in (16).[3] If semantic dominance is a discourse-structural notion, then this is another way in which discourse can call the shots.

   Proponents of this approach (e.g. Erteschik-Shir and Lappin 1979) claim that it has empirical advantages over purely geometric approaches, in that it can be extended to cover Ross's core island effects, but also predict that some exceptional cases of extraction from

---

[3] This is not to suggest that this is the last word in research into factivity and locality. See de Cuba (2007) for a thorough analysis of the syntax of factive predicates.

islands are grammatical, when a syntactic approach might rule them out. Kuno's original contrast in (3)–(4) is an example of this: both examples involve relativization out of adverbial clauses, which would be ruled out by purely syntactic bans on extraction from adjuncts such as the ones proposed by Cattell (1976) and Huang (1982) (see discussion in Section 4.3.4). The ability to discriminate between cases like these, which are often lumped together on purely syntactic approaches, is one of the main empirical attractions of Kuno's and Erteschik-Shir's approaches.

In the paragraphs that follow, we run through Ross's constraints from the perspective of Erteschik-Shir (1973) (the same argument was later made by Morgan 1975 using the 'ah'-test and by Kuno 1976 with reference to his Topichood Condition for Extraction). We only briefly recap Ross's formulation of the constraints here—for more detail, consult Section 4.3. The point here is the correspondence with semantic dominance.

Sentential Subject Constraint
The Sentential Subject Constraint is given in (17).

(17) **The Sentential Subject Constraint**
      No element dominated by an S may be moved out of that S if that node S is dominated by an NP which itself is immediately dominated by S.   (Ross 1967: 243)

This constraint was proposed by Ross to account for contrasts like (18): it is possible to extract from the same clause as a complement of *expect* in (18a), and as an extraposed clause associated with *it was expected* in (18c), but not from the in situ passive subject position in (18b).

(18)   a. The teacher who [the reporters expected [that the principal would fire __]] is a
           crusty old battleax.
       b. *The teacher who [[that the principal would fire __] was expected by the
           reporters] is a crusty old battleax.
       c. The teacher who [it was expected by the reporters [that the principal would fire
           __]] is a crusty old battleax.   (Ross 1967: 241)

Erteschik-Shir (1973) showed, though, that sentential subjects never contain semantically dominant material, citing the contrast between (19) (with extraposed sentential subject) and (20) (with in situ sentential subject).

(19)   Bill said: 'It's likely that Sheila knew all along.'
       a. ..., which is a lie—it isn't.
       b. ..., which is a lie—she didn't.

(20)   Bill said: 'That Sheila knew all along is likely.'
       a. ..., which is a lie—it isn't.
       b. *..., which is a lie—she didn't.

The Sentential Subject Constraint can therefore be seen as a special case of Erteschik-Shir's dominance-based principle.

The Complex Noun Phrase Constraint
The Complex Noun Phrase Constraint is given in (21).

(21) **The Complex NP Constraint**
No element contained in a sentence dominated by a noun phrase with a lexical head noun may be moved out of that noun phrase by a transformation.

(Ross 1967: 127)

The job of the CNPC is to explain contrasts like (22).

(22) a. The man [who I read [$_{NP}$ a statement [$_{PP}$ about __]]] was sick.
b. *The man [who I read [$_{NP}$ a statement [$_{S}$ which was [$_{PP}$ about __]]]] was sick.

(Ross 1967: 119)

In Kiparsky and Kiparsky's (1970) approach to factivity, factive complement clauses are in fact also analyzed as complex noun phrases, with a silent *the fact that*, as in (23).

(23) ??What did Bill confirm [~~the fact that~~ Roger had eaten __]?

Morgan (1975) gives (24) as evidence that material within the complex NP cannot be semantically dominant. Relying on the *ah*-test, Morgan notes that (24) can be used only to express surprise that the man came in the door, not at Kissinger's vegetarianism.

(24) Ah, [a man [who says that Kissinger is a vegetarian]] just came in the door.

(Morgan 1975: 296)

Like the Sentential Subject Constraint, then, the CNPC can be considered as a special case of Erteschik-Shir's dominance constraint.

Ross (1967) had already discussed a class of exceptions to the CNPC, involving contrasts like (25).

(25) a. What did she claim that he had done?
b. ?What did she make the claim that he had done?
c. *What did she discuss the claim that he had done? (Erteschik-Shir 1973: 146)

(25a) is a straightforward case of extraction from a potentially semantically dominant complement clause. (25c) is a regular CNPC violation. The interesting case is (25b), which has the surface syntax of a CNPC violation but is relatively acceptable. For Ross, this indicated that *make the claim* was structurally identical to the verb *claim* at the level of representation at which the island constraints are evaluated. However, it is not clear how that line of analysis could be formalized in any current syntactic theory. Erteschik-Shir offers an alternative analysis, showing that the judgments in (25) correspond with the potential for treating the subordinate clause as semantically dominant, as shown in (26).

(26) a. She claimed that John would certainly marry her, but it is not at all certain.
b. ?She made the claim that John would certainly marry her, but it is not at all certain.
c. *She discussed the claim that John would certainly marry her, but it is not at all certain. (Erteschik-Shir 1973: 149)

This again shows the potential for approaches based on topichood or semantic dominance to make distinctions which are beyond the reach of Ross's original syntactic formulations of the island constraints. In the next subsection, we turn our attention to the consequences of the Kuno/Erteschik-Shir approach for extraction from coordinate structures.

6.2.2 Topichood, semantic dominance, and the CSC

The same authors all made a case for reducing the CSC to considerations of topichood or semantic dominance, along the lines just described for the Sentential Subject Constraint and Complex Noun Phrase Constraint. Erteschik-Shir offers (27) to show that single conjuncts cannot ordinarily be semantically dominant, but that it is possible for dominant material to be spread across all conjuncts.

(27) Bill said: '[[The nurse polished her trombone] and [the plumber computed my tax]].'
    a. *..., which is a lie—(s)he didn't.
    b. ..., which is a lie—they didn't.   (Erteschik-Shir 1973: 160)

The implications of this for extraction are more subtle than it might appear. Clearly both conjuncts can jointly contribute to the dominant material—this is the point of (27b)—but that isn't sufficient to allow extraction from the dominant material in just one conjunct. In other words, the dominance constraint alone does not capture the ATB extraction pattern, although Erteschik-Shir states that it 'can possibly be extended' to capture the ATB pattern (p. 160).

If this extension is possible, then it is likely that some asymmetric extraction patterns will also follow automatically. For instance, Morgan (1975) notes that it is possible to find semantically dominant material in a single conjunct in one of Ross's cases of asymmetric extraction. That is, (28a) can be used to express surprise at just the fact that John bought ouzo, and not necessarily at the fact that John went to the store, predicting the familiar extraction pattern in (28b).

(28) a. Ah, John [[went to the store] and [bought some ouzo]].
    b. This is the ouzo which I [[went to the store] and [bought __]].
                  (Morgan 1975: 296–7)

Kuno's (1976) Topichood Condition for Extraction arguably offers a more complete account than Erteschik-Shir's dominance-based approach. Kuno demonstrated that in symmetrical coordination, a topic (identified by the *speaking of X* test) cannot be embedded within a single conjunct.[4]

(29) *Speaking of the lute, Henry [[plays it] and [sings madrigals]].

---

[4] We suspect that the *speaking of X* test is not a fully reliable test for topichood, because it is infelicitous with continuing topics (*Kate is speaking in the meeting now. #Speaking of Kate, she's asking when to file her report*). Clearly, out-of-the-blue judgments about the felicity of *speaking of X* require a certain amount of accommodation, which we do not understand well. We will nevertheless use it as a good first-pass heuristic.

A year earlier, in the context of a seminal investigation of left dislocation and topic–comment structures, Gundel (1975) had already claimed that Ross's cases of asymmetric extraction corresponded to cases in which a topical, left-dislocated NP was related to a single conjunct. That is, Gundel predicts correspondences like those in (30) and (31).[5]

(30)   a. It was the bread which Jim [[went to the store] and [picked __ up]].

(Gundel 1975: 96)

   b. The bread, Jim [[went to the store] and [picked it up]].

(31)   a. The guitar which Jim [[saved $50] and [bought __]] was a Yamaha.

(Gundel 1975: 96)

   b. The Yamaha guitar, Jim [[saved $50] and [bought it]].

In the wake of Lakoff (1986), several researchers investigated the connection between topichood and/or dominance, and extraction from coordinate structures, in greater depth. Na and Huck (1992) drew a distinction between 'primary' and 'secondary' clauses, a distinction clearly reminiscent of Erteschik-Shir's notion of dominance. A primary clause is one which cannot be omitted without seriously distorting the message, and Na and Huck claim that extraction must be only from primary clauses. This captures the extraction patterns described by Lakoff if the initial clause is primary in Type B and Type C scenarios, but not in Type A scenarios. Na and Huck claim that this is the case, but unfortunately do not offer an independent test to establish which clauses are primary. They claim, for instance, that the initial conjunct is primary in (32a) (an example of a Type C scenario), and that this explains the preference for extraction from an initial conjunct in Type C scenarios, as in (32b). However, this seems dubious: part of the message of (32a) is about the effects of babies always eating 'that'.

(32)   a. Babies always [[eat that] and then [get sick]].   (Na and Huck 1992: 257)
   b. This is the thing that babies always [[eat __] and then [get sick]].

Deane (1991), in contrast, adopts the *lie*-test from Erteschik-Shir (1973) to investigate dominance in coordinate structures. This is part of Deane's project, developing ideas from Kuno and from Takami (1989), of accounting for Lakoff's data in terms of sentence processing. Deane's idea is that the acceptability of long-distance extraction is related to attention, and the task of attending to both the filler and the gap site is facilitated by information-structural factors. Among these factors, Deane considers topic, focus, and semantic dominance, but does not consistently distinguish them, nor develop a theory of how these different notions affect attention. We repeat his evidence concerning semantic dominance here, as the most systematic data set that he presents.

Using Erteschik-Shir's *lie*-test, Deane claims that almost none of the different kinds of background conjunct that he identified (see Section 5.4) are semantically dominant.

---

[5] We give these pairs, where the (a)-examples come from Gundel (1975), in preference to the pair that Gundel herself gave on p. 93 of her paper, because of a clear confound in her pair. The (b)-examples with left dislocation are ungrammatical for one of the authors. If the same is true for the reader, the same point can be made using *as for*-clauses, as in (i).

(i)   a. As for the bread, Jim [[went to the store] and [picked it up]].
   b. As for the Yahama guitar, Jim [[saved $50] and [bought it]].

This applies to preparatory actions like (33), scene-setters like (34), and incidental events like (35).

(33) Bill said: Here's the cheese I [[went to the store] and [bought __]].
    a. *Which is a lie; he didn't go to the store.
    b. Which is a lie; he didn't buy any.

(34) Bill said: Sue's the one I [[stood in the parlor] and [told jokes about __]].
    a. *Which is a lie; he didn't stand in the parlor.
    b. Which is a lie; he didn't tell jokes about her.

(35) Bill said: This is the job that I [[worked on __ all morning], [took a lunch break], and [finished off __ by 2 p.m.]].
    a. *Which is a lie; he didn't take a lunch break.
    b. Which is a lie; he didn't work on it all morning.
    c. Which is a lie; he didn't finish it off by 2 p.m.   (Deane 1991: 50)

This is preliminary evidence that the prospects are good for an Erteschik-Shir-style explanation of Lakoff's Type A scenarios. However, Deane claims that the same is not true for one type of backgrounded Type A conjunct, namely 'internal causes' like (36), as well as Types B and C, illustrated in (37) and (38). In all of these cases, the *lie* test suggests that either conjunct can be treated as dominant, even in examples with asymmetric extraction.

(36) Bill said: This is the problem I [[got bored] and [gave up on __]].
    a. Which is a lie; he didn't get bored (he just has low self-esteem).
    b. Which is a lie; he didn't give up on the problem.

(37) Bill said: Seven courses is the most I have [[taken __] and [still remained sane enough to carry on a coherent conversation]].
    a. Which is a lie; he didn't take seven courses.
    b. Which is a lie; he didn't remain that sane.

(38) Bill said: This is the machine gun you can [[shoot __ off] and [kill a thousand men a minute]].
    a. Which is a lie; you can't shoot it off (it's fake).
    b. Which is a lie; it won't kill a thousand men a minute.   (Deane 1991: 51)

Deane states that extraction is possible from the final conjunct only in (36) and the initial conjunct only in (37) and (38). These examples therefore do not correlate perfectly with the evidence that either conjunct can be semantically dominant in these examples.

We do not understand what lies behind Deane's data in (36)–(38), but it is important to remember that we documented a wider range of extraction patterns in Chapter 5 than Lakoff had recognized. We claimed in that chapter that we find extraction from either conjunct in Type A and Type B scenarios.[6] However, we will discuss the interaction of

---

[6] It is worth noting that there is almost nothing to extract from the initial conjunct in (36). The only candidate example of extraction from the initial conjunct would be (i), which admittedly isn't great.

(i) ??How bored did he [[get __] and [give up on the problem]]?

dominance with Types B and C further on. These data are of particular interest to us because we still have not seen any examples of extraction from final conjuncts in Type C scenarios, despite the fact that those conjuncts can be semantically dominant, as in (38b).

Kehler (2002), building on Kuno (1976, 1987), paints a more optimistic picture of the extent to which discourse relations predict asymmetric extraction patterns. Kehler proposes an analysis in which the distribution of topics differs across the Humean classes of relations, based on the following two hypotheses:

(39)   **Kehler's Hypothesis 1 (KH1):**
       Arguments of Humean Resemblance relations have a common topic.

(40)   **Kehler's Hypothesis 2 (KH2):**
       Arguments of Humean Cause/Effect and Contiguity relations do not impose constraints on topics.

Let's consider these two hypotheses in turn. Kehler's idea in positing KH1 is that if a moved element must be topical, and the movement is not ATB, then the topic is not shared across conjuncts. This hypothesis is motivated by examples which harbor Resemblance relations. For example, using Kuno's *speaking of X* test, (41), harboring the Resemblance relation CONTRAST, shows that *the book* can be the topic of *John enjoyed the book* and *Bill hated the book*, thus satisfying KH1.

(41)   Speaking of the book, [[John enjoyed it] and [Bill hated it]].

If *the book* is not an argument in each conjunct, it is not available as a common topic, as shown in (42).[7]

(42)   a. #Speaking of the book, [[John enjoyed it] and [Bill hated the movie]].
       b. #Speaking of the book, [[John enjoyed the movie] and [Bill hated it]].
                                                             (Kehler 2002: 125)

Instead, a common topic shared between the conjuncts in such cases must be a kind of generalization over *the book* and *the movie*, not corresponding directly to a constituent of either conjunct (we describe the nature of this generalization in Section 6.5).

(43)   a. Speaking of that franchise, [[John enjoyed the book] and [Bill hated the movie]].
       b. Speaking of junk from Joe's garage sale, I hear that [[John bought the book] and [Bill bought the magazine]].   (Kehler 2002: 124)

These facts, together with Kuno's Topichood Condition for Extraction, predict that only ATB extraction is permitted with Resemblance relations like CONTRAST in (44a). In (44b) *the book* cannot extract from the first conjunct alone, as it cannot be a common topic of the two conjuncts, and any structure in which *the book* is topical in the first conjunct but not the second will violate KH1. The same reasoning applies to (44c) (we return briefly to other Resemblance relations in Section 6.2.4.).[8]

---

[7] Kehler classes these examples as instances of PARALLEL, rather than CONTRAST, but we think that this is likely to be inaccurate, because the sentences become infelicitous if the cue-phrase *too* is added.

[8] Kehler's analysis does not explain why (44b) and (44c) are odd, only why Resemblance relations cannot hold here. Kehler's claim is presumably that (44b) and (44c) are not ungrammatical, but rather infelicitous because no discourse relation other than a Resemblance relation can plausibly be inferred.

(44)   a.   What book did [[John enjoy __] and [Bill hate __]]?
       b.   ??What book did John [[enjoy __] and [hate the movie]]?
       c.   ??What magazine did John [[enjoy the book] and [hate __]]?

Let us now consider KH2, Kehler's hypothesis that Contiguity and Cause/Effect relations do not impose constraints on topics. Recall from Section 5.2 that Kehler proposes only one Humean Contiguity relation, namely OCCASION, while proposing the four Cause/Effect relations below:

- **Cause/Effect relations**:
  RESULT, EXPLANATION, DENIAL OF PREVENTER, VIOLATED EXPECTATION

All else being equal, Kehler's prediction about extraction from coordinate structures with these families of relations is that anything goes: the discourse relations in question do not impose constraints on the distribution of topical items, so discourse structure does not combine with the Topichood Condition for Extraction to directly rule out extraction from either conjunct. Based on data such as (45) and (46),[9] he argues that with RESULT and OCCASION, this is the correct prediction.

(45)   Extraction with RESULT
       a.   Which dish is it that [[people always order __ here] and [get sick as a result]]?
       b.   Which dish is it that [[people always order __ here] and [get sick from __]]?

(46)   Extraction with OCCASION
       a.   What did he [[go to the store] and [buy __]]?
       b.   Which student did the teacher [[scold __] and then [send __ to the principal's office]]?

It will be immediately obvious, though, that these paradigms are incomplete, with no examples of extraction from only the final conjunct in (45) and no examples of extraction from only the initial conjunct in (46). Kehler acknowledges that these possibilities are less typical than the patterns illustrated in (45) and (46), though he stops short of calling them impossible. His account of these cases is framed in terms other than the distribution of sentence topics: he follows Na and Huck (1992) in claiming that the initial conjunct is typically semantically dominant (or primary, in Na and Huck's terms) with RESULT, while in the case of OCCASION, he claims that final conjuncts without gaps are typically not 'topic-relevant', although it is not clear exactly what this follows from. We return to these problematic cases in Section 6.2.4.

In short, the literature on information structure and extraction from coordinate structures leaves a clear impression that there is real explanatory potential, but the picture is quite complex and remains somewhat imprecise, both in terms of the theoretical devices used in the analysis, and the assumptions about the empirical fact of the matter to be explained. It appears that two distinct but related information-structural notions are implicated in these analyses, namely semantic dominance and topichood, but the relationship between the two is not clear. Meanwhile, the relation of these notions to the facts about

---

[9] All examples besides (46b) are from Kehler (2002).

extraction from coordinate structures has moments of clarity (for instance, the link between Resemblance relations and ATB extraction patterns), but also moments of apparent disconnect (particularly concerning RESULT, where the facts about dominance from Deane given in (38), and the predictions about topicality from Kehler summarized in KH2, do not seem to fit the patterns observed in Chapter 5). In the next subsection, we aim to sharpen the theoretical picture outlined here. This will allow us to identify some of its limitations in Section 6.2.4.

6.2.3 Refinements and extensions

We take it that the attractions of the approach described in the previous two subsections are clear. The attempt to ground island effects in independently motivated principles of information structure and discourse structure promises to simultaneously simplify syntactic theory (by reducing the empirical burden on constraints like those formulated by Ross) and improve empirical accuracy (by providing a unified explanation for the patterns Ross described and the exceptions to those patterns).

However, the discussion at the end of the previous subsection indicates that the insights from Erteschik-Shir, Morgan, Gundel, Kuno, Deane, and Kehler are not in themselves sufficient to scaffold a precise and accurate theory of extraction from coordinate structures. In this subsection, we discuss a string of questions left open in Section 6.2.2.

What is the relevant notion of topic?
Different conceptions of topic and related notions have proliferated throughout the development of linguistic theory (see Kruijff-Korbayová and Steedman 2003 for an attempt to clarify the terminology used and relationships among different traditions of information structure research). We will be concerned here with the distinction between **sentence topic** and **discourse topic**. Reinhart (1982) gave (47)–(48) as an illustration of the difference between the two notions. (48a) characterizes the sentence topic, while (48b) characterizes the discourse topic.

(47)   Mr. Morgan is a careful researcher and a knowledgeable semiticist, but his originality leaves something to be desired.

(48)   a. [(47)] is about Mr. Morgan.
       b. [(47)] is about Mr. Morgan's scholarly ability.   (Reinhart 1982: 54)

We won't say anything much about *how* we decide what (47) is about (a complex and multifaceted question which underlies much of the complexity that Kruijff-Korbayová and Steedman aim to disentangle). Reinhart's point is independent of that: the two types of statement in (48) demonstrate that (47) can be construed as being about two different types of objects, where aboutness is plausibly derivative of a procedure for updating the Common Ground (Stalnaker 1978).

There are several distinctions between these two types of aboutness (which are both useful in different ways). First, (48a), describing the sentence topic, identifies (47) as being about an individual, while (48b), describing the discourse topic, identifies (47) as being about something else, perhaps a (concealed) question. Second, the topic picked out by (48a) is a constituent of (47), while the topic in (48b) is not.

This latter difference hints at an important distinction in the treatment of sentence topics and discourse topics. Although both types of topic are best construed as phenomena at the interface between pragmatics and grammar, discourse topics are primarily pragmatic, and largely determined by context of utterance. Sentence topics, in contrast, are more narrowly grammatical objects (they reside in sentences). As a consequence, **topic-marking** (morphosyntactic devices used to identify topics) targets sentence topics, not discourse topics. For this reason, the sentence topic is the most important type of topic in most syntactic research on information structure, from Rizzi (1997) and Benincá and Poletto (2001) to Erteschik-Shir (2007).

Sentence topics always denote individuals. The evidence for this view comes from a wide range of topic-marking constructions. For instance, É. Kiss (2002: Ch. 2) demonstrates that Hungarian sentences instantiate a topic–predicate articulation, with a dedicated left-peripheral position for the sentence topic, and observes that topics correspond to referential, rather than quantificational, DPs. Her characterization of the 'topic function' is reproduced in (49), while (50) and (51) illustrate the empirical consequences of the topic–predicate articulation. In (50a), a referential subject occupies the initial topic position, and in (50b) a referential object occupies this position, with equal grammaticality but different information-structural status. The contrast with (51) demonstrates that quantificational NPs, whether subjects or objects, cannot occupy this position.

(49) *The topic function*
      The topic foregrounds an individual (a person, an object, or a group of them) from among those present in the universe of discourse as the subject of the subsequent predication.   (É. Kiss 2002: 9)

(50) a. [$_{Topic}$ A védők] sokáig tartották a   várat   a   törökök ellen.
           the defenders long   held   the fort-ACC the Turks   against
        'The defenders held the fort against the Turks for a long time.'
      b. [$_{Topic}$ A várat] sokáig tartották a   védők   a   törökök ellen.
           the fort-ACC long   held   the defenders the Turks   against
        'The defenders held the fort against the Turks for a long time.'   (É. Kiss 2002: 8)

(51) a. *[$_{Topic}$ Kik]   meg védték   a   várat   a   törökök ellen?
            who-PL VM defended the fort-ACC the Turks against
        'Who defended the fort against the Turks?
      b. *[$_{Topic}$ Kevés várat]   meg védtek   a   zsoldosok   a   törökök ellen
             few   fort-ACC VM defended the mercenaries the Turks against
        'Few forts were defended against the Turks by the mercenaries.'
                                                                           (É. Kiss 2002: 10)

This restriction to referential topics can be understood in terms of Karttunen (1976) proposal that there are abstract topical entities, called 'discourse referents' (DREFS), whose 'lifespan' determines how long they can serve as antecedents for anaphoric expressions later in the discourse. A DREF can be thought of as a variable under an assignment function that stands for an individual introduced in the discourse. This idea was influential in the development of Discourse Representation Theory (DRT) by Hans Kamp and colleagues (Kamp 1981, Kamp and Reyle 1993), as well as in the development of File Change Semantics by Irene Heim (1982, 1983). In this vein, McNally (1995) notes several approaches that adopt Heim's File Change Semantics, defining a topic of a sentence S as a 'file card' onto which the information contained in S is entered, or a referent with which the information in S is associated (Reinhart 1982, Portner and Yabushita 1998, 2001).

As for the nature of a discourse topic, this is the focus of Section 6.5. Here, we provide a short preview by outlining the influential **Question Under Discussion** model developed by Roberts (1996), Büring (2003), and others. This is not the model of discourse topic that we ultimately adopt. However, it is a simple and powerful model, widely used among information structure researchers, that is suitable for our immediate needs.

Roberts (1996) models a discourse context as a set of questions that are answerable, but as yet unanswered. A question at the top of the stack represents the question which has been most recently accepted by the discourse participants as being answerable but unanswered. Its relation to the other questions has to do with 'a combination of Relevance, entailing a commitment to answering prior questions, and logical constraints on the way that the stack is composed' (Roberts 1996). At the bottom of the stack is the 'big question', *What is the way things are?*, of which all other questions are subquestions.

Büring (2003) models a context as a tree, with a question corresponding to multiple subquestions, which in turn have subquestions of their own. Following Hamblin (1973), a question can be modeled as a set of propositions. This, in turn, allows us to think of the relationship between a discourse topic and an assertion as simply the relationship between a question and its answer.

Returning now to Kuno's (1973) Topichood Condition for Extraction, the notion of topic that Kuno had in mind must be the sentence topic. We know this because Kuno's original insight concerned an observation about a topic-marking device, *wa*-marking in Japanese, and we have noted that topic-marking pertains specifically to sentence topics. Moreover, it is much easier to make sense of that condition in terms of a notion of sentence topic, simply because sentence topics are sentential constituents, and extraction targets sentential constituents. Discourse topics are not typically sentential constituents, so they cannot map so neatly to a sentence-grammar phenomenon like movement.

Nevertheless, the notion of discourse topic is surely relevant to Kehler's use of Kuno's ideas. The reason in a nutshell, though we will be able to state this more precisely in Section 6.5, is that the discourse relations that are a key component of Kehler's theory are typically not represented sententially (except for the handful of cue-phrases that we discussed in Chapter 5). Rather, they hold at a suprasentential level. If discourse relations are to condition any kind of topic, then, we would expect them to condition discourse topics.

Therefore, to understand how Kehler might intend to make use of Kuno's condition, we need to consider the relation between sentence topic and discourse topic. This is purely in the interest of sharpening Kehler's proposal—we will critique, and in fact reject, this sharpened version later in this subsection.

There is no consensus in the literature on the nature of the relationship between sentence topics and discourse topics. McNally (1995) states that sentence topics are dispensable if the notion of discourse topic is fully worked out, while Kehler (2004) states the opposite. We will rely on both notions, because we don't see how to go about a complete reconstruction of either notion within the terms of the other, and look for a formal relationship between them.

Such a relationship is described by von Fintel (1994). Von Fintel proposes that a sentence topic stands in an anaphoric relation to the discourse topic. More precisely, in a sentence where the sentence topic is the proper name *Ana*, denoting *a*, the discourse topic must be a subset of $\{p|\exists P.p = P(a)\}$, the set of propositions which predicate something of Ana. This ensures that the discourse topic, the question under discussion, is a subquestion of *What about Ana*.[10] Discourse topics, in practice, are richer, more specific, and more context-dependent than this, and this is what motivates McNally's (1995) claim that von Fintel's notion of sentence topic is so weak as to be dispensable. However, the importance of von Fintel's claim is that it shows that formal statements of the relationship between sentence topic and discourse topic are possible, even if there may be more to be said about the nature of that relation.

The relationship between topichood and dominance

Erteschik-Shir's notion of semantic dominance, as well as Na and Huck's notion of 'primary conjunct', are surely related to topicality (indeed, the authors all assume as much). However, in much of the literature, the notions are assumed to be independent to a degree (e.g. Deane 1991), or the nature of the relationship between these notions is left implicit (e.g. Kehler 2002). We will say a little here about how these notions fit into the understanding of sentence topic and discourse topic that we just sketched.

First, we assume that semantic dominance and 'primary conjunct' are two terms for the same thing. In characterizing dominance, Erteschik-Shir (1973) states that 'it is only the dominant part of the sentence which it is natural to comment on' (p. 16), while Erteschik-Shir and Lappin (1979) characterize dominant constituents as those that 'the speaker intends to direct the attention of his hearers to the intension of' (p. 43). Meanwhile, Na and Huck (1992) talk about 'propositions of unequal importance', and characterize the primary proposition as the more important one. They offer a heuristic that 'if the clause can be deleted without seriously distorting the message expressed, then we will say that the clause is secondary' (p. 256). It is reasonable to suppose that these are different ways of characterizing the same property.

Semantic dominance is clearly a property of propositions, rather than of individuals. We know this because tests for semantic dominance, such as the *lie*-test, target propositions. Semantic dominance is therefore more likely related to discourse topics than to sentence topics. Continuing for now to think of a discourse topic as a question, or a set of propositions, we might suppose that the proposition expressed by the semantically dominant material, possibly without the nondominant material, is a member of the set of propositions corresponding to the discourse topic.

---

[10] See Ginzburg (1995a,b, 1996, 2012), Büring (1997, 1999, 2007), Constant (2014), and references therein for related ideas on how sentence topics and discourse topics are related.

If there is an identifiable sentence topic, then von Fintel's model of the relationship between sentence topics and discourse topics will force the other propositions in the set corresponding to the discourse topic to be predications of that sentence topic. For instance, if our utterance is *Jessica went to the store and bought some whiskey*, with *Jessica* as sentence topic and *Jessica ... bought some whiskey* as semantically dominant, then the discourse topic could correspond to questions such as *Tell me something about Jessica*, *What did Jessica do*, *What did Jessica buy*, or *What did Jessica go to the store and buy*. It could not, on the other hand, correspond to *Where did Jessica go*, because answers to that question may exclude the dominant material *bought some whiskey*. It also could not correspond to *Who went to the store and bought some whiskey*, because not all possible answers to that question are predications of the sentence topic *Jessica*.

We hope that this is a useful way to make sense of the different information-structural notions that have been used in the analysis of exceptional extractions such as asymmetric extraction from coordinate structures. Despite the proliferation of terms, there is some reason to believe that sentence topic, semantic dominance, and discourse topic are related in ways that can be formally stated: the semantically dominant material is a proposition derived by predicating something of the sentence topic (if there is one), and that proposition stands in a close relation to the discourse topic (for instance, if a discourse topic is modeled as a question, then the semantically dominant proposition is an answer to that question).

Not all extracted phrases are topical

Earlier in this subsection, we discussed the common idea that a sentence topic denotes an individual. This has immediate consequences for how we think of the relationship between topicality and extraction. Put simply, not every extracted phrase denotes an individual. Therefore, not every extracted phrase can correspond to a sentence topic. To give one example, returning to the discussion in Section 5.4.1, the extracted phrase in (52a) ranges over amounts, not individuals, and therefore cannot correspond to a sentence topic. Kuno's *speaking of* test, in (52b), confirms this.[11]

(52)   a.   How much can you [[drink __] and [still stay sober]]?
        b.   #Speaking of a gallon of fermented mare's milk, I can [[drink one] and [still stay sober]].

We can gain more insight into the limits of the relation between extractees and sentence topics by considering the class of **aggressively non-D-linked** *wh*-phrases identified by Pesetsky (1987), such as *who the hell* in (53).

(53)   Who the hell broke the vase?

---

[11] Julian Schlöder (pers. comm.) points out that the following example, a minimal modification of (52b), is more acceptable.

(i)   Speaking of gallons of fermented mare's milk, I can [[drink one] and [still stay sober]].

An approach to the contrast between (i) and (52) would be to treat the bare plural *gallons of fermented mare's milk* as the proper name of a kind, as in Carlson (1977), and *one* as anaphoric to that kind. This would imply that *gallons of fermented mare's milk* in (i) is referential, while nonspecific *a gallon of fermented mare's milk* in (52b) is not.

In the analysis of Den Dikken and Giannakidou (2002), *who the hell* differs from most *wh*-phrases in that it cannot be linked to familiar discourse referents. This can be seen in the impossibility of establishing an anaphoric link between *who the hell* and *someone* in the sluicing example in (54).

(54)   Someone bought the book. John knows {who/*who the hell}.

(Den Dikken and Giannakidou 2002: 42)

Because sentence topics are necessarily familiar, or given, it follows that aggressively non-D-linked *wh*-phrases such as *who the hell* are necessarily not topical.

Pesetsky opposed aggressively non-D-linked *wh*-phrases like *who the hell* to **D-linked** *wh*-phrases like *which person*, which range over a familiar set of individuals. By virtue of the reference to 'familiar' and 'individual', the properties of D-linked phrases are fairly similar to those of sentence topics.

D-linked phrases have a special status in locality theory because they are insensitive to certain locality constraints that restrict movement of non-D-linked phrases. For instance, they can violate the Superiority condition (that is, they can move across another *wh*-phrase), while aggressively non-D-linked phrases cannot.

(55)   a.   Which book did [which kid buy __]?
        b.   *What did [who the hell buy __]?
        c.   *What the hell did [who buy __]?

Moreover, building on ideas we discussed in Section 4.3, D-linked phrases can extract from weak islands.[12] This could lead us to hope that the D-linked phrases are the sentence topics that Kuno refers to in his Topichood Condition for Extraction.

There are some subtle issues to work through, though, to relate this notion of specificity to Kuno's condition. It doesn't seem plausible to claim that all A'-extracted elements are topics, even if they are D-linked.[13] Here is an example that demonstrates why not. Assume a contextually given group of three kids, Alexa, Ben, and Charlie, and the question in (56), with a D-linked *wh*-phrase.

(56)   Which kid ate the cake I left on the table?

The discourse topic, which we continue to model as a question under discussion, corresponds to the following set of three possible answers.

(57)   {Alexa ate the cake, Ben ate the cake, Charlie ate the cake}

In this context, the subject cannot function as a sentence topic, according to the *speaking of*-test, as (58) shows.

---

[12] See Starke (2001) for a survey of different analyses of the interpretive effect of extraction from weak islands. Starke's conclusion is that the noun phrases that can extract are distinguished by a syntactic feature [SpecificQ], corresponding to a specific interpretation.

[13] It may be that the extractee can be construed as a sentence topic in some A' constructions, but not others. The types of A'-dependency discussed in Lasnik and Stowell (1991), for instance, such as *tough*-movement and topicalization, may have extractees which are good candidates for sentence topics. However, the point of the discussion of questions in the main text is to illustrate that there is no necessary connection between a D-linked extractee and the sentence topic.

(58) A: Which kid ate the cake I left on the table?
      B: Alexa ate the cake.
      B': #Speaking of Alexa, she ate the cake.

However, there is a broad similarity between D-linked phrases and sentence topics, in that sentence topics must be familiar individuals, while D-linked phrases range over a set of familiar individuals. In a question–answer pair, a D-linked *wh*-phrase will therefore typically correspond to an answer which makes a good sentence topic in *other* contexts. (59) is an example of such a context.

(59) A: I just saw Alexa in the park.
      B: Speaking of Alexa, she ate the cake you left on the table.

Moreover, there is morphosyntactic evidence that D-linking and sentence topic are related. Polinsky (2001) discusses patterns of long-distance agreement in Tsez. Long-distance agreement is restricted to agreement with topical, absolutive-marked constituents of embedded clauses like (60).

(60) Enir   [užā   magalu-gon   bāc'ruλi]   b-iy-xo.
      mother boy   bread.ABS.III-TOP ate   III-know-PRS
      'The mother knows that the bread, the boy ate.'

The same agreement pattern is available to *wh*-phrases only when they have a D-linked interpretation, as in (61).

(61) Dār   [nāsi   keč'   nesir   b-āti-ru-λi]
      me.DAT which song.III.ABS him.DAT   III-like-PSTPRT-NMLZ
      b-iy-x-ānu.
      III-know-PRS-NEG
      'I don't know which song he liked.'

Polinsky's conclusion is that the similarity between sentence topics and D-linked *wh*-phrases is not just a point of contact in the semantics, but is actually reified in the grammar (in fact, in her analysis, D-linked *wh*-phrases move to a designated left-peripheral topic position, while other *wh*-phrases move elsewhere). This kind of similarity raises the possibility that D-linked phrases and sentence topics, even if different in the fine detail, form a natural class in the syntax and semantics.

To our knowledge, there is no consensus on the issue of the relationship between D-linking, sentence topic, and weak islands. We will therefore frame this as a choice point.

Choice Point 5 What is the relationship between D-linking, sentence topic, and weak islands?

   Option 1: D-linking and sentence topic form a natural class; only D-linked/topical phrases can be extracted from weak islands.
   Option 2: D-linking is distinct from sentence topic; sentence topics can be extracted from weak islands.
   Option 3: D-linking is distinct from sentence topic; D-linked phrases can be extracted from weak islands.

We tentatively assume Option 1 as we develop our analysis. However, further research is needed here. Note that both Options 1 and 2 are consistent with Kuno's Topichood Condition for Extraction.

Our tentative choice of Option 1 makes an interesting point of contact between D-linking and the adjunction-based analysis of coordinate structures discussed in Section 4.6 (this was Option 3 of Choice Point 4). On the adjunction analysis, noninitial conjuncts are adjoined to the initial conjunct. In languages like English, the noninitial conjuncts are weak islands (in contrast to languages like German, where they are strong islands, from which nothing can extract). This means that only D-linked phrases should be able to extract asymmetrically from noninitial conjuncts.

However, this approach also implies that initial conjuncts are not islands, in any language. This predicts that there is no D-linking requirement on extraction from an initial conjunct. This is the basis for the generalization we stated in (1), in the introduction to this chapter: extraction from a coordinate structure must be either ATB, from the initial conjunct, or of a D-linked phrase.

In terms of the extraction patterns that Lakoff (1986) described for his three scenario types, and disregarding the more complex patterns that we described in Chapter 5, this makes the following predictions.

- Type A: extraction from noninitial conjunct(s), extractee must be D-linked;
- Types B, C: extraction from initial conjunct, extractee need not be D-linked.

We believe that the empirical data support this approach better than the classical approach based on Ross's purely syntactic formulation of the CSC. However, we emphasize again that this is a preliminary hypothesis; our goal here is to lay out a framework for further empirical exploration of this rich theoretical terrain.

6.2.4 Outstanding problems

The previous subsection was an exercise in theoretical and terminological tidying up, trying to draw out similarities and sharpen distinctions between clearly related terms and concepts used in different corners of this literature. We now turn to a series of problems concerning the Erteschik-Shir/Kuno approach to extraction from coordinate structures, particularly in light of the empirical patterns reported in Section 5.4. Some of these matters don't have a straightforward resolution within the terms used so far in this section. This motivates the search for alternative formulations in the rest of this chapter.

The problem with RESULT
The first three problems concern what we called Kehler's Hypothesis 2, in (40), repeated below.

(40)   **Kehler's Hypothesis 2 (KH2):**
       Arguments of Humean Cause/Effect and Contiguity relations do not impose constraints on topics.

For Kehler, because topicality is a major constraint on extraction, KH2 implies that Cause/Effect and Contiguity relations do not impose constraints on extraction. However, in Chapter 5, we suggested that RESULT does not allow asymmetric extraction from the final conjunct, citing contrasts like the following.

(62)   a.   What can you [[swallow __] and, as a result, [feel instant euphoria]]?
       b.   What can you [[swallow __] and, as a result, [feel instant euphoria from __]]?
       c.   ??Who did Kharms [[swallow a pill] and, as a result, [feel instant euphoria toward __]]?

If that suggestion is accurate (and, unlike some of what we presented in Chapter 5, it is in line with the received wisdom from Lakoff 1986, Deane 1991, and Kehler 2002), then it is puzzling from the perspective of KH2. On its own, KH2 does not explain why one cannot extract from only the second conjunct with RESULT, because KH2 essentially predicts that anything goes with Cause/Effect relations: by hypothesis, Cause/Effect relations do not impose constraints on topics, so topics can go anywhere, and that means that topicality does not constrain extraction with Cause/Effect relations. That means that the problem with RESULT is simply stated: we expect to be able to extract from any conjunct, so why can't we?

The problem with VIOLATED EXPECTATION

The problem with VIOLATED EXPECTATION, in short, is that it doesn't behave exactly like RESULT. More specifically, Chapter 5 gave (63) as an example of asymmetric extraction from the final conjunct with VIOLATED EXPECTATION, exactly the pattern which we have just claimed to be impossible with RESULT.

(63)   This is an argument that you can [[get blind drunk] and [still understand __]].

This is a surprise from the perspective of KH2, because KH2 implies that these two Cause/Effect relations should be equally unconstrained in terms of the distribution of topical material. Any differences between the two relations would then require a different analysis.

In Section 5.4, we raised several further questions about Lakoff's Type B scenarios and their relation to VIOLATED EXPECTATION. Moreover, SDRT, the theory of discourse structure that we will explore in the following sections, does not have a relation labeled VIOLATED EXPECTATION (as we will see, the nearest match is CONTRAST, whose semantics involve what Asher and Lascarides 2003 describe as 'violation of expectation'). A better statement of this problem is therefore that we do not know what discourse relation is instantiated in Type B scenarios, and we do not know to what extent that relation is responsible for observed extractions, particularly as they differ from Type C scenarios with RESULT.

The problem with OCCASION

OCCASION may initially seem like the most straightforward case to explain in Kehler's terms. KH2 states that OCCASION, as a Contiguity relation, does not impose constraints on the distribution of topical material. This would imply that we can scatter topical material around any conjuncts we like, and extract from any set of conjuncts that suits us. This is essentially Lakoff's characterization of extraction in Type A scenarios, motivated by examples like (64) (again repeated from example (73) in Chapter 5, and lightly modified from Lakoff's own example).

(64)   This is the kind of brandy that you can [[sip __ after dinner], [watch tv for a while], [sip some more of __], [work a bit], [finish __ off], [go to bed], and [enjoy __ again the following evening]].

There are several details of implementation, though, which need attention. Many of these relate to the fact that OCCASION, unlike RESULT and VIOLATED EXPECTATION, allows the creation of *n*-ary coordinate structures. That is, Type A scenarios are not limited to two conjuncts, while Types B and C are. OCCASION, like all discourse relations in Kehler's system, is a binary relation, so an *n*-ary coordinate structure like (64) as analyzed by Kehler could, in principle, involve repeated use of OCCASION to relate ever more complex discourse units.

When one looks at the fine structure of a complex OCCASION example like (64), though, the impression of unified OCCASION structure quickly disappears. The conjuncts without gaps in (64) are all of the type that Deane (1991) calls 'incidental events' (as opposed to 'preparatory actions' or 'scene setters,' which are more clearly related to the topical conjuncts—see discussion in Section 5.4). If one considers the relationship between *work a bit* and *finish [brandy] off*, for instance, there is nothing more than spatiotemporal contiguity. Any sense of a natural course of events disappears when one zooms in, and it is only when one looks at the whole coordinate structure that the coherence emerges. But we claimed throughout Chapter 5 that OCCASION is more than just contiguity.

Deane's purpose in classifying nontopical conjuncts in Type A scenarios is to make it clear that topichood is quite tightly regulated in such coordinate structures. Topical material typically doesn't occur in any of the four categories that Deane identifies (preparatory actions, scene setters, internal causes, and incidental events), and it typically occurs in all other conjuncts. Moreover, once we classify nontopical conjuncts according to Deane's scheme, something of an ATB character emerges in Type A scenarios, in that extraction from Type A scenarios is more acceptable if all topical conjuncts contain gaps (see also many of the structures for Type A scenarios proposed in Neeleman and Tanaka 2020). Indeed, interpolating topical conjuncts without gaps in a complex Type A scenario like (64) is typically degraded, as in (65).

(65)   #This is the kind of brandy that you can [[sip some wine after dinner], [watch tv for a while], [sip some of __], [work a bit], [finish the wine off], [go to bed], and [enjoy __ again the following evening]].

It is hard to say exactly what is wrong with (65). Two natural hypotheses are either that there are not enough topical conjuncts, or that there are topical conjuncts which don't contain gaps. However, on our current understanding of the Kuno/Kehler approach to extraction from coordinate structures, neither of these hypotheses follows from any principle. KH2 states that OCCASION doesn't place constraints on the distribution of topical material, which suggests that 'not enough topical conjuncts' can't be a problem, and Kuno's Topichood Constraint on Extraction states that extracted elements must be topics, not that topical elements must extract.

In short, OCCASION is not as simple as it might look. The patterns of extraction make a good deal of intuitive sense, but there are several respects in which it is not clear that these patterns follow from Kehler's characterization of OCCASION, together with the Topichood Constraint on Extraction.

The problem with PARALLEL *and* CONTRAST

We turn now to a problem related to Kehler's Hypothesis 1, repeated below, which regulates the distribution of topics with Resemblance relations such as PARALLEL and CONTRAST.

(39)   **Kehler's Hypothesis 1 (KH1):**
        Arguments of Humean Resemblance relations have a common topic.

One of the problems just identified for OCCASION also surfaces for these Resemblance relations. KH1 does impose a constraint on topicality with these Resemblance relations: the conjuncts must share a common topic. However, that does not in itself explain why extraction must follow the ATB pattern with these coordinate structures. That is, why is (66a) more acceptable than (66b) or (66c), when they all presumably have the same topic? We doubt that statements about topicality alone will be able to fully account for the ATB requirement with these relations.

(66)   a.   This is a book that [Sue loves __] and [Carol hates __].
        b. ??This is a book that [Sue loves it] and [Carol hates __].
        c.   ?This is a book that [Sue loves __] and [Carol hates it].

The other readings of coordinate structures

Returning to a point we made in Chapters 3 and 5, Lakoff's three scenarios do not exhaust the range of interpretations of coordinate structures with extraction. At least four others have surfaced in our discussions so far: the SLF construction in (67), the 'Type D' scenario from Na and Huck (1992) in (68), the conditional family of interpretations (including 'threat-*or*') in (69), and the examples with ⇒BACKGROUND like (70), discussed in Section 5.4.4 (see (79)), which behave like Type A scenarios but do not fall under the description of OCCASION.

(67)   In den Wald ging der Jäger   und fing   einen Hasen.
        in the forest went the hunter and caught a   hare
        'Into the forest went the hunter and caught a hare.'   (Wunderlich 1988: 289)

(68)   Which baserunner was Doc [[following his coach's instructions] and [keeping __
        close to first]]?   (Na and Huck 1992: 260)

(69)   a. ?This is the loot that [[you just identify __] and [we arrest the thief on the spot]].
        b. ?This is the thief that [[you just identify the loot] and [we arrest __ on the spot]].
                                                      (Culicover and Jackendoff 1997: 206)

(70)   Who did you [[stand in the hallway] and [scream at __]]?

The problem with all of these examples is straightforward: we don't know how they fit. Kehler's taxonomy of discourse relations is fairly brittle, being based on a limited set of manipulations of Hume's three types of association of ideas. A case in point is that it is unclear how the taxonomy applies to the examples just given. Hence, we need to find a way to characterize these examples, without having the list of discourse relations descend into a free-for-all.

How do coordinating conjunctions relate to the Humean taxonomy?

One glaringly incomplete aspect of Kehler's proposal, and in fact all of its precursors in the extraction literature, is that no attention is paid to the discourse relations in which extraction from coordinate structures is impossible a fortiori, because the relations in question cannot be expressed by coordinate structures.

For instance, Section 5.2 reported that Kehler identifies four Resemblance relations in addition to PARALLEL and CONTRAST:

- **Resemblance relations in addition to PARALLEL and CONTRAST**
  EXEMPLIFICATION, GENERALIZATION, EXCEPTION, ELABORATION

Hence, without additional assumptions, KH1 predicts that the four additional Resemblance relations above should give rise to extraction patterns that we see with PARALLEL.

However, these other Resemblance relations are all allergic to *and*, and most are allergic to all coordinating conjunctions. First consider the minimal pairs in (71), from Blakemore and Carston (1999), which differ solely in whether *and* is present:

(71)   ELABORATION
    a. I had a great meal last week. I went to Burger King.
    b. I had a great meal last week and I went to Burger King.

While one infers ELABORATION in (71a), this interpretation is not possible in (71b).[14]

The data below show that no coordinating conjunction can co-occur with EXEMPLIFICATION, GENERALIZATION, or EXCEPTION:

(72)   EXEMPLIFICATION
    a. Emar bought many things at the fish market in Groningen. For example, he bought smoked eel.
    b. ??Emar bought many things at the fish market in Groningen and/or/but, for example, he bought smoked eel.

(73)   GENERALIZATION
    a. Ava owns chihuahuas, Afghan hounds, and terriers. Clearly, she loves dogs.
    b. ??Ava owns chihuahuas, Afghan hounds, and terriers, and/or/but clearly she loves dogs.

Meanwhile, EXCEPTION can be expressed by *but*, but not with *and* or *or*.

(74)   EXCEPTION
    a. Children love to play in the snow after the storm. But today, Jill stayed inside.
    b. ??Children love to play in the snow after the storm. And/or today, Jill stayed inside.

Likewise, KH2 predicts, all else being equal, that all Cause/Effect relations should give rise to extraction patterns like those we see with VIOLATED EXPECTATION and RESULT. There are two other Cause/Effect relations to consider in Kehler's taxonomy, namely DENIAL OF PREVENTER and EXPLANATION, and again, these cannot be expressed by a coordinate structure.

---

[14] The incompatibility of *and* with ELABORATION in (71b) is one reason to believe that the 'Type D' scenarios introduced in example (25) of Chapter 3 cannot harbor ELABORATION, despite initial appearances.

(75)   DENIAL OF PREVENTER[15]

    a.   I hope it does not snow this weekend, even though I love building snowmen.

    b.   ??I hope it does not snow this weekend and/but/or I love building snowmen.

(76)   EXPLANATION

    a.   I broke the vase. I hit it with my elbow.

    b.   ??I broke the vase and/but/or I hit it with my elbow.

In (75b), the discourse is odd; *even though* is required here, as in (75a). The discourse in (76b) with *and* or *but* is interpretable, but not as an instance of EXPLANATION. Rather, OCCASION is salient with *and*, and CONTRAST with *but*.

Nothing in Kehler's analysis, or indeed in any published discourse-calls-the-shots approach to extraction that we know of, has anything to say about these data. Moreover, the observation that *and*, *or*, and *but* are infelicitous with most Humean Resemblance relations undermines KH1 and KH2; it is not clear that the patterns of topicality that Kehler identifies are derived from the Humean Resemblance, Contiguity, and Cause/Effect families of relations, rather than idiosyncratic properties of the specific relations PARALLEL, CONTRAST, OCCASION, RESULT, and VIOLATED EXPECTATION, because many Resemblance relations don't behave like PARALLEL and CONTRAST, and some Cause/Effect relations don't behave like RESULT or VIOLATED EXPECTATION.

In sum, Kehler's hypotheses about links between discourse relations and topicality are clearly along the right lines. However, we are some way from deriving a genuinely explanatory theory of these links, particularly as they apply to coordination, from an approach to discourse structure grounded in Humean principles of idea association.

Summary

We have accumulated quite a list of challenges to Kehler's development of Kuno's ideas about topichood and extraction, but we do not want this to become an exercise in beating up an approach which has real explanatory potential, and in some respects clearly surpasses purely syntactic alternatives in empirical accuracy. We think that the long list of problems just constructed can be boiled down to the following handful of more focused challenges.

1.   Topichood may sometimes condition extraction, but not all extractees are topical. We entertain an approach to this state of affairs which recasts Kuno's notion of topichood in terms of the observations of Pesetsky (1987) and Rizzi (1990), among others, about the special status of referential, or D-linked, noun phrases in extracting from weak islands, aiming to preserve the spirit of Kuno's hypotheses, while rejecting the letter of his analysis. However, the nature of the relationships between D-linking, sentence topic, and locality are not clear (see Choice Point 5), and the links from any of these notions to discourse structure are not yet clear.

2.   KH1 and KH2 do not make many predictions. KH1 gives only a partial account of the ATB requirement with Resemblance relations, where we still need a better understanding of the hypothesized link between topicality and extraction. Meanwhile,

---

[15] Unlike the other relations just considered, DENIAL OF PREVENTER cannot usually be expressed using plain juxtaposition of independent sentences. Rather, a conjunction like *(even) though* is required. The point of interest is the contrast between this conjunction in (75a) and the coordinating conjunctions in (75b).

KH2's only function is to exempt Cause/Effect and Contiguity relations from the ATB requirement. We need to understand the way in which RESULT and OCCASION allow different extraction patterns, and KH2 won't help us.

3. Kehler's Humean taxonomy of discourse relations appears to be a stumbling block, as already suggested in Chapter 5. Not every observed relation fits well in the taxonomy, and if you make them fit, it is often at the cost of less precise or less accurate empirical predictions.

Starting in Section 6.3, we will investigate the predictions of SDRT with respect to discourse structure, information structure, and conjunction. This gives us more ammunition to return to the relationship of all of these factors to extraction, at the end of this chapter.

6.3 SDRT's model of discourse structure

SDRT is a formal, integrated theory of discourse relations. It aims to model: (i) what discourse relations *mean*, and (ii) how discourse structures (modeled as graphs) are constructed. We have surveyed one approach to (i) by considering Kehler's definitions in Chapter 5. However, neither Kehler nor the work he builds on implement discourse relations within a theory of how logical forms of discourses are constructed. SDRT is the best worked out theory that we know of that has this aim.

In this section we spell out the graph-theoretic basics that underlie SDRT's analysis of discourse structure. This will provide the adequate background for Section 6.4, where we discuss constraints imposed by the lexical entries of different coordinating conjunctions. Then, in Section 6.5, we provide a brief overview of the more technical aspects of SDRT, focusing on the treatment of topics and the related notion of 'common theme'.

SDRT models discourse structure as a graph over semantic representations called **discourse representation structures** (DRSs). These representations are of discourse units (DUs), which come in two types: (i) elementary discourse units (EDUs), which are the atoms of a given discourse, and (ii) complex discourse units (CDUs), which are built out of EDUs and may include only two or three EDUs or correspond to several paragraphs or even multiple pages of text. While SDRT does not provide an official definition of EDUs, Afantenos et al. (2012) loosely describe them as 'clauses, appositions, some adverbials,' and mention that 'each EDU contains at least one eventuality description, and often only one.' On this view, a **discourse** is simply two or more EDUs that are connected by edges of a graph. In other words, every discourse (regardless of length) is, simply, a CDU.[16]

In Section 6.3.1, we briefly summarize the logics that build representations of the meaning of CDUs. In Section 6.3.2 we (i) show how these representations imply a representation of discourse structure as a graph with labeled edges, (ii) give definitions of 'coherent' and 'incoherent discourse' in terms of that graph, and (iii) consider the relationship between

---

[16] The idea that a discourse has to describe more than one eventuality (and hence cannot be an EDU) can be ascribed to pioneering work by Labov (1972), who proposed that a narrative discourse must contain at least two clauses (see also discussion in Cumming 2021 and Anand and Toosarvandani forthcoming). Labov was thinking about language here, though recent research has explored the possibility that DUs need not be representations of language; see work by Cumming et al. (2017) on DU segmentation in film and discourse relations that are defined in terms of space, and see Altshuler and Schröder (2021a,b) for an SDRT analysis of pictorial narrative.

those graphs, as discrete objects, and the gradience which is often perceived in interpreting naturally occurring discourses. In Section 6.3.3, we introduce an important structural distinction defined over these graphs, namely between coordinating and subordinating discourse relations.

6.3.1 A brief overview of two component logics

SDRT features two main component logics: (i) **Glue Logic** to construct logical forms, and (ii) **Logic of Information Content** for the truth-conditional semantics of logical forms. Glue Logic is employed in a construction algorithm to pragmatically enrich **underspecified logical forms** (ULFs), which are generated by the syntax and the compositional semantics. The specified ULFs output by the Glue Logic, called **Segmented Discourse Representation Structures** (SDRSs), describe discourse structures. The Logic of Information Content is then used to compute plausible model-theoretic interpretations of the SDRSs. We summarize this schema in Figure 6.1.

In this subsection, we will provide an illustration of the first two components of this schema, following an overview chapter by Lascarides and Asher (2007). Throughout, we will leave many of the formal details aside, and assume some familiarity with the 'box' notation of classical DRT (Kamp 1981, Kamp and Reyle 1993). For those interested in these details, we encourage reading: (i) the original proposal by Asher and Lascarides (2003), (ii) an extended account by Lascarides and Asher (2009), which introduces the 'modern' notation of an SDRS, and (iii) a recent proposal by Altshuler and Schlöder (2019, 2021b) to enrich the SDRT architecture in Figure 6.1 with an additional event-structural layer.

We begin our illustration of the first component of the schema in Figure 6.1 with a language for incomplete descriptions of SDRSs. Lascarides and Asher (2007) call this language 'the Language $\mathcal{L}_{ulf}$ of Semantic Underspecification' and apply it to the following example, which has two truth-conditionally distinct readings, whereby the indefinite *a man* may have wide or narrow scope with respect to the modal *might*. Moreover, without further context, there is no particular antecedent that can be assigned to the pronoun *him*.

(77)   A man might push him.

Assuming, for sake of illustration, two possible antecedents for *him*, z_1 and z_2, there are a total of four *specified* logical forms. Lascarides and Asher provide two of these forms in

Linguistic Forms

are interpreted to

Underspecified Logical Forms   partially describe content

are specified to

SDRSs   describe discourse structure

are evaluated in

Models

Fig. 6.1 The SDRT architecture

(78), where the one on the left corresponds to the indefinite ($\exists$) with widest scope and *him* resolved to z_1, while the one on the right corresponds to *might* with widest scope and *him* resolved to z_2.

(78)

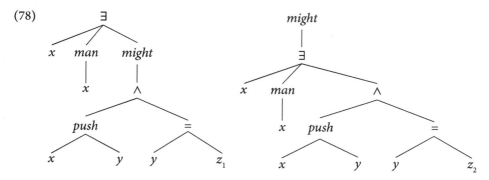

These two trees each correspond to a **model** M of $\mathcal{L}_{ulf}$. We say that a given ULF φ partially describes the unique specified logical form that corresponds to M. For example, the ULF of (77) partially describes one of four possible trees (two of which are in (78)).

To express partial descriptions of such trees, Asher and Lascarides follow Bos (1995) and Asher and Fernando (1997) in assuming that the vocabulary of $\mathcal{L}_{ulf}$ consists of **labels**, which 'tag' bits of the logical form. In particular they pick out nodes in the trees (that correspond to a model of $\mathcal{L}_{ulf}$, e.g. the trees in (78)).

These labels, which Lascarides and Asher represent as l_1, l_2 (taking variable symbols for labels), allow them to treat connectives, predicate symbols, and variables in the specified language of SDRSs (e.g. '$\wedge$', '$=$', 'z_2', '*man*') as predicates over labels in $\mathcal{L}_{ulf}$. Lascarides and Asher (2007: 22) write:

> We can then express partial information about semantic scope by underdetermining the outscopes constraints on labels (in this case, the ULF will underdetermine the relative semantics scopes [sic] of the label that tags $\exists$ and the label that tags *might*). Information about anaphoric conditions amounts to not knowing the value of an SDRS-discourse referent (at least, for pronouns referring to individuals). Discourse referents become *one-place predicates* in $\mathcal{L}_{ulf}$, the argument of the predicate being reserved for the label that tags its position in the 'trees' of the kind shown [in (78)].

Accordingly, the example in (77) would be represented as (79), which (for simplicity) includes the anaphoric condition $x =$? (the '?' showing that the antecedent to x is unknown).[17] The ULF for (77) (in this simplified notation, where labels that don't contribute to the semantic ambiguities are ignored) is in (80), where the curved arrows convey the 'outscopes' conditions.[18]

---

[17] As noted by Lascarides and Asher (2007), this condition is a matter of convenience, adding that 'one should think of "x" and "?" as one-place predicate symbols in $\mathcal{L}_{ulf}$, and one should also bear in mind that this gloss ignores the labels indicating their position in the trees of [(78)]' (ibid., 22).

[18] Note that *outscopes*(l_i, l_j) means that the content that l_i labels has semantic scope over the content that l_j labels. For a more discussion of these conditions, including their formal definitions, see Asher and Lascarides (2003: §4.3).

(79) $l_1: \exists\,(x, man), l_2) \wedge$
    $l_3: might(l_4) \wedge$
    $l_5: \wedge(l_6, l_7) \wedge l_6 : push(x, y) \wedge l_7 : x =? \wedge$
    $outscopes(l_4, l_5) \wedge outscopes(l_2, l_5)$

(80)

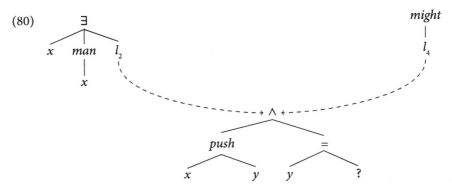

In addition to expressing underspecified conditions for scope and anaphora, $\mathcal{L}_{ulf}$ can also express underspecified information about discourse relations. Lascarides and Asher use '$?(\pi_1, \pi_2, \pi_0)$' to express the information that the DUs π_1 and π_2 are connected by some underspecified discourse relation (as shown by the higher-order variable ?) and this resulting connection is part of the CDU π_0.[19] Lascarides and Asher demonstrate how this is useful for spelling out the compositional semantics of *but*, which entails CONTRAST between two DUs. In particular, they propose that sentence-initial *but* includes the underspecified condition CONTRAST$(?_1, \pi_2, ?_2)$, where π_2 is the top label of the clause that is syntactically outscoped by *but* in the grammar. Lascarides and Asher write: 'This indicates that sentence-initial *but* generates a Contrast relation between the label of a proposition that's not determined by the grammar (although it may be by some other knowledge source) and the label of the proposition denoted by the clause that's syntactically outscoped by *but*, and the label that's assigned to this Contrast connection in the SDRS is also unknown.'

Glue Logic pragmatically enriches ULFs and any model of an enriched ULF is an SDRS. Usually, there won't be a unique SDRS since Glue Logic only accesses ULFs; it has no access to the interpretation of ULFs. It does, however, have access to domain knowledge, the lexicon, and cognitive states. Lascarides and Asher propose that Glue Logic determines the following logically dependent information:[20]

(81)   a.   the (pragmatically preferred) values of certain underspecified conditions that are generated by the grammar;
    b.   which labels are connected to which other labels by a discourse relation;
    c.   the values of the discourse relations.   (Lascarides and Asher 2007: 24)

---

[19] The resulting connection is *part* of the CDU π_0 because π_0 can label multiple discourse relations.

[20] In addition to Glue Logic, Lascarides and Asher propose that a principle of Maximize Discourse Coherence (MDC) helps to determine the information in (81). MDC consists of three sub-principles: (i) all else being equal, the more rhetorical connections there are between two items in a discourse, the more coherent the interpretation, (ii) all else being equal, the more anaphoric expressions whose antecedents are resolved, the higher the quality of coherence of the interpretation, and (iii) all else being equal, an interpretation which maximizes the quality of its discourse relations is more coherent than one that doesn't. We come back to (iii) in the next subsection. For more discussion of (i) and (ii), see Asher and Lascarides (2003).

This information is computed on the basis of inferences over default axioms within the Glue Logic. These axioms are written with a ceteris paribus conditional > that is commonly used in logics of nonmonotonic inference (Asher and Moreau 1991). The idea is that $p > q$ is true if in all circumstances where p holds and these are normal circumstances for p, then q holds.[21] Such axioms express information about pragmatically preferred values of underspecified conditions in a given ULF. Lascarides and Asher (2007: 24) write: 'SDRT thus enriches dynamic semantics with contributions from pragmatics in a constrained way. It's a contribution from pragmatics in that the default axioms are justified on the basis of pragmatic information such as domain knowledge and cognitive states; it's constrained because of its limited access to these information sources.'

Axiom schemata in Glue Logic often take the form in (82), where α, β, and λ are metavariables over **speech act discourse referents** π_1, π_2, and π_3.[22]

(82) $(?(\alpha, \beta, \lambda) \wedge Info(\alpha, \beta, \lambda)) > R(\alpha, \beta, \lambda)$

This says that if: (i) β is to be attached to α with some unspecified discourse relation and the result is labeled λ, and (ii) information $Info(\alpha, \beta, \lambda)$ about α, β, λ, that is transferred into the Glue Logic (from SDRS, the lexicon, domain knowledge, and cognitive states) holds, then normally, the inferred discourse relation is R.[23]

We end this section by considering an instantiation of (82). It involves the discourse relation RESULT:

(83) $(?(\alpha, \beta, \lambda) \wedge cause_D(\alpha, \beta)) > \text{RESULT}(\alpha, \beta, \lambda)$

As we have proposed, RESULT can be inferred when there is evidence in the discourse that α causes β. It is important to note that evidence of a causal relation is distinct from a causal relation's actually holding. The Glue Logic axiom in (83) uses $cause_D(\alpha, \beta)$ to merely express evidence in the discourse of a causal relation. To express that an actual causal discourse relation holds between events, $cause(e_\beta, e_\alpha)$ is used.[24]

Below is a Glue Logic axiom that Lascarides and Asher (2007) provide for inferring $cause_D(\alpha, \beta)$, which can be applied to (85):

(84) $(change(e_\beta, y) \wedge cause.change.force(e_\alpha, x, y)) \rightarrow cause_D(\alpha, \beta)$

(85) π_1: Wonder Woman pushed the awful dude.
       π_2: He fell.

---

[21] We could also express the truth conditions in modal terms. See Asher and Moreau (1991) for more discussion.

[22] These discourse referents are also sometimes called 'labels' and are crucially different from the labels defined earlier in this section. Rather than being defined in terms of ULFs, they are defined in terms of SDRSs. For more discussion of speech-act discourse referents, see Lascarides and Asher (2007: §4).

[23] Lascarides and Asher (2007: 24) stress that $Info(\alpha, \beta, \lambda)$ 'expresses information from rich knowledge sources that contribute to discourse interpretation in a shallow form: for example the discourse content present in SDRSs is transferred into the Glue Logic in a shallow form, as expressed in $\mathcal{L}_{ulf}$.' This 'shallow form' is in contrast to 'deep' truth-conditional/compositional information. Glue Logic is 'shallow' in that it only makes sense of explicit surface information (such as domain knowledge, the lexicon, and cognitive states).

[24] According to Schlöder (2018), given two DUs α and β, if it is possible to infer $cause(e_\alpha, e_\beta)$, then RESULT(α, β). Moreover, if it is possible to infer the inverse, namely $cause(e_\beta, e_\alpha)$, then EXPLANATION(α, β). In other words, if a causal discourse relation can be inferred, it will normally be inferred. See Altshuler (2021) for further discussion.

According to Lascarides and Asher, the lexical semantics of *fall* describes a change in location and the lexical semantics of *push* describes a force that causes a change in location.[25] Thus the information about content that is transferred into the Glue Logic from $\mathcal{L}_{ulf}$ and the lexicon verifies the antecedent of (84), and so the consequent $cause_D(\alpha, \beta)$ is inferred. Now, we know that (π_1, π_2, π_0) holds if we assume that π_2 is connected to π_1 with a discourse relation (i.e. that it is a coherent discourse). Putting these two observations together means that the antecedent to (83) is verified, and so RESULT(π_1, π_2, π_0) is nonmonotonically inferred.

6.3.2 Discourse relations and discourse structure in SDRT

In the SDRSs output by the Glue Logic, the discourse relations holding among DUs constitute a graph, in which the edges connecting DUs are labeled with discourse relations. Hence, in SDRT, a discourse relation holds between two nodes of a graph. In principle, an edge may have several (nonconflicting) labels.[26] For example, (86), repeated from Chapter 5, is understood as harboring both OCCASION and PARALLEL, and includes a cue-phrase for each relation.[27] That is, we understand that (i) Julian and Yu'an engaged in an event of the same kind, and (ii) Yu'an's petting followed Julian's petting as a natural course of events.

(86)   a.   Julian petted his cat.   } OCCASION, PARALLEL
       b.   Then, Yu' an did too.

Analogously, (87) is naturally understood as harboring both EXPLANATION and ⇐BACKGROUND. That is, we naturally understand that (i) the speaker painted the barn *because* it was an ugly brown, and (ii) the speaker's painting event serves as a figure against a ground, which describes an ugly brown barn; the painting event and the state of being brown are understood to overlap.

(87)   a.   I painted the barn.   } EXPLANATION, ⇐ BACKGROUND
       b.   It was an ugly brown.

This graph-theoretic approach to discourse structure is an important innovation of SDRT. We can use it to define coherent and incoherent discourse, by saying that a **coherent discourse** is a CDU whose edges are all labeled, while an **incoherent discourse** is either a disconnected graph or a CDU which contains an unlabeled edge.

This view assumes that SDRSs are discrete objects: either a relation labels an edge or it doesn't. One piece of evidence in favor of this view comes from contrasts in discourses like the following, first discussed in the previous chapter:

(88)   John took a train from Paris to Istanbul.
       a.   ... He has family there.
       b.   ??... He likes spinach.

---

[25] Hence, the change in location doesn't come from the world and it need not even be a fact. It is just something contributed by surface information (here, from the lexicon applied to surface vocabulary).

[26] While SDRT does not specify how many nonconflicting labels are possible, Kamp (2013) suggests that three is the maximum. For an exploration of this question, as well as the question of which discourse relations can be used as nonconflicting labels, see Avery (2019).

[27] In fact, OCCASION is not a discourse relation in SDRT, and (86) is actually taken to harbor NARRATION (in addition to PARALLEL). For now, we continue to use the term OCCASION, from Chapter 5.

(89)   Arash came over to see Akna.
    a.   ... They had lunch.
    b.   ?... He drank a glass of water.

Using the SDRT terminology developed thus far, we would say that (88) + (88a) is a CDU, whose edge is labeled with EXPLANATION: we understand that John took a train from Paris to Istanbul *because* he has family there. What about (88) + (88b)? Despite the oddness of (88b) as a continuation of (88), we nevertheless infer EXPLANATION. We ask: how does liking spinach explain John taking a train from Paris to Istanbul? We do not ask: does liking spinach explain John's taking a train from Paris to Istanbul or does liking spinach result from John's taking a train from Paris to Istanbul? Similarly, there is no question as to what relation holds in (89): OCCASION holds whether we continue with (89a) or (89b). In the case of (89b), we ask why Arash would merely drink a glass of water if his intention was to see Akna.

One question that comes up is why these particular relations are inferred in (88) and (89). This question was briefly discussed in the previous section. Recall that SDRT posits axiom schemata that determine which discourse relation is chosen when there is competing information. For example, Schlöder (2018: 170) proposes that all else being equal it is maximally coherent to interpret a potential causal relation as an actual causal relation (see footnote 24). This axiom alone would explain why we infer EXPLANATION in (88).[28] As for (89), things are more complex as a causal interpretation is not warranted (given world knowledge reasoning). Understanding why OCCASION is typically inferred here involves a full-fledged theory of temporal anaphora in which default axioms interact with grammatical information about tense and aspect (see Webber 1988, Lascarides and Asher 1993, Bary 2009, Kamp et al. 2011, Bittner 2014, Altshuler 2012, 2016, 2021).

In what follows, the main point to take away from (88) and (89) is that a discourse relation either holds between DUs or it doesn't. However, the *acceptability* of a given discourse, assigned a particular structure, is a gradient matter. This gradience has at least two components.[29] First, we will see in Section 6.5 that certain discourse relations have gradient 'quality'. To get an initial feeling for what this entails, consider that both (90) and (91) can be understood as harboring PARALLEL, but (90) is 'more parallel' than (91), by virtue of the fact that (90) contains semantically identical elements (*saw Teia, saw her*) where (91) has similar but different elements (*organized rallies, distributed pamphlets*).[30] PARALLEL still holds in the two cases, but the content of the DUs supports PARALLEL to a greater extent in (90) than in (91). We define this notion of 'support' more precisely in Section 6.5.

(90)   Justin saw Teia and Anna saw her too.

(91)   Dick Gephardt organized rallies for Gore, and Tom Daschle distributed pamphlets
      for him.
                                                              (Kehler 2002: 16)

---

[28] Schlöder's idea is that 'people go places for reasons' is a topos that one is actively applying when trying to make sense of a discourse like (88).

[29] It is very likely that there are more than two sources of gradience related to the assignment of structures to discourses. Processing factors may be a third, although we are unaware of any studies trying to tease processing apart from the considerations in the main text. We thank Alex Lascarides for discussion of the ideas in this passage.

[30] Example (91) was also used as example (26) in Chapter 5.

The second source of gradience is the more slippery notion of the extent to which world knowledge supports a postulated structure. Our understanding of (91) is facilitated by large amounts of background knowledge: Al Gore is a former presidential candidate, presidential candidates need to orchestrate electoral campaigns, and rallies and pamphlets are typical components of such campaigns. People with long memories for less prominent American politicians may recognize Gephardt and Daschle as Democrats (members of Gore's party) in positions of power around 2000 (the year of Gore's most recent presidential campaign). All of this knowledge is important in helping interlocutors to see that the parallelism in (91) extends beyond 'NP1 VP1 for Gore, and NP2 VP2 for him'. The same would not be true of a superficially similar example like (92), which does not have the same coherence of script. Again, the parallelism (though still perceivable) is less well-supported as a result.

(92)   Dick Gephardt organized rallies for Gore, and Richard Sullivan drew pictures of him.

A more involved example of the same kind of interaction between linguistic structure, world knowledge, and gradient quality of discourse relation can be found in (93) and (94), due to Julian Schlöder (pers. comm.).

(93)   I was looking for John by the river. But I found him at the bank.

(94)   I was looking for John by the river. I found him at the bank.

In (93), *but* cues CONTRAST, which drives an ambiguity resolution strategy whereby we understand *the bank* to pick out a financial institution (because 'riverbank' doesn't contrast with 'river'). Moreover, OCCASION holds in addition to CONTRAST, as we understand that the looking led to the finding, a narrative progression. In (94), without *but*, we only infer OCCASION, and not CONTRAST. Our default understanding of *the bank* in (94) is as a riverbank. While it is much harder to understand *the bank* as picking out a financial institution, it could be resolved in this way if, say, there is a financial institution by the river.

Hence, what is at stake is not what discourse relation holds. Rather, what is at stake is what resolution leads to a *better* OCCASION. Without more context, a better OCCASION is one in which *the bank* is resolved to a riverbank. We will return, again, to what makes this resolution 'better' in Section 6.5.

6.3.3 Coordinating and subordinating discourse relations

A property of SDRT which will assume central importance when we return to coordinate structures is the distinction between two classes of discourse relations in their representations of discourse structure: a vertical edge represents a **subordinating** discourse relation, while a horizontal edge represents a **coordinating** discourse relation.

Example (95), from Altshuler and Schlöder (2019), provides an intuitive way of illustrating this distinction: coordinating relations change the scene, and hence *move forward* the narrative (see the horizontal move below), while subordinating relations detail the scene, and thereby *deepen* the narrative (see the vertical move below):

(95) *There were three circles.*   *Later, there were three squares.*

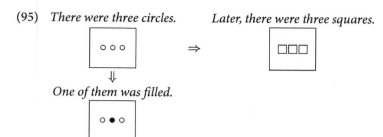

One of them was filled.

Below is a literary discourse which mostly exemplifies subordinating relations (see (96a)), before ending with coordinating relations (see (96b)):

(96)   'Blue notebook No. 10' (from *Today I Wrote Nothing* by Daniil Kharms; translated by Matvej Yankelevich)

   a. Once there was a redheaded man without eyes and without ears. He had no hair either, so that he was a redhead was just something they said. He could not speak, for he had no mouth. He had no nose either. He didn't even have arms or legs. He had no stomach either, and he had no back, and he had no spine, and no intestines of any kind. He didn't have anything at all.

   b. So it is hard to understand whom we are really talking about. So it is probably best not to talk about him any more.

In (96a), details of an alleged, redheaded man are provided. In particular, we see a series of instances of ELABORATION, which is the quintessential subordinating relation (Asher 1993, Asher and Lascarides 2003, Asher and Vieu 2005). The effect of establishing this relation again and again is to detail all the properties that are missing of the alleged man. Once there is nothing left to detail, the discourse moves forward in (96b), which evaluates the alleged man who can no longer be seen as a man. With the information that (96) was written in Leningrad during the Great Terror, when Stalin's purges were at their height and people were 'disappearing,' the reader appreciates the absurd duality that the subordinating discourse moves create: a funny depiction of an alleged man on the one hand, and a tragic disappearance of the same man on the other.

   Let us now consider a discourse by the same author, during the same time period, but now with a series of coordinating discourse relations:

(97)   'Hunger' (from *Today I Wrote Nothing* by Daniil Kharms; translated by Matvej Yankelevich)

   In the morning you wake lively,
   Then weakness,
   Then boredom,
   Then comes the loss
   Of quick reason's strength –
   Then comes calm,
   And then horror.

Here we are constantly asked to imagine new scenes in a quick succession. The temporal demonstrative *then* cues OCCASION, which—along with RESULT—is the quintessential coordinating relation (Asher 1993, Asher and Lascarides 2003, Asher and Vieu 2005). To appreciate the power of establishing OCCASION in this poem, consider the slightly altered version below, without the temporal cues:

(98)   In the morning you wake,
       weakness,
       boredom,
       the loss
       of quick reason's strength –
       calm,
       horror.

Here it is possible to understand that the event of waking serves as the figure, and the various feelings described serve as the ground, although the reader may also perhaps infer a temporal succession between some of these feelings. That is, it is possible to infer a series of ⇐BACKGROUNDs in (98), possibly interspersed with instances of OCCASION. Unlike OCCASION, ⇐BACKGROUND is a subordinating relation (Asher and Lascarides 2003, Asher et al. 2007).

While also powerful—highlighting the complexity and contradictory nature of hunger— (98) does not speak to the ever-changing nature of hunger (at least not to the same extent that (97) does); the evolution of feelings that end in sheer horror. (97) achieves this by establishing a series of coordinating moves through OCCASION, all cued by *then*.

The distinction between coordination and subordination is often visible in patterns of anaphora resolution, and resolution of third-person pronouns in particular. Since coordinating discourse relations change the scene while subordinating discourse relations deepen the description of the scene, only subordination keeps the things we talk about around, and hence available for anaphora. Put differently, we cannot detail scenes that have been changed. Hence, coordinating discourse moves block accessibility for anaphora. This blocking effect is usually described in graph-theoretic terms: the anaphora-accessible referents are on the rightmost branch of the graph. This generalization is known as the **Right Frontier Constraint** (Polanyi 1985, 1988), which amounts in informal terms to 'look left one step only or look up'. Or, more formally:

(99)   Right Frontier Constraint: Let Δ be a discourse structure with α the current DU. A new DU β can be attached to a DU γ in Δ iff (a) or (b) holds:
       a. $\gamma = \alpha$;
       b. α is connected to γ by at least one subordinating discourse relation.

Assume that a new DU β contains an anaphoric expression whose antecedent is in γ. If (a) or (b) holds, then the resolution is predicted to be possible because β can attach to γ. However, if neither (a) nor (b) holds, the resolution is predicted not to be possible because β will have to attach to some other DU that is not on the Right Frontier.[31]

Let's consider a concrete example:

(100)   a. John dropped off his car for repairs.
         b. Then he got a rental.

$$\pi_a \xrightarrow{\text{OCCASION}} \pi_b$$

---

[31] For other characterizations of the Right Frontier, see Asher (1993: 302–3), Asher and Lascarides (2003: 118). For more recent discussion, see Hunter and Thompson (forthcoming).

Here we infer OCCASION, cued by *then*. Notice that only π_b is on the right edge of the graph. This is because we have changed the scene from π_a to π_b by coordinating with OCCASION. As such, *it* in (101c) can only refer to the rental car described in (101b), and not John's car described in (101a), which would be a more likely interpretation given world knowledge. That is, rather than understanding John to have gotten a rental because it had a broken fuel pump, we understand John to have gotten a damaged rental car.

(101)   a. John dropped off his car for repairs.
        b. Then he got a rental.
        c. It had a broken fuel pump.

The graph representation below makes it clear how the Right Frontier Constraint ensures that (101) receives this less likely interpretation. π_c attaches to π_b with ELABORATION and not to π_a with EXPLANATION, because only π_b is on the rightmost branch of the graph. As such, *it* is resolved to the rental, and not John's car.[32]

(102)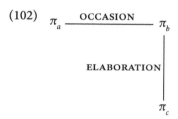

In sum, if π_b is a coordinating discourse move from π_a, then one can continue by either co-ordinating or subordinating from π_b, but not π_a. If, on the other hand, π_b is a subordinating discourse move from π_a, then two kinds of continuations are possible:

- we can continue the subordinating discourse move by either subordinating or coordinating on π_b;
- we can go back to π_a and either coordinate (providing a new scene) or subordinate (detailing π_a further).

These two possibilities are displayed in (103) and (104),[33] which we consider in turn.

(103)   [Arash doesn't trust Akna](π_1) because [she lied to him once](π_2) and [it was about something really important](π_3).

(104)   [Arash doesn't trust Akna](π_1) because [she lied to him once](π_2), so [he's not going to let her babysit his kids](π_3).

In (103) we have two subordinating discourse moves, namely EXPLANATION(π_1, π_2) and ELABORATION(π_2, π_3):

---

[32] Unlike third-person pronouns, definite descriptions and demonstratives can sometimes override the Right Frontier Constraint owing to the way they accommodate presuppositions. The accommodation is sometimes cued by phrases like *by the way*.

(i)   a. John dropped off his car for repairs.
      b. Then he got a rental.
      c. The car had a broken fuel pump (by the way).

[33] These examples come from Julie Hunter (pers. comm.).

(105) π_1

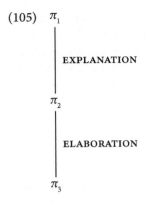

Let us now consider (104). Here we have a coordinating discourse move RESULT(π_1, π_3), in addition to the subordinating discourse move EXPLANATION(π_1, π_2) that we saw in (103):[34]

(106)

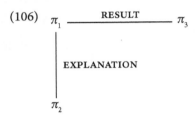

In fact, there is nothing preventing us from combining these two structures, by elaborating on π_2 and then returning to π_1, because π_1 (along with π_2) is on the Right Frontier. This is illustrated in (107) and the graph representation in (108).[35]

(107)   [Arash doesn't trust Akna](π_1) because [she lied to him once](π_2) and [it was about something really important](π_3). So [he's not going to let her babysit his kids](π_4).

(108)

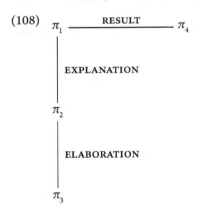

---

[34] One may also analyze this discourse by saying that the first argument of RESULT is a CDU that consists of π_1 and π_2. The discussion that follows does not rest on this choice.

[35] The Right Frontier Constraint also predicts that we can coordinate π_4 from π_2. This prediction is borne out in (i):

(i)   Arash doesn't trust Akna because she lied to him once and it was about something really important. Weeks later, she apologized but it was too late.

In contrast, we cannot start with (104), as diagrammed in (106), and then elaborate on π_2. The reason is that nothing other than π_3 is accessible, because of the coordinating discourse move that introduces π_3. That is, only π_3 is on the Right Frontier. As such, the continuation in π_4 below is infelicitous; we cannot resolve *it* to the lie described by π_2. Doing so would violate the Right Frontier Constraint.

(109)   [Arash doesn't trust Akna](π_1) because [she lied to him once](π_2). So [he's not going to let her babysit his kids](π_3). [??It was about something really important](π_4).

In sum, we have motivated a distinction between discourse coordination and subordination though intuitive semantic features ('changing/detailing the scene') and in terms of a linguistic diagnostic, namely anaphora resolution of third-person pronouns, which is sensitive to the Right Frontier Constraint.[36] There have been many other characterizations of this dichotomy, usually in terms of semantic features (Asher 1993, van Kuppevelt 1995, Asher and Vieu 2005, Jasinskaja and Karagjosova 2020).

We will now consider the structural properties of each of the discourse relations that feature in the extraction patterns that we considered in Chapter 5. We have already considered OCCASION and RESULT, concluding that they are coordinating (see (100a) and (109) respectively). Moreover, we considered ⇐BACKGROUND in connection with (98), claiming that it was subordinating based on intuitive semantic features. The discourse in (110) shows that we reach the same conclusion when we consider anaphora resolution contexts:[37]

(110)   [During her lunch break, Ava bought a whole fish](π_1). [She always buys the catch of the day from the Covered Market](π_2). [When she got home, she scaled, gutted, breaded, and fried it for dinner](π_3).

---

[36] Below is the so-called 'salmon example' that is often used to motivate the coordination/subordination dichotomy through anaphora resolution. Examples (if) and (ig) are both intended to be continuations of (ie).

(i)   a. John had a great evening last night.
      b. He had a great meal.
      c. He ate salmon.
      d. He devoured lots of cheese.
      e. He then won a dancing competition ...
      f. ?... Then he had a great dessert.
      g. ??... It was a beautiful pink.   (Asher and Lascarides 2003)

The continuation in (if) is pragmatically deviant insofar as people typically eat dessert after their main course and not after a dancing competition. We are forced to attach (if) to (ie) rather than (id) because (ie), but not (id), is on the Right Frontier. This is so because (ie) attaches to (ib) via OCCASION. The continuation in (ig) is more clearly odd because we cannot resolve the third-person pronoun to the salmon described in (ic). Once again, the reason why we cannot attach (ig) to (ic) is that the latter is not on the Right Frontier (for the same reason that (id) is not on the Right Frontier). Finally, note that changing the third-person pronoun in (ig) to *the salmon* or *that salmon* improves the continuation slightly; also adding *by the way* makes the continuation perfectly acceptable. This is a further illustration of the phenomenon described in footnote 32.

[37] Quite surprisingly, Asher and Lascarides (2003: 166) take ⇐BACKGROUND to be a coordinating relation, albeit a *complex* one; complex because it only 'acts' like a subordinating relation with respect to the tests just noted. However, this position is based on an earlier version of SDRT (Asher 1993), and has since then been revised (see Asher et al. 2007). In what follows, we will assume—following the current line of thinking—that ⇐BACKGROUND is in fact a subordinating discourse relation, as our tests indicate. The reason ⇐BACKGROUND 'acts' this way, according to Asher (1993), is that it factors in the construction of a topic that is unlike that of any other discourse relation. We will discuss topic construction in relation to ⇐BACKGROUND and other discourse relations in Section 6.5, where we will see that topicality is neither a necessary nor a sufficient condition for coordinating discourse relations.

It is quite easy to resolve *it* to the fish in (110). If we assume $\Leftarrow$BACKGROUND(π_1, π_2) and take $\Leftarrow$BACKGROUND to be a subordinating relation, then we can attach π_3 to π_1:

(111)   No violation of the Right Frontier Constraint:

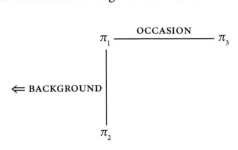

As for the other BACKGROUND, Asher and Lascarides (2003: 208) write: 'On the other hand, Background$_2$ [i.e. $\Rightarrow$BACKGROUND] seems to be a simple coordinating relation.' The discourse below provides evidence for this view.[38]

(112)   [Ava lay on a new couch](π_1). [Teia turned to look at her](π_2). [??It was upholstered in soft Bandero grey microfiber](π_3).

Here, we cannot easily resolve *it* to the couch, despite the fact that the couch was the only inanimate object mentioned in prior discourse. If we assume $\Rightarrow$BACKGROUND(π_1, π_2) and take $\Rightarrow$BACKGROUND to be a coordinating relation, then we cannot attach π_3 to π_1. Doing so would violate the Right Frontier Constraint:

(113)   Violation of the Right Frontier Constraint:

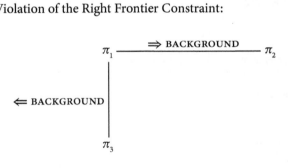

A similar point can be made about (114), where we cannot easily resolve *it* to 'the road,' despite the fact that the road was the only inanimate object mentioned in prior discourse. Again, this is expected if we assume $\Rightarrow$BACKGROUND(π_1, π_2) and take $\Rightarrow$BACKGROUND to be a coordinating relation.

(114)   [Raindrops were falling on the road](π_1). [Suzo began her long walk back](π_2). [??It was made of cobblestones](π_3).

PARALLEL and CONTRAST also pattern with coordinating discourse relations (Asher 1993, Asher and Lascarides 2003, Asher and Vieu 2005). The discourses in (115) and (116)

---

[38] Example (112) is based on an example from Alex Lascarides (pers. comm.), discussed in footnote 39 of Chapter 5.

provide evidence for this view with respect to PARALLEL, while (117) and (118) provide evidence for this view with respect to CONTRAST.[39]

(115)   [Ava lay on a new couch](π_1). [Justin did too](π_2). [??She was tired from the long day](π_3).

(116)   [Suzo saw Lev](π_1). [She also saw Dina, Anna, Ava, and Teia](π_2). [??But he was the only one to notice her](π_3).

(117)   [Ava lay on a new couch](π_1). [Justin did not](π_2). [??She was tired from the long day](π_3).

(118)   [Suzo saw Lev](π_1). [She did not see Dina, Anna, Ava, and Teia](π_2). [??He was the only one to notice her](π_3).

In (115) and (117) we cannot easily resolve *she* to Ava despite the fact that Ava was the only female individual mentioned in prior discourse.[40] Similarly, in (116) and (118), we cannot easily resolve *he* to Lev despite the fact that Lev was the only male individual mentioned in prior discourse. These observations are expected if we assume that PARALLEL and CONTRAST are coordinating relations.

Below, we summarize our assumptions about which discourse relations are coordinating and which are subordinating. In addition to the coordinating discourse relations already discussed, we also include CONTINUATION, which is another prototypical coordinating relation (Asher and Lascarides 2003, Asher and Vieu 2005), to be defined in Section 6.5. Moreover, in addition to ⇐BACKGROUND, we include ELABORATION and EXPLANATION, which are prototypical subordinating discourse relations (Asher and Lascarides 2003, Asher and Vieu 2005).

- **Coordinating relations**:
  RESULT, OCCASION, PARALLEL, CONTRAST, CONTINUATION, ⇒BACKGROUND

- **Subordinating relations**:
  ELABORATION, EXPLANATION, ⇐BACKGROUND

These distinctions will play a vital role in Section 6.4, where we make sense of *and*'s discourse-structural properties, and again in Section 6.6, where we attempt to make sense of the extraction data that we considered in Chapter 5 through the lens of SDRT.

It is important to keep this structural distinction between coordination and subordination separate from the distinction between symmetrical and asymmetrical coordination discussed at several points in this survey. Many authors have used 'subordination' and 'coordination' to describe various forms of what we have called asymmetry and symmetry. Deane (1991), following Hobbs (1979, 1985), Mann and Thompson (1986), view subordination and coordination in terms of functional symmetry: if the segments linked are on an equal footing, they are coordinated; if there is an asymmetry between them, one is

---

[39] Example (116) becomes acceptable if *he* and *her* are pronounced with contrastive stress, for reasons that are not clear to us.

[40] As noted by Martin Van Den Berg (pers. comm.), (115) is OK with focal stress on *she*, and an additional conjunct such as *but he just wanted to see how it felt*, which would attach to π_3 via CONTRAST and form a CDU. For a discussion of how focal stress affects discourse structure and anaphora resolution, see Schlöder and Lascarides (2020).

subordinate (in Deane's terms) to the other. Culicover and Jackendoff (1997: 196) discuss 'left-subordinating *and*,' where the initial conjunct 'functions semantically as if it were a subordinate clause.' Other notable claims about semantic asymmetry include Bar-Lev and Palacas's (1980) claim that *P and Q* is asymmetric in that *Q* must not temporally precede *P*, and the idea noted in Chapter 2 that 'asymmetric' conjunction describes those cases in which *P and Q* is not truth-conditionally equivalent to *Q and P*.

In what follows, we treat all of these distinctions as cases of semantic asymmetry, while reserving the term 'subordination' for the SDRT sense, which is quite independent. A case in point is OCCASION, which is coordinating in SDRT. However, *P and Q*, interpreted as harboring OCCASION, is asymmetric in many of the senses we have given: it is truth-conditionally distinct from *Q and P*, and it is subordinating according to Deane (1991) notion of functional asymmetry. Although we have been exploring the connection between 'asymmetric interpretation' and asymmetric extraction patterns at some length, this notion must be kept apart from SDRT's subordination/coordination distinction. It will become apparent in Section 6.4 that the latter distinction plays an important role in a general characterization of the semantics of *and*.

In sum, this section has outlined those core properties of SDRT which allow us to make sense of discourse-structural properties of discourse relations. We refer the reader to Asher and Lascarides (2003), Lascarides and Asher (2009), Hunter et al. (2018), Altshuler and Schlöder (2019) for further information on aspects of SDRT not discussed here. In the next section, we consider the relationship of *and* to this conception of discourse structure.

6.4 The discourse semantics of conjunctions

In this section, we discuss claims made within the SDRT framework about the effects of coordinating conjunctions on discourse structure. We begin in Section 6.4.1 with the striking claim that *and* requires its conjuncts to be related by a coordinating discourse relation (Txurruka 2003). This claim has the potential to explain why many discourse relations simply cannot be expressed by *and*, which directly addresses one of the challenges for Kehler's account identified in Section 6.2.4. As such, to the extent that the claim is accurate, it constitutes a strong motivation for an SDRT approach to the discourse semantics of *and*.

Moreover, Txurruka's claim may be able to simultaneously explain why *and* is so flexible with respect to the interpretation of its conjuncts, within the limitations imposed by the restriction to coordinating relations. This constrained flexibility fits well with research like that inspired by Lakoff, in which a small set of interpretations of *and* are identified, and this small set is treated as representative. The literature on extraction from coordinate structures has focused to a large extent on *and*, probably for this reason. In contrast, *but* and *or* have more tightly constrained semantic ranges. According to Asher and Lascarides (2003), among others, *but* is a cue-phrase for the discourse relation CONTRAST (because CONTRAST is a coordinating relation, this implies that *but* is appropriate in a proper subset of the cases in which *and* is appropriate), while Asher (2004) adopts an analysis of *or* as a cue-phrase for ALTERNATION (also a coordinating relation), whose arguments are 'epistemic alternatives'. In Section 6.4.2 we briefly cover the discourse semantics of *or* and *but*.[41]

---

[41] To our knowledge, conjunctions in other languages have not been investigated in SDRT to the same extent as these three English conjunctions (see Jasinskaja and Karagjosova 2020: §2.2.3 for discussion). One notable exception is the work on the Russian conjunctions *i* and *a* by Jasinskaja (2010).

6.4.1 *And* as a marker of discourse coordination

In Chapter 2, we described two kinds of approaches to the semantics of *and*: 'meaning-minimalist' approaches, such as that of Grice (1975), according to which the meaning of *and* is semantically equivalent to logical conjunction and more specific interpretations arise as implicatures; and 'meaning-maximalist' approaches exemplified by the claim that *and* is temporally loaded (Bar-Lev and Palacas 1980). Txurruka's (2003) approach is intermediate in a sense: it is not strictly meaning-minimalist in that the semantics that she provides for *and* is richer than logical conjunction, but it is only a little richer, and doesn't carry anything like the specific temporal entailments that Bar-Lev and Palacas attribute to *and*. Rather, Txurruka claims that *and* signals that its conjuncts are related by a coordinating discourse relation. The different interpretations sometimes ascribed to *and* are then analyzed as epiphenomena of the establishment of certain discourse relations.

Let us consider these three different approaches in more detail. We begin with the data below, from Txurruka (2003), which are examples of narrative progression:

(119)   Mary put on her tutu and (she) pruned the apple tree.

(120)   Bill went to bed and (he) took off his shoes.

The key question is whether the understood narrative progression is tied to the meaning of *and*. Grice (1975) famously argued that we can maintain *and* as being semantically equivalent to logical conjunction if we invoke the **Maxim of Manner**: be as clear, brief, and orderly as possible. The most orderly way to represent the temporal order of eventualities is by reflecting it iconically in the temporal order of the sentences that describe them.

This view was further motivated by Blakemore and Carston (1999), who consider the example below, from Kempson (1975), which is a bizarre case of narrative progression:

(121)   She [[rode into the sunset] and [jumped on her horse]].

Here we are we forced to imagine a bizarre scenario, e.g. one in which an individual was riding on a train that was headed toward the setting sun and then, from the train, this individual jumped on to her (moving) horse. Why are we forced to imagine such a bizarre scenario? One possibility, proposed by Blakemore and Carston (1999), is that in the absence of any highly accessible scheme or script, the hearer will 'tend to take the natural processing track, that is, the chronological one.' This principle as it applies in the *and*-case would be a special case of a general principle for interpreting juxtaposed sentences, and would be a way to save the meaning-minimalist, Gricean view of *and*.

Another possibility is to reject the Gricean view. According to Bar-Lev and Palacas (1980), the meaning of *and* is temporally loaded: *and* disallows narrative regression, while allowing narrative progression (as in the examples discussed) and temporal overlap, as in (122):

(122)   [[He walked into the room] and [the director was slumped in her chair]].

(Dowty 1986)

On this meaning-maximalist view, the fact that (121) forces such a bizarre interpretation is a matter of the temporally loaded lexical semantics of *and*, rather than Gricean pragmatics.

Txurruka (2003) follows Bar-Lev and Palacas (1980) in rejecting the Gricean view, but proposes that the impossibility of narrative regression with *and* is an epiphenomenon of the discourse relations established: *and* is not temporally loaded, but selects for certain discourse relations. For example, Txurruka argues that coordinate structures with *and* are sometimes interpreted as instances of OCCASION, and in those cases we infer narrative progression *because* we establish OCCASION.

To motivate her claim, Txurruka provides the discourse below, which serves as a minimal pair to (119) above:

(123)   [[Mary put on her tutu] and [Melissa pruned the apple tree]].

(123) differs from (119) solely in that Mary is no longer the agent of the tree-pruning event. However, there is a second, less obvious difference in how we interpret (123): we can now infer any temporal relation we like between the two eventualities described. It is even possible for the tree-pruning to have preceded the tutu-wearing.

This change in temporal order is challenging to Bar-Lev and Palacas (1980), because it speaks against their claim that *and* is temporally loaded. However, it correlates with a change in discourse structure: in (123), OCCASION is no longer inferred; a weaker relation, CONTINUATION, is inferred instead. We will introduce CONTINUATION in Section 6.5, but the important point in connection to (123) is that it does not impose the same temporal constraints as OCCASION. Rather, the two events described could be understood to overlap, or precede one another (in either direction). This observation drives Txurruka's point that if we have an adequate theory of discourse relations, the temporal inferences will fall out. Clearly, *and* is robust in cases of narrative progression, i.e. with OCCASION, and in cases where there are no constraints on temporal order, e.g. with CONTINUATION.

Similarly, as we already saw in Chapter 5, RESULT and PARALLEL are also natural with *and*. Below are two examples, taken from Section 5.3.1 (see (23) and (24) there), which exemplify these two discourse relations respectively; RESULT triggers a narrative progression in (124), while PARALLEL imposes no temporal constraints in (125).

(124)   [[Teia asked for this problem to be looked into], and so, [Ava did]].

(125)   [[Teia looked into this problem] and [Ava did too]].

What all these relations (OCCASION, CONTINUATION, RESULT, and PARALLEL) have in common is that they are coordinating. This is not accidental, according to Txurruka, but rather reflects the key property of *and*: if *and* joins two discourse units π_1, π_2, it signals that those discourse units are joined by a coordinating discourse relation.

As an indication of what this rules out, recall the contrast below, from Section 6.2.2:

(126)   a. I broke the vase. I hit it with my elbow.
         b. I [[broke the vase] and [hit it with my elbow]].

In (126a), EXPLANATION is salient. However, once we add *and*, as in (126b), OCCASION becomes salient despite what world knowledge reasoning suggests.

Let us now reconsider the discourse in (121), repeated below:

(121)   She [[rode into the sunset] and [jumped on her horse]].

Recall that OCCASION holds here despite the fact that one is forced to imagine an unlikely scenario. According to Txurruka, this is so because, once again, subordinating discourse relations which entail temporal simultaneity, inclusion, and overlap are ruled out.[42]

Let us now consider a case where temporal overlap is favored by world knowledge. An obvious case involves ELABORATION, which entails that its second argument provides more information about an event described by the first argument (e.g. by providing more information about the thematic structure). Recall the examples below, from Section 6.2.2, which differ solely in the presence of *and* in (127b):

(127)   a. I had a great meal last week. I went to Burger King.
        b. [[I had a great meal last week] and [I went to Burger King]].

One infers ELABORATION in (127a), while in (127b), ELABORATION is not possible; only a coordinating relation can be inferred (e.g. OCCASION, PARALLEL, and/or CONTINUATION). That *and* biases us to ditch ELABORATION (a subordinating relation) in favor of a coordinating relation is, of course, expected on Txurruka's proposal.

Now consider the contrast in (128a) and (128b), which was also mentioned in Section 6.2.2. In both examples, we see the phrase *for example*, which entails the subordinating relation EXEMPLIFICATION.[43] And, as expected on Txurruka's proposal, (128b) is odd because the semantic requirements of *for example* clash with the semantic requirements of *and*.

(128)   a. Emar bought many things at the fish market in Groningen. For example, he
           bought smoked eel.
        b. ??[[Emar bought many things at the fish market in Groningen] and, for example,
           [he bought smoked eel]].

Finally, consider (129a) and (129b):

(129)   a. Justin plays the trumpet. Ava does too.
        b. [[Justin plays the trumpet] and [Ava does too]].

These examples are truth-conditionally equivalent. This is so, despite the fact that only (129b) contains *and*. This is expected on Txurruka's proposal since (129) exemplifies the coordinating discourse relation, PARALLEL, which, as we have seen, *and* has an affinity for.

In sum, Txurruka's proposal is able to explain our intuitions about *and* in a wide array of discourse contexts. In particular, we have seen that *and*'s affinity for coordinating discourse relations explains the key examples that fuel both 'meaning-minimalist' approaches and 'meaning-maximalist' approaches. We think this is an important result and in what follows, assume that Txurruka's approach to the meaning of *and* is correct. We end this subsection by considering data which Txurruka's account cannot explain without additional

---

[42] Coordinating relations which do not force temporal progression, such as PARALLEL and CONTINUATION, are of course possible with (121). This is what explains the interpretability of *She rode into the sunset and jumped on her horse at the same time!* However, interpreting such a discourse requires even more unlikely scenarios than those conjured up by (121). We assume that that is ultimately why (121) is interpreted as an unlikely OCCASION rather than an unlikely PARALLEL: again, gradient factors concerning quality of support for a postulated discourse relation are at play.

[43] In SDRT, EXEMPLIFICATION is often thought of as a special case of ELABORATION. Regardless of the name, the discourse relation is clearly subordinating.

assumptions. Below we review some of these data, describing Txurruka's proposal for addressing them, and offering suggestions for future research.

Apparent subordinating relations with and

Txurruka notes that there are examples in which *and* appears to co-occur with subordinating discourse relations. Our assessment of this challenge is that it is unlikely to seriously undermine Txurruka's hypothesis, but nonetheless merits further investigation as a potentially rich source of information about complex interactions of subordinating and coordinating relations.

We focus on examples involving EXPLANATION and ⇐BACKGROUND. Consider the minimal pair below, differing solely in whether *and* is present:

(130) a. Anna fell; she slipped on a banana peel.
        b. [[Anna fell], and [she slipped on a banana peel]].

What is surprising, given the data and generalizations given in this subsection, is that in certain contexts, both (130a) and (130b) are understood as describing the cause for Anna's fall. That is, both seem to exemplify EXPLANATION, which Txurruka (2003: 267) assumes to be subordinating, following the standard view in SDRT (Asher and Vieu 2005). For instance, Txurruka considers the discourse below:

(131) If Max fell, and he slipped on a banana peel, and his slipping explains his falling, we don't need to resort to any esoteric or voodoo-related explanation to understand what happened.

In contrast, examples like (132), without such contextual support, do not harbor EXPLANATION. Rather, we understand that Anna was the patient of two unfortunate eventualities that are not causally related.

(132) a. What happened to Anna today?
        b. She fell, and she slipped on a banana peel.

Txurruka addresses this seeming counterexample by claiming that in (131) the interpreter infers only nonmonotonically that the speaker is communicating that the slipping event explains the falling event. Txurruka maintains that at the truth-conditional level, a coordinating relation is being asserted.

Txurruka's (2003) DRS for the antecedent of the conditional in (131) is replicated in (133). The three inner DRSs correspond to the three conjuncts in the antecedent. The conditions in these DRSs include familiar predicates like 'Max' and 'fall', as well as temporal conditions, e.g. 'holds(e, t)', which says that the run time of the event holds at an interval t, and 't < now', which ensures that this time is prior to the time of utterance. The truth conditions require that the event e is a past falling event by Max, the event e_1 is a past slipping event by Max,[44] and finally, the two past events of slipping and falling are such that the former explains the latter. Finally, in the global DRS, i.e. the outermost box, we see two further conditions that ensure that each conjunct is related by a coordinator.

---

[44] To ensure that the second conjunct is about Max, we would have to say more about anaphora resolution. As discussed in Chapter 5, anaphora resolution and the establishment of discourse relations are mutually constraining tasks.

(133)

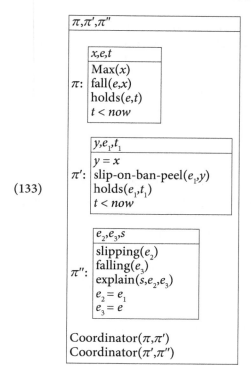

Txurruka's argument is that the predicate *explains*, by virtue of its semantics, constrains the temporal relation between the falling and the slipping. Without it, as in (130b), Txurruka claims that there is no assertion about the temporal ordering. In other words, (130b) does not require a relation of EXPLANATION between the conjuncts, but certain broader contexts, like that in (131), may lead us to construe the relationship between the two conjuncts of (130b) as one of explanation, with the associated temporal constraints.

Txurruka talks about such examples as 'implicating' EXPLANATION. However, this raises several questions. The first concerns the soundness of the assumption that you can assert a coordinating discourse relation while implicating a subordinating discourse relation.[45] This assumption is especially surprising given the principle in (134), which Txurruka (2003: 267) endorses:

(134)   *Incompatibility of Coordinators and Subordinators*
         Coordinator$(\pi, \pi') \rightarrow \neg$Subordinator$(\pi, \pi')$

This principle is foundational in SDRT (Altshuler and Schlöder 2021a). Since an edge cannot be horizontal and vertical simultaneously, we would not be able to construct an SDRT graph of a discourse that exemplifies a subordinating and a coordinating discourse relation simultaneously. And we cannot imply a discourse relation unless we also imply its structural properties; these are an integral part of a discourse relation.

---

[45] Unfortunately, Txurruka does not state what coordinating discourse relation is involved in (130b). It is hard to think what coordinating discourse relation could be asserted in this example, though the most likely candidate is CONTINUATION, discussed briefly earlier in this subsection and in more depth in Section 6.5.

As such, what Txurruka must really mean when she says 'implicate a subordinating relation ρ_2 with the use of a coordinating relation ρ_1 (or vice versa)' is more that we pragmatically enrich the constraints imposed by ρ_1 with some constraints (e.g. temporal constraints) which are imposed, in other cases, by ρ_2 (or vice versa).

This point also applies when we consider Larry Horn's example below, cited by Txurruka, which indicates focal stress with SMALL CAPS:

(135)   A: Did John break the vase?
        B: WELL/the VASE BROKE/and HE dropped it.

Txurruka observes that B asserts that two events occurred, and only implicates that John did, in fact, break the vase. We know that there is an implicature here due to the use of *well*, which indicates that only a partial answer to the question is provided (Carlson 1984). That is, since what is at issue is whether a causal relationship holds, the use of *well* indicates that no such assertion is made on the part of Speaker B.

There are also instances in which discourse relations are presupposed. Asher and Vieu (2005) credit Caroline Heycock (pers. comm.) for providing relevant examples involving clefts. Here are two examples of this kind:

(136)   [[Anna fell], and [it was a banana that she slipped on]] (can you believe it?!).

(137)   [[Anna fell], and [it was Teia who pushed her]].

The explanans in these examples is not asserted, but presupposed—an observation that is correlated with the meaning of clefts (see, e.g., Velleman et al. 2012 and references therein). For example, (137) can only be uttered in a context in which it is already known that someone pushed Anna. So the asserted content doesn't involve EXPLANATION—the explanation is presupposed.[46]

In light of these data, a reasonable hypothesis is that particular information-structural cues (e.g. clefts, prosody) can license inferences with *and* which are normally associated instead with subordinating relations. This hypothesis may well also extend to cover the examples without clefts such as (130b). We expect that this hypothesis could be modeled in SDRT using the techniques for representing presupposition developed by Asher and Lascarides (1998b). One of their key insights is that presupposed content constitutes its own DU. Given this assumption, we could further hypothesize that such (presupposed) DUs don't care if their triggers come with *and*. For example, we could analyze the cleft in (136) as follows. *She slipped* and *it was a banana peel* are related via CONTINUATION. This CDU is then related to the DU, *Anna fell*, via EXPLANATION. This analysis could also be extended to cases like (135), if we further assume that focus triggers presuppositions (Schlöder and Lascarides 2020), which (as we just assumed) constitute their own discourse units.[47] We don't pursue this idea further here, but will be able to expand briefly in Section

---

[46] As it turns out, EXPLANATION is not the only subordinating discourse relation that can co-occur with *and* in clefts. Example (i) has ELABORATION, with a pseudocleft in the second conjunct:

(i)   [[Lev had a big meal] and [lamb was what he chose as his main course]].

[47] Thanks to Julian Schlöder (pers. comm.) for discussing this possible analysis with us.

6.5, when we discuss the relationship between discourse structure, discourse topic, and information structure.

In the remainder of this section, we consider cases in which Txurruka claims that temporal constraints imposed by OCCASION are pragmatically enriched with temporal constraints imposed by ⇐BACKGROUND (or, in her words, ⇐BACKGROUND is implicated when OCCASION is asserted). At first blush, this may seem counterintuitive: while OCCASION entails temporal sequencing, ⇐BACKGROUND entails temporal overlap. And, indeed, when OCCASION holds of two eventive DUs, it is not possible to pragmatically strengthen from temporal sequencing to temporal overlap. However, when stative DUs are involved, things are different.

To see why, consider Altshuler and Schwarzschild (2013) Temporal Profile of Statives (TPS) below, which we assume is respected by ⇐BACKGROUND.

(138)   TPS: For any tenseless stative clause ϕ, if a moment m is in $[\![\phi]\!]$, then there is a moment m' preceding m and a moment m'' following m such that m' and m'' are in $[\![\phi]\!]$.[48]

TPS has been important for calculating temporal implicatures that arise with statives (like those below) called **cessation** by Altshuler and Schwarzschild.

(139)   How is Barrie doing?
   a. Her heart was racing.   (Cessation implicature: it isn't racing now)
   b. Her heart will be racing.   (Cessation implicature: it isn't racing now)

According to TPS, (139a) is entailed by its present-tense counterpart: if *Her heart be racing* is true at the moment of utterance, then, by TPS, *Her heart be racing* is true at some moment m' prior to the moment of utterance and the truth of *Her heart be racing* at that prior moment verifies (139a). The entailment is asymmetric since if (139a) is true at a moment m that is prior to the utterance, then, by TPS, (139a) is true at some moment m' after m. However, there is no guarantee that m' is the moment of utterance. Hence, the truth of (139a) at m' need not verify the present-tense *Her heart be racing*. We can run analogous reasoning for the present-tense counterpart of (139b).

With this in place, we could offer the following implicature account of cessation in (139a): in uttering (139a), the speaker could have uttered the stronger present-tense counterpart. Given that the speaker is opinionated on the matter (e.g. the speaker is a doctor), the speaker reasons that the present-tense counterpart must be false, so it cannot be what speaker intended (by the **Maxim of Quality**).[49] After all, if the intent of the speaker is not

---

[48] On the first reading of TPS, one may be tempted to reject it. A common misconception is that TPS entails that states must hold for arbitrarily large temporal intervals. This is not true. TPS says that no isolated moments can be in the denotation of tenseless statives: there are always infinitely many points in the denotation of a tenseless stative if it is not empty. This, of course, is not a problem since infinitely many points can be packed into a finite interval, for example if we have a densely ordered set. See Altshuler (2016) for further discussion and a way to derive TPS given further assumptions about statives and an axiom which ensures that infinitely many moments in $[\![\phi]\!]$ take the form of convex sets (i.e. intervals). Tenseless statives, then, are true at moments as well as (open) intervals.

[49] Grice (1975) defines the Maxim of Quality as follows:

(i)   a. Do not say what you believe is false.
      b. Do not say that for which you lack adequate evidence.

to convey that they Barrie's heart is still racing, then why was the logically stronger present not used? It would allow the speaker to convey vital information (to a worried parent) (by the **Maxim of Quantity**).[50] An analogous derivation can be run for (139b).

Let us now consider the pair of discourses below from Txurruka (2003); (140a) differs from (140b) in not containing *and*.

(140)   a. He walked into the room. The director was slumped in her chair.
   b. [[He walked in to the room] and [the director was slumped in her chair]].

                                                                    (Dowty 1986)

Txurruka argues that while (140a) entails temporal overlap by establishing ⇐BACKGROUND, (140b) asserts OCCASION, but nevertheless implies ⇐BACKGROUND.[51] As noted, a coordinating relation cannot, strictly speaking, imply a subordinating relation. What she means is that the temporal constraints imposed by OCCASION are pragmatically enriched with temporal constraints imposed by ⇐BACKGROUND. With this in mind, Txurruka's proposal amounts to the following: (140b) asserts that there was an event of some prominent male having walked into the room; given the temporal constraints imposed by OCCASION, the state of the director being slumped in her chair held when the prominent male was already in the room, i.e. we infer a narrative progression (first the walking in, then the being slumped).

So far so good. The additional inference that we draw, based on world knowledge, is that the director was also slumped *when* the prominent male walked into the room, and presumably before the walking in as well. 'Stretching the state' in this way is in line with TPS, as we have seen.[52]

One question that arises is whether this analysis is, in fact, the correct one, or whether both (140a) and (140b) assert ⇐BACKGROUND and what is implicated, given TPS, is that the director was slumped (*before* and) *after* the prominent male walked into the room. It turns out that this is a difficult question to address and would take us too far afield.[53] Hence, rather than addressing this question directly, we would like to briefly discuss how Txurruka's analysis could account for an intriguing contrast that we considered in Section 5.4.4, repeated in (141)–(142), where the (a)-examples exemplify ⇒BACKGROUND, while the (b)-examples cannot easily be understood as exemplifying ⇐BACKGROUND.

(141)   a.   Teia [[stood in the hallway] and [screamed at Ava]].
   b.   ??Teia [[screamed at Ava] and [stood in the hallway]].

(142)   a.   Anna [[lived with Ava] and [read *Grumpy Monkey* to her]].
   b.   ??Anna [[read *Grumpy Monkey* to Ava] and [lived with her]].

---

[50] Grice (1975) defines the Maxim of Quantity as follows:

(i)   a. Make your contribution as informative as is required (for the current purposes of the exchange).
   b. Do not make your contribution more informative than is required.

[51] Txurruka does not distinguish ⇐BACKGROUND from ⇒BACKGROUND. However, she clearly means the former here.

[52] Because *slumped* is an adjective in these examples, there is no entailment that the state of being slumped results from a prior slumping event. The only relevant temporal relation is that between the walking-in event and the being-slumped state.

[53] For a discussion of this question, see classic work by Dowty (1986) and Webber (1988), as well as more recent work by Bary (2009) and Altshuler (2012, 2016, 2021).

Rather than exemplifying $\Leftarrow$BACKGROUND, (141b)—to the extent that it can be construed as a felicitous utterance—is more easily understood as exemplifying OCCASION, along the lines of (143):

(143)   Teia [[screamed at Ava] and then [stood in the hallway (with her head down in frustration)]].

We also note that (141b) can be made more natural when the second conjunct makes reference to the event described by the first conjunct:

(144)   Teia [[screamed at Ava] and [stood in the hallway during the screaming/while the screaming was going on]].

Adding the additional modifier in (144), however, introduces $\Rightarrow$BACKGROUND, i.e. *stood in the hallway {during the screaming/while the screaming was going on}* exemplifies this discourse relation. This construction is therefore a close cousin of the bridging construction discussed in Section 5.4.4.

These data support our conclusion from Chapter 5 that *and* is allergic to $\Leftarrow$BACKGROUND, while having an affinity for $\Rightarrow$BACKGROUND. This is expected on Txurruka's proposal given the insight, introduced in Section 6.3, that $\Rightarrow$BACKGROUND is coordinating, while $\Leftarrow$BACKGROUND is subordinating.

What remains to be answered, on Txurruka's proposal, is why it seems easier to assert OCCASION with (140b) than it is with (141b) (and then 'implicate $\Leftarrow$BACKGROUND' by pragmatically strengthening the duration of the described state). We leave this question open for further research, noting here that one may be tempted to seek a difference in the lexical semantics of the stative verbs; while both *be slumped* and *stand* are stage-level predicates, world knowledge reasoning may suggest that slumping is more likely to be a reaction to some prior event than standing.[54]

In sum, there are a few prima facie challenging cases for Txurruka's (2003) proposal that *and* selects for coordinating discourse relations. Txurruka's response is to argue that those cases which appear to *assert* subordinating discourse relations are really cases in which content associated with a subordinating discourse relation is instead being *implicated*. Moreover, we have seen cases in which that content is *presupposed*. The details of this approach are still clearly in need of development, but we will assume that Txurruka's insight about the discourse semantics of *and* is essentially correct. If this assumption is justified, Txurruka answers a question that was unresolved in Kehler (2002) and raised in Section 6.2.4, namely why only some discourse relations are expressed by *and*. That answer constitutes a strong argument in favor of using SDRT, which embodies the coordinating/subordinating distinction, for the analysis of the discourse semantics of coordination.

---

[54] Another possibility, suggested by Julian Schlöder (pers. comm.) is to say that *and*'s selection of coordinating discourse relations is a mere default that can be overridden. In SDRT, default rules are often used to explain infelicities: if there is no 'defeater' for the default, the default applies, even if this results in an incoherent discourse. We leave it open for further research whether a pragmatic analysis of this kind can be worked out for the many discourses considered in this section. An analysis of this kind would, on the one hand, undermine Txurruka's proposal that $and(\pi_1, \pi_2)$ entails that π_1 and π_2 are related by a coordinating relation. On the other hand, the analysis would preserve the spirit of Txurruka's proposal that *and* has an affinity for coordinating discourse relations.

6.4.2 Discourse semantics of *or* and *but*

We will not cover other conjunctions in the same depth as *and*, partly because the extraction data are less rich and partly because the proposed semantic analyses hold less interest for us. Nevertheless, SDRT-based hypotheses concerning the semantics of *or* and *but* will turn out to have interesting consequences when we return to extraction data in Section 6.6.[55]

Asher and Lascarides (2003) treat *or* as a cue-phrase for the relation ALTERNATION. The conjuncts related by *or* typically range over what Asher (2004), following Zimmermann (2000), calls **epistemic alternatives**.[56] Epistemic alternatives are more restricted than what logical disjunction would allow. For instance, (145a) and (145b) are coherent discourses, and it is possible that both π_1 and π_2 are true in each case.

(145)   a. Chris is eating a steak (π_1). It's raining (π_2).
        b. Chris is eating a steak (π_1). Pat bought it (π_2).   (Asher 2004: 174)

Logically, if π_1 and π_2 are true, then $\pi_1 \vee \pi_2$ is true. So if *or* simply signalled logical disjunction, the sentences in (146) should be acceptable, contrary to fact.

(146)   a. #Either Chris is eating a steak or it's raining.
        b. #Either Chris is eating a steak or Pat bought it.   (Asher 2004: 174)

Asher attributes the ill-formedness of the examples in (146) to the fact that the disjuncts are not epistemic alternatives. This distinguishes them from well-formed disjunctions like (147).

(147)   Chris is eating a steak or a salad.

(147) is a plausible answer to a question like *What is Chris eating?* More involved examples of epistemic alternatives include the 'bathroom-sentence' in (148), which plausibly offers alternative answers to *Why can't I find a bathroom in this house?*

(148)   Either [[there's no bathroom in this house] or [it's in a funny place]].

(Asher 2004: 171)

Asher's characterization even extends to the 'threat-*or*' identified by Culicover and Jackendoff (1997) and discussed in Chapter 3. (149) is syntactically unusual in that it coordinates an imperative and a declarative, but semantically regular from Asher's perspective in that the two disjuncts describe alternatives.[57]

(149)   [[Stand up] or [I'll break your arm]].   (Asher 2004: 175)

---

[55] In what follows, we therefore consider only SDRT-based hypotheses concerning the semantics of *or* and *but*. Readers interested in further discussion about the semantics of *or*, see, e.g., Zimmermann (2000), Simmons (2001), Alonso-Ovalle (2006), Roelofsen and van Gool (2010), and references therein. For further discussion about the semantics of *but*, see, e.g., Blakemore (2000), Umbach (2005), Toosarvandani (2014), and references therein.

[56] We will be able to be more precise about this notion in Section 6.5, but an informal characterization is that they are different answers to a question of relevance to the discourse context. For a recent overview of the role that alternatives play in formal semantics and pragmatics, see Westera (forthcoming).

[57] Strictly speaking, this is not quite true, because (149) does not concern *epistemic* alternatives. Asher characterizes (149) instead as describing deontic alternatives.

While *or* cues ALTERNATION, *but* cues CONTRAST. Asher and Lascarides actually distinguish two different varieties of CONTRAST. The first ('formal contrast') is illustrated in (150).

(150)   [[John speaks French] (but) [Bill speaks German]].

(Asher and Lascarides 2003: 168)

This type of CONTRAST is very close to the relation of PARALLEL discussed in Chapter 5, except that it emphasizes dissimilarity among discourse units, whereas PARALLEL emphasizes similarity. We return to the nature of the similarity between PARALLEL and CONTRAST in Section 6.5.

The second type of CONTRAST occurs when π_2 violates an expectation (for instance, a default inference) generated by π_1. This is illustrated in (151).

(151)   John loves sport. But he hates football.   (Asher and Lascarides 2003: 168)

The first sentence of (151) might be taken by default to imply a universal quantification: John loves all kinds of sport. The second sentence violates that default expectation.

Recall that VIOLATED EXPECTATION is a crucial component of Kehler (2002) analysis of Lakoff's Type B scenarios, and that VIOLATED EXPECTATION, unlike Kehler's Resemblance relation CONTRAST, is part of the Cause/Effect family of discourse relations for Kehler. Here, however, 'violated expectation' and 'formal contrast' are grouped together as two types of CONTRAST. This exemplifies a pattern that we will see repeatedly in Section 6.5, and in fact have already seen in Section 6.3: SDRT groups discourse relations in different ways from Kehler's, and new predictions follow from those groupings.

That said, it is not clear that the unification of 'formal contrast' and 'violated expectation' as two subcases of CONTRAST carries real weight. The main unifying criterion is that they are cued by *but*, but even there, the similarity is only partial. As Asher and Lascarides note, (151) requires *but* (or some other cue-phrase such as *and still*), while *but* is optional in (150). We return to further differences between these two subcases of CONTRAST in the following section, but we will continue to use a single term for these two cases, following Asher and Lascarides.

6.5 Constructing topics and themes

A subtle but important difference between SDRT and approaches such as Kehler's concerns the relationship between the notion of discourse coherence and the entailments of different discourse relations. Under Kehler's Humean view, the discourse relations holding between the ideas expressed are themselves the guarantors of discourse coherence. The same is sometimes true in SDRT, but sometimes more is needed to guarantee discourse coherence: hidden pieces of discourse structure which augment the relations between overtly expressed discourse units, and without which the discourse is incoherent, or less coherent. In this section, we will discuss two such pieces of hidden structure: certain discourse relations require a partial isomorphism between the DUs in question, known as a **common theme**, while others require a particular relation to a **discourse topic**.

This suggests a new classification of discourse relations in terms of their relationship to information structure: some discourse relations require a particular relation to a common discourse topic, some require a particular relation to a common theme, and some impose no such requirements. In turn, this means that only a few discourse relations require an explicit representation of discourse topics in logical forms. In SDRT, discourse topics are not a ubiquitous organizing principle of discourse structures, but rather an occasional presence.

This has important implications for our investigation of extraction from coordinate structures, because of the relationships between discourse topic, sentence topic, and extraction sketched in Section 6.2. We are building toward a contrast between two schools of thought: the Kuno/Kehler approach, in which topicality is a ubiquitous factor conditioning extraction, and a new approach, in which topicality is only a factor in some syntactic environments (including asymmetric extraction from noninitial conjuncts) and in some discourse contexts (relations which require the presence of a topic in the logical form). One of the important questions for this chapter is the extent to which the syntactic and discourse-semantic aspects of topics align in this empirical domain.

In Section 6.5.1, we cover discourse relations which require a common topic for their arguments. In Section 6.5.2, we cover relations which require partially isomorphic arguments. In Section 6.5.3, we cover relations which do not fall into either of these categories, and identify the properties which permit these relations to guarantee coherence without requiring a common topic or theme.

With this information-structural taxonomy in place, we will return to extraction from coordinate structures in Section 6.6. With an eye on that plan, we concentrate in the following subsection mainly on coordinating relations expressible by *and*, *or*, and *but*. However, it is important to appreciate that the distinctions drawn in this section are applicable quite generally. In Section 6.5.3 in particular, we will consider the place of subordinating relations within this new taxonomy.

6.5.1 Relations requiring a common discourse topic

In Section 6.2, we provisionally followed von Fintel (1994), Roberts (1996), Büring (2003) in adopting the well-established analysis which treats a discourse topic as a set of questions under discussion partially ordered by specificity. This partial order implies a model of discourse structure. For instance, a contrastive topic in an utterance can be analyzed as indicating that the utterance does not address the current QUD, but answers another question which stands in a certain well-defined relation to that QUD. (152) illustrates the broad idea: (152b) does not completely answer the question in (152a), but it could form part of a strategy to completely answer that question, by breaking it down into a set of subquestions, as in (152c).

(152)   a. What did the pop stars wear?
        b. The FEMALE$_{CT}$ pop stars wore CAFTANS$_F$.   (Büring 2003: 525)
        c. What did the female pop stars wear? What did the male pop stars wear? ....

A similar, but slightly more complex, analysis can be applied to classic examples like (153).

(153)   a. What about Bill? What did he eat?
        b. Well, FRED$_{CT}$ ate the BEANS$_F$.

In this case, the response in (153b) does not help to answer the question in (153a), but it can form part of a strategy to answer a superquestion like (154a), by breaking it down into a set of subquestions including *What did Bill eat* and *What did Fred eat.*

(154)   a. Who ate what?
        b. What did Bill eat? What did Fred eat? What did Jane eat? ...

However, SDRT researchers have argued for a richer and more formally varied conception of discourse topic and discourse structure than that afforded by the QUD model. Two distinct arguments for this claim have been developed. The most straightforward, from Hunter and Abrusán (2017), is that the QUD model is insufficiently expressive to capture important properties of discourse structures. Hunter and Abrusán consider the hypothesis that on a QUD model, different discourse relations correspond to different relations among QUDs (Onea 2013). For instance, EXPLANATION could correspond to an answer to *why?* This would entail that the partial order over questions of the kind we have described would define the structure of discourse relations as a tree (this assumption is developed in Büring 2003, where discourse structures are characterized as 'discourse trees,' or d-trees).

However, SDRT research since at least Asher and Lascarides (2003) has argued that discourse structure cannot be represented in a tree, because a node in the discourse structure can have multiple mothers. In (155), for instance, we infer $\text{EXPLANATION}(\pi_1, \pi_2)$, $\text{RESULT}(\pi_2, \pi_3)$, and $\text{ELABORATION}(\pi_1, \pi_3)$. These three relations cannot fit in a tree because π_3 is the second argument of both RESULT and ELABORATION. This implies that the QUD model cannot be a complete model of discourse structure, because the QUD model defines discourse structure as a tree, and examples like (155) require more structural flexibility.

(155)   Sam is being punished (π_1). She took her parents' car without permission (π_2), so they've grounded her for 2 weeks (π_3).   (Hunter and Abrusán 2017)

Another argument against a general notion of discourse topics as questions is sketched by Asher (2004). The gist of Asher's arguments is that topics as questions don't have the right 'granularity' (Asher's term) to distinguish between coherent and incoherent discourses. The argument is built around the two discourses in (156a–b), with the former originally from Moens and Steedman (1988).

(156)   a. My car broke down. Then the sun set.
        b. My car broke down. Then the sun set and I knew I was in trouble.

                                                          (Asher 2004: 181)

(156b) is more coherent than (156a). However, it is hard to see how to distinguish them in terms of a QUD: both apparently only address the QUD *what happened?*, and nothing more specific than that. Moreover, both are equally coherent as answers to *what happened?*. Asher therefore claims that QUDs do not make distinctions that are needed for a complete model of discourse coherence.

What seems to be going on in (156) is that the final conjunct in (156b) specifies the otherwise elusive topic for the whole discourse (roughly, *several things happened which landed me in trouble*). However, that topic is not obviously statable as a question. Because of considerations like these, SDRT conceives of discourse topics not specifically as questions, but as discourse units of the same form as any other discourse unit, which may be only implicit in the overt discourse.[58]

Asher's position on discourse topics has two main properties which distinguish it from the QUD model. First, discourse topics are not questions, as just discussed. Secondly, only certain discourse relations require explicit representation of a discourse topic. NARRATION, exemplified in (156), is one such relation: (156a) is an incoherent narrative, on Asher's analysis, because it requires a common topic and no common topic is discernible. In fact, a major property which distinguishes the SDRT relation of NARRATION from Kehler's relation of OCCASION is this topic requirement.

SDRT actually construes OCCASION not as a discourse relation, but as a relation between eventualities: $OCCASION(e_1, e_2)$ holds iff the post-state of e_1 stands in the appropriate relation to the pre-state of e_2 (compare Section 5.3.2, and see Asher and Lascarides 2003: §5.6 for more discussion.) In turn, Asher and Lascarides propose that $NARRATION(\alpha, \beta)$ is typically inferred if $OCCASION(e_\alpha, e_\beta)$ holds, i.e. if OCCASION relates the events described by α and β. $NARRATION(\alpha, \beta)$ is not, however, entailed by $OCCASION(e_\alpha, e_\beta)$, because NARRATION has the additional topicality requirement just mentioned.

The process of identifying a discourse topic is somewhat mysterious on both the SDRT approach and the QUD approach—in fact, much of Asher (2004) is taken up with demonstrating the difficulties inherent in straightforward approaches to the identification of discourse topics. It is best to think of various aspects of sentence structure as placing constraints on the nature of the discourse topic, without necessarily fully determining it. The relationship between sentence topic and discourse topic, as discussed in Section 6.2, is one such constraint, as well as the relationship between contrastive topic and discourse topic articulated by Roberts (1996) and Büring (2003). Constraints imposed by the local discourse structure, including the relation holding between two discourse units, are yet another kind of factor conditioning the discourse topic.

In fact, constraints imposed by local discourse structure can be cashed out in terms of other discourse relations. For instance, Asher (2004) claims that a coherent NARRATION is an ELABORATION of a discourse topic. This means that certain discourse relations relate to discourse topics through statements of the following approximate form.

(157)   If $NARRATION(\alpha, \beta)$ then $\exists\pi.ELABORATION([\alpha, \beta], \pi)$, where π is a topic for $[\alpha, \beta]$.

The discourse relations discussed in this section are all coordinating relations, which bear this kind of relationship with a discourse topic. We begin with a relation, CONTINUATION, which can be considered to instantiate this relationship in a 'pure' form.

CONTINUATION

As just previewed, Asher and Lascarides (2003) define CONTINUATION as a coordinating discourse relation which attaches two DUs to form a CDU. In turn, the CDU is an elaboration of a DU, π, that constitutes the discourse topic. That is, following Asher (2004), we assume:

---

[58] Although this has not been demonstrated to our knowledge, we assume that Asher's position can be unified with Hunter and Abrusán's if one assumes that the extra flexibility Asher requires in identifying discourse topics and relating them to discourse structure is sufficient to meet the need identified by Hunter and Abrusán for expressive power beyond that afforded by the QUD model.

(158) If CONTINUATION(α, β) then $\exists \pi.$ELABORATION($[\alpha, \beta], \pi$), where π is a topic for $[\alpha, \beta]$.

This assumption can be graphically represented as follows, where we use dashed lines to represent that the CDU consisting of α and β is π':

(159)

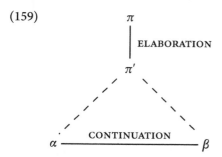

Now, let us also assume, following Lascarides and Asher (1993), that (160) holds. That is, if ELABORATION holds between two DUs, α, β, then the event described by β, namely e_β, is a part of the event described by α, namely e_α.[59]

(160) If ELABORATION(α, β), then part-of(e_β, e_α).

With (159) and (160) in mind, we can now be explicit about what requirement CONTINUATION and other related discourse relations impose on the **topical event**, i.e. the event described by the discourse topic. This will be helpful when we correlate the requirements imposed by discourse relations with the patterns of extraction that we have observed.

For example, given CONTINUATION(α, β), we have the requirement in (161), where the events described by α and β are both parts of an event described by the topic π. In other words, e_π is the topical event whose parts are e_α and e_β. The condition '$(K_\alpha \sqcap K_\beta)^{e_\pi}$' is the DRS that records 'the common content' of the DRSs of α and β, namely K_α and K_β respectively, with respect to what they contribute to the topical event e_π.[60] As such, CONTINUATION is **veridical**: it composes to content that entails its parts.

(161)
$$\boxed{\begin{array}{l} e_\pi \\ \hline \text{part-of}(e_\alpha, e_\pi) \\ \text{part-of}(e_\beta, e_\pi) \\ (K_\alpha \sqcap K_\beta)^{e_\pi} \end{array}}$$

Let's now apply this analysis of CONTINUATION to some examples, beginning with (162). Notice that *this* in π_4 could be anaphorically linked to the content of π_3, but the more salient reading is that *this* in π_4 refers to the common content of π_{1-3}, roughly that 'three plaintiffs make three claims that they are ill-treated'.

(162) One plaintiff was passed over for promotion three times (π_1). Another didn't get a raise for five years (π_2). A third plaintiff was given a lower wage compared to males who were doing the same work (π_3). But the jury didn't believe this (π_4).

(Asher and Lascarides 2003: 15)

---

[59] We come back to this assumption when we further describe ELABORATION.
[60] Asher and Lascarides (2003) admit that this is 'a very difficult operation to define in practice,' though as we show in what follows, the intuitive idea can be easily grasped. For more discussion of this operation, see Altshuler and Schlöder (2019, 2021b).

Given (158), an appropriate discourse structure for (162) would include at least the following relations, where π is an implicit topic.

(163)   CONTINUATION(π_1, π_2)
   CONTINUATION(π_2, π_3)
   ELABORATION(π, π_{1-3})
   CONTRAST(π, π_4)

Moreover, given (160), we would say that each event described by π_{1-3} is a part of the event described by π, i.e. the topical event, which here is something like labor exploitation. The power of the contrast comes from inferring this topical event: despite three events that all constitute labor exploitation, the jury wasn't moved to action.

The truth conditions of CONTINUATION are weak and compatible with many other discourse relations. For example, in (164), we would most probably treat (164b) and (164c) in isolation as an instance of PARALLEL, given the structural and semantic similarities between the two DUs. However, in the context of (164a), they are better considered as jointly elaborating a discourse topic of 'the children search for the cat'. Therefore, we would again consider (164b) and (164c) to be related by CONTINUATION, possibly in addition to PARALLEL.

(164)   a.   Essun told the children to search for the cat (π_1).
   b.   Binof searched the garden (π_2).
   c.   Tonkee searched upstairs (π_3).

Given (158), an appropriate discourse structure for (164) would thus include at least the relations in (165), where π is an implicit topic.

(165)   CONTINUATION(π_2, π_3)
   ELABORATION$(\pi, [\pi_{2-3}])$
   RESULT(π_1, π).

Moreover, given (160) and (161), we can represent (164b) and (164c) as follows:

(166) $K_b =$

e_b, b, x, g
Binof(b)
searching(e_b)
actor(e_b, b)
object(e_b, x)
location(e_b, g)
garden(g)

$K_c =$

e_c, t, k
Tonkee(t)
searching(e_c)
actor(e_c, t)
object(e_c, x)
location(e_c, k)
upstairs(k)

$(K_b \sqcap K_c)^e =$

e, x
searching(e)
object(e, x)

In this representation, the anaphor for the search-event object is resolved to the same x in K_b and K_c.[61] Moreover, $(K_b \sqcap K_c)^e$ yields a DRS that represents the common content of K_b and K_c. This establishes the searching event as topical.

---

[61] Technically speaking, a distinct discourse referent y would be introduced in K_b, along with the condition that both x and y pick out the same cat. This shows that topic 'intersection' of DRSs is really intersection modulo identity conditions. We overlook this complexity here for ease of exposition. Thanks to Julian Schlöder for bringing this point to our attention.

NARRATION

Like CONTINUATION, NARRATION is a veridical coordinating relation. In addition to what CONTINUATION contributes, NARRATION adds a constraint that OCCASION holds between the events described by the DUs in question.[62] That is, given NARRATION(α, β) we have the following requirement on the topical event:

(167)

$$
\begin{array}{|l|}
\hline
e_\pi \\
\hline
\text{part-of}(e_\alpha, e_\pi) \\
\text{part-of}(e_\beta, e_\pi) \\
(K_\alpha \sqcap K_\beta)^{e_\pi} \\
\text{post}(e_\alpha) \approx \text{pre}(e_\beta) \\
\hline
\end{array}
$$

The condition $\text{post}(e_\alpha) \approx \text{pre}(e_\beta)$ should be understood as follows: the post-state of the event represented in a DRS α constitutes the pre-state of the event described by the DRS β. It would also be possible to add constraints in the manner described in Section 5.3.2, when we considered Altshuler and Varasdi's (2015) proposal for defining this discourse relation.

Let's illustrate the proposal with an example. In the discourse below, the post-state of Binof going to the garden, i.e. Binof being in the garden, is understood to be a nontrivial precondition for the pre-state of his looking for the cat, since the search is outdoors.

(168) a. Binof went to the garden.
       b. And looked for the cat.

Here, then, is a representation of this discourse, deriving the topical event that has Binof as the actor:

(169)

$$
K_b = \begin{array}{|l|}
\hline
e_a, b, g \\
\hline
\text{Binof}(b) \\
\text{going}(e_a) \\
\text{actor}(e_a, b) \\
\text{object}(e_a, g) \\
\text{garden}(g) \\
\hline
\end{array}
\quad
K_c = \begin{array}{|l|}
\hline
e_b, c \\
\hline
\text{cat}(c) \\
\text{searching}(e_b) \\
\text{actor}(e_b, b) \\
\text{object}(e_c, c) \\
\hline
\end{array}
\quad
(K_b \sqcap K_c)^e = \begin{array}{|l|}
\hline
e \\
\hline
\text{actor}(e, b) \\
\hline
\end{array}
$$

The characterization of (169) involves an inference that the search is outdoors. This follows from the condition: $\text{post}(e_\alpha) \approx \text{pre}(e_\beta)$.

Asher and Lascarides provide the discourse in (170) to motivate this condition. It is perfectly possible for (170b) to occur after (170a) (if Kim moved from Austin to New York in the interim). However, (170) is a poor NARRATION. This indicates that temporal succession is not enough to allow NARRATION.[63] This is expected given (167) because the post-state in (170a) (being in Austin) is not a possible pre-state for (170b) (the required pre-state is being in New York).

---

[62] Asher and Lascarides (2003) frame this constraint in terms of spatiotemporal contiguity. We discuss this idea with respect to (170).

[63] For more recent discussion of this point, see Cumming (2021).

(170)   a.   In 1982, Kim moved from LA to Austin.

  b.   ??She moved from New York to Austin.   (Asher and Lascarides 2003)

In what follows, we shall assume that $\text{post}(e_\alpha) \approx \text{pre}(e_\beta)$ is sufficient to explain why spatiotemporal contiguity is often inferred with NARRATION, and that the infelicity in (170b) is due to a failure to satisfy $\text{post}(e_\alpha) \approx \text{pre}(e_\beta)$.[64]

BACKGROUND

Asher and Lascarides (2003) state that ⇐BACKGROUND contributes the constraint of spatiotemporal overlap between two events, and the same is true of ⇒BACKGROUND. This insight is captured in (171) and (172), which provide requirements on the topical event for ⇐BACKGROUND(α, β) and ⇒BACKGROUND(α, β) respectively.[65]

(171)

$$
\begin{array}{|l|}
\hline
e_\pi \\
\hline
\text{overlap}(e_\alpha, e_\beta) \\
e_\pi = e_\alpha \\
\hline
\end{array}
$$

(172)

$$
\begin{array}{|l|}
\hline
e_\pi \\
\hline
\text{overlap}(e_\alpha, e_\beta) \\
e_\pi = e_\beta \\
\hline
\end{array}
$$

While these are necessary conditions, they are not sufficient. Asher and Lascarides (2003: 165) provide the following discourse to illustrate this point:

(173)   ??Max smoked a cigarette. Mary had black hair.

One can certainly imagine (173) describing a situation in which Max smoked a cigarette in front of Mary, who happened to have black hair at the time. However, this isn't sufficient to warrant either BACKGROUND relation (or indeed any other discourse relation). In particular, Mary's black hair is not understood as being the ground for the event of smoking (the figure), or vice versa. This raises again the difficult question, already discussed in Section 5.4.4, of how the ground/figure inference comes about.

Asher et al. (1996), Asher and Lascarides (2003) take steps in addressing this challenge when they write:

Intuitively, a discourse structure containing [⇐BACKGROUND(π_1, π_2)] where K_{π_1} describes a (foregrounded) event and K_{π_2} describes the (background) state should encode the fact that K_{π_1} is the 'main story line' or the foreground; K_{π_1} is the thing that 'matters' in that events from subsequent utterances will be related to it. In SDRT, this is captured in the topic. If an SDRS includes [⇐BACKGROUND(π_1, π_2)], then this text segment has a topic whose content is constructed by *repeating* (rather than summarising) the contents of K_{π_1}

---

[64] We don't say more about this constraint here, but direct the reader to Truswell (2019), who shows that while spatial contiguity between the events in a narrative is common in human experience, it does not seem to be a necessary condition.

[65] Note that e_π is identified with the foregrounded event: e_α for ⇐BACKGROUND and e_β for ⇒BACKGROUND. See Altshuler and Schlöder (2021b) for more discussion.

and K_{π_2}. This topic is related to the background segment with a relation called *Foreground–Background Pair* or *FBP* for short.   (Asher and Lascarides 2003: 166)

More concretely, Asher and Lascarides's idea is as follows. Assume that the text segment $\Leftarrow$BACKGROUND(π_1, π_2) is the CDU π'. π' factors in the construction of a topic π and a (subordinating) relation FBP. π results from performing set union over the discourse referents and the conditions in K_{π_1} and K_{π_2}. FBP is a relation between π and π' and has the following constraint: it can hold only if there is a thematic link between the two constituents, that can either be determined already from the discourse context or from world knowledge. With respect to (173), Asher and Lascarides note that 'we can't form an FBP because neither the context nor conventional knowledge have made clear any link between Mary's hair being black and Max's smoking a cigarette.'

Unfortunately, Asher and Lascarides do not say anything about the semantics of $\Rightarrow$BACKGROUND, beyond noting that 'it seems to be a simple coordinating relation' (Asher and Lascarides 2003: 208). In later work, however, Asher et al. (2007) propose that both $\Rightarrow$BACKGROUND and $\Leftarrow$BACKGROUND elaborate on a topic just like CONTINUATION and NARRATION. The difference is that for CONTINUATION and NARRATION, the topic is a summary, i.e. what is common to both of its arguments, whereas for BACKGROUND, the topic is a sum, i.e. it is the by product of summing up the 'at-issue' content from its two arguments. We do not outline the details of this analysis here because the underlying aim of Asher et al.'s analysis is to take strides in having an account of presupposition in SDRT, and further discussion would take us too far afield.[66] What matters to us is that in addition to (172), $\Rightarrow$BACKGROUND also factors in the construction of a topic. Moreover, we assume that topicality constraints on $\Rightarrow$BACKGROUND capture the clear notion that a DU with $\Rightarrow$BACKGROUND(π_1, π_2) is about π_2, just as a DU with $\Leftarrow$BACKGROUND(π_1, π_2) is about π_1. In what follows, we will sometimes talk, for simplicity's sake, as if π_2 is the topic of $\Rightarrow$BACKGROUND(π_1, π_2).

ALTERNATION

Discourse topics figure in ALTERNATION relations in yet another way, according to Asher (2004). ALTERNATION is the label for the most common (but not the only) interpretation of disjunctions with *or*, and in most cases *or* can be treated as a cue-phrase for ALTERNATION.[67] Asher's claim is that DUs related by ALTERNATION are alternative possible answers to a question that functions as discourse topic. For instance, (174) (lightly modified from Asher 2004: 175) offers alternative possible answers to the question 'where is the intruder'.

(174)   The intruder is [[in the living room] or [in the study]].

The same account can be extended to cover 'bathroom-sentences' like (148), repeated below and first discussed by Partee: each disjunct is a possible answer to the question 'where

---

[66] There is, of course, something quite intuitive about BACKGROUND being related to presupposition, i.e. 'not at issue' or 'backgrounded' content. For more discussion, see Abrusán (forthcoming).

[67] The exceptions to these statements include certain cases of 'logical *or*', in statements like 'If *P*, then *P* or *Q*', and uses of *or in other words* for rephrasing an utterance.

is the bathroom', and that topical question is sufficient to license the resolution of *it* in the second disjunct to the bathroom.

(148)   Either [[there's no bathroom in this house] or [it's in a funny place]].

(Asher 2004: 171)

In some cases, such as (149) (repeated below), particularly relevant to the 'threat-*or*' reading discussed in Section 3.4.1, the alternatives are not obviously alternative answers to a topical question, but they are still topical alternatives.

(149)   [[Stand up] or [I'll break your arm]].   (Asher 2004: 175)

However, when a discourse cannot easily be construed as presenting alternatives, *or* can often sound ill-formed. (175) is a case in point. (175a) entails (175b). However, Chris's eating of a steak and Pat's buying of a steak are not straightforwardly construed as alternatives (this may change in response to an overt question like *Tell me what happened to a steak*). Therefore, *or*, as a cue-phrase for ALTERNATION, is not licensed in (175b).

(175)   a.   Chris is eating a steak. Pat bought it.
         b.   #Either [[Chris is eating a steak] or [Pat bought it]].

Although Asher (2004) does not indicate how to give a semantics for ALTERNATION at the same level of precision as we have for the other discourse relations in this section, we can see the outlines of such a semantics, as follows.

(176)   If ALTERNATION(α, β) then $\exists \pi.R([\alpha, \beta], \pi)$, where π is a topic for $[\alpha, \beta]$.

In (176), the relation R may vary between instances of ALTERNATION. In most of the cases we have just discussed, the relevant relation is most likely QAP, or QUESTION–ANSWER PAIR.[68] However, in the case of 'threat-*or*', this is clearly not appropriate. Asher and Lascarides (2003) discuss related examples with *and* in terms of the relations DEF-CONSEQUENCE$_r$ and RESULT$_r$, and it is likely that similar relations will be appropriate here. However, to the best of our knowledge, the precise labels in question have not been worked out, and there is no principled hypothesis as to the possible values of R in (176).

Summary

The discourse relations covered in this section are distinguished by the fact that they all require explicit representation of discourse topics in logical forms, even when those topics are implicit. Exactly how they relate to those topics is a matter of some variation: CONTINUATION(π_1, π_2) states only that π_1 and π_2 each contribute to the characterization of a common topic by elaborating on it; and NARRATION does the same but with an added constraint on the relationship between the post-state of π_1 and the pre-state of π_2. However, in $\Rightarrow$BACKGROUND(π_1, π_2), the discourse is 'about' π_2, and, on the original SDRT formulation, the relationship of the discourse topic to π_1 is characterized as a Foreground–Background Pair.[69] On a more recent formulation, however, $\Rightarrow$BACKGROUND(π_1, π_2) states that π_1 and

---

[68]   This discourse relation features prominently in dialogue, which we have not discussed, but is a vibrant area of research in SDRT (see, e.g., Asher and Lascarides 2003: Ch. 7, and Hunter et al. 2018).

[69]   The same is true of $\Leftarrow$BACKGROUND(π_1, π_2), only with the discourse 'about' π_1. However, $\Leftarrow$BACKGROUND, as a subordinating relation, is of less interest to our study of coordination.

π_2 each contribute to the characterization of a topic by elaborating on it, but this topic is not 'common' in the sense that it does not summarize the contribution of π_1 and π_2 (vis-à-vis CONTINUATION and NARRATION). Rather, the topic is the by product of summing up the at-issue content from π_1 and π_2. Finally, ALTERNATION, at least in its most common use, requires that π_1 and π_2 are possible answers to a topical question.

6.5.2 Relations requiring a common theme

We now turn to two relations, PARALLEL and CONTRAST, whose interpretation involves something very close to a discourse topic, namely some shared semantic material on which the DUs in question expand. Asher et al. (1997) and Asher and Lascarides (2003) refer to this as a **common theme**.

A major difference between theme and discourse topic is that theme is not explicitly represented in the logical form. There is no sense, then, in which DUs related by PARALLEL or CONTRAST are explicitly represented as, for instance, ELABORATIONS of their theme. Rather, these relations entail that such a theme exists, and the quality of these relations is determined by the richness of the common theme inferable from the DUs that appear as arguments of these relations.

This entails a second difference between theme and discourse topic: the common theme of two DUs can serve as a clue to the relevant discourse topic, but the discourse topic does not have to be identical to the theme. It can be more, or less, fully specified. In contrast, with respect to determining the quality of a PARALLEL or CONTRAST relation, only the Maximal Common Theme (MCT) matters.

A third difference is that the MCT of two DUs can be calculated algorithmically. An algorithm of this kind is proposed by Asher et al. (1997), with further developments in Asher and Lascarides (2003) and Schlöder and Lascarides (2020). A core component of this algorithm is that MCT defines a partial isomorphism between the arguments of PARALLEL and CONTRAST. The nonisomorphic elements of these arguments relate to the MCT in different ways. PARALLEL emphasizes semantic similarity,[70] while CONTRAST emphasizes dissimilarity.

Apart from these differences, these two discourse relations behave in broadly similar ways. We will discuss PARALLEL in detail, and then briefly compare it to CONTRAST. In Section 6.6, we will see that there is a close connection between the notion of theme described here and the ATB movement pattern described by Ross (1967). The notion of 'common theme' in this context recapitulates many of Kehler's ideas about effects of Resemblance relations (including PARALLEL and CONTRAST), which we referred to as 'Kehler's Hypothesis 1' (KH1) in Section 6.2.

PARALLEL

Let us consider a few examples of PARALLEL. We begin with (177), along with its representation in (178):[71]

---

[70] Similarity, not identity: *love* and *like* are similar in this sense, while *love* and *hate* contrast. It is sometimes useful to think of PARALLEL as presupposing that the nonisomorphic parts of its arguments are similar, while CONTRAST presupposes the opposite.

[71] Here we ignore event-structural information since it does not factor in what follows.

(177)   [[Justin saw Teia] and [Anna saw her too]].

(178)

x,y,z
justin(x)
teia(y)
anna(z)
see(x,y)
see(z,y)

According to the algorithm in Asher et al. (1997), the Maximal Common Theme of these two examples is as in (179), representing the information that someone saw Teia.

(179)

u,t
teia(t)
see(u,t)

This can also be seen as a partial isomorphism between aspects of (178), with PARALLEL telling us that the nonidentical elements are similar.

Now consider the pair of discourses below:

(180)   [[Anna saw Justin] and [Ava saw Teia (??too)]].

(181)   [[Justin saw Ava] and [he saw Teia (too)]].

(180) plausibly exemplifies CONTINUATION, but the infelicity of *too* in (180), as a cue for PARALLEL, indicates that there is only weak support for PARALLEL. This is because no isomorphic element is identical: Anna isn't Ava, Justin isn't Teia, and neither are the two events the same. If we apply the algorithm from Asher et al. (1997) to (180), the result is (182), where the only content is that someone saw someone, a much less impressive maximal common theme.

(182)

u,v
see(u,v)

On the other hand, in (181), Justin is the actor of both seeing events. As a result, the maximal common theme for (181) is in (183), roughly 'Justin saw someone.' The fact that the two conjuncts have more in common makes *too* more natural.

(183)

j,v
justin(j)
see(j,v)

Similar considerations apply in cases where different predicates appear in the different conjuncts. Imagine that the speaker is describing what happened in a game of poker and says:

(184)   [[Teia had a high card] and [Ava had a great hand too]]![72]

---

[72] Thanks to Julian Schlöder for providing this example.

Either one finds this discourse odd, or one attributes to the speaker the erroneous belief that a high card constitutes a good hand. The algorithm for finding the maximal common theme of the conjuncts in (184) produces (185).

(185)

u,v
poker-hand(v)
have(u,v)

Relative to that common theme, Teia and Ava, as the different values of u in the two conjuncts, are plausibly similar, as required by PARALLEL, but *high card* and *great hand* are dissimilar. The use of *too* in (184) presupposes that PARALLEL holds, but a suitably rich MCT for PARALLEL would require that a high card and a great hand are similar, and knowledge of poker hands blocks accommodation of that presupposition.

CONTRAST

The functioning of CONTRAST is very similar to that of PARALLEL. The main difference is that, while PARALLEL emphasizes the similarity of the elements excluded from the maximal common theme, CONTRAST emphasizes the dissimilarity. We can appreciate the effect of CONTRAST by comparing (184) to (186), where *but* is a cue for CONTRAST.

(186)   [[Teia had a high card], but [Ava had a great hand]]!

This example is felicitous, because now we are emphasizing the dissimilarity of a high card and a great hand, relative to the same MCT diagrammed in (185).

According to Asher and Lascarides (2003), though, CONTRAST does not always refer to a common theme. In Section 6.4.2, we noted a second kind of CONTRAST, described by Asher and Lascarides as 'violation of expectation' and illustrated with (151), repeated below.

(151)   John loves sport. But he hates football.   (Asher and Lascarides 2003: 168)

CONTRAST qua violation of expectation is equally present in examples like (187). However, the maximal common theme of (187), according to the Asher et al. algorithm, is just (188): John and sport exist.

(187)   John loves sport. But he only watches it on TV.

(188)

j,s
john(j)
sport(s)

Perhaps this means that Asher and Lascarides are simply mistaken in conflating these two varieties of CONTRAST, with their different structural requirements. But a more intriguing possibility suggests itself. We have seen that *and* sometimes requires a common theme (these are the cases of PARALLEL we have discussed) and sometimes doesn't (when used with any of the other coordinating relations described by Txurruka). And the same is in fact true for *or*: canonical examples of *or* like (189), describing alternative answers to a topical question, imply a common theme relating to the presupposed material in the question, while other examples, like (149), discussed in the previous section and repeated here, do not.

(189)   Either [[Chris ate the rice], or [Jane ate the beans]].

(149)   [[Stand up] or [I'll break your arm]].   (Asher 2004: 175)

So in fact none of *and*, *or*, and *but* requires a common theme, but all have distinctive interpretations in the presence of a common theme. The current orthodoxy is to give a privileged label (PARALLEL) to the relation inferred when *and* is paired with a common theme, but not when *but* or *or* is paired with a common theme. However, the rationale for this distinction is not clear to us.

6.5.3   Relations without topic or theme constraints

In the previous subsections, we have described relations where coherence is guaranteed through constraints on discourse topic or a maximal common theme. These are of particular importance to us because of links between topic, theme, and extraction, which we introduced in Section 6.2 and will return to in Section 6.6. However, there are ways in which coherence can be established, by other discourse relations, without a common topic or theme being required. In many of these other cases, event-structural considerations underpin the coherence: for a discourse relation $R(\pi_1, \pi_2)$, some specified relation holds between the eventualities e_1, e_2, described by π_1 and π_2 respectively. We discuss two such cases here: the subordinating relation ELABORATION and the coordinating relation RESULT. As a subordinating relation, ELABORATION is not directly expressible by any coordinate structure. However, as we have seen, it figures in coordinate structures insofar as CONTINUATIONS and NARRATIONS are ELABORATIONS of a discourse topic. It will also be relevant to our discussion of extraction in Section 6.6.

ELABORATION
In our discussion of CONTINUATION and NARRATION, we assumed (160), repeated below:

(160)   If ELABORATION(α, β), then part-of(e_β, e_α).

However, we did not motivate this assumption. The classic example that motivates (160) is the 'salmon' example, which features alarmingly often in all SDRT texts (see discussion in footnote 36).

(190)   a. John had a great evening last night.
        b. He had a great meal.
        c. He ate salmon.
        d. He devoured lots of cheese.
        e. He then won a dancing competition.   (Asher and Lascarides 2003)

(190a) describes an event (the great evening), of which two subparts (the meal and the dancing) are described in (190b) and (190e) respectively. Two further subparts of the meal are described in (190c) and (190d). All of these subpart relations correspond to ELABORA-TIONS in the discourse structure: the meal and the dancing elaborate on the great evening; the salmon and the cheese elaborate on the meal.

In fact, Asher and Lascarides claim that coherence is also guaranteed here by a constraint on topic: if ELABORATION(π_1, π_2) holds, then π_1 is the topic for π_2. Our impression is that this is not an independent constraint, but actually reflects the primary event-structural constraint on ELABORATION. Regardless, it captures the use of ELABORATION as a label for the relationship between a NARRATION or CONTINUATION, and a discourse topic. (190a) establishes the discourse topic; (190b) elaborates on it and establishes a more specific topic, upon which (190c–d) elaborate in turn, and so on.

The discourse in (191), from Asher (2004: 185–6), is a similar example.

(191)   a.   Chris and Pat took really neat vacations this year.
        b.   In September, Chris went to Madagascar.
        c.   From there, he went to the island of Maurice, and
        d.   he returned to Madagascar via the Kerguelen islands.
        e.   A little later in the year, Pat also went on a boat trip.
        f.   She visited all the Greek islands, one by one.

(191b–f) elaborate on (191a). Moreover, there is a bifurcation between (191b–d) and (191e–f). (191b–d) is a chain of NARRATIONS, while (191f) is an ELABORATION of (191e). The point of interest is that *also* in (191e) is a cue to a PARALLEL relation, and we need to know the other term of that relation. Intuitively, the other term is 'Chris's boat trip' (and even if your geographical knowledge doesn't tell you that Chris's trip should be undertaken by boat—the only means of access to the Kerguelen islands—you should accommodate that information). Asher therefore argues that 'Chris's boat trip' is a discourse topic which isn't introduced by any single DU, but upon which (191b–d) are ELABORATIONS. The structure proposed by Asher (p. 187) for (191) is as in (192).[73]

(192)

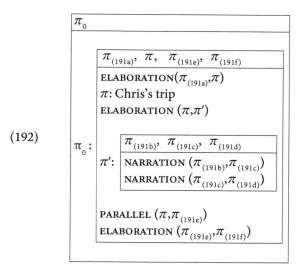

---

[73] We have modified a few details in (192) for clarity and consistency. The fact that (191e) is an elaboration of (191a) is not explicitly represented, but follows from the facts that the covert topic π is an ELABORATION of (191a) and that PARALLEL holds between π and (191e).

RESULT

According to Asher and Lascarides (2003) and Asher (2004), RESULT—while veridical like the rest of the coordinating relations—does not contribute a topic to logical form or require a common theme.[74] Rather, RESULT guarantees coherence by the causal relation that holds between the eventualities described by its arguments. More precisely, we can say that RESULT(α, β) contributes the following information:

(193)

$$
\begin{array}{|l|}
\hline
e_\pi \\
\hline
\text{cause}(e_\alpha, e_\beta) \\
\neg\text{before}(e_\beta, e_\alpha) \\
e_\pi = e_\alpha + e_\beta \\
\hline
\end{array}
$$

According to the first condition, first mentioned in Section 6.3.1, an event described by α causes an event described by β. According to the second condition, which follows from commonsense understanding of causation, an event described by β does not occur before its causing event. And, finally, according to the third condition, e_π is the event recording the causative effect of e_α on e_β. For reasons related to those mentioned in Sections 5.3.1 and 5.3.2, SDRT does not spell out what it means to be a **causative effect**, assuming that this is a primitive notion (McCawley 1968).[75]

There is some subtlety required here to clarify the relationship between RESULT and NARRATION. We saw in Chapter 5 that there is an entailment relation between RESULT and OCCASION. However, we have seen that OCCASION is different from NARRATION, because NARRATION requires a discourse topic. This gives rise to a prediction that it is possible to find cases in which RESULT holds, but NARRATION does not. Asher (2004) claims that (194), repeated from (156b), is such an example.

(194)   My car broke down (π_1). Then the sun set (π_2) and I knew I was in trouble (π_3).

(Asher 2004: 181)

If the three EDUs in (194) shared a common topic, then a fortiori the first two EDUs would also share a common topic. This would mean that (195), repeated from (156a), should be a coherent NARRATION. The relative unacceptability of (195) suggests that this is not the case, or at least that the common topic is not readily identified.

(195)   #My car broke down. Then the sun set.

Asher suggests that π_3 in (194) allows us to retrospectively assign a discourse structure in which CONTINUATION(π_1, π_2) holds, along with RESULT(π_{1-2}, π_3), but not NARRATION because the common topic of π_1 and π_2 (roughly, things which happened and got me into trouble) does not also extend to π_3.

This subtle argument is useful for us in that it finally allows us to drive a wedge between Lakoff's Type A scenarios (with NARRATION) and Type C scenarios (with RESULT), and avoid the apparently incorrect prediction from Chapter 5 that RESULT should allow all the

---

[74] In this way, Asher and Lascarides's proposal converges with Kehler (2002) claim, discussed in Section 6.2.2, that RESULT is unlike PARALLEL in that it doesn't contribute a discourse topic.

[75] For more discussion of causality in SDRT, see Schlöder (2018: Ch. 7). For an attempt to unpack what it means to be a causative effect, including a discussion of why it is fruitful to do so, see Copley and Wolff (2014).

extraction patterns that OCCASION does, because RESULT entails OCCASION. We return to this point in Section 6.6.

6.5.4 Summary

This section has considered how discourse relations contribute in different ways to the construction of discourse topics, and the different constraints they impose in terms of common themes. In Section 6.5.1, we looked at CONTINUATION, NARRATION, ⇒BACKGROUND, and ALTERNATION. CONTINUATION contributes the most basic of all SDRT topic constraints: it requires its arguments to be elaborations of a common discourse topic. As for NARRATION, it stands in the same relation to a discourse topic, but also contributes the information that events described by its two arguments are temporally close and reported in order. ⇒BACKGROUND is different again: its first argument must be stative, and overlap temporally with the eventuality described by the second event. On the original version of SDRT, the two arguments also form a Foreground–Background Pair, which constrains their relation to the discourse topic. In more recent work, however, ⇒BACKGROUND is assumed to be like CONTINUATION and NARRATION in requiring its arguments to be elaborations of a discourse topic, though this topic is not common, but rather a sum of what is at issue. Finally, ALTERNATION, at least in its canonical use, describes alternative answers to a topical question.

Next, in Section 6.5.2, we considered PARALLEL and CONTRAST, whose semantics references the maximal common theme of the two arguments. Although a theme is similar to a discourse topic, a major difference is that discourse topics are explicitly represented in logical forms, while themes are instead implicit in the nature of the arguments of relations like PARALLEL and CONTRAST. The greater the similarity between those arguments, the richer the common theme. This in turn entails more support for these relations, so the relations are of higher 'quality'. PARALLEL and CONTRAST differ in the relation that they stand in to this common theme: PARALLEL entails that elements excluded from the common theme are similar, while CONTRAST entails that they are dissimilar.

Finally, we considered relations like RESULT, which differ from the above relations in several important respects. RESULT is a coordinating relation, but does not impose any constraints on a topic or theme. Instead, the coherence of a discourse structure with RESULT is guaranteed by the causal relation that is entailed to hold between its arguments.

In the next section, we take this new taxonomy and revisit the extraction data from this new perspective. In particular, we want to see whether this more nuanced theory of the relationships between sentence topic, discourse topic, theme, and discourse relation allows for any progress with respect to the questions raised for Kehler's account at the end of Section 6.2.4.

6.6 Back to extraction from coordinate structures

We are now ready to return to the unresolved puzzles from the end of Chapter 5 and from Section 6.2.4, about discourse relations, information structure, and extraction patterns. Recall that Sections 5.4 and 5.5 demonstrated that Lakoff's (1986) three scenario types—identified as permitting different asymmetric extraction patterns—do not actually behave as Lakoff predicts. More or less any extraction pattern can be found with more or less any of Lakoff's scenarios: from just the initial conjunct, just the final conjunct, ATB, or from any subset of the conjuncts in the type of n-ary Type A coordination (taken by Kehler 2002 to exemplify a string of OCCASION relations; Lakoff only discussed strictly binary coordinate structures with Types B and C). The only exception to this observation is that we have no convincing examples of extraction from only the final conjunct in Type C scenarios, exemplifying RESULT.[76]

Despite this negative conclusion, we nevertheless found that there are clear links between discourse relations (not always construed in the way that Lakoff or Kehler construed them) and patterns of extraction from coordinate structures. We identified four classes of discourse relations, with distinctive interactions with coordinate structures.

1. Many discourse relations cannot be expressed by coordination, including ⇐BACKGROUND, EXPLANATION, and ELABORATION, among others.
2. Some relations, like PARALLEL and CONTRAST, allow only ATB extraction.
3. Relations like RESULT and ALTERNATION allow extraction from the initial conjunct, or ATB extraction, but not extraction from the final conjunct alone.
4. Relations like NARRATION and ⇒BACKGROUND do not impose constraints on the conjuncts from which extraction takes place in languages like English, although asymmetric extraction from noninitial conjuncts is impossible in languages like French.

In Section 6.2 we discussed the possibility that topicality may be the link between discourse structure and extraction patterns, following Kuno (1976), Kehler (2002), and others. However, there are several points of unclarity where further research is needed, and we framed the discussion in terms of Choice Point 5, concerning the relationship between D-linking, sentence topic, and weak islands. In fact, Section 6.2 is essentially an exploration of a particular option listed under Choice Point 5. Citing Polinsky's (2001) data concerning topic-marking of D-linked phrases in Tsez, we tentatively assumed that D-linking and sentence topic are, if not identical, at least a natural class, and that only D-linked/topical phrases can be extracted from weak islands. In this section, we explore the relationship between this notion of sentence topic and the SDRT notion of topicality.

We left Section 6.2 with a list of further unanswered questions pertaining to this topic-based analysis. We summarize this to-do list below.

1. We need to expand the empirical coverage beyond Lakoff's three scenarios and ATB movement, to include at least the SLF construction, the examples from Culicover and Jackendoff (1997), and the Type D scenario of Na and Huck (1992).

---

[76] As noted in Chapter 5 (see in particular the end of Section 5.4.2), the judgments for such examples are subtle, and merit a controlled study that considers (among other things) how extraction from coordinate structures is processed in real time. For example, consider the question below. Of thirty-two native speakers that we asked, thirty found this somewhat odd, though these speakers differed as to the degree of oddity, with some speakers reporting that this question would never be uttered in conversation, while others could imagine asking this question in some context.

(i)   Who did [[John drunk drive] and [kill __]]?   (Julian Schlöder, pers. comm.)

2. The demonstration at the end of Chapter 5 that extraction from coordinate structures with 'pure' RESULT is more restricted than extraction from coordinate structures with VIOLATED EXPECTATION or 'pure' OCCASION is particularly difficult to make sense of given the entailment relations between VIOLATED EXPECTATION, RESULT, and OCCASION (or, in SDRT terms, NARRATION). We therefore would consider it a success for a topic-based approach if it could make some progress in explaining the extraction patterns that we observe in light of the noted entailment relations.

3. Coordinate structures with NARRATION are challenging in a different respect: these structures are highly flexible in that it is possible to create an example with extraction from any arbitrary set of conjuncts, and yet for any given example, the extraction possibilities are typically quite fixed. Moreover, extraction from the final conjunct is normally, but not always, required.

4. We still need to understand why PARALLEL and CONTRAST require ATB extraction, rather than simply permitting it.

The reason for introducing SDRT in detail in this chapter is to give us a framework for exploring the above patterns more precisely in the terms of a more nuanced theory of discourse structure, in which topics play a role, as in the Kuno/Kehler vision outlined in Section 6.2, but only as one of many moving parts. The crucial ingredients in SDRT are the following:

- A structural distinction between coordinating and subordinating discourse relations (Section 6.3), with both an intuitive basis and a diagnostic based on patterns of anaphora and the Right Frontier Constraint.
- Particular constraints that lexical items place on discourse structure (Section 6.4): *and* requires a coordinating discourse relation (Txurruka 2003), *but* is a cue for CONTRAST (Asher and Lascarides 2003), and *or* typically, but not exclusively, triggers ALTERNATION and ranges over epistemic alternatives (Asher 2004).
- A set of statements on which discourse relations require explicit representation of discourse topic in logical form, and the nature of that representation (the majority of Section 6.5).
- A related notion of 'maximal common theme', which features in the interpretation of discourse relations (e.g. PARALLEL and CONTRAST) that are sensitive to the internal notions of their arguments (Section 6.5.2).

These elements of discourse structure complement the syntactic generalizations about extraction from coordinate structures from Chapters 3 and 4. In fact, because of the different behaviors of initial and noninitial conjuncts revealed by the summary above, in this section we will not remain neutral with respect to the options laid out in Choice Points 2–4, in Chapters 3 and 4, but explicitly assume the adjunction analysis of Munn (1993) and the generalization derived from Postal (1998), that initial conjuncts are not islands for extraction, while noninitial conjuncts are weak islands in languages like English, and strong islands in languages like German. We assume these options in this section because they articulate well with the topic-based approach that we are exploring. Our evaluation of this topic-based approach could be seen to reflect indirectly on the strengths and weaknesses of these syntactic choices, because we have seen that these syntactic options do need to be supplemented by a rich discourse-semantic theory if they are to avoid overgeneration.

Below, we consider discourse relations in three classes: those that explicitly represent a discourse topic in logical form (NARRATION, CONTINUATION, ⇒BACKGROUND, ALTERNATION); those that rely on a notion of 'maximal common theme' (PARALLEL, CONTRAST); and those that do neither (particularly RESULT). Within each group, we consider extraction from initial and noninitial conjuncts, and where appropriate the effect of conjunction choice (although the majority of the relations mentioned in this paragraph are only compatible with *and*). We restrict ourselves to binary coordination in what follows, because all SDRT relations are strictly binary. We consider extraction from more complex coordinate structures in Section 6.7.

Our initial aim is to correlate these classes of discourse relations, identified on the basis of how they interact with topic and theme, with the different extraction patterns enumerated at the start of this section. The following generalizations will emerge from this exercise:

- ATB extraction is always permitted, all else being equal.
- Extraction from the initial conjunct is possible, except with those relations with maximal common themes.
- Extraction (possibly ATB) of topical material from weak islands is possible only for those relations with discourse topics explicitly represented in logical forms.

The statements with which we began this section are a very close match for these three generalizations. In our opinion, this represents clear progress in understanding symmetrical and asymmetric patterns of extraction from coordinate structures. Nevertheless, there are some clear empirical discrepancies which will emerge in what follows. Moreover, we do not fully understand these generalizations in detail: there is more work to be done to explain *why* these discourse-structural classes align with extraction patterns in precisely this way. We will therefore continue to evaluate the progress, and its limits, in the remainder of this chapter and the next.

6.6.1 Relations with explicit representation of discourse topic

Relations like NARRATION and ⇒BACKGROUND are permissive in terms of extraction patterns: they allow the Type A pattern identified by Lakoff, but also allow extraction from only the initial conjunct (as demonstrated by Neeleman and Tanaka 2020 for NARRATION), and ATB extraction.

(196) **NARRATION: solely 1st; solely 2nd; ATB**
       a. What city did Mary [[go to __] and [buy a modernist painting]]?
       b. What modernist painting did Mary [[go to NYC] and [buy __]]?
       c. What did Ava [[write __ all night] and then [discuss __ with Teia]]?

(197) **⇒BACKGROUND: solely 1st; solely 2nd; ATB**
       a. Where did Ava [[stand __] and [scream at Teia]]?
       b. Who did you [[stand in the hallway] and [scream at __]]?
       c. Who does Anna [[live with __] and [read *Grumpy Monkey* to __]]?

We learned in Section 6.5.1 that from the perspective of SDRT these two relations are co-ordinating and require explicit representation of discourse topics. Following Asher et al. (2007), we assume that NARRATIONS and BACKGROUNDS are elaborations of the discourse topic. From this perspective, it may be possible to make sense of the permissiveness of these relations, if we adopt a particular set of assumptions about discourse topic, sentence topic, and extraction. Specifically, to make sense of the data, we need to follow von Fintel (1994) in assuming an anaphoric relation between sentence topic and discourse topic, as discussed in Section 6.2, and assume that sentence topics are uniquely able to extract from weak islands (this corresponds to Option 1 or 2 of Choice Point 5, from Section 6.2.3).

If we adopt these assumptions, all the pieces fit neatly together: an extracted phrase in a noninitial conjunct must correspond to a sentence topic, the discourse topic must be a predication of the sentence topic, and the semantics of NARRATION and ⇒BACKGROUND tells us that it is appropriate to put such topical material in noninitial conjuncts with these relations.

It is also not surprising, for different reasons, that it is possible to extract from initial conjuncts as in (196a) and (197a). On the syntactic hypothesis adopted for the purposes of developing this analysis, initial conjuncts are not islands. This means that extraction is generally possible from initial conjuncts, and in fact only blocked for relations which make reference in their semantics to a maximal common theme, as discussed in the following subsection.

Because initial conjuncts are, by hypothesis, not islands, elements extracted from initial conjuncts do not have to be topical, and therefore are not subject to the constraints on sentence topic described in Section 6.2. As discussed in that section, sentence topics are typically referential NPs. It is therefore significant that the extracted element in (197a) is not an NP. A similar example, with extraction of a non-D-linked NP from the initial conjunct of a NARRATION, is in (198).

(198)   How much money did you [[take __ out of the bank] and [buy that modernist painting]]?

Unsurprisingly, the extracted phrase in (198) fails tests for sentence topichood.

(199)   a.   #Speaking of $175,000, I took it/them out of the bank and bought that modernist painting.
        b.   Speaking of that modernist painting, I took $175,000 out of the bank and bought it.

There are further questions here about the relationship of these apparently nontopical initial conjuncts to the discourse topic, particularly in the case of NARRATION. SDRT principles have it that, if a NARRATION is an ELABORATION of the discourse topic, then every argument of the NARRATION should likewise be an ELABORATION of the discourse topic. In other words, in the examples labeled as NARRATION in (196), both conjuncts should be on an equal footing with respect to the discourse topic, apparently contrary to fact. We put these questions aside until Section 6.7, where they are central to the analysis of more complex examples of Lakoff's Type A scenarios. Moreover, we defer discussion of ATB extraction with these relations until we have a better handle of ATB extraction with PARALLEL and CONTRAST.

6.6.2 Relations with maximal common themes

The relations considered in this subsection only allow ATB movement:

(200)   **PARALLEL: ??solely 1st; ??solely 2nd; ATB**
    a. ??What book did John [[buy __] and [read a magazine]]?
    b. ??What magazine did John [[buy a book] and [read __]]?
    c. What book did [[John buy __] and [Bill read __]]?

(201)   **CONTRAST: ??solely 1st; ??solely 2nd; ATB**
    a. ??Which drink did [[Mike like __] but [Kate hate schnapps]]?
    b. ??Which drink did [[Mike like kefir] but [Kate hate __]]?
    c. Which drink did [[Mike like __] but [Kate hate __]]?

From an SDRT perspective, these are the relations that require a maximal common theme. To make sense of this pattern, we therefore need to understand better what a theme is, and how it relates to extraction. What we need to say is intuitively clear: these relations are distinguished by the extent to which they require semantic parallelism at the subsentential level. Furthermore, any traces must fall within the common theme, the portions of the semantic representation which are common to the conjuncts.

In this respect, an SDRT-based approach fits well with the claims of Ruys (1992) and Fox (2000) about semantic parallelism and extraction from coordinate structures. As discussed in Chapter 3, Ruys was interested in minimal pairs like (202). On Ruys's account, the acceptability of (202b) and unacceptability of (202a) derive from the fact that the covertly moved *what* binds a variable in each conjunct in (202b), but not in (202a), despite the fact that it has covertly moved only from the first conjunct.

(202)   a. *I wonder who [[took what from Mary] and [gave a book to Fred]].
    b. I wonder who [[took what from Mary] and [gave it to Fred]].

(Ruys 1992: 36)

This pattern is on a par with the examples given immediately above. The only difference is that the parallelism requirement is satisfied by a variable which corresponds to a pronoun in the syntax, rather than a trace. In other words, the heart of an ATB structure is the semantic configuration in (203), rather than a particular syntactic configuration of moved phrases and traces.

(203)   ... Wh_i ...[[... x_i ...] and [... x_i ...]]

It is also possible to see echoes of the analysis of Kehler (2002) in these claims, although we cannot follow Kehler in the details. Kehler claimed that the semantic material common to the conjuncts constituted a common topic for the two sentences, and indeed we have seen that common themes are quite close to discourse topics. However, common themes are not the same as topics. Most importantly, ATB-extracted phrases do not have to be sentence topics, and need not have the syntactic and semantic properties required of sentence topics. (204a) is an example of ATB extraction of an adverbial with PARALLEL, while (204b) is an example of ATB extraction of a nonreferential NP with NARRATION, possibly in addition to PARALLEL.

(204) a. How quickly can [[Mary swim __] and [Jo sail __]]?
       b. How many stories did the author [[dream up __] and then [write down __]]?

This indicates that the common theme in such examples does not entail that the extracted element corresponds to a sentence topic, unlike the genuinely topical extractees just discussed in the context of NARRATION and ⇒BACKGROUND.

SDRT therefore suggests a neat correlation: relations which require ATB extraction are just those defined with reference to a common theme. However, it is not clear precisely why this correlation holds. This question has never been posed in SDRT terms before, to our knowledge, and even the empirical facts are less clear-cut than the foregoing would suggest, as we will see presently, so all we can do is sketch some initial directions for future research. We will list some possible approaches here, and then discuss them each in turn.

Choice Point 6 What is the relationship between a common theme and the ATB constraint?

Option 1: The ATB constraint does not align with maximal common themes: there are cases of PARALLEL or CONTRAST with asymmetric extraction;
Option 2: The ATB constraint follows from interactions between maximal common themes and the syntax of canonical A'-extraction;
Option 3: The ATB constraint follows from interactions between maximal common themes and the semantics of canonical A'-constructions;
Option 4: Something else.

Option 1 initially sounds contrary to the spirit of this section, but there are some data that call into question the correlation proposed here. It is accordingly worthwhile to consider the possibility that the generalization presented in this section is simply wrong, and that the examples which only permit ATB extraction are not identical to the examples with relations that make reference to a maximal common theme. This would imply that we should not be looking for a connection between common themes and ATB extraction in the first place.

The main evidence in support of this option comes from cases where it apparently is possible to extract asymmetrically from the initial conjunct, despite the presence of a relation which requires a maximal common theme. (205) illustrates one such set of examples. As discussed in Section 3.5.3, Johnson (2004) claimed that (205a) is derived from an underlying structure approximately as in (205b), which transparently reflects the interpretation of the sentence.

(205) a. [[Ward can't eat caviar] and [Mary eat beans]].   (Johnson 2004)
       b. [not [can [[Ward eat caviar] and [Mary eat beans]]]]

The same is true of the following examples of asymmetric coordination discussed in Section 3.6.

(206) Äpfel ißt der Hans [[drei __] und [zwei Bananen]].
       apples eats the Hans three   and two   bananas
       'Hans eats three apples and two bananas.'   (Schwarz 1998: 195)

(207)   Leider   [[haben viele Kinder   Probleme mit   dem Gewicht]
        unfortunately have   many children problems with   the   weight
        und [können nicht lesen]].
        and can   not   read
        'Unfortunately, many children have weight problems and are unable to read.'

(Mayr and Schmitt 2017: 7)

However, we are ultimately unenthusiastic about Option 1, for two reasons. The first is that it is not clear precisely which discourse relation, if any, holds in the examples we've presented. For instance, the point of (205) is the contrast between caviar and beans, which would suggest that the discourse relation in question should be CONTRAST, but the example is significantly less acceptable if *and* is replaced by *but*, the cue-phrase for CONTRAST.

In fact, in these three examples, it is not even clear that we are dealing with two discourse units: in (205), negation and *can* must outscope *Ward eat caviar* and *Mary eat beans*; in (206) the conjoined elements are NPs, and in (207), *viele Kinder* must outscope both conjuncts. (207) is truth-conditionally distinct from either of the paraphrases in (208), and must instead be understood as in (209): many children are such that they have weight problems and are unable to read. Johnson described similar truth-conditional distinctions with respect to (205). In short, in each case, there are grounds to suspect that the constituents in question do not translate as independent DUs, either because they are not clausal (in the case of (206)) or because the first conjunct should not be interpreted independently of the second (as in the other two examples).

(208)   a. Many children have weight problems and many children are unable to read.
        b. Many children have weight problems and they are unable to read.

(209)   MANY x.[child(x)][weight-problem(x) $\wedge$ can't-read(x)]

The second reason why we are skeptical about Option 1 is that the examples listed in (205)–(207) are plausibly the opposite of Ruys's variable-binding example. Ruys demonstrated that a covertly moved *wh*-phrase can move asymmetrically out of a single conjunct if it binds a variable in the other conjunct. In contrast, in these examples, it is plausible that an asymmetrically extracted phrase reconstructs into the initial conjunct at LF, and therefore does not bind a variable in any conjunct. Johnson made this argument for (205) (see discussion in Chapter 3), and it seems possible that this argument could be extended to cover (206) and (207). For these three examples to count as clear counterexamples to the generalization that relations with common themes are subject to the ATB constraint, it would need to be demonstrated that the initial phrase binds a variable in one conjunct but not the other. To our knowledge, this has not been demonstrated, so from a Ruysian perspective, these examples may be simply irrelevant to the discussion of extraction patterns.

If one were to choose **Option 2**, a natural place to start would be Bošković and Franks (2000) observation, based on the contrast in (210), that the extracted element in an ATB construction behaves like a single phrase, as opposed to multiple identical phrases each originating in a different conjunct.

(210)   a. What did Mary say [[that John bought __] and [that Bill sold __]]?
        b. Who said [[that John bought what] and [that Bill sold what]]?

(210a) is interpreted as asking about a single object, but (210b) doesn't have that reading, and is taken instead to ask about objects that John is claimed to have bought and other objects that Bill is claimed to have sold. This contrast suggests that the two gap sites in (210a) are, in some sense, the same, an intuition which is cashed out in different ways from Williams (1978) through Gazdar (1981) to Nunes (2005) and Citko (2005).

It is tempting to try to leverage this understanding of (210a) to build an account of the ATB pattern. One way of building such an account would be to claim that there is actually only a single trace in a sentence like (210a), on a multidominance analysis such as Citko's. It would then be possible to claim that, if that trace is part of the maximal common theme, it must be interpreted in a parallel way within each conjunct.

However, the weakness of such an analysis is that it is not clear why the trace would have to be part of the common theme. Syntax doesn't care, because 'common theme' is not a syntactic notion. And discourse semantics doesn't care, because a common theme is just the common content of two DUs. If a trace happens to be present in one DU but not the other, then it falls outside the common theme and nothing more needs to be said.

We think the most promising of the options listed above is **Option 3**. In order to flesh this option out, we will look in a little more detail at the semantics of PARALLEL and CONTRAST, which are defined in relation to a maximal common theme. If PARALLEL(π_1, π_2) or CONTRAST(π_1, π_2) holds, then the common theme of π_1 and π_2 is information which is either common to π_1 and π_2, or inferable from each of π_1 and π_2. Moreover, some material in each of π_1 and π_2 is excluded from the common theme. In other words, the relations PARALLEL and CONTRAST divide a logical form into a common theme shared between the two conjuncts, and the nonthematic material which is not shared between the two conjuncts.

It may be helpful, following Kehler (2002), to think of this nonthematic material as a vector of paired elements of a logical form. For instance, the examples in (211a–b) both have a common theme as in (211c), according to Asher et al. (1997). What differs across the two conjuncts is the identity of u and v. For a simple example like (211), we can think of this nonthematic material as a list of pairs of corresponding elements, as in (211d): in the first conjunct, u is Mary and v is pizza; in the second conjunct, u is Sue and v is lasagne. (211a), with PARALLEL, implies that Mary is similar to Sue and pizza is similar to lasagne. (211b), with CONTRAST, implies that at least one of these pairs is dissimilar.

(211)   a. Mary ordered pizza and Sue ordered lasagne.
       b. Mary ordered pizza, but Sue ordered lasagne.

       c.
u, v
order(u, v)

       d. $\langle\langle \text{mary}(u), \text{sue}(u)\rangle, \langle \text{pizza}(v), \text{lasagne}(v)\rangle\rangle$

We now need to consider how this partition relates to extraction. In the case of ATB movement, following the insight from Bošković and Franks we have discussed, a single trace is common to both conjuncts. It is therefore part of the common theme. In cases of asymmetric extraction, the trace is not associated with both conjuncts.[77] It is therefore not part of the

---

[77] We will put aside the Ruys/Fox variable-binding effects discussed earlier in this section. Everything we say here applies equally to those cases, if we talk about ATB variable binding rather than ATB extraction.

common theme. If we believe that PARALLEL and CONTRAST require ATB extraction (that is, if we reject Option 1), then Option 3 requires us to explain why a trace of movement, or a variable A'-bound by an operator, must be part of the common theme.

One possible way of addressing this challenge would be to examine the information-structural status of elements outside the common theme: if variables bound by A'-operators are somehow incompatible with that status, then that would entail that the traces have to be located within the common theme. Specifically, what we have in mind is that the elements of the pairs in (211d) contrast with each other, this contrast being signaled with the distinctive fall–rise accent sometimes known as the 'B-accent' (Jackendoff 1972, Büring 2003). If a variable bound by an A'-operator is not able to contrast with a paired element in another conjunct, if a trace cannot be similar or dissimilar to a paired element in another conjunct,[78] or perhaps if the B-accent is obligatory but cannot be borne by a trace, we would have an explanation for why the trace must be within the common theme, and this in turn would yield an information-structural account for why the ATB pattern is obligatory in the case of PARALLEL or CONTRAST.

Although this seems like a promising line of inquiry, we are unaware of any current theory of information structure or prosody which would derive this result (see Steedman 2014, Schlöder and Lascarides 2020 for recent theories of information structure and prosody). Accordingly, Option 3 must wait for attention from researchers with more expertise than we have in this area.

The options listed with respect to Choice Point 6 are quite speculative, and it is therefore highly likely that there are good answers that we simply haven't considered. This is **Option 4**. We don't know what other options are worth considering, of course, and the SDRT-based approach to extraction from coordinate structures sketched in this chapter will remain incomplete until some more clarity emerges here. However, we would like to emphasize that this unfinished business isn't confined to the SDRT approach. We have already seen that the approach of Kehler (2002) to ATB extraction and Resemblance relations, in terms of the distribution of topics, is problematic because ATB-extracted phrases are not always plausible topics. The considerations in this chapter also have troubling implications for approaches like the Ruys/Fox approach based on semantic parallelism. It is clearly not always the case that conjuncts must be semantically parallel, so semantic parallelism clearly doesn't hold in the general case. It may well be possible to claim that ATB movement follows from a semantic parallelism constraint, broadly as in Munn (1993), but the value of such a claim is limited in the absence of a clear account of when parallelism does, and doesn't, obtain.

From that perspective, a virtue of the SDRT approach is that it has highlighted gaps in our current understanding, and in Option 3, it may have the germ of a way of plugging those gaps.

6.6.3   RESULT: Neither topic nor theme

We will move on to consider RESULT, which disallows asymmetric extraction from the final conjunct, while allowing it from the initial conjunct, as well as ATB movement:

---

[78] This possibility was suggested to us by Julian Schlöder.

(212)   **RESULT: solely 1st; ??solely 2nd; ATB**

    a.   What's the stuff the guys in the Caucasus [[drink __] and, as a result, [live to be 100]]?

    b.   ??Who did Kharms [[hear a news story] and, as a result, [think of __]]?

    c.   What did you [[hear __] and, as a result, [think of __]]?

According to SDRT, RESULT is coordinating but does not require explicit representation of a discourse topic in logical form.[79] However, to make sense of (212), we would require a stronger statement: noninitial conjuncts in RESULT-coordinations *cannot* contain sentence topics, and therefore cannot contain material able to extract from a weak island. In other words, it is not enough to state that a discourse topic is unnecessary—a sentence topic in a noninitial conjunct with RESULT must be impossible.

The *speaking of* test suggests that this may be the case. The examples in (213), using *speaking of X* to identify a sentence topic in the second conjunct, are approximately as degraded as the cases of extraction from the noninitial conjunct.[80,81]

(213)   a.   ?Speaking of the local hospital, people always [[eat that chili dish] and, as a result, [end up there]].

    b.   ?Speaking of Lenin, Kharms [[heard a news story] and, as a result, [thought of him]].

(214)   a.   *Which hospital do people always [[eat that chili dish] and, as a result, [end up at __]]?

    b.   *Who did Kharms [[hear a news story] and, as a result, [think of __]]?

We do not know exactly why this should be, and the judgments are very subtle, but it is nevertheless another case where the predictions of SDRT align suggestively with observed extraction patterns: extraction from the initial conjunct is possible, but there is no possibility of asymmetric extraction from a noninitial conjunct.

6.6.4 More challenging cases

Finally, we consider some cases where the SDRT-based approach that we have been developing either does not make clear predictions, or makes apparently incorrect predictions.

---

[79] Recall from Section 6.2.2 that Kehler (2002) also proposes that Humean Cause/Effect relations (and hence RESULT) do not factor into topic construction.

[80] We do not report judgments on sentence topics in initial conjuncts, because extraction from initial conjuncts does not impose any topicality constraint. As discussed in Chapter 5, the phrase *as a result* disambiguates in favor of RESULT but leads to some degradation of all extraction examples. The reader can check that omitting *as a result* is not enough to make the examples in (214) fully grammatical, though.

[81] Julian Schlöder offers the following example of RESULT with a topic in the second conjunct.

(i)   Speaking of Yu'an, I just [[felt my wedding band] and, as a result, [thought of her]].

We do not know how this is different from the examples in (213), but it may well relate to the possibility, discussed in Section 5.4, that the characterization of Type C scenarios like those in (213) involves more than just RESULT. We are not sure whether it is possible to extract out of the noninitial conjunct in (i) (*This is the person who I just [[felt my wedding band] and, as a result, [thought of __]]*): there was variation in the judgments of the native speakers we asked.

Type B scenarios

For all the ground that we have covered since Chapter 5, we still do not really know what to do about Lakoff's Type B examples, like (215).

(215)   How many lakes can we [[destroy __] and [not arouse public antipathy]]?

Kehler (2002) analyzed these as harboring VIOLATED EXPECTATION, which, as a Cause/Effect relation, was predicted not to impose constraints on the distribution of topical material. Accordingly, within his framework of assumptions about topicality and extraction, Kehler predicted that extraction from either conjunct would be possible, a prediction which is borne out, at least in English: the following examples are all repeated from Section 5.4.1.

(216)   a.   How much can you [[drink __] and [still stay sober]]?
      b.   This is an argument that you can [[get blind drunk] and [still understand __]].
      c.   This is the kind of meal that you know you're going to [[pay too much for __] but [still enjoy __]].

However, this correct prediction—that anything goes with extraction from Type B scenarios—was derived from assumptions that we challenged repeatedly in Chapter 5 and Section 6.2. Moreover, in Section 5.4.1 we discussed regularities in canonical Type B examples which seem to have nothing to do with discourse relations: the extracted phrase is a measure phrase, the coordinate structure is in the scope of a possibility modal, there is a gap in the first conjunct only, and the second conjunct specifies a 'threshold' for the relevant instances of the event described in the first conjunct. With so much going on which is apparently orthogonal to the discourse relation in question, it is tempting to push back against the Lakoff/Kehler project of correlating the extraction pattern in (216a) with a specific discourse relation.

SDRT doesn't give us a single clear way to approach these data. There is no relation called VIOLATED EXPECTATION in SDRT. The nearest equivalent, as mentioned in Section 6.2.4, is a variety of CONTRAST ('a violation of expectations' in the terms of Asher and Lascarides 2003) which does not require a maximal common theme. Because that variety of CONTRAST does not require a maximal common theme, it will not be restricted to ATB movement, and will allow at least asymmetric extraction from the initial conjunct, as in (216a). Whether it also allows asymmetric extraction from the final conjunct depends on the relationship between this form of CONTRAST and a discourse topic, a relationship which has not been investigated to our knowledge. If it does not have a discourse topic, we would have to conclude that CONTRAST should not allow extraction from the final conjunct, and (216b) must harbor some other relation, most likely NARRATION.[82]

However, it is not even clear that classic Type B examples harbor CONTRAST. As noted in Section 5.4.1, we do not know whether an expectation is violated in (216a) unless we know the amount that was drunk: if 'you' drank a very small amount of alcohol, then it would be unsurprising if you stayed sober. With this in mind, it is quite plausible that a less contentful discourse relation, such as CONTINUATION, holds between the conjuncts in (216a). Supporting this conclusion, the example is less natural with *but* replacing *and*.

---

[82] Note that one infers spatiotemporal contiguity between the described events of getting drunk and understanding the argument.

(217)   ??How much can you [[drink __] but (still) [stay sober]]?

In short, there is a range of fairly clearly defined options here:

Choice Point 7   What is the correct analysis of Type B scenarios?

> Option 1:   Examples of Type B scenarios harbor CONTRAST, possibly without reference
> to a maximal common theme; CONTRAST allows asymmetric extraction from
> either conjunct.
>
> Option 2:   Examples like (216a) harbor CONTRAST; CONTRAST only allows asymmetric
> extraction from initial conjuncts; examples like (216b) should be analyzed in
> terms of some other discourse relation.
>
> Option 3:   Examples like (216a) harbor some less contentful relation like CONTINUA-
> TION; factors not closely related to discourse structure explain the distinctive
> properties of such examples; examples like (216b–c) should be analyzed in
> terms of some other discourse relation.

It is probably clear that our sympathies lie with Option 3, because it has the greatest potential for explaining the whole range of properties of Type B scenarios. However, the choice
between these three options is relatively inconsequential for the broad shape of the analysis
developed in this chapter.

Type D scenarios
Little attention has been paid to Type D examples such as (218), other than by Schmerling
(1975) and Na and Huck (1992).

(218)   Which baserunner was Doc [[following his coach's instructions] and [keeping __
close to first]]?   (Na and Huck 1992: 260)

This is one place where the SDRT-based approach appears to make an incorrect prediction.
The natural label for the relation exemplified in (218) is ELABORATION: the second conjunct
describes the same event as the first, or perhaps part of that event, in more detail than the
first conjunct provides. However, ELABORATION is a subordinating relation, rather than a
coordinating relation—in fact, it is in many respects the central example of a subordinating
relation. Therefore, according to the hypothesis of Txurruka (2003) (see Section 6.4.1), it
should be incompatible with *and*, regardless of whether extraction takes place.

It seems unpromising to claim that *and* is somehow compatible with a subordinating
relation in this case. For one thing, we have no theory of why this case is special, in comparison to all the subordinating relations that Txurruka's theory correctly rules out. For another
thing, patterns of anaphora suggest that examples like (218) are coordinating rather than
subordinating.

(219)   Doc [[followed some very clear instructions$_i$] and [kept the baserunner close to
first]]. *They$_i$ were repeated to him several times by the coach before the match
began.

So it is more likely that Type D scenarios either involve an exceptionally coordinating version of ELABORATION (which would be a surprise in itself, though see Asher and Vieu 2005)
or some other coordinating relation (perhaps ⇒BACKGROUND, although (218) would be

an unusual instantiation of ⇒BACKGROUND because both conjuncts describe events rather than states).[83]

We will introduce a label, ⇒ELABORATION, in Section 6.7 to describe a related class of examples, but we emphasize that this is only a placeholder for an actual analysis.

Culicover and Jackendoff's examples with CONSEQUENCE

The 'left-subordinating *and*' pattern identified by Culicover and Jackendoff (1997) involves a conditional interpretation of the relationship between the two conjuncts.

(220)   a. ?This is the loot that [[you just identify __] and [we arrest the thief on the spot]].
        b. ?This is the thief that [[you just identify the loot] and [we arrest __ on the spot]].

                                                      (Culicover and Jackendoff 1997: 206)

The SDRT label for conditional-like relations is CONSEQUENCE. We can see from (220) that examples harboring this relation allow extraction from either conjunct, at least marginally.[84] This is somewhat surprising because one might initially expect CONSEQUENCE to be a subordinating relation, where the second conjunct (or the consequent more generally, regardless of how it is expressed syntactically) elaborates on a situation described by the first conjunct (or the antecedent). However, the Right Frontier Constraint again says otherwise. In (221), *it* can only relate to *a hamburger* if the latter is interpreted, oddly, as referring to a specific hamburger, outside the scope of the conditional. If *a hamburger* remains within the scope of the conditional, then the discourse referent that it introduces is inaccessible to anaphors introduced after the consequent, as is familiar from classic work on donkey anaphora in DRT (Kamp 1981).[85]

(221)   a. If [you eat a hamburger$_i$], [you will get sick]. You ate one/*it$_i$, so you will get sick.
        b. [[You eat a hamburger$_i$] and [you get sick]]. You ate one/*it$_i$, so you will get sick.

So CONSEQUENCE is a coordinating relation, at least in those cases which correspond to Culicover and Jackendoff's left-subordinating *and*. It would be natural to assume that the antecedent and consequent somehow relate to a superordinate topic, as for NARRATION and other relations discussed in Section 6.6.1. However, these aspects of CONSEQUENCE have not received very much scrutiny yet in SDRT,[86] so the nature of that relation, and whether all conditional-like cases should be analyzed in similar terms, are currently open questions.

---

[83] Another possibility, suggested by Julian Schlöder (pers. comm.) is that (218) harbors RESULT. Potential evidence for this view is the observation that (218) is compatible with the cue-phrase *as a result*:

(i)   Which baserunner was Doc [[following his coach's instructions] and, **as a result**, [keeping __ close to first]]?

Note, however, that there is no cue-phrase that stands in a one-to-one correspondence with a discourse relation (Jasinskaja and Karagjosova 2020). For example, *as a result* is also compatible with the mathematical discourse below, which clearly is not causal:

(ii)   For all real numbers x, $x^2 = (-x^2)$. As a result, $2^2 = (-2^2)$.

According to our intuitions, to the extent that (i) is natural with *as a result*, it is on a par with (ii).

[84] The question marks in (220) are Culicover and Jackendoff's.

[85] In this case, one would have to use *one*. For more discussion of *one*-anaphora, see, e.g., Dahl (1984).

[86] Thanks to Alex Lascarides and Julian Schlöder for discussion of what *has* been done so far.

Culicover and Jackendoff's examples with ALTERNATION

The other pattern identified by Culicover and Jackendoff (1997) is 'threat-*or*', as in (222).

(222)   a.   This is the loot that [[you hide __ right now] or [we're in big trouble]].
        b.   Which kind of candy do [[you spit __ right out] or [you get real sick]]?

(Culicover and Jackendoff 1997: 215)

In Sections 6.4 and 6.5.1, we talked about *or*, including threat-*or* as a cue-phrase for the relation of ALTERNATION. In Chapter 5, we cited the contrast in (223) as evidence that ALTERNATION allows asymmetric extraction from the initial conjunct, but not the noninitial conjunct.

(223)   ALTERNATION: solely 1st; ??solely 2nd; ATB
        a.   This is the loot that [[you hide __ right now] or [we're in big trouble]].
        b.   ??This is the loot that [[you tell us what you know] or [you never see __ again]].
        c.   This is the loot that [[you hide __ from the thieves] or [we never see __ again]].

The challenge here is that we would not predict this pattern on the basis of the considerations laid out in this chapter. We have reviewed the evidence from Asher (2004) that DUs related by ALTERNATION relate to a discourse topic represented in logical form, and we have also suggested in Section 6.6.1 that such a relation to a discourse topic is a precondition for asymmetric extraction of elements corresponding to sentence topics from noninitial conjuncts. That is precisely what we do not see in (223). Instead, (223) shows the extraction pattern associated with RESULT, which we attributed in Section 6.6.3 to the fact that RESULT does not stand in such a relation to a discourse topic.

There are a handful of possibilities for explaining this discrepancy. The first is that we may simply be wrong about the facts: (223) may be inaccurate and/or unrepresentative. The second is that Asher may be wrong about the relation between ALTERNATION and discourse topics. The third is that the contrast between ALTERNATION and NARRATION, if better understood, might tell us something about the different ways in which DUs can relate to a discourse topic. Asher hints that this relation is unusual in the cases of ALTERNATION but does not provide any detail. We expect that the contrast in (223), if robust, will ultimately be illuminating in this way, but for now have nothing concrete to add.

6.6.5 Summary

Even limiting ourselves to binary coordinate structures, we can see that the SDRT-based approach developed in this chapter offers new insight into the extraction behavior of different relations, despite all the loose ends just documented. We have been assuming that the empirical picture is quite different to how it is usually laid out: rather than Lakoff's project of associating different relations with different sets of conjuncts which allow extraction, we have argued in Chapter 5 for an implicational relation: some relations are incompatible with coordinate structures, some only allow ATB extraction, some also allow asymmetric extraction from initial conjuncts, and some allow asymmetric extraction from any conjunct, at least in languages like English.

In Sections 6.4.1 and 6.6.1–6.6.3, we correlated these four patterns with a principled taxonomy of SDRT discourse relations: subordinating relations are incompatible with coordinate structures; relations requiring a common theme only allow ATB extraction; relations without a discourse topic or a common theme also allow asymmetric extraction from the initial topic; and relations with a discourse topic allow asymmetric extraction from any conjunct.

This taxonomy relies on two essential ingredients of SDRT which do not feature, or at least do not feature in the same way, in other theories of discourse structure. The first is the distinction between subordinating and coordinating relations, as diagnosed by the Right Frontier Constraint. The second is the way in which discourse topics structure some, but not all, discourse relations. Our reason for focusing on SDRT in this chapter is because these properties of SDRT open up new structural possibilities.

None of this means that the SDRT-based approach sketched here is correct! Firstly, we must acknowledge the loose ends and apparently incorrect predictions listed in Section 6.6.4, as well as the lack of clarity about the relationship between common themes and the ATB requirement in Section 6.6.2. Secondly, this theory depends on a syntactic distinction between initial and noninitial conjuncts along the lines of Munn (1993) (see Choice Point 4 in Chapter 4), and the jury is still out on those aspects of the syntax of coordination, as well.

We do not believe that this account is any more incomplete or inaccurate in these respects than accounts like Lakoff's, Deane's, or Kehler's, but this list reinforces how much is left to do in order to evaluate competing theories of extraction, and thereby make progress in resolving the tension between syntax and discourse.

6.7 More complex discourse structures and extraction

We limited ourselves in Section 6.6 to strictly binary conjunction, reflecting the fact that discourse relations are strictly binary in the theories of discourse structure we have considered. However, we know that coordinate structures sometimes contain more than two conjuncts. We discussed the syntactic distinction between binary and n-ary coordination briefly in Chapter 2; in this section we complement that discussion by covering the discourse semantics of n-ary coordination.

In SDRT, representations of n-ary coordination must be built up recursively from binary coordination. For instance, we might arrive at the logical form for (224) by first positing PARALLEL(π_1, π_2), and only then adding π_3 to arrive at a representation where all three conjuncts are parallel.

(224)   Sam read *Dubliners* (π_1), Kate read *Ulysses* (π_2), and Heather read *Finnegans Wake* (π_3).

In what follows, we will not develop a compositional mechanism for achieving this. Instead, we will describe some desiderata for the output of such a mechanism. One of the most important desiderata is that the logical form for examples like (225) must be 'flatter' than might be expected from recursive binary application of discourse relations. In the case of (224), it would be inappropriate to end up with an (abbreviated) representation of discourse structure as in (225), with PARALLEL holding of π_1 and π_2, and PARALLEL holding again of the CDU containing π_1 and π_2 (that is, π_4 in (225)) and π_3.

(225) π_4: PARALLEL(π_1, π_2)
      π_5: PARALLEL(π_4, π_3)

The first reason is that it is not clear what this would mean. The maximal common theme of the three conjuncts in (224) is as in (226). PARALLEL then entails that the elements outside the common theme are similar.

(226)

u,v
read(u,v)

But what is Heather, in π_3, similar to? She is presumably similar to Sam in π_1 and Kate in π_2. It is not so clear that she is similar to whatever the corresponding object in π_4 is—perhaps she is, but working out the details of such an approach would require some sharpening of the definition of PARALLEL in such cases. Similar considerations apply to the three books in (224). For ease of exposition, we will pretend that these complications do not exist, and talk instead as if there were an *n*-ary PARALLEL relation, such that PARALLEL(π_1, π_2, π_3) holds in (224).

A more concrete (and less lazy) independent justification for this approach is that *n*-ary coordination must be distinguishable from nested binary coordinations (see the discussion, based on Borsley 2005, in Section 2.4.3). There may be a marginally grammatical reading of (227a), where the correlative coordination marker *both* forces binary conjunction, but it is not the same as the most straightforward interpretation of (227b). In (227b), all three conjuncts are presented on an equal footing, while (227a) forces us to compare the first two conjuncts as a unit to the last alone.

(227) a. ??Sam both [[[read *Dubliners*], [recited *Ulysses*]], and [gave up on *Finnegans Wake*]].
      b. Sam [[read *Dubliners*], [recited *Ulysses*], and [gave up on *Finnegans Wake*]].

We want the flexibility to represent the reading that is only available in (227b), as well as the reading that (227a) and (227b) share. We believe that a 'flat' representation, with an *n*-ary PARALLEL relation, is a necessary step toward achieving this.[87]

Because we need such flat structures for PARALLEL, we will assume that the same considerations apply to *n*-ary NARRATIONS. That is, in a discourse like (228) (a lightly modified part of (191)), the relevant discourse relations that Asher (2004) postulated are in (229) (a lightly modified part of (192)). Note the flat structure of the NARRATION relations, implied by the fact that $\pi_{(228c)}$ is the first argument of one NARRATION relation and the second argument of the other.[88]

---

[87] Another possibility is to say that there are actually three PARALLEL relations in (224), namely PARALLEL(π_1, π_2), PARALLEL(π_2, π_3), and PARALLEL(π_1, π_3). Such an analysis, would, however, have to provide independent motivation for PARALLEL(π_1, π_3), which violates the Right Frontier Constraint. For this reason, we do not pursue this analysis here. Thanks to Julian Schlöder for discussing this possibility with us.

[88] Recall that graphs of discourse structure are not trees, because a node can have multiple mothers. The flat structure described here could not be represented in a tree, but is still a valid discourse structure under SDRT assumptions.

(228)   a. Chris took a really neat vacation this year.
         b. In September, he went to Madagascar.
         c. From there, he went to the island of Maurice, and
         d. he returned to Madagascar via the Kerguelen Islands.

(229)

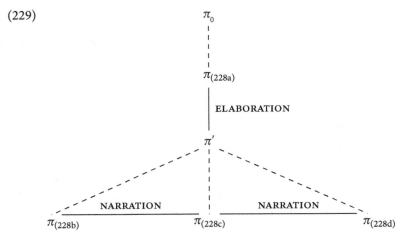

Such a structure, together with general SDRT principles, guarantees that each of the three EDUs contained within π' in (229) is an ELABORATION of the discourse topic, Chris's vacation.

Against this background, we turn to examples of extraction from n-ary coordination structures. There is not much to add concerning examples with PARALLEL, at least considering the current state of our understanding of such cases in Section 6.6.2. However, there are additional complexities concerning examples like (230), which we have already discussed in several places.

(230)   This is the kind of brandy that you can [[sip __ after dinner], [watch TV for a while], [sip some more of __], [work a bit], [finish off __], [go to bed], and [still feel fine in the morning]].   (Lakoff 1986)

This is a complex relative clause, with gaps in several noninitial conjuncts corresponding to the relative head *(the) kind of brandy*. We can infer that the relative head is the sentence topic. Von Fintel's (1994) theory of the relationship between sentence topic and discourse topic (see Section 6.2.3), recast in SDRT terms, leads us to expect the discourse topic to be a discourse unit which includes the sentence topic and which stands in a relationship of ELABORATION with the material in the relative clause.

Now, if all of the conjuncts in (230) formed a chain of NARRATIONS as in (229), each conjunct should contribute an EDU which is an elaboration of the discourse topic. We do not believe that this is plausible in cases like (230). In particular, almost all of the gapless conjuncts (with the possible exception of the final conjunct) have no evident relation to brandy: watching TV, working a bit, and so on.[89] These are the conjuncts that Deane

---

[89] In this respect, note that (230) does not feel borderline incoherent, which is what we would expect if this discourse formed a chain of NARRATIONS with discourse topics that are only common in the very general sense, e.g. 'events in temporal sequence,' as in the discourse below:

(i)   #Christ was born no later than 4 B.C. and today Fortuna won the match.   (Altshuler and Melkonian 2014)

Of course, one could deny our assumption about the nature of the discourse topic in (230), and claim that it is more complex—e.g. the discourse topic concerns one's evening plans in addition to the brandy. Such a complex

(1991) identified as 'background' (see Section 6.2.2): preparatory actions, scene-setters, and (particularly prominent in (230)) incidental events. If NARRATION requires conjuncts all to stand in the same relation to the discourse topic, then clearly not all of the conjuncts in (230) are related by NARRATION.

We are unaware of a standard SDRT label for the relation between such EDUs and their sisters. It is tempting to say that, for example, *watch TV for a while* stands in a relation of ⇒BACKGROUND to *sip some more of (this kind of brandy)*. However, we have consistently taken ⇒BACKGROUND to be a relation between a state and an event. It is therefore inappropriate as a label for a relation between two events. We will use the label ⇒ELABORATION to describe this relation, though this should of course be taken with a hefty pinch of salt: all we intend is a coordinating discourse relation holding between two DUs which describe events (not states), and only the second of which is an elaboration of the discourse topic. This is related to a problem discussed in Section 6.6.4 with respect to the interpretation of Type D scenarios: we do not appear to have a good understanding of the relationship between two events in cases such as this; we are using the label ⇒ELABORATION as an ad hoc device to give us a way of incorporating Deane's insight about 'background' conjuncts into SDRT representations.

An approximate representation for (230) is then as in (231).

(231)

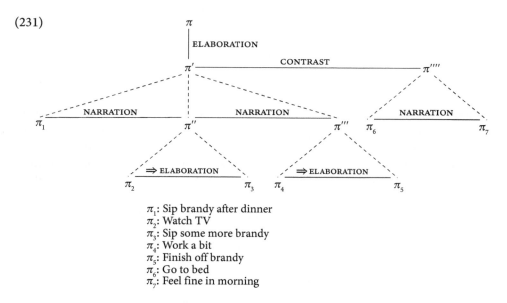

π_1: Sip brandy after dinner
π_2: Watch TV
π_3: Sip some more brandy
π_4: Work a bit
π_5: Finish off brandy
π_6: Go to bed
π_7: Feel fine in morning

Within this structure, three discourse units (π_1, π'', and π''') are related by NARRATION. Each of them relates to the discourse topic (something to do with 'this kind of brandy', the sentence topic). Two of them (π'' and π''') happen to be CDUs, each containing one topical DU and one background DU, related by ⇒ELABORATION. ⇒ELABORATION allows us to represent more accurately the structure of this discourse: there is a discourse topic (π),

discourse topic would, then, allow an analysis in which the discourse harbors a chain of NARRATIONS. The problem with such an analysis, however, is how to motivate, without circularity, the claim that the discourse topic is, in fact, complex in this way.

which is then elaborated upon, but not every conjunct in the coordinate structure does so to the same extent.

The structure in (231) has a syntactic analog in the approach of Neeleman and Tanaka (2020) to such complex Type A coordinate structures. Neeleman and Tanaka assume a distinction between two structural relations, one of which ('subordination') is a strictly binary, asymmetric relation, and one of which ('coordination') is n-ary and symmetrical.[90] In subordination structures, particularly Lakoff's Type A, extraction must take place from the final conjunct only; in coordination structures extraction must be ATB.

This means that examples like (230) require some kind of hybrid analysis: the presence of gaps in some but not all conjuncts rules out a fully symmetrical analysis, while the presence of more than two conjuncts rules out a fully asymmetrical analysis. Discussing Lakoff's example (232), Neeleman and Tanaka demonstrate that two such hybrid examples in fact exist, given schematically as in (233).

(232)   What did he [[go to the store], [buy __], [load __ in his car], [drive home], and [unload __]]?

(233)   a. What did he $\begin{bmatrix} \text{[go to the store]} & \begin{bmatrix} \text{[buy __]} \\ \text{[load __ in his car]} \end{bmatrix} \\ \text{[drive home] and [unload __]?} \end{bmatrix}$

b. What did he $\begin{bmatrix} \text{[go to the store], [buy __]} \\ \text{[load __ in his car]} \\ \text{[drive home] and [unload __]?} \end{bmatrix}$

(Neeleman and Tanaka 2020: 7–8)

In these schematic diagrams, vertically aligned constituents correspond to Neeleman and Tanaka's iterable 'coordination' structure, while horizontally aligned constituents correspond to the binary 'subordination' structure. Within each 'coordination' structure, extraction is ATB (there are gaps in each constituent), while within each 'subordination' structure, extraction is from the final conjunct only. The complex patterns that Lakoff describes arise from interleaving of these two basic structures.

What we have been suggesting in this section is a discourse-structural analog of this syntax. The vertically aligned units are related by NARRATION; the horizontally aligned units by the relation that we have been calling ⇒ELABORATION.

We have discussed n-ary coordinate structures with relations like PARALLEL, which are defined with reference to a maximal common theme, and relations like NARRATION, which are defined with reference to a discourse topic. On the basis of Lakoff (1986) and subsequent work along those lines, it would be natural to assume that these two relations are special in that they are n-ary, whereas Type B and Type C scenarios appear always to be binary. If that is the case, then there is no obvious general explanation within the terms of SDRT. We have seen that n-ary NARRATION relations are composed from iterating binary relations, so if any relations only feature in binary coordinate structures, we would have to hope that the semantics of those relations is incompatible with iteration for some reason.

---

[90] Neeleman and Tanaka attribute this distinction and its characterization to Lakoff (1986). As discussed, these terms have been used by various authors, with different and perhaps even incommensurate denotations. We preserve their terms in this passage, and trust that this won't lead to confusion with the way we've used these terms elsewhere.

However, it seems that at least RESULT, implicated in Type C scenarios, can feature in n-ary coordinate structures. Examples like (234) involve more than two conjuncts, and involve at least one instance of RESULT, and probably two.

(234) This is the chili dish that people always [[order __], [eat __], [get sick], and [end up in hospital]].

Such examples are probably strictly binary as far as RESULT is concerned, but each of the arguments of RESULT is itself complex. That is, we assume a structure like (235) for (234), where extraction does indeed take place from only the first argument of RESULT, which happens to be a CDU containing two conjuncts, each with a gap.

(235)

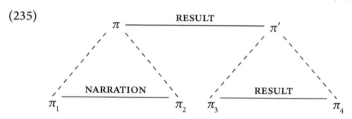

π_1: People order chili
π_2: People eat chili
π_3: People get sick
π_4: People in hospital

It may be that there is still a structural difference between NARRATION and PARALLEL on the one hand, and RESULT on the other: perhaps the former two relations admit flatter structures than RESULT, because any number of conjuncts can be structurally parallel, and any number of conjuncts in a narration can stand as elaborations of a discourse topic, but the link between cause and effect is strictly binary. Intuitions along these lines (that is, that the difference between binary and n-ary coordination must somehow relate to the semantics of the different discourse relations involved) have been stated repeatedly in prior literature. The assumptions of SDRT about different classes of coordinating discourse relations give us a way to make these intuitions precise.

6.8 Summary

We have covered a lot of ground in this chapter, and nevertheless arrived at a position which is programmatic and incomplete. In this summary, we lay out what we have, and haven't, done in this chapter.

The overarching purpose of the chapter is to continue to develop possible discourse-based approaches to patterns of extraction from coordinate structures, documented by Lakoff (1986) and others following him, and refined in Chapter 5 and this chapter. This will allow us, in Chapter 7, to return to an evaluation of the relative roles of syntax and discourse structure in this area.

In Chapter 5, we saw that analyses such as Lakoff's, which attempted to correlate discourse relations directly with patterns of extraction, faced significant empirical challenges. Therefore, in this chapter we turned to an alternative approach, perhaps first glimpsed by

Deane (1991) but stated most clearly by Kehler (2002), developing work by Kuno (1973, 1976, 1987). Kehler's leading idea is that A'-extracted elements correspond to sentence topics, and that discourse relations constrain the distribution of sentence topics.

Kehler's presentation of this idea is quite cursory and incomplete, and developing it in the most simple-minded ways very quickly reveals problems. In Section 6.2.4, we addressed some of these by moving to a more subtle position, integrating Kehler's leading idea with the syntax of Munn (1993), and the refinements we had proposed to that syntax in Section 4.6 based on Postal (1998). The key refinement that this integration allows is the following: not all A'-extractees need to correspond to sentence topics; only extractees from noninitial conjuncts in languages like English require such a correspondence. This is because noninitial conjuncts are weak islands in languages like English (as opposed to languages like German, where asymmetric extraction from noninitial conjuncts is ungrammatical), and the restrictions on possible extractions from weak islands may correspond closely to restrictions on sentence topics, as discussed in relation to Choice Point 5.

Even with this refinement of Kehler's leading idea, there were still several empirical challenges which had not been addressed by Kehler. The aim for this chapter, from Section 6.3 onward, was to make sense of a four-way distinction among discourse relations, glimpsed at the end of Chapter 5, with respect to their behavior in coordinate structures.

1. Some discourse relations, such as EXPLANATION or ELABORATION, are not expressed by coordinate structures.
2. Some discourse relations, such as PARALLEL, only allow ATB extraction.
3. Some discourse relations, such as RESULT, only allow ATB extraction or asymmetric extraction from the initial conjunct.
4. Some discourse relations, such as NARRATION, allow any extraction pattern in some instances.

These patterns have not previously been reported in the literature, and the implicational relation that they imply does not correspond to the presentations by Lakoff, Deane, Kehler, or anyone else. We think that they emerge straightforwardly from the systematic investigation of English data in Chapter 5. However, it goes without saying that these empirical generalizations need more rigorous scrutiny, particularly on the basis of data from languages other than English.

The factors that Kehler considered were not subtle enough to allow for this four-way distinction, because he was mainly concerned with a two-way distinction between: (i) Resemblance relations, where structural constraints on topic placement derived a requirement that any extraction be ATB, and (ii) other relations, which have no such constraints. This motivated the introduction of SDRT, a more elaborated theory of discourse structure.

SDRT has several properties which we believe are promising for going beyond Kehler's implementation of his leading idea. First, it is an investigation of discourse *structure*, as opposed to Kehler's emphasis on the relations themselves in isolation from the structures they generate. We have made increasing use of the hierarchical aspects of SDRT's model of discourse structure, particularly when investigating extraction from *n*-ary coordinate structures in Section 6.7. One aspect of the SDRT model of discourse structure which was of particular relevance is the distinction between coordinating and subordinating discourse relations introduced in Section 6.3.

Second, SDRT is a more clearly linguistic theory of discourse structure than Kehler's, which is grounded in Humean notions of association of ideas (whether linguistic or not). As a linguistic theory, SDRT allows for modeling of the constraints that the semantics of individual lexical items may place on discourse structure. The SDRT literature has developed hypotheses about the lexical semantics of three coordinating conjunctions, namely English *and, or,* and *but.* We discussed these in Section 6.4. Of most interest was the analysis of *and* by Txurruka (2003), which claims that *and* can express only coordinating discourse relations.

Finally, SDRT provides a limited role for discourse topics in its representation of discourse structure. They are not fully reducible to more narrowly grammatical notions like sentence topic, and they are not omnipresent in representations of discourse structure. They are explicitly represented in the logical forms for relations like NARRATION, but not for relations like RESULT or PARALLEL. The job that discourse topic does in guaranteeing the coherence of well-formed discourses with NARRATION is done instead by causal relations in the case of RESULT, and by the notion of 'maximal common theme' in the case of PARALLEL.

In Section 6.6, we revisited the extraction data in the light of this new typology of discourse relations. We proposed the following correspondences.

1. Subordinating discourse relations are not expressed by coordinate structures.
2. Discourse relations such as PARALLEL, whose semantics makes reference to a maximal common theme, only allow ATB extraction.
3. Discourse relations such as RESULT, whose semantics does not make reference to a maximal common theme and which do not include a discourse topic in their structural representations, only allow ATB extraction or asymmetric extraction from the initial conjunct.
4. Discourse relations such as NARRATION, which stand as ELABORATIONS of a discourse topic represented in their logical form, allow any extraction pattern in some instances.

We believe that it is an empirical and theoretical advance even to be able to state those correspondences in terms of the natural classes of discourse relations that SDRT implies, and we take it as encouraging that the aspects of SDRT used here have been taken more or less off the shelf, with minimal tinkering. However, we emphasize that the correspondences proposed here are only a starting point. In particular, Section 6.6.2 and Choice Point 6 make it very clear that we have only a partial understanding of why these correspondences might hold, and Section 6.6.4 shows the extent of the empirical work which is left to do, even in English.

In Chapter 7, we will consider the analysis developed in the last couple of sections, in the context of the other approaches discussed in Chapters 3–5. We hope that this will help to identify the important open questions in this area, as a stimulus to further research.

7

Conclusion

7.1 So who does call the shots?

In the introduction to this book, we pointed out a paradoxical aspect of the syntax–discourse interface: from a certain perspective, there should be no such interface, because it would straddle the competence–performance divide. But there is ample empirical evidence suggesting that the interface is real, in that there are phenomena which appear to be conditioned by some interaction of syntactic and discourse-related factors.

We chose extraction from coordinate structures as an example of the challenges that arise in squaring this circle. The topic seems irreducibly syntactic in that it involves a syntactic structure (coordination), a syntactic relation (movement, or extraction), and specific constraints on that syntactic relation in the context of that syntactic structure. However, it also seems undeniable that the distribution of the different extraction patterns, and particularly the distribution of gaps across conjuncts, can be explained in terms that derive from the interpretation of discourse. Both horns of this dilemma can be traced back to Ross (1967), the foundational study of syntactic constraints on movement, and also the source for observations about the interpretive characteristics of certain non-ATB extraction patterns.

We sketched two simple-minded approaches to this challenge, both based on reassessing the division of labor between syntax and discourse (competence and performance, grammar and use). The first approach (**syntax calls the shots**) assumes that the relevant discourse properties are somehow prefigured in syntactic representations, and syntactic wellformedness conditions may then force certain effects related to discourse interpretation. The second (**discourse calls the shots**) put all the eggs into the discourse-structural basket. Discourse wellformedness conditions may then rule out the syntactic structures in question.

Neither of these positions is a straw man: Lakoff (1986) and Kehler (2002) embody a discourse-calls-the-shots approach in that they provide a purely pragmatic account of the distribution of gaps in coordinate structures, while Ross (1967) and Postal (1998) claimed that the interpretive distinctions that Lakoff drew are prefigured by differences in the underlying syntactic representation. This allows a syntax-calls-the-shots approach to the different extraction patterns: both Ross and Postal claimed, in different ways, that certain asymmetric interpretations of coordinate structures, with asymmetric extraction patterns, were syntactically not true coordinate structures, and that this explained their different extraction behavior. Moving beyond this narrow empirical domain, the field of cognitive linguistics often aims to ground syntactic patterns in patterns of language use (including discourse), as well as domain-general cognitive properties, while cartography

Coordination and the Syntax–Discourse Interface. Daniel Altshuler and Robert Truswell, Oxford University Press.
© Daniel Altshuler and Robert Truswell (2022). DOI: 10.1093/oso/9780198804239.003.0007

involves the reification of interpretive differences through elaborated sequences of functional heads. These can include discourse-oriented heads, such as the range of different topic, focus, and force projections in Rizzi (1997) and Benincá and Poletto (2001).[1]

In the particular case of extraction from coordinate structures, though, neither the syntax-calls-the-shots nor the discourse-calls-the-shots approach fared very well on its own. We can see this by comparing how the two approaches handle Lakoff's original claims about the difference between Type A scenarios (with extraction from some set of noninitial conjuncts according to Lakoff's presentation, namely those that are not backgrounded in the sense of Deane 1991), and Type B and C scenarios (with extraction from the initial conjunct only, according to Lakoff). The syntax-calls-the-shots approach could only capture that distinction through some syntactic reification of NARRATION (or OCCASION), VIOLATED EXPECTATION, and/or RESULT, such as Postal's claim that only the former features in true coordinate structures. Such a claim is unappealing because there does not seem to be independent evidence to support it: extraction aside, all three scenarios look like regular coordinate structures.

However, the discourse-calls-the-shots method had no easy way of approaching crosslinguistic variation in extraction from coordinate structures. For instance, we saw in Section 4.6 that some languages allow the Type B/C pattern but not the Type A pattern. Compare French (1a) (repeated from (128) in Chapter 4) with English (1b), for example. Assuming that the discourse structure of the two examples is the same (both are NARRATIONS), a pure 'discourse calls the shots' approach offers no easy way to approach the contrast.

(1) a. *le   pain   que Jacques [[a   couru au   marché], [(a)   acheté
        the   bread that Jacques has   run   to.the market   has   bought
        ___],   [(a)   foncé chez   lui],   et   [(a)   mangé   ___]]
        has   rushed to.home.of him and   has   eaten
        'the bread that Jacques ran to the market, bought, rushed home, and ate'
                                                                    (Postal 1998: 75)
    b. the bread that Jacques [[ran to the market], [bought ___], [rushed home], and
        [ate ___]]

Although we did not offer an account of this difference, the crosslinguistic variation coupled with interpretive uniformity is crying out for a wholly or partially syntactic explanation. It may be possible, for instance, to investigate crosslinguistic variation in the relationship between A'-extraction and sentence topics, or constraints on the distribution of sentence topics in coordinate structures. On a purely discourse-based approach, it i not even clear where one could start.

Equally mysterious on a 'discourse calls the shots' approach is the fact that the range of possible extractees is greater for the Type B/C pattern than for the Type A pattern (which is limited to extraction of referential noun phrases), or more generally, asymmetric extraction from initial conjuncts is possible for a greater range of extractees than from noninitial conjuncts. A minimal pair illustrating this is (2) ((2a) is repeated from (198) in Chapter 6):

---

[1] Again, Ross blazed a trail of sorts here, with his 'performative hypothesis' that every declarative sentence includes a syntactic representation of illocutionary force through a possibly covert performative verb (see Ross 1970b).

although Type A scenarios allow asymmetric extraction from any conjunct, asymmetric extraction of a nonreferential NP is only possible from the initial conjunct. Again, it is completely unclear what this could follow from on a purely discourse-based approach.

(2) a. How much money did you [[take __ out of the bank] and [buy that modernist painting]]?

   b. *How much money did you [[go to the gallery] and [spend __ on that modernist painting]]?

Therefore, no-one calls all the shots: we need to analyze both the syntax and the discourse structure to fully understand patterns of extraction from coordinate structures. The next question, then, is how this works. How do syntax and discourse talk to each other, when we might expect that they can't?

In the next two sections, we will lay out the choice points that we have considered with respect to first the syntax, and then the discourse semantics, of coordination.[2] When discussing the discourse semantics, we will also be able to consider the relationships between our semantic choices and our syntactic choices. Following that, we wrap up in a way which we think is appropriate to a survey, by pointing out what is left to do. To this end, in Section 7.4 we consider the descriptive generalizations about extraction from coordinate structures which, to our mind, remain unaddressed in the frameworks we have considered, while in Section 7.5 we consider the implications of the ideas we have surveyed, beyond extraction from coordinate structures.

7.2 Two syntactic approaches

The most important choice point in Chapter 2, Choice Point 1, is between **symmetrical** and **asymmetric** structures for coordination. No current analysis is fully symmetrical, because it is more or less universally accepted since Ross (1967) that a coordinating conjunction attaches more closely to one conjunct than another. However, some analyses are *almost* symmetrical. For instance, Gazdar (1981) proposes a flat structure for English coordination, with all conjuncts as daughters of the same mother, and the final conjunct marked with a diacritic which leads to attachment of the coordinating conjunction. Steedman's work on coordination (1985, 1989, 1990) mainly assumes a derivation in which the coordinating conjunction attaches to conjuncts one by one, but where the resulting semantic representation is symmetrical in the sense of Chapter 2. And Neeleman and Tanaka (2020) propose a rule of 'mutual adjunction' in which (the position of *and* aside) each conjunct has equal status as an adjunct.

A distinctive class of symmetrical structures are the **multiplanar** analyses of Williams (1978), Goodall (1987), Muadz (1991), Moltmann (1992), and others. These are symmetrical to the extent that each conjunct has an equal status as a separate 'plane'.

In contrast, asymmetrical analyses propose that different conjuncts have different phrase-structural statuses. We discussed two main asymmetrical analyses in Section 2.4.3: according to one (e.g. Johannessen 1998), the first conjunct is a specifier and the second

---

[2] The choice points are reproduced in Appendix in the form in which they appear in the preceding chapters.

a complement; according to the other (e.g. Munn 1993), the second conjunct is adjoined to the first. Both approaches rely on recursive embedding of binary coordinate structures in the analysis of *n*-ary coordinate structures (*n* > 2). Although Johannessen's analysis appears currently to be the most popular, we concentrated on Munn's analysis, in part because of Borsley (2005) critique of Johannessen's structure and in part because we developed ideas from Munn in Chapter 6.

It is not surprising that these differences in syntactic analysis yield different predictions with respect to extraction patterns, summarized in Choice Point 2. Most symmetrical analyses (the exception being Neeleman and Tanaka 2020) adopt, or even aim to derive, the CSC as Ross stated it: a symmetrical pattern of extraction. In contrast, the symmetry of the CSC does not fit well with most asymmetrical analyses. There are two obvious kinds of response to this. Munn (1993) agreed that the ATB extraction pattern had a special status, but (like Ruys 1992 and Fox 2000) invoked extrasyntactic factors to explain it. The alternative, developed in Section 4.6 and later chapters, is to reject the CSC as a generally applicable description of extraction from coordinate structures, in favor of an analysis in which asymmetric extractions from coordinate structures may be well-formed.

The consequences of the dichotomy between symmetrical and asymmetric analyses run deeper than this, though. If we consider the syntactic state of the art of the early–mid 1970s, three properties are of interest to us: movement is treated as a nonlocal, transformational operation, the syntax of coordination is taken to be more or less as described by Ross (1967) or Dougherty (1970a,b), and the CSC is treated as an essentially correct statement of the facts. It appears, though, that at least one of these three properties must be given up. Choice Points 3 and 4 were about what to give up.

As noted in Section 4.3, the CSC does not fit naturally with the direction of travel of Chomskyan locality theory since Chomsky (1973): the general principles, such as Subjacency, which have superseded Ross's original enumeration of specific constraints do not automatically extend to the CSC, because of the distinctive properties of the CSC. As a result, theories which aim to derive the CSC have typically either moved away from Chomsky's approach to locality, or radically reimagined the syntax of coordination.

The approaches to locality which integrate the CSC tend to have the property that nonlocal movement relations are replaced or supplemented by local, mother–daughter relations, through the rules governing SLASH features in Gazdar (1981), the notion of 'path' in Pesetsky (1982), and the strictly local combinatory system of Steedman (1985). The point is that if information about unbounded dependencies is represented at every step between the head and the foot of the dependency, and if the dependency originates within a coordinate structure and terminates outside the structure, then the CSC reduces to the law of coordination of likes: if one conjunct contains an unbounded dependency, then they all must. On these approaches, Chomsky's locality theory is rejected, but a more or less standard syntax of coordination—as well as the CSC—can be maintained.

Multiplanar structures stand in the opposite relation to Chomskyan syntax: they are able to adopt Chomsky's locality theory, because they pair it with a radically different syntax for coordination. Multiplanar structures allow for locality constraints in the Chomskyan mold to be implemented separately within each plane: if an operator does not bind a variable in each conjunct, then that operator will violate the ban on vacuous quantification in the plane corresponding to that conjunct. In this way, multiplanar approaches maintain Chomsky's locality theory and the CSC, at the expense of a conventional syntax of coordination.

As for asymmetric analyses, these often reject the CSC as a syntactic constraint, and also the conventional analysis of coordination (though in a less radical way than the multiplanar analyses), but they can incorporate a Chomskyan take on locality theory.

Choosing between these options should be a straightforward empirical exercise, of unusual theoretical significance. However, it is not straightforward. The reason is that ill-formedness is not a matter of syntax alone. In this particular case, theories of discourse structure must be given equal consideration. It has been clear since at least Lakoff (1986), and arguably since Ross (1967), that the CSC undergenerates with respect to attested patterns of extraction from coordinate structures: asymmetric extraction does exist, and the CSC predicts that it does not. This means that the two types of approach we have identified face different problems. Symmetrical approaches risk undergeneration, and need to explain why asymmetrical extraction from coordinate structures is sometimes possible. Asymmetric approaches risk overgeneration, and need to explain why extraction from coordinate structures is not free.

We are not aware of any worked-out proposals for avoiding undergeneration with symmetrical approaches, and this is a significant problem that these approaches face. Normally, if a sentence is ill-formed at any level of representation, then the sentence is ill-formed. According to symmetrical approaches which derive the CSC, asymmetric extraction should be syntactically ill-formed. It is often asserted in the literature that examples of asymmetric extraction are marginal, or exceptional. We are not aware of any concrete evidence supporting this claim, though, and even if they are marginal, our grammars still generate them.[3]

The question, then, is how to rescue an ill-formed structure. The simplest approach would be to claim that there is some extra structural analysis available in cases of asymmetric extraction, where even symmetrical theories would not expect the CSC to hold. Postal (1998) is an example of this approach, following the lead of Ross (1967). Postal claims that Lakoff's Type B and C scenarios, with extraction from the initial conjunct, are examples of subordination rather than coordination. However, as Levine (2001) argues, there is no clear noncircular basis for Postal's claims.[4]

The way forward for asymmetric approaches is a little more straightforward: they risk overgeneration, so they need to find complementary, often extrasyntactic, ways to rule out extraction patterns which, as a matter of fact, are ill-formed. There are reasons to believe that discourse-semantic theories of coordination could complement syntactic analyses in this way, particularly because Kehler (2002) develops an approach in which the symmetrical, ATB extraction pattern would sometimes be required for nonsyntactic reasons. However, there has been little, if any, previous work which aimed to connect a discourse semantics of coordination to a worked-out syntax of extraction from coordinate structures: syntax does no real empirical heavy lifting for Kehler, for instance. Therefore, one reason for investigating the discourse semantics of coordination (aside from its intrinsic interest) is that it can help us discriminate between *syntactic* analyses.

---

[3] Mark Steedman (pers. comm.) suggests that instances of asymmetric extraction, although acceptable and interpretable, are strictly ungrammatical, similarly to *that*–trace violations such as *Who did Seymour tell you that would win the match?* Such violations, although judged as ungrammatical, are frequently produced and readily interpreted, possibly in part through general inferential processes rather than strictly compositional semantics. However, as Steedman also notes, 'The problem is in defining the limits of such processes.' In our opinion, this is a real problem, given the complexity of some of the empirical patterns we have discussed.

[4] However, Mark Steedman (pers. comm.) has described ongoing research in CCG which aims to link certain asymmetric extraction patterns to Gapping, which is undoubtedly asymmetric and for which CCG analyses exist.

7.3 Two approaches to discourse structure

After the many earlier hints (Ross 1967, Schmerling 1975, Goldsmith 1985), it was Lakoff (1986), in our opinion, who first demonstrated not only that discourse structure conditions asymmetric extraction, but also that it conditions the distribution of gaps in extraction from coordinate structures, through his opposition between Type A scenarios and Type B/C scenarios, correlating interpretations with extraction patterns.

As we understand Lakoff, his proposal is that these interpretations directly determine extraction (the title of his paper is 'Frame semantic *control* of the Coordinate Structure Constraint', emphasis added). This is one approach to the discourse semantics of extraction from coordinate structures. It was developed in various respects by Deane (1991) and Kehler (2002), neither of whom fully adopted it. As shown in Chapter 5, it has a range of problems. The most challenging problem, described in Section 5.3.2, is that two core Hobbsian/Kehlerian discourse relations (RESULT and OCCASION) stand in an entailment relation (on reasonable assumptions about their truth conditions): RESULT is a special case of OCCASION. This means that, in purely truth-conditional terms, we expect that every instance of RESULT could also be construed as OCCASION. However, the extraction patterns associated with these relations do not match that prediction. Specifically, there are extraction patterns which are possible with OCCASION but not with RESULT, and that should be impossible if every instance of RESULT can also be construed as an instance of OCCASION. We take this as a strong empirical argument that discourse relations do not directly condition extraction patterns.

Another, more basic problem for Lakoff's approach is that it is essentially correlational: it pairs discourse relations (the natural way of cashing out Lakoff's use of 'frames', following Kehler 2002) with patterns of extraction, but it is not clear why a given relation pairs with a given extraction pattern. Kehler (2002) in fact addresses this question, by proposing a structural distinction between Resemblance relations and others, but his empirical predictions are quite weak and, in strictly these terms, limited to a distinction between Resemblance relations (which require ATB extraction) and others (which do not).

Our conclusion is that Lakoff (1986) has provided some very interesting and challenging data, but interpretive factors such as semantic frames, 'scenarios', or discourse relations are not promising devices for explaining those data. Therefore, in Chapter 6, we instead developed some hints from Deane (1991) and Kehler (2002) about an alternative approach whereby discourse relations indirectly condition extraction patterns, through an intermediary of topicality. That is, discourse relations condition the distribution of sentence topics, and extraction is sensitive to the notion of 'sentence topic'.

As described by Deane and Kehler, following Kuno (1973, 1976, 1987), information structure (including topicality) is a pervasive factor conditioning extraction from coordinate structures. We did not accept that position, because the canonical set of examples of asymmetric extraction includes many where the extractee is not plausibly a sentence topic. Instead, from Section 6.3 onward, we set about reconstructing the Deane/Kehler insights about topicality within a framework which afforded topicality a more limited role in conditioning extraction. On the syntactic side, we suggested that topicality is only a factor conditioning extraction from noninitial conjuncts, grounding this suggestion in the observation from Postal (1998) that only noninitial conjuncts behave like weak islands (this is not an innocent choice: we framed the discussion of the alternatives as Choice Point

5, and noted that it presupposed certain options in Choice Points 2–4). On the semantic side, we built on von Fintel (1994) claim that sentence topics are anaphorically related to discourse topics, and adopted Segmented Discourse Representation Theory because it has several structural properties that make it an ideal framework for investigating relationships between discourse relations, topicality, and coordinate structures.

What emerged from our review of relevant aspects of SDRT is a tripartition: the most basic pattern is exemplified by relations like RESULT, which do not represent a discourse topic in their logical form and do not reference a maximal common theme in their semantics. Relations like RESULT allow asymmetric extraction from the initial conjunct, or ATB extraction. There are then two possible manipulations of this base pattern: (i) relations like NARRATION, whose arguments stand in a specific relation to an explicitly represented discourse topic, allow extraction of topical elements from noninitial conjuncts in addition to the patterns which RESULT allows, while (ii) relations like PARALLEL, whose semantics refers to a maximal common theme, are more restricted than RESULT in that they require symmetrical ATB extraction.

Drawing out these SDRT-based predictions, and pairing them with the syntactically motivated distinction between initial and noninitial conjuncts, is the most significant original research contribution of this survey. We think that it is a promising direction for future research. However, we emphasize that it is new, and not thoroughly tested, and therefore an atypical inclusion in a survey. Our reason for including it in the survey is because of the type of survey that this is. We have been focusing on extraction from coordinate structures as a case study in the kinds of empirical phenomena which require sustained research in both syntax and discourse semantics, illustrating the kinds of challenges which arise in research like this. One pervasive practical challenge is that the required expertise is very diverse. We would expect that many syntacticians have been persuaded for years that discourse-structural factors condition extraction from coordinate structures, but have not been able to develop a theoretical account of those factors because they lack an up-to-date theoretical understanding of discourse semantics (at the outset of this project, one of the authors matched this description). On the other hand, discourse semanticists may be unaware of the assumptions that syntacticians are making about discourse structure, when in fact they are well placed to help develop and critically evaluate those assumptions (the other author matched this description). Regardless of whether the approach described in Chapter 6, pairing Munn and Kehler with SDRT, ultimately stands or falls, it is at least interesting, and stands as an indication of the benefits of collaborating beyond one's comfort zone. Work on the syntax–discourse interface will surely require more collaborations like this.

7.4 Unanswered questions

So far in this summary, we have identified two main types of syntactic approaches (symmetrical and asymmetrical), and also identified the major challenge facing the symmetrical approach: how to exceptionally rule asymmetrical extractions back in. In Section 7.3, we extolled the virtues of an asymmetrical syntax, paired with an SDRT-based analysis of topicality in coordinate structures. In this section, in the interests of balance, we first discuss two major outstanding challenges for this approach. We then go on to discuss some problems which remain unanswered to our knowledge under *any* approach.

7.4.1 Unfinished business for the topicality approach

What are the facts?

The simplest question for the topicality approach is whether we have the correct empirical generalizations about the discourse relations which allow different asymmetric extraction patterns. In particular, a lot hangs on the claim that RESULT only allows asymmetric extraction from the initial conjunct, whereas relations like NARRATION are more permissive. We have also considered various strategies for making sense of Lakoff's Type B scenarios (Kehler's VIOLATED EXPECTATION) in Chapters 5 and 6—these strategies were summarized in Choice Point 7.

These empirical issues are subtle, not least because of the entailment relations which hold between Kehler's definitions of VIOLATED EXPECTATION, RESULT, and OCCASION. In order to fill in the gaps in the previous literature, we have done some preliminary, informal empirical work—just enough to give us some faith in the generalizations that we have presented—but there is clearly scope for a more thorough, controlled investigation of the effects of the different factors we have considered.

We also note that the empirical scope of Chapters 5 and 6 is significantly smaller than that of Chapters 3 and 4. In these later chapters, we only talk about A'-movement in any depth, while in the earlier chapters we cover a much wider range of movement types and related dependencies. There is still plenty of work to do in exploring the broader implications of the discourse-based theories that we have been considering.

Crosslinguistic variation in extraction from coordinate structures

The incompleteness of our crosslinguistic empirical coverage is particularly clear. Chapters 2–4 demonstrated that there is crosslinguistic variation in both the syntax of coordination and the availability of asymmetric extraction from coordinate structures. The former type of variation has been covered in reasonable detail in both the descriptive literature (e.g. Haspelmath 2004, 2007) and the theoretical literature (e.g. Johannessen 1998), but we still know very little about crosslinguistic variation in extraction. What is known is that Lakoff's patterns can broadly be replicated in some other languages (e.g. Kubota and Lee 2015), and that some Germanic and Romance languages are more restrictive, particularly with respect to extraction from noninitial conjuncts (as discussed in Postal 1998, among others). However, the scattered data points that we have are clearly some way from a robust crosslinguistic typology of extraction patterns.

More seriously, the focus on English may be obscuring important questions about the syntax and semantics of asymmetric extraction, in particular. We are thinking, for instance, about the parallels that Weisser (2015) draws between coordinate structures and clause-chaining. Such parallels could not emerge from a consideration of English, or even western European data, because western European languages do not have clause-chaining structures. Our own discussion of the discourse semantics of coordination in Chapters 5 and 6 was almost entirely based on English. The current state of research in these areas necessitated that decision. Only time will tell what we are missing because of that limitation.

Moving beyond correlation

Even if we have the correct empirical generalizations, the considerations in Section 6.6 only go so far in helping us understand them. What we have done is correlate generalizations about extraction patterns with independently motivated aspects of SDRT's treatment of discourse relations. Certain promising themes have emerged. For instance, relations like NARRATION obligatorily stand in a particular relation to a discourse topic represented in logical form, and NARRATION allows extraction of elements corresponding to sentence topics. Likewise, the distinguishing characteristic of relations like PARALLEL is the partitioning of DUs into a maximal common theme and a residue of items which are not common, which is surely related to the fact that traces of movement with such relations must be shared across all conjuncts.

None of this amounts to a complete account of the discourse semantics of A'-extraction from coordinate structures, though. Consider first the point about NARRATION and discourse topics. This, on the account we sketched in Section 6.6, is what permits extraction of phrases corresponding to sentence topics from noninitial conjuncts with NARRATION in languages like English. But that is not enough, because it does not explain why we cannot also extract topical NPs from noninitial conjuncts with relations like RESULT. To explain that, we would need a stronger statement, for instance that sentence topics cannot occur in noninitial conjuncts with RESULT, or that a CDU formed with RESULT cannot be related to a discourse topic explicitly represented in a discourse structure. We currently do not know what either of these stronger statements could follow from. As a result, we don't really know why we apparently cannot just extract a phrase which happens to correspond to a sentence topic from a noninitial conjunct with RESULT.

As for PARALLEL and the maximal common theme, the outstanding questions were the subject of Choice Point 6. We could make fairly precise predictions about ATB extraction if we could guarantee firstly that traces of movement must be part of the common theme (if there is one), and secondly that the common theme is literally shared between conjuncts at the relevant level of representation. The first statement is a way of linking discourse relations with common themes to ATB extraction: if the traces are not part of the common theme, then they should differ across conjuncts, and extraction would therefore not be ATB. Meanwhile, the point of this second statement is to capture the generalization from Bošković and Franks (2000) that ATB movement behaves as if there is only a single base position for the extracted phrases. Without these two statements, we cannot derive a requirement for ATB extraction from the semantics of PARALLEL or other relations with a common theme.

This is the major unfinished theoretical business in the topicality-based account that we developed in Chapter 6. We hope it goes without saying that, for all the promise of that approach, it will be possible to evaluate it only once these theoretical gaps have been filled.

7.4.2 Challenges for any approach

Typological considerations

In keeping with the literature on extraction from coordinate structures, this book has been overwhelmingly based on English data. We have seen enough crosslinguistic data to convince us that there is substantial variation in this domain. Some languages violate the Conjunct Constraint; most, apparently, do not. Some languages allow asymmetric extraction from noninitial conjuncts; most, apparently, do not. There are even hints that languages differ with respect to the interpretation of extraction from initial conjuncts:

Type B scenarios, with VIOLATED EXPECTATION (in Kehler's terms) and extraction of a *wh*-measure phrase from the initial conjunct, were acceptable in English but less so in Swedish.[5]

(3) *Hur mycket kan du   [[dricka __] och [inte bli   full]?
    how   much   can you   drink   and not become   drunk
    'How much can you drink and not get drunk?'

This is despite the fact that Swedish allows the Type A extraction pattern.

(4) Detta är   whiskeyn   som jag [[gick till affären] och [köpte   __]].
    it.here is   whiskey.DEF that I   went to   store.DEF and bought
    'This is the whiskey that I went to the store and bought.'

We must admit that we have only the faintest outline of a crosslinguistic typology of extraction patterns, with patchy data from Romance and Germanic, and even less from beyond. Further crosslinguistic data would be extremely useful in evaluating the hypotheses laid out in this book.

It is worthwhile to think about the types of variation that we predict on the theories considered here. It is hard to be precise about the predictions of the symmetrical syntactic approach described in Section 7.2, except that ATB extraction is predicted to be the default pattern of extraction, if any extraction at all is possible. Any other extraction patterns would be exceptional in some way, and so the typology of those other patterns would depend on the nature of those extensions.

As for the asymmetric theory that we stitched together in Chapter 6 by pairing Munn's syntax with an SDRT semantics, the predictions are somewhat different. The asymmetric theory apparently makes the striking prediction that asymmetric extraction from the initial conjunct is at least as available as ATB extraction. Indeed, we do not know of any language which allows ATB extraction but disallows asymmetric extraction from the initial conjunct, but this is not particularly surprising given such a small crosslinguistic sample.[6]

In short, the predictions, although quite approximate, have the potential to give us some traction in discriminating between different theoretical approaches to extraction from coordinate structures, if appropriate data are collected. This is potentially a very rich avenue for future exploration.

Syntax and lexical semantics of coordinating conjunctions

A lot of the finer-grained descriptions of extraction patterns in Chapter 6 were grounded in statements about the lexical semantics of *and*, *or*, and *but*. We have spent most of our energy on *and*, again following the majority of the literature. As discussed in Section 6.4, it is also not surprising that research has focused on *and*, because *and* has the most general meaning, requiring only that its arguments are related by a coordinating discourse relation. *But* and *or* are more specialized: *but* is a cue-phrase for CONTRAST, while *or* describes alternatives, as required by ALTERNATION.

---

[5] Thanks to Lisa Gotthard for these examples and judgments.

[6] Asymmetric theories may have an advantage in explaining the Conjunct Constraint violations described by Bošković (2019a,b,c, 2020), although our understanding of these extractions is still very limited. The reason for suggesting that these theories might have an advantage is that the conjunct which is extracted is always the initial conjunct, and a symmetrical theory does not grant a special status to the initial conjunct, or indeed to any conjunct.

These statements about the semantics of coordinating conjunctions are much richer than anything grounded in the classical view of conjunctions as propositional connectives, as outlined in Chapter 2. Given the richness of the representational tools that SDRT makes available, it is natural to ask: are these the only possible conjunctions? If so, why? If not, what else is possible, and what would we predict about extraction patterns with other conjunctions? These are again typological questions in essence.

The questions are not just about meaning. Because of the work of researchers like Gazdar et al. (1985), van Oirsouw (1987), and Haspelmath (2004, 2007), we have a pretty good understanding of a range of syntactically differentiated coordinate structures. NP coordination can have a special, group-forming semantics. Some conjunctions, like *but*, only allow binary coordination, while others, like *and*, allow *n*-ary coordination. Some conjunctions allow coordination of a wide range of categories, while others are restricted to a limited subset (for instance, *but* does not allow NP coordination; and Haspelmath 2004 has examples of conjunctions which only allow VP coordination, or only allow S coordination, among other patterns). We know that there is significant crosslinguistic variation in this regard, but we do not yet know much about how this variation interacts with extraction patterns. Another promising future research direction would therefore be a syntactic–semantic typology of conjunctions, with special reference to effects on extraction patterns.

Is VP coordination special?

Virtually all of our examples of asymmetric extraction involve VP coordination, with the subject excluded from the coordinate structure (the only likely exceptions to this status that we have come across are some of the cases discussed in Section 3.6, including apparent asymmetric extraction from NP coordination). In contrast, asymmetric *interpretations* of coordinate structures, although still subject to size constraints discussed in Section 3.3.2, are not restricted to VP coordination. Moreover, it is possible to ATB-extract from coordinate structures of many different categories. In fact, many of the canonical examples of ATB extraction with CONTRAST involve contrasting subjects, like (5).

(5)   What does [[Kim like __] but [Mary hate __]]?

We have not seen any robust and general explanation for this restriction of asymmetric extraction to VP coordination. For symmetrical analyses, this is because of the general lack of in-depth analysis of asymmetrical extraction. As for asymmetrical analyses, only Neeleman and Tanaka (2020) have an account of the restriction, but their account is only designed to cover Type A scenarios, and the extraction to other scenario types, with extraction from initial conjuncts, is not straightforward, for reasons discussed in Section 4.6. The special status of VP coordination is therefore in need of further investigation.

7.5 Extensions and implications for locality theory

We conclude by considering the implications of the different approaches we have laid out for locality theory beyond extraction from coordinate structures. Again, the implications of the symmetrical approach will not occupy too much space. This is not to disregard that approach but because there isn't much to say: if the symmetrical approach is maintained, then we need a theory of locality, and indeed a theory of syntax, which explains the special symmetrical syntax of coordinate structures, including their symmetrical extraction patterns, as in Williams (1978), Gazdar (1981), or the other symmetrical analyses discussed in Chapters 3 and 4. However, we also need a robust analysis of the asymmetrical extraction patterns.

The alternative that we have stitched together in Section 4.6 and Chapter 6 makes more interesting predictions. We have already, in Section 6.2, described the claim of Erteschik-Shir (1973), Morgan (1975), Kuno (1976), and Erteschik-Shir and Lappin (1979) that core Ross island effects can be reduced to information-structural concerns like topicality. We will not discuss this further here, although there is obviously much work to do in the future to repeat the exercise of Chapter 6 for other island effects—that is, to try to pair these findings about topicality and islandhood to a well-developed theory of discourse structure.

In this section, we discuss two other, less obvious ways of extending the ideas developed in this book. Section 7.5.1 is concerned with the extent to which coordinate structures behave like adjunction structures, syntactically and semantically. Then, Section 7.5.2 asks what locality effects *aren't* touched by these information-structural considerations.

7.5.1 Conjuncts and adjuncts: Similarities and differences

A key component of the asymmetric analysis that we have considered is Munn's adjunction analysis of coordinate structures. From a syntactic perspective, what Munn's analysis buys us is a distinction between initial and noninitial conjuncts: noninitial conjuncts are adjuncts, and therefore are subject to locality constraints that do not affect initial conjuncts. However, we have not explored any *interpretive* similarities between conjuncts and adjuncts.

Adjunction structures are more heterogeneous than coordinate structures in many respects, and it is not clear that there are meaningful generalizations to be made about the discourse semantics of all adjuncts. However, there is potential for an interesting comparison to be made between extraction from coordinate structures, and extraction from adjuncts. As discussed in Section 4.6, Postal (1998) demonstrated some suggestive syntactic similarities between extraction from Type A coordinate structures and from adjuncts, while Munn (1992, 1993, 2000, 2001) demonstrated similarities between ATB movement and parasitic gap constructions. It would be worthwhile to ask how far-reaching those similarities are, and in particular whether they extend to semantic constraints on extraction.

The question is particularly acute because the currently predominant theory of the semantics of adjunction claims that, semantically, adjuncts just are conjuncts. This was a seminal claim regarding adverbial modification by Davidson (1967), adapted to adnominal modification by Higginbotham (1985), Parsons (1990) among others, and reified as the rule of Predicate Modification by Heim and Kratzer (1998) and Predicate Conjunction by Altshuler et al. (2019).

Davidson's main claim is that *Mary danced at midnight* entails *Mary danced* because the modifier denotes a conjoined predicate of events. The inference from (6a) to (6b) is just a case of conjunct elimination, on Davidson's analysis.

(6) a. $\exists e.\mathrm{dance}(m, e) \wedge \mathrm{at}(e, \mathrm{midnight})$
     b. $\exists e.\mathrm{dance}(m, e)$

Likewise, the extension of *red car* is logically related to the extension of *car*: the set of objects picked out by (7a) is a proper subset of the set of objects picked out by (7b).

(7) a. $\lambda x.\mathrm{red}(x) \wedge \mathrm{car}(x)$
     b. $\lambda x.\mathrm{car}(x)$

This implies that the semantics of adjunction (at least, of these classes of adjuncts) is very similar to a semantics for conjunction. We should therefore ask whether the semantic and pragmatic considerations from the previous two chapters apply to adjunction structures in the same way as they apparently apply to coordinate structures.

To our knowledge, the most extensive study of semantic constraints on extraction from adjuncts is by Truswell (2011). He claims that extraction from adjuncts is possible only if the adjunct and its host jointly describe a single event. This has a range of consequences. For instance, on the semantic side, it predicts (given Truswell's theory of event structure) the contrast between (8a), where the adjunct modifies an achievement, and (8b), where the adjunct modifies an activity.

(8) a. What did John arrive [whistling __]?
     b. #What does John work [whistling __]?

From a syntactic perspective, it predicts that the adjunct must be adjoined no higher than VP (or possibly *v*P), and must not contain any functional structure above VP (or *v*P) itself. The reason is that any such functional structure would bind the event variable introduced by the main verb, or the event variable introduced by the adjunct. This predicts, for instance, that only nonfinite adjuncts allow extraction.

(9) a. #Which movie did Harry cry [after he watched __]?
     b. ?Which movie did Harry cry [after watching __]?

A central part of Truswell's analysis is a range of relations which allow event descriptions to combine into larger event descriptions. There are four such relations in Truswell's theory:[7]

1. Causation: What did John drive Mary crazy [whistling __]?
2. Temporal precedence: What did John die [whistling __]?
3. Intention: What did you come here [to talk about __]?
4. Background: What did you stand in the corner [screaming __]?

It is easy to see a loose similarity between this set of relations and those which featured prominently in Chapters 5 and 6. At least, Causation is very similar to RESULT, and Background is very similar to ⇒BACKGROUND.

---

[7] Truswell did not phrase things in this way, but this presentation facilitates comparison with the approach to extraction from coordinate structures in Section 6.6.

There are reasons to think that asymmetric extraction from coordinate structures is also conditioned by a notion of single eventhood. A persuasive argument in support of this conclusion was outlined by Carlson (1987). Carlson argues that a 'sentence-internal' *same* and *different* can be licensed by VP coordination, as in (10), where each conjunct describes a different eventuality, and those eventualities are either distributed over the individuals picked out by the subject (in (10a)), or asserted to have involved a single individual (in (10b)).

(10)   a.   Different people [[changed the oil] and [greased the chassis]].
       b.   The same person [[changed the oil] and [greased the chassis]].

However, instances of VP coordination which allow asymmetric extraction do not license *same* or *different* in this way: although the examples in (11) are grammatical, the sentence-internal reading (where, for example, one person in (11a) went to the store and another bought ice cream) does not have the NARRATION interpretation required for asymmetric extraction.

(11)   a.   Different people [[went to the store] and [bought ice cream]].
       b.   The same person [[went to the store] and [bought ice cream]].

Accordingly, examples like (12) are ungrammatical, unless *same* or *different* are interpreted 'sentence-externally', as involving comparison with some other, discourse-given women.

(12)   *What did different women/the same woman [[go to the store] and [buy __]]?

(Carlson 1987: 540)

The ungrammaticality is explained by an interpretive clash: asymmetric extraction requires that the coordinated VPs be interpreted as describing a single event; sentence-internal readings of *same* and *different* require that the coordinated VPs be interpreted as describing multiple events, and the two requirements cannot be satisfied simultaneously. This is a strong argument that asymmetric extraction from coordinate structures requires single eventhood. Although Carlson does not give the data, the same effect can be reproduced in at least Type B and C scenarios with extraction from initial conjuncts.[8]

(13)   a.   *How much can the same person/different people [[drink __] and [stay sober]]?
       b.   *This is that dish that the same person/different people always [[order __ here] and [get sick]].

This pattern suggests that the notion of single event conditions asymmetric extraction from coordinate structures, just as it does with extraction from adjuncts. However, it is easy to see differences between the two extraction types. Most strikingly, the interpretive relations found in Truswell's account of extraction from adjuncts do not match those that we have described for asymmetric extraction from coordinate structures. Temporal

---

[8] Reich (2009) argued that asymmetric coordinations, with or without extraction, describe single events. However, it is not clear to us what independent tests Reich uses to recognize single events.

precedence does not correspond to any one discourse relation, and although a notion of continuity of intention will often be sufficient to guarantee NARRATION, it is clear that intention is not the same as NARRATION. Conversely, relations like VIOLATED EXPECTATION do not license extraction from adjuncts (compare (14a) to the familiar (14b)).

(14) a. *How much can you [stay sober [after/despite drinking __]]?
      b. How much can you [[drink __] and [still stay sober]]?

So the challenge for future research is to make sense of this family resemblance between theories of extraction from adjuncts and from coordinate structures (see Neeleman and Tanaka 2020 for initial steps in this direction). When Truswell (2007) compared the interpretive constraints on extraction from adjuncts and from coordinate structures, he was skeptical about the prospects for a unification of the two sets of constraints. However, that assessment was based on the approach to coordinate structures described in Chapter 5, where discourse relations directly condition extraction patterns. It is not clear that his skepticism would be warranted if one adopted the information-structural alternative sketched in Chapter 6, and the asymmetric syntactic option outlined in Section 4.6, where extraction from initial conjuncts is relatively unconstrained.

The most informative comparisons will instead be between extraction from noninitial conjuncts and from adjuncts. The issue isn't necessarily which interpretive relations are encoded in the two cases: as discussed in Chapter 3, (15a) and (15b) encode different relations between going and buying, but we take that to be a relatively mundane fact about the lexical semantics of *and* and *to*.

(15) a. What did you [[go to the store] and [buy __]]?
      b. What did you [[go to the store] to [buy __]]?

The more interesting question is whether there is some overarching set of principles which predict the similar-but-different semantic patterns observed in extraction from adjuncts and from coordinate structures.[9]

Differences between the two cases are to be expected, because Truswell's event relations range over objects of different types from the DUs that serve as arguments of discourse relations. Although EDUs, for Asher and Lascarides (2003), are typically eventuality descriptions, they correspond to larger syntactic units than Truswell's adjuncts: a typical EDU is finite, and roughly sentential, whereas Truswell's theory necessarily pertains to nonfinite, subsentential event descriptions. That syntactic difference will surely have visible consequences in the semantic representation.

In recognition of this difference, let us talk about 'event relations' to describe the family of relations between events that Truswell describes, as opposed to discourse relations. The question about interpretive similarities between extraction from adjuncts and from noninitial conjuncts is then this: is there a unified analysis of extraction from adjuncts and from coordinate structures, for instance in terms of topicality, which simultaneously

---

[9] The most salient similarity between extraction from coordinate structures and extraction from adjuncts is the similarity between ATB movement and parasitic gap constructions. We discussed that similarity in Section 4.6, and endorsed the conclusion of Postal (1993) that there are real differences as well as the similarities. In this respect, too, then, extraction from adjuncts and extraction from coordinate structures are tantalizingly similar but irreducibly different.

derives Truswell's generalizations about the effect of event relations on extraction from adjuncts, and the findings described in Chapters 5 and 6 about the effect of discourse relations on extraction from noninitial conjuncts?

It is not the case that any old sentence topic can be extracted from an adjunct. Using the *speaking of*-test, we do not detect a clear difference in topicality between those cases which allow extraction and those that do not.

(16) a. (i)   Speaking of the *Marseillaise*, John drove Mary crazy whistling it.
      (ii) What did John drive Mary crazy [whistling __]?
    b. (i)   ?Speaking of the *Marseillaise*, John works whistling it.
      (ii) #What does John work [whistling __]?

(17) a. Speaking of whiskey, I came here to buy some.
    b. What did you come here [to buy __]?

(18) a. (i)   Speaking of *Terminator 2*, Harry cried after watching it.
      (ii) ?Which movie did Harry cry [after watching __]?
    b. (i)   Speaking of *Terminator 2*, Harry cried after he watched it.
      (ii) *Which movie did Harry cry [after he watched __]?

But we also know that not just any old sentence topic licenses extraction from a noninitial conjunct—this was one of the problems described in Section 7.4.1. It may then be the case that the question is not about sentence topics, but about the special relationship that discourse relations like NARRATION bear with the discourse topic, and whether that has any analog in the domain of event relations. At this point, we don't even have speculations to offer.

7.5.2   What is left for syntactic locality theory?

Ross's (1967) discovery of island effects (see Section 4.3.2) is one of the central achievements of generative syntactic theory. However, a recurring question in the second half of this book is whether the basis for Ross's island effects really is syntactic, or whether discourse calls the shots. The answer of Erteschik-Shir (1973), Morgan (1975), Kuno (1976), and the other references cited in Section 6.2 is that discourse structure and information structure predict island effects such as the Complex NP Constraint and the Sentential Subject Constraint, and their exceptions, at least as well as Ross's syntactic account. And regardless of the theoretical choices that one makes with respect to the CSC, it seems inevitable that an accurate theory of extraction from coordinate structures will be partly discourse-based, for reasons outlined at the start of this chapter.

This could lead to a suspicion that locality theory is syntactically trivial: Ross invented island constraints, and Erteschik-Shir, Morgan, and Kuno collectively pushed the explanation for island constraints into pragmatics. In reality, though, this is far from the case. The pursuit of unified syntactic explanations for Ross's constraints, particularly by Chomsky (1973) (see Section 4.3 for discussion) uncovered new types of locality effects, which cannot plausibly be treated in the above 'discourse calls the shots' fashion.

A clear example of this is successive-cyclic movement, a direct consequence of Subjacency. Subjacency places limits on the amount of distance that a single movement step can cover. Chomsky (1973) proposed that movement could only cross a single bounding node, as part of a program of unifying Ross's island constraints. While the details have changed (the current descendant of this approach is the Phase Impenetrability Condition of Chomsky 2000, 2001, which limits extraction out of phases), the major consequence remains the same: apparent long-distance movement must be composed of multiple shorter steps. A range of empirical evidence supports this broad approach, as mentioned in Section 4.3.

This locality effect cannot plausibly be reduced to the approach outlined in the previous two chapters, because that approach only regulates the distribution of base positions of moved phrases. To our knowledge, there are no proposals to reduce the distribution of intermediate traces, of the sort generated by successive-cyclic movement, to discourse structure or indeed any other semantic property. Their distribution is also not plausibly phonologically conditioned (after all, traces of any sort have a very limited phonological effect, restricted to effects like *wanna*-contraction), so they stand as strong evidence that there *is* a syntactic locality theory, or, in other words, that not every locality effect can be derived from pragmatic conditions, interface considerations, and so on.

This raises the question of the division of labor between different aspects of competence and performance in jointly explaining locality phenomena. What kinds of phenomena are best handled in the syntax, and which are best handled in terms of meaning (semantics or pragmatics)? A full answer to this question lies some way in the future, but the following strong hypothesis suggests itself. Some locality constraints concern extraction from 'domains': Ross's original island constraints concern domains from which extraction is impossible, while other examples of this kind are the CED effects of Cattell (1976) and Huang (1982) described in Section 4.3.4, where extraction from subjects and from adjuncts is degraded. *All* of these constraints on extraction from certain domains have plausible nonsyntactic etiologies: in terms of topicality and other semantic factors as discussed in Chapter 6 and earlier in this chapter, or for instance in terms of 'left branch' effects, which prohibit extraction from subjects in languages like English because they occur on left branches.[10]

According to this strong hypothesis, what would be left for syntax is to regulate the length of movement steps, intervention effects, and the form of chains (including the distribution of traces or copies). The factors mandating successive cyclicity, discussed earlier in this section, are an example of this. Others include the Relativized Minimality effects described by Rizzi (1990) and discussed in Section 4.3.5.

In the context of this monograph, this hypothesis would imply that it wasn't an accident that the original formulation of the CSC has fallen by the wayside in Chomskyan locality theory, because the original CSC restricted extraction from a certain type of domain (coordinate structures), and prohibition of extraction from designated domains is a type of locality effect that Chomskyan syntax often handles badly, and nonsyntactic accounts often handle quite well. Nevertheless, even if one adopts the Chomskyan approach,

---

[10] See Kayne (1983) for an early example of an approach to subject islands in which branching direction plays a crucial role—because linear order has been taken to be determined postsyntactically since Chomsky (1995), any approach which references linear order must necessarily have a postsyntactic element.

there is an irreducibly syntactic component to locality theory, and that component may even constrain extraction out of coordinate structures in nontrivial ways, as described in Section 4.6 and incorporated into the asymmetric approach to coordination described at the start of this chapter.

Neither syntactic locality theory nor a purely discourse-based approach to islands fully accounts for observed patterns of extraction from coordinate structures, but there are prospects for real advances in a theory which combines the best of both. We hope that this book has demonstrated both the empirical and the theoretical payoffs of such a pluralistic approach to locality effects, some of the challenges, and a plethora of exciting prospects for further research.

List of choice points

Choice Point 1 What is the structure of coordination?

Option 1: Gazdar's symmetrical structure (all conjuncts c-command each other);
Option 2: Progovac's or Neeleman and Tanaka's symmetrical structure (no conjunct c-commands any other);
Option 3: Johannessen's and Zoerner's asymmetrical structure (specifier–head–complement);
Option 4: Munn's asymmetrical structure (all noninitial conjuncts adjoined to initial conjunct);
Option 5: Something else.

Choice Point 2 What is the relationship between symmetrical and asymmetric patterns of extraction from coordinate structures?

Option 1: The unmarked pattern of extraction is symmetrical ATB extraction; all asymmetric extraction patterns are marked in some way (e.g. Postal 1998, Haspelmath 2004, Steedman 2011).
Option 2: ATB extraction has no special status in the syntax vis-à-vis asymmetric extraction patterns (though it may have a special status in the semantics, for instance because of a parallelism constraint, e.g. Ruys 1992, Munn 1993).

Choice Point 3 What do the CSC and its exceptions derive from?

Option 1: Coordination is syntactically unique; the CSC follows from the unique syntax of coordination, together with general syntactic locality principles; apparent exceptions to the CSC can also be explained in syntactic terms;
Option 2: Coordination is not syntactically unique; the CSC and its exceptions follow from general syntactic locality principles;
Option 3: Coordination is not syntactically unique; the CSC follows from a semantic parallelism constraint as in Ruys (1992), Fox (2000); exceptions to the CSC follow from nonsyntactic considerations of the sort sketched by Lakoff (1986).

Choice Point 4 What is the relationship between the CSC and Chomskyan locality theory?

Option 1: Chomskyan locality theory should be rejected in favor of alternatives in which the CSC is not an outlier (e.g. Gazdar 1981, Pesetsky 1982).
Option 2: The CSC can be integrated into Chomskyan locality theory (e.g. Takahashi 1994). This may require a novel, multiplanar syntax of coordination (e.g. Williams 1978).
Option 3: The CSC should be rejected as a syntactic constraint, although it may be reinterpreted as a semantic parallelism constraint. Syntactic locality theory may make other predictions about extraction from coordinate structures (e.g. the adjunction theory of Munn 1993 implies that extraction from an initial conjunct is syntactically unmarked).

Choice Point 5 What is the relationship between D-linking, sentence topic, and weak islands?

Option 1: D-linking and sentence topic form a natural class; only D-linked/topical phrases can be extracted from weak islands.
Option 2: D-linking is distinct from sentence topic; sentence topics can be extracted from weak islands.
Option 3: D-linking is distinct from sentence topic; D-linked phrases can be extracted from weak islands.

Choice Point 6 What is the relationship between a common theme and the ATB constraint?

Option 1: The ATB constraint does not align with maximal common themes: there are cases of PARALLEL or CONTRAST with asymmetric extraction;

Option 2: The ATB constraint follows from interactions between maximal common themes and the syntax of canonical A'-extraction;

Option 3: The ATB constraint follows from interactions between maximal common themes and the semantics of canonical A'-constructions;

Option 4: Something else.

Choice Point 7 What is the correct analysis of Type B scenarios?

Option 1: Examples of Type B scenarios harbor CONTRAST, possibly without reference to a maximal common theme; CONTRAST allows asymmetric extraction from either conjunct.

Option 2: Examples like (216a) in Chapter 6 harbor CONTRAST; CONTRAST only allows asymmetric extraction from initial conjuncts; examples like (216b) in Chapter 6 should be analyzed in terms of some other discourse relation.

Option 3: Examples like (216a) in Chapter 6 harbor some less contentful relation like CONTINUATION; factors not closely related to discourse structure explain the distinctive properties of such examples; examples like (216b–c) in Chapter 6 should be analyzed in terms of some other discourse relation.

Bibliography

Abels, Klaus (2003). *Successive Cyclicity, Anti-locality and Adposition Stranding*. Ph.D. thesis, University of Connecticut.

Abrusán, Márta (2014). *Weak Island Semantics*. Oxford University Press, Oxford.

Abrusán, Márta (forthcoming). Presuppositions. In *Linguistics meets Philosophy* (ed. D. Altshuler). Cambridge University Press, Cambridge.

Ades, Anthony and Steedman, Mark (1982). On the order of words. *Linguistics and Philosophy*, **4**, 517–58.

Adger, David and Ramchand, Gillian (2005). Merge and Move: *Wh*-dependencies revisited. *Linguistic Inquiry*, **36**, 161–93.

Afantenos, Stergos, Asher, Nicholas, Benamara, Farah, Bras, Myriam, Fabre, Cécile, Ho-Dac, Lydia-Mai, Le Draoulec, Anne, Muller, Philippe, Péry-Woodley, Marie-Paule, Prévot, Laurent, Rebeyrolle, Josette, Tanguy, Ludovic, Vergez-Couret, Marianne, and Vieu, Laure (2012). An empirical resource for discovering cognitive principles of discourse organisation: The ANNODIS corpus. In *Proceedings of the Eighth International Conference on Language Resources and Evaluation (LREC'12)* (ed. N. Calzolari, K. Choukri, T. Declerck, M. U. Dogan, B. Maegaard, J. Mariani, A. Moreno, J. Odijk, and S. Piperidis.), pp. 2727–34. European Language Resources Association, Istanbul.

Alonso-Ovalle, Luis (2006). *Disjunction in Alternative Semantics*. Ph.D. thesis, University of Massachusetts, Amherst.

Altshuler, Daniel (2012). Aspectual meaning meets discourse coherence: A look at the Russian imperfective. *Journal of Semantics*, **29**, 39–108.

Altshuler, Daniel (2016). *Events, States and Times: An Essay on Narrative Discourse in English*. De Gruyter, Berlin/Warsaw. Open access, available at: www.degruyter.com/document/doi/10.1515/9783110485912/html. Last accessed December 7, 2021.

Altshuler, Daniel (2021). A puzzle about narrative progression and causal reasoning. In *The Language of Fiction* (ed. A. Stokke and E. Maier), pp. 255–76. Oxford University Press, Oxford.

Altshuler, Daniel and Haug, Dag (2017). The semantics of provisional, temporal anaphors and cataphors. Talk presented at Deutsche Gesellschaft für Sprachwissenschaft, Saarland University, Saarbrücken.

Altshuler, Daniel and Haug, Dag (under contract). *Literature as a Formal Language*. Routledge, Abingdon.

Altshuler, Daniel and Melkonian, Susanna (2014). In defense of the reference time. *Semantics–Syntax Interface*, **1**, 133–49.

Altshuler, Daniel, Parsons, Terence, and Schwarzschild, Roger (2019). *A Course in Semantics*. MIT Press, Cambridge, MA.

Altshuler, Daniel and Schlöder, Julian (2019). Anaphora and ambiguity in narratives. Lecture notes from ESSLLI 2019, University of Latvia. Available at http://jjsch.github.io/teaching/esslli2019.html. Last accessed December 7, 2021.

Altshuler, Daniel and Schlöder, Julian (2021a). If pictures are stative, what does this mean for discourse interpretation? In *Proceedings of Sinn und Bedeutung 25*. Edited by P. Grosz, L. Martí, H. Pearson, Y. Sudo, and S. Zobel.), pp. 19–36. Available online at https://ojs.ub.uni-konstanz.de/sub/index.php/sub/article/view/922/846. Last accessed January 21, 2022.

Altshuler, Daniel and Schlöder, Julian (2021b). Super pragmatics of pictorial and mixed linguistic–pictorial discourse. Under review.

Altshuler, Daniel and Schwarzschild, Roger (2013). Correlating cessation with double access. In *Proceedings of the 19th Amsterdam Colloquium* (ed. M. Aloni, M. Franke, and F. Roelofsen), pp. 43–50. Institute for Logic, Language, and Computation, Amsterdam.

Altshuler, Daniel and Stojnić, Una (2015). The attention–coherence model of prominence: A look at 'now'. Presented at the International Conference on Prominence in Language, June 15–17, University of Cologne.

Altshuler, Daniel and Varasdi, Károly (2015). An argument for definitional adequacy of RESULT and NARRATION. In *Proceedings of SALT 25* (ed. S. D'Antonio, C.-R. Little, M. Moroney, and M. Wiegand), pp. 38–56. CLC Publications, Ithaca, NY.

Anand, Pranav and Toosarvandani, Maziar (forthcoming). Narrative and point of view. In *Linguistics meets Philosophy* (ed. D. Altshuler). Cambridge University Press, Cambridge.

AnderBois, Scott (2021). Switch reference in A'ingae. Ms., Brown University.

AnderBois, Scott and Silva, Wilson (2018). Kofán collaborative project: Collection of audio–video materials and texts. SOAS, Endangered Languages Archive, London. https://www.elararchive.org/dk0466/. Last accessed January 21, 2022.

Andersson, Marta and Spenader, Jennifer (2014). RESULT and PURPOSE relations with and without 'so'. *Lingua*, **148**, 1–27.

Aoun, Joseph, Hornstein, Norbert, Lightfoot, David, and Weinberg, Amy (1987). Two types of locality. *Linguistic Inquiry*, **18**, 537–77.

Artstein, Ron (2005). Coordination of parts of words. *Lingua*, **115**, 359–93.

Asher, Nicholas (1993). *Reference to Abstract Objects in Discourse*. Springer, Dordrecht.

Asher, Nicholas (1999). Discourse and the focus/background distinction. In *Focus: Linguistic, Cognitive, and Computational Perspectives* (ed. P. Bosch and R. van der Sandt), pp. 247–67. Cambridge University Press, Cambridge.

Asher, Nicholas (2004). Discourse topic. *Theoretical Linguistics*, **30**, 163–202.

Asher, Nicholas, Aurnague, Michel, Bras, Myriam, Sablayrolles, Pierre, and Vieu, Laure (1996). De l'espace–temps dans l'analyse du discours. *Sémiotiques*, **9**, 13–62.

Asher, Nicholas and Fernando, Tim (1997). Labelling representation for effective disambiguation. In *Proceedings of the 2nd International Workshop on Computational Semantics*. Tilburg University.

Asher, Nicholas, Hardt, Daniel, and Busquets, Joan (1997). Discourse parallelism, scope, and ellipsis. In *SALT VII* (ed. A. Lawson), pp. 19–36. CLC Publications, Ithaca, NY.

Asher, Nicholas and Lascarides, Alex (1998a). Bridging. *Journal of Semantics*, **15**, 83–113.

Asher, Nicholas and Lascarides, Alex (1998b). The semantics and pragmatics of presupposition. *Journal of Semantics*, **15**, 239–300.

Asher, Nicholas and Lascarides, Alex (2003). *Logics of Conversation*. Cambridge University Press, Cambridge.

Asher, Nicholas and Moreau, Michael (1991). Common sense entailment: A modal theory of nonmonotonic reasoning. In *Proceedings of the Twelfth International Joint Conferences on Artificial Intelligence, vol. 1*, pp. 387–92.

Asher, Nicholas, Prévot, Laurent, and Vieu, Laure (2007). Setting the background in discourse. *Discours*, **1**, 1–30.

Asher, Nicholas and Vieu, Laure (2005). Subordinating and coordinating discourse relations. *Lingua*, **115**, 591–610.

Avery, Walden (2019). Co-occurrence of multiple coherence relations between pairs of discourse segments. Division III (Senior) Thesis, Hampshire College.

Avrutin, Sergey (1999). *Development of the Syntax–Discourse Interface*. Kluwer, Dordrecht.

Bach, Emmon (1986). The algebra of events. *Linguistics and Philosophy*, **9**, 5–16.

Bar-Lev, Zev and Palacas, Arthur (1980). Semantic command over pragmatic priority. *Lingua*, **51**, 137–46.

Bary, Corien (2009). *Aspect in Ancient Greek. A Semantic Analysis of the Aorist and Imperfective*. Ph.D. thesis, Radboud University, Nijmegen.

Benincà, Paola and Poletto, Cecilia (2001). Topic, focus, and V2: Defining the CP sublayers. In *The Structure of CP and IP: The Cartography of Syntactic Structures, Volume 2* (ed. L. Rizzi), pp. 52–75. Oxford University Press, Oxford.

Bennett, Jonathan (2003). *A Philosophical Guide to Conditionals*. Oxford University Press, Oxford.

Bittner, Maria (2014). *Temporality: Universals and Variation*. Wiley Blackwell, Chichester.

Bjorkman, Bronwyn Moore (2013). A syntactic answer to a pragmatic puzzle: The case of asymmetric *and*. In *Syntax and its Limits* (ed. R. Folli, C. Sevdali, and R. Truswell), pp. 391–408. Oxford University Press, Oxford.

Bjorkman, Bronwyn Moore (2014). Accounting for unexpected subject gaps in TP coordination. *The Linguistic Review*, **31**, 487–513.

Black, Maria, Coltheart, Max, and Byng, Sally (1985). Forms of coding in sentence comprehension during reading. In *Attention and Performance XII: The Psychology of Reading* (ed. M. Coltheart), pp. 655–72. Lawrence Erlbaum, Hillsdale, NJ.

Blakemore, Diane (2000). Indicators and procedures: *Nevertheless* and *but*. *Journal of Linguistics*, **36**, 463–86.

Blakemore, Diane and Carston, Robyn (1999). The pragmatics of and-conjunctions: The non-narrative cases. *UCL Working Papers in Linguistics*, **11**, 1–20.

Blakemore, Diane and Carston, Robyn (2005). The pragmatics of sentential coordination with *and*. *Lingua*, **115**, 569–89.

Boeckx, Cedric (2012). *Syntactic Islands*. Cambridge University Press, Cambridge.

Borgonovo, Claudia and Neeleman, Ad (2000). Transparent adjuncts. *Canadian Journal of Linguistics/Revue canadienne de linguistique*, **45**, 199–224.

Borsley, Robert (2005). Against ConjP. *Lingua*, **115**, 461–82.

Bos, Johan (1995). Predicate logic unplugged. In *Proceedings of the 10th Amsterdam Colloquium* (ed. P. Dekker and M. Stokhof), pp. 133–43. Institute for Logic, Language, and Computation, Amsterdam.

Bošković, Željko (2008). What will you have, DP or NP? In *Proceedings of NELS 37, Volume 1* (ed. E. Elfner and M. Walkow), pp. 101–14. GLSA, Amherst, MA.

Bošković, Željko (2019a). On the Coordinate Structure Constraint, islandhood, phases, and rescue by PF-deletion. Ms., University of Connecticut.

Bošković, Željko (2019b). On the Coordinate Structure Constrant and labeling. In *Proceedings of the 36th West Coast Conference on Formal Linguistics* (ed. R. Stockwell, M. O'Leary, Z. Xu, and Z. Zhou), pp. 71–80. Cascadilla Proceedings Project, Somerville, MA.

Bošković, Željko (2019c). On the limits of Across-The-Board movement. Ms., University of Connecticut.

Bošković, Željko (2020). On the Coordinate Structure Constraint and the adjunct condition. In *Syntactic Architecture and its Consequences II: Between Syntax and Morphology* (ed. A. Bárány, T. Biberauer, J. Douglas, and S. Vikner), pp. 227–58. Language Science Press, Berlin.

Bošković, Željko and Franks, Steven (2000). Across-The-Board movement and LF. *Syntax*, **3**, 107–28.

Breitholtz, Ellen (2021). *Enthymemes and Topoi in Dialogue*. Brill, Leiden.

Bresnan, Joan (1978). A realistic transformational grammar. In *Linguistic Theory and Psychological Reality* (ed. M. Halle, J. Bresnan, and G. Miller), pp. 1–59. MIT Press, Cambridge, MA.

Brown, Jessica (2017). *Heads and Adjuncts: An Experimental Study of Subextraction from Participials and Coordination in English, German and Norwegian*. Ph.D. thesis, University of Cambridge.

Bruening, Benjamin and Al Khalaf, Eman (2020). Category mismatches in coordination revisited. *Linguistic Inquiry*, **51**, 1–36.

Büring, Daniel (1997). *The Meaning of Topic and Focus: The 59th Street Bridge Accent*. Routledge, London.

Büring, Daniel (1999). Topic. In *Focus: Linguistic, Cognitive, and Computational Perspectives* (ed. P. Bosch and R. van der Sandt), pp. 142–65. Cambridge University Press, Cambridge.

Büring, Daniel (2003). On D-trees, beans, and B-accents. *Linguistics and Philosophy*, **26**, 511–45.

Büring, Daniel (2005). *Binding Theory*. Cambridge University Press, Cambridge.

Büring, Daniel (2007). Semantics, intonation, and information structure. In *The Oxford Handbook of Linguistic Interfaces* (ed. G. Ramchand and C. Reiss), pp. 445–74. Oxford University Press, Oxford.

Büring, Daniel and Hartmann, Katharina (1998). Asymmetrische Koordination. *Linguistische Berichte*, **174**, 172–201.

Burkhardt, Petra (2005). *The Syntax–Discourse Interface: Representing and Interpreting Dependency*. John Benjamins, Amsterdam.

Burton, Strang and Grimshaw, Jane (1992). Coordination and VP-internal subjects. *Linguistic Inquiry*, **23**, 305–13.

Carlson, Greg (1977). *Reference to Kinds in English*. Ph.D. thesis, University of Massachusetts, Amherst.

Carlson, Greg (1987). *Same* and *different*: Some consequences for syntax and semantics. *Linguistics and Philosophy*, **10**, 531–65.

Carlson, Katy (2001). *Parallelism and Prosody in the Processing of Ellipsis Sentences*. Ph.D. thesis, University of Massachusetts, Amherst.

Carlson, Lauri (1984). *'Well' in Dialogue Games: A Discourse Analysis of the Interjection 'Well' in Idealized Conversation*. John Benjamins, Amsterdam.

Carston, Robyn (1993). Conjunction, explanation and relevance. *Lingua*, **90**, 27–48.

Carter, Sam and Altshuler, Daniel (2017). 'Now' with subordinate clauses. In *Proceedings of SALT 27* (ed. D. Burgdorf, J. Collard, S. Maspong, and B. Stefánsdóttir), pp. 358–76. CLC Publications, Ithaca, NY.

Cattell, Ray (1976). Constraints on movement rules. *Language*, **52**, 18–50.

Chaves, Rui (2012). On the grammar of extraction and coordination. *Natural Language & Linguistic Theory*, **30**, 465–512.

Chomsky, Noam (1956). Three models for the description of language. *IRE Transactions on Information Theory*, **2**, 113–24.

Chomsky, Noam (1957). *Syntactic Structures*. Mouton, The Hague.

Chomsky, Noam (1964). *Current Issues in Linguistic Theory*. Mouton, The Hague.

Chomsky, Noam (1965). *Aspects of the Theory of Syntax*. MIT Press, Cambridge, MA.

Chomsky, Noam (1973). Conditions on transformations. In *A Festschrift for Morris Halle* (ed. S. Anderson and P. Kiparsky), pp. 232–86. Holt, Rinehart and Winston, New York.

Chomsky, Noam (1976). Conditions on rules of grammar. *Linguistic Analysis*, **2**, 303–51.

Chomsky, Noam (1977). On wh-movement. In *Formal Syntax* (ed. P. Culicover, T. Wasow, and A. Akmajian), pp. 71–132. Academic Press, New York.

Chomsky, Noam (1981). *Lectures on Government and Binding*. Foris, Dordrecht.

Chomsky, Noam (1982). *Some Concepts and Consequences of the Theory of Government and Binding*. MIT Press, Cambridge, MA.

Chomsky, Noam (1986). *Barriers*. MIT Press, Cambridge, MA.

Chomsky, Noam (1993). A minimalist program for linguistic theory. In *The View from Building 20: Essays in Honor of Sylvain Bromberger* (ed. K. Hale and S. J. Keyser), pp. 1–52. MIT Press, Cambridge, MA.

Chomsky, Noam (1995). *The Minimalist Program*. MIT Press, Cambridge, MA.

Chomsky, Noam (2000). Minimalist inquiries: The framework. In *Step by Step: Essays on Minimalist Syntax in Honor of Howard Lasnik* (ed. R. Martin, D. Michaels, and J. Uriagereka), pp. 89–115. MIT Press, Cambridge, MA.

Chomsky, Noam (2001). Derivation by phase. In *Ken Hale: A Life in Language* (ed. M. Kenstowicz), pp. 1–52. MIT Press, Cambridge, MA.

Chomsky, Noam (2004). Beyond explanatory adequacy. In *Structures and Beyond: The Cartography of Syntactic Structures, Volume 3* (ed. A. Belletti), pp. 104–31. Oxford University Press, Oxford.

Chomsky, Noam (2008). On phases. In *Foundational Issues in Linguistic Theory: Essays in Honor of Jean-Roger Vergnaud* (ed. R. Freidin, C. Otero, and M. L. Zubizarreta), pp. 133–66. MIT Press, Cambridge, MA.

Chomsky, Noam and Lasnik, Howard (1977). Filters and control. *Linguistic Inquiry*, **8**, 425–504.

Chomsky, Noam and Lasnik, Howard (1993). The theory of principles and parameters. In *Syntax: An International Handbook of Contemporary Research* (ed. J. Jacobs, A. von Stechow, W. Sternefeld, and T. Vennemann), pp. 506–69. De Gruyter, Berlin. Reprinted as Chapter 2 of Chomsky (1995).

Cinque, Guglielmo (1990). *Types of A̅-dependencies*. MIT Press, Cambridge, MA.

Citko, Barbara (2005). On the nature of Merge: External Merge, internal Merge, and parallel Merge. *Linguistic Inquiry*, **36**, 475–96.

Constant, Noah (2014). *Contrastive Topic: Meanings and Realizations*. Ph.D. thesis, University of Massachusetts, Amherst.

Copley, Bridget and Harley, Heidi (2015). A force-theoretic framework for event structure. *Linguistics and Philosophy*, **38**, 103–58.

Copley, Bridget and Martin, Fabienne (2014). *Causation in Grammatical Structures*. Oxford University Press, Oxford.

Copley, Bridget and Wolff, Philip (2014). Theories of causation should inform linguistic theory and vice versa. In *Causation in Grammatical Structures* (ed. B. Copley and F. Martin), pp. 11–57. Oxford University Press, Oxford.

Cormack, Annabel and Breheny, Richard (1994). Projections for functional categories. In *UCL Working Papers in Linguistics* (ed. J. Harris), pp. 35–61.

Cormack, Annabel and Smith, Neil (2005). What is coordination? *Lingua*, **115**, 395–418.

Culicover, Peter and Jackendoff, Ray (1997). Semantic subordination despite syntactic coordination. *Linguistic Inquiry*, **28**, 195–217.

Culicover, Peter and Jackendoff, Ray (1999). The view from the periphery: The English comparative correlative. *Linguistic Inquiry*, **30**, 543–71.

Culicover, Peter and Jackendoff, Ray (2005). *Simpler Syntax*. Oxford University Press, Oxford.

Culicover, Peter and Postal, Paul (2001). *Parasitic Gaps*. MIT Press, Cambridge, MA.

Cumming, Samuel (2021). Narrative and point of view. In *The Language of Fiction* (ed. A. Stokke and E. Maier), pp. 221–54. Oxford University Press, Oxford.

Cumming, Samuel, Greenberg, Gabriel, and Kelly, Rory (2017). Conventions of viewpoint coherence in film. *Philosopher's Imprint*, **17**, 1–28.

Dahl, Deborah (1984). *The Structure and Function of* One-*anaphora in English*. Ph.D. thesis, University of Minnesota.

Dalrymple, Mary and Nikolaeva, Irina (2006). Syntax of natural and accidental coordination: Evidence from agreement. *Language*, **82**, 824–48.

Dalrymple, Mary, Shieber, Stuart, and Pereira, Fernando (1991). Ellipsis and higher-order unification. *Linguistics and Philosophy*, **14**, 399–452.

Davidson, Donald (1967). The logical form of action sentences. In *The Logic of Decision and Action* (ed. N. Rescher), pp. 81–95. University of Pittsburgh Press, Pittsburgh, PA.

de Cuba, Carlos (2007). *On (Non)factivity, Clausal Complementation and the CP-field*. Ph.D. thesis, Stony Brook University.

de Swart, Henriette (1998). Aspect shift and coercion. *Natural Language & Linguistic Theory*, **16**, 347–85.

de Vos, Mark (2005). *The Syntax of Verbal Pseudo-coordination in English and Afrikaans*. Ph.D. thesis, Universiteit Leiden.

de Vries, Mark (2005). Coordination and syntactic hierarchy. *Studia Linguistica*, **59**, 83–105.

de Vries, Mark (2017). Across-the-board phenomena. In *The Wiley Blackwell Companion to Syntax, Volume 1* (2nd edn) (ed. M. Everaert and H. van Riemsdijk), pp. 1–31. Wiley Blackwell, Hoboken, NJ.

Deane, Paul (1991). Limits to attention: A cognitive theory of island phenomena. *Cognitive Linguistics*, **2**, 1–63.

Den Dikken, Marcel and Giannakidou, Anastasia (2002). From *hell* to polarity: "Aggressively non-D-linked" *wh*-phrases as polarity items. *Linguistic Inquiry*, **33**, 31–61.

Dong, Quang Phuc (1971). A note on conjoined noun phrases. In *Studies out in Left Field: Defamatory Essays Presented to James D. McCawley on the Occasion of his 33rd or 34th Birthday* (ed. A. Zwicky, P. Salus, R. Binnick, and A. Vanek), pp. 11–18. John Benjamins, Amsterdam.

Dougherty, Ray (1970a). A grammar of coördinate conjoined structures I. *Language*, **46**, 850–98.

Dougherty, Ray (1970b). A grammar of coördinate conjoined structures II. *Language*, **47**, 298–339.

Dowty, David (1986). The effects of aspectual class on the temporal structure of discourse: Semantics or pragmatics? *Linguistics and Philosophy*, **9**, 37–62.

Dubey, Amit, Sturt, Patrick, and Keller, Frank (2005). Parallelism in coordination as an instance of syntactic priming: Evidence from corpus-based modeling. In *Proceedings of the Conference on Human Language Technology and Empirical Methods in Natural Language Processing* (ed. R. Mooney, C. Brew, L.-F. Chien, and K. Kirchhoff), pp. 827–34. Association for Computational Linguistics, East Stroudsburg, PA.

Ducrot, Oswald (1984). *Le dire et le dit*. Les Éditions de Minuit, Paris.

É. Kiss, Katalin (2002). *The Syntax of Hungarian*. Cambridge University Press, Cambridge.

Erteschik-Shir, Nomi (1973). *On the Nature of Island Constraints*. Ph.D. thesis, Massachusetts Institute of Technology.

Erteschik-Shir, Nomi (2007). *Information Structure: The Syntax–Discourse Interface*. Oxford University Press, Oxford.

Erteschik-Shir, Nomi and Lappin, Shalom (1979). Dominance and the functional explanation of island phenomena. *Theoretical Linguistics*, **6**, 41–86.

Fiengo, Robert (1974). *Semantic Conditions on Surface Structure*. Ph.D. thesis, Massachusetts Institute of Technology.

Fillmore, Charles (1975). An alternative to checklist theories of meaning. In *Proceedings of the First Annual Meeting of the Berkeley Linguistics Society* (ed. C. Cogan, H. Thompson, G. Thurgood, K. Whistler, and J. Wright), pp. 123–31. Berkeley Linguistics Society, Berkeley, CA.

Fillmore, Charles (1976). Frame semantics and the nature of language. *Annals of the New York Academy of Sciences*, **280**, 20–32.

Fortmann, Christian (2005). Die Lücken im Bild von der Subjektlücken-Koordination. *Linguistische Berichte*, **204**, 441–76.

Fox, Danny (2000). *Economy and Semantic Interpretation*. MIT Press, Cambridge, MA.

Fox, Danny and Hackl, Martin (2007). The universal density of measurement. *Linguistics and Philosophy*, **29**, 537–86.

Frank, Anette (2002). A (discourse) functional analysis of asymmetric coordination. In *Proceedings of the LFG02 Conference* (ed. M. Butt and T. H. King), pp. 175–96. CSLI, Stanford, CA.

Frazier, Lyn and Fodor, Janet Dean (1978). The sausage machine: A new two-stage parsing model. *Cognition*, **6**, 291–325.

Frazier, Lyn, Munn, Alan, and Clifton, Charles (2000). Processing coordinate structures. *Journal of Psycholinguistic Research*, **29**, 343–70.

Frazier, Lyn, Taft, Lori, Roeper, Tom, Clifton, Charles, and Ehrlich, Kate (1984). Parallel structure: A source of facilitation in sentence comprehension. *Memory and Cognition*, **12**, 421–30.

Frey, Werner (2005). Zur Syntax der linken Peripherie im Deutschen. In *Deutsche Syntax: Empirie und Theorie* (ed. F. J. d'Avis), pp. 147–71. Acta Universitatis Gothoburgensis, Gothenburg.

Fukui, Naoki and Speas, Margaret (1986). Specifiers and projection. In *Papers in Theoretical Linguistics* (ed. N. Fukui, T. Rapoport, and E. Sagey), pp. 128–72. MIT Working Papers in Linguistics, Cambridge, MA.

Gazdar, Gerald (1979). *Pragmatics*. Academic Press, New York.

Gazdar, Gerald (1980). A cross-categorial semantics for coordination. *Linguistics and Philosophy*, **3**, 407–9.

Gazdar, Gerald (1981). Unbounded dependencies and coordinate structure. *Linguistic Inquiry*, **12**, 155–84.

Gazdar, Gerald, Klein, Ewan, Pullum, Geoffrey, and Sag, Ivan (1985). *Generalized Phrase Structure Grammar*. Blackwell, Oxford.

Gazdar, Gerald, Pullum, Geoffrey, Sag, Ivan, and Wasow, Thomas (1982). Coordination and transformational grammar. *Linguistic Inquiry*, **13**, 663–77.

Georgopoulos, Carol (1985). Variables in Palauan syntax. *Natural Language & Linguistic Theory*, **3**, 59–94.

Ginzburg, Jonathan (1995a). Resolving questions, I. *Linguistics and Philosophy*, **18**, 459–527.

Ginzburg, Jonathan (1995b). Resolving questions, II. *Linguistics and Philosophy*, **18**, 567–608.

Ginzburg, Jonathan (1996). Dynamics and the semantics of dialogue. In *Logic, Language and Computation, Volume 1* (ed. J. Seligman and D. Westerståhl), pp. 221–37. CSLI, Stanford, CA.

Ginzburg, Jonathan (2012). *The Interactive Stance: Meaning for Conversation*. Oxford University Press, Oxford.

Gleitman, Lila (1965). Coordinating conjunctions in English. *Language*, **41**, 260–93.

Godard, Danièle (1989). Empty categories as subject of tensed Ss in English or French? *Linguistic Inquiry*, **20**, 497–506.

Goldsmith, John (1985). A principled exception to the coordinate structure constraint. In *CLS 21, Part 1: The General Session*, pp. 133–43. Chicago Linguistic Society, Chicago, IL.

Goodall, Grant (1987). *Parallel Structures in Syntax: Coordination, Causatives, and Restructuring.* Cambridge University Press, Cambridge.

Goodluck, Helen and Rochemont, Michael (1992). *Island Constraints.* Kluwer, Dordrecht.

Goodman, Nelson (1947). The problem of counterfactual conditionals. *Journal of Philosophy*, **44**, 113–28.

Grice, Herbert Paul (1975). Logic and conversation. In *Syntax and Semantics, Volume 3: Speech Acts* (ed. P. Cole and J. Morgan), pp. 41–58. Academic Press, New York.

Grohmann, Kleanthes (2003). *Prolific Domains: On the Anti-locality of Movement Dependencies.* John Benjamins, Amsterdam.

Grønn, Atle (2003). *The Semantics and Pragmatics of the Russian Factual Imperfective.* Ph.D. thesis, Universitetet i Oslo.

Grosu, Alexander (1972). *The Strategic Content of Island Constraints.* Ph.D. thesis, Ohio State University.

Grütera, Theres, Takedaa, Aya, Rohde, Hannah, and Schafera, Amy (2018). Intersentential coreference expectations reflect mental models of events. *Cognition*, **177**, 172–6.

Guérin, Valérie (2019). *Bridging Constructions.* Language Science Press, Berlin.

Gundel, Jeanette (1975). Left dislocation and the role of topic–comment structure in linguistic theory. In *Ohio State University Working Papers in Linguistics 18*, pp. 72–131. Ohio State University, Columbus, OH.

Haïk, Isabelle (1985). *The Syntax of Operators.* Ph.D. thesis, Massachusetts Institute of Technology.

Hamblin, Charles (1973). Questions in Montague English. *Foundations of Language*, **10**, 41–53.

Hardt, Daniel (1992). VP ellipsis and contextual interpretation. In *COLING 1992 Volume 1: The 14th International Conference on Computational Linguistics*, pp. 303–9.

Hardt, Daniel (1993). *Verb Phrase Ellipsis: Form, Meaning and Processing.* Ph.D. thesis, University of Pennsylvania.

Hardt, Daniel (1999). Dynamic interpretation of verb phrase ellipsis. *Linguistics and Philosophy*, **22**, 187–221.

Harris, Jesse (2011). Extraction from coordinate structures: Evidence from language processing. In *Proceedings of the 45th Annual Meeting of the Chicago Linguistic Society* (ed. M. R. Bochnak, P. Klecha, A. Lemieux, N. Nicola, J. Urban, and C. Weaver), pp. 73–88. Chicago Linguistic Society, Chicago, IL.

Haspelmath, Martin (2004). Coordinating constructions: An overview. In *Coordinating Constructions* (ed. M. Haspelmath), pp. 3–39. John Benjamins, Amsterdam.

Haspelmath, Martin (2007). Coordination. In *Language Typology and Syntactic Description, Volume 2: Complex Constructions* (2nd edn) (ed. T. Shopen), pp. 1–51. Cambridge University Press, Cambridge.

Heim, Irene (1982). *The Semantics of Definite and Indefinite Noun Phrases.* Ph.D. thesis, University of Massachusetts, Amherst.

Heim, Irene (1983). File change semantics and the familiarity theory of definiteness. In *Meaning, Use, and Interpretation of Language* (ed. R. Bäuerle, C. Schwarze, and A. von Stechow), p. 164–89. De Gruyter, Berlin.

Heim, Irene and Kratzer, Angelika (1998). *Semantics in Generative Grammar.* Blackwell, Oxford.

Henstra, Judith-Ann (1996). *On the Parsing of Syntactically Ambiguous Sentences: Coordination and Relative Clause Attachment.* Ph.D. thesis, University of Sussex.

Heycock, Caroline and Kroch, Anthony (1994). Verb movement and coordination in a dynamic theory of licensing. *The Linguistic Review*, **11**, 257–83.

Higginbotham, James (1985). On semantics. *Linguistic Inquiry*, **16**, 547–93.

Hirschbühler, Paul (1982). VP-deletion and across-the-board quantifier scope. In *Proceedings of NELS 12* (ed. J. Pustejovsky and P. Sells), pp. 132–9. GLSA, Amherst, MA.

Hobbs, Jerry (1979). Coherence and coreference. *Cognitive Science*, **3**, 67–90.

Hobbs, Jerry (1985). On the coherence and structure of discourse. Technical Report CSLI–85–37, CSLI, Stanford, CA.

Hobbs, Jerry (1990). *Literature and Cognition.* CSLI, Stanford, CA.

Hobbs, Jerry (2010). Clause-internal coherence. In *Constraints in Discourse 2* (ed. P. Kuhnlein, A. Benz, and C. L. Sidner), pp. 15–34. John Benjamins, Amsterdam.

Hobbs, Jerry and Kehler, Andrew (1997). A theory of parallelism and the case of VP ellipsis. In *Proceedings of the 35th Annual Meeting of the Association for Computational Linguistics and the 8th Conference of the European Chapter of the Association for Computational Linguistics*, pp. 394–401. Association for Computational Linguistics.

Höhle, Tilman (1983). Subjektlücken in Koordinationen. Ms., published (2018) in S. Müller, M. Reis, and F. Richter (Eds.), *Beiträge zur deutschen Grammatik: Gesammelte Schriften von Tilman N. Höhle.* Language Science Press, Berlin.

Höhle, Tilman (1990). Assumptions about asymmetric coordination in German. In *Grammar in Progress: GLOW Essays for Henk van Riemsdijk* (ed. J. Mascaró and M. Nespor), pp. 221–35. Foris, Dordrecht.

Hornstein, Norbert and Nunes, Jairo (2002). On asymmetries between parasitic gap and across-the-board constructions. *Syntax*, **5**, 26–54.

Huang, Cheng-Teh James (1982). *Logical Relations in Chinese and the Theory of Grammar.* Ph.D. thesis, Massachusetts Institute of Technology.

Hume, David (1748/1999). *An Enquiry Concerning Human Understanding.* Oxford University Press, Oxford.

Hunter, Julie (2016). Reports in discourse. *Dialogue & Discourse*, **7**, 1–35.

Hunter, Julie and Abrusán, Márta (2017). Rhetorical structure and QUDs. In *New Frontiers in Artificial Intelligence: JSAI–isAI 2015 Workshops, LENLS, JURISIN, AAA, HAT-MASH, TSDAA, ASD-HR, and SKL Kanagawa, Japan, November 16–18, 2015, Revised Selected Papers* (ed. M. Otake, S. Kurahashi, Y. Ota, K. Satoh, and D. Bekki), pp. 41–57. Springer, Dordrecht.

Hunter, Julie, Asher, Nicholas, and Lascarides, Alex (2018). A formal semantics for situated conversation. *Semantics & Pragmatics*, **11**, Article 10.

Hunter, Julie and Thompson, Kate (forthcoming). On the role of relations and structure in discourse interpretation. In *Linguistics meets Philosophy* (ed. D. Altshuler). Cambridge University Press, Cambridge.

Jackendoff, Ray (1972). *Semantic Interpretation in Generative Grammar.* MIT Press, Cambridge, MA.

Jasinskaja, Katja (2010). Corrective contrast in Russian, in contrast. *Oslo Studies in Language*, **2**, 433–66.

Jasinskaja, Katja and Karagjosova, Elena (2020). Rhetorical relations. In *Companion to Semantics* (ed. D. Gutzmann, L. Matthewson, C. Meier, H. Rullmann, and T. E. Zimmermann). Wiley.

Jespersen, Otto (1924). *The Philosophy of Grammar.* Allen & Unwin, London.

Johannessen, Janne Bondi (1998). *Coordination.* Oxford University Press, Oxford.

Johnson, Kyle (2000). Few dogs eat Whiskas or cats Alpo. In *UMOP 23: Issues in Semantics* (ed. K. Kusumoto and E. Villalta), pp. 59–82. GLSA, Amherst, MA.

Johnson, Kyle (2002). Restoring exotic coordinations to normalcy. *Linguistic Inquiry*, **33**, 97–156.

Johnson, Kyle (2003). Towards an etiology of adjunct islands. *Nordlyd*, **31**, 187–215.

Johnson, Kyle (2004). In search of the English middle field. Ms., University of Massachusetts, Amherst.

Johnson, Kyle (2009). Gapping is not (VP-)ellipsis. *Linguistic Inquiry*, **40**, 289–328.

Johnson, Kyle (2014). Gapping. Ms., University of Massachusetts, Amherst.

Joshi, Aravind K. (1985). Tree adjoining grammars: How much context-sensitivity is required to provide reasonable structural descriptions? In *Natural Language Parsing: Psychological, Computational, and Theoretical Perspectives* (ed. D. Dowty, L. Karttunen, and A. Zwicky), pp. 206–50. Cambridge University Press, Cambridge.

Kaiser, Elsi (2011). On the relation between coherence relations and anaphoric demonstratives in German. In *Proceedings of Sinn und Bedeutung 15* (ed. I. Reich, E. Horch, and D. Pauly), pp. 337–51. Saarland University Press, Saarbrücken.

Kaiser, Elsi and Cherqaoui, Boutaina (2016). Effects of coherence on anaphor resolution, and vice versa: Evidence from French personal pronouns and anaphoric demonstratives. In *Empirical Perspectives on Anaphora Resolution* (ed. A. Holler and K. Suckow), pp. 51–78. De Gruyter, Berlin.

Kamp, Hans (1981). A theory of truth and semantic representation. In *Formal Methods in the Study of Language* (ed. J. Groenendijk, T. Janssen, and M. Stokhof), pp. 277–322. Mathematisch Centrum, Amsterdam.

Kamp, Hans (2013). Deixis in discourse: Reichenbach on temporal reference. In *Meaning and the Dynamics of Interpretation: Selected Papers of Hans Kamp* (ed. K. von Heusinger and A. ter Meulen), pp. 105–59. Brill, Leiden.

Kamp, Hans and Reyle, Uwe (1993). *From Discourse to Logic: Introduction to Modeltheoretic Semantics of Natural Language, Formal Logic and Discourse Representation Theory*. Kluwer, Dordrecht.

Kamp, Hans and Rohrer, Christian (1983). Tense in texts. In *Meaning, Use, and Interpretation of Language* (ed. A. von Stechow, C. Schwarze, and R. Bäuerle), pp. 391–408. De Gruyter, Berlin.

Kamp, Hans, van Genabith, Josef, and Reyle, Uwe (2011). Discourse Representation Theory. In *Handbook of Philosophical Logic* (ed. D. Gabbay and F. Guenthner), pp. 125–394. Springer, Dordrecht.

Kaplan, Ronald and Maxwell, John (1988). Constituent coordination in Lexical–Functional Grammar. In *Proceedings of COLING-88, Vol.1*, pp. 303–5.

Karttunen, Lauri (1976). Discourse referents. In *Syntax and Semantics 7* (ed. J. McCawley), pp. 363–85. Academic Press, New York.

Kathol, Andreas (1993). Linearization and coordination in German. In *Ohio State University Working Papers in Linguistics 42* (ed. A. Kathol and C. Pollard), pp. 117–52. Ohio State University, Columbus, OH.

Kayne, Richard (1981a). ECP extensions. *Linguistic Inquiry*, **12**, 93–133.

Kayne, Richard (1981b). Two notes on the NIC. In *Theory of Markedness in Generative Grammar: Proceedings of the 1979 GLOW Conference* (ed. A. Belletti, L. Brandi, and L. Rizzi), pp. 317–46. Scuola Normale Superiore, Pisa.

Kayne, Richard (1983). Connectedness. *Linguistic Inquiry*, **14**, 223–49.

Kayne, Richard (1994). *The Antisymmetry of Syntax*. MIT Press, Cambridge, MA.

Kazenin, Konstantin and Testelets, Yakov (2004). Where coordination meets subordination: Converb constructions in Tsakhur (Daghestanian). In *Coordinating Constructions* (ed. M. Haspelmath), pp. 227–39. John Benjamins, Amsterdam.

Kearney, Kevin (1983). Governing categories. Ms., University of Connecticut, Storrs.

Kehler, Andrew (1993). The effect of establishing coherence in ellipsis and anaphora resolution. In *ACL '93: Proceedings of the 31st Annual Meeting of the Association for Computational Linguistics*, pp. 62–9. Association for Computational Linguistics.

Kehler, Andrew (2002). *Coherence, Reference, and the Theory of Grammar*. CSLI, Stanford, CA.

Kehler, Andrew (2004). Discourse topics, sentence topics, and coherence. *Theoretical Linguistics*, **30**, 227–40.

Kehler, Andrew (2019). Coherence relations. In *The Oxford Handbook of Event Structure* (ed. R. Truswell), pp. 583–604. Oxford University Press, Oxford.

Kehler, Andrew, Kertz, Laura, Rohde, Hannah, and Elman, Jeffrey L. (2008). Coherence and coreference revisited. *Journal of Semantics*, **25**, 1–44.

Kempson, Ruth (1975). *Presupposition and the Delimitation of Semantics*. Cambridge University Press, Cambridge.

Kertz, Laura, Kehler, Andrew, and Elman, Jeffrey L. (2006). Grammatical and coherence based factors in pronoun interpretation. In *Proceedings of the 28th Annual Meeting of the Cognitive Science Society*, pp. 1605–10.

Kiparsky, Paul and Kiparsky, Carol (1970). Fact. In *Progress in Linguistics* (ed. M. Bierwisch and K. E. Heidolph), pp. 143–73. Mouton, The Hague.

Klein, Ewan and Sag, Ivan (1985). Type-driven translation. *Linguistics and Philosophy*, **8**, 163–201.

Knoeferle, Pia and Crocker, Matthew (2009). Constituent order and semantic parallelism in on-line comprehension: Eye-tracking evidence from German. *Quarterly Journal of Experimental Psychology*, **62**, 2338–71.

Koffka, Kurt (1935). *Principles of Gestalt Psychology*. Kegan Paul, Trench, Trubner & Co., London.

Koopman, Hilda and Sportiche, Dominique (1991). The position of subjects. *Lingua*, **85**, 211–58.

Kratzer, Angelika (1981). The notional category of modality. In *Words, Worlds, and Contexts: New Approaches in Word Semantics* (ed. H. Eikmeyer and H. Rieser), pp. 38–74. De Gruyter, Berlin.

Kratzer, Angelika (1991). Modality. In *Semantics: An International Handbook of Contemporary Research* (ed. A. von Stechow and D. Wunderlich), pp. 639–50. De Gruyter, Berlin.

Kratzer, Angelika (1998). More structural analogies between pronouns and tenses. In *Proceedings of SALT VIII* (ed. D. Strolovich and A. Lawson), pp. 36–54. CLC Publications, Ithaca, NY.

Kroch, Anthony (1989). Amount quantification, referentiality, and long wh-movement. Ms., University of Pennsylvania.

Kruijff-Korbayová, Ivana and Steedman, Mark (2003). Discourse and information structure. *Journal of Logic, Language and Information*, **12**, 249–59.

Kubota, Yusuke and Lee, Jungmee (2015). The coordinate structure constraint as a discourse-oriented principle: Further evidence from Japanese and Korean. *Language*, **91**, 642–75.

Kuno, Susumu (1973). *The Structure of the Japanese Language*. MIT Press, Cambridge, MA.

Kuno, Susumu (1976). Subject, theme, and the speaker empathy: A reexamination of the relativisation phenomena. In *Subject and Topic* (ed. C. Li), pp. 419–44. Academic Press, New York.

Kuno, Susumu (1987). *Functional Syntax: Anaphora, Discourse and Empathy*. The University of Chicago Press, Chicago.

Kuno, Susumu and Robinson, Jane (1972). Multiple wh questions. *Linguistic Inquiry*, **3**, 463–87.

Kuno, Susumu and Takami, Ken-Ichi (1997). Remarks on negative islands. *Linguistic Inquiry*, **28**, 553–76.

Kusmer, Leland Paul (2018). An itsy-bitsy puzzle: Asymmetric coordination in Khoekhoegowab. Paper presented at WCCFL 36.

Labov, William (1972). *Language in the Inner City: Studies in the Black English Vernacular*. University of Pennsylvania Press, Philadelphia, PA.

Lakoff, George (1970). Repartee, or a reply to 'Negation, conjunction and quantifiers'. *Foundations of Language*, **6**, 153–65.

Lakoff, George (1986). Frame semantic control of the Coordinate Structure Constraint. In *Papers from the Parasession on Pragmatics and Grammatical Theory*, pp. 152–67. Chicago Linguistic Society, Chicago, IL.

Lakoff, George and Peters, Stanley (1967). Phrasal conjunction and symmetric predicates. In *Modern Studies in English: Readings in Transformational Grammar* (ed. D. Reibel and S. Schane), pp. 113–42. Prentice-Hall, Englewood Cliffs, NJ.

Lakoff, Robin (1971). Ifs, ands, and buts about conjunction. In *Studies in Linguistic Semantics* (ed. C. Fillmore and D. T. Langendoen), pp. 114–49. Holt, Rinehart, and Winston, New York.

Larson, Richard (1988). On the double object construction. *Linguistic Inquiry*, **19**, 335–91.

Larson, Richard (1990). Extraction and multiple selection in PP. *The Linguistic Review*, **7**, 169–82.

Lascarides, Alex and Asher, Nicholas (1993). Temporal interpretation, discourse relations, and common sense entailment. *Linguistics and Philosophy*, **16**, 437–95.

Lascarides, Alex and Asher, Nicholas (2007). Segmented Discourse Representation Theory: Dynamic semantics with discourse structure. In *Computing Meaning, Volume 3* (ed. H. Bunt and R. Muskens), pp. 87–124. Kluwer, Dordrecht.

Lascarides, Alex and Asher, Nicholas (2009). Agreement, disputes, and commitments in dialogue. *Journal of Semantics*, **26**, 109–58.

Lascarides, Alex and Stone, Matthew (2009). A formal semantic analysis of gesture. *Journal of Semantics*, **26**, 393–449.

Lasnik, Howard and Kupin, Joseph (1977). A restrictive theory of transformational grammar. *Theoretical Linguistics*, **4**, 173–96.

Lasnik, Howard and Saito, Mamoru (1984). On the nature of proper government. *Linguistic Inquiry*, **15**, 235–89.

Lasnik, Howard and Stowell, Tim (1991). Weakest crossover. *Linguistic Inquiry*, **22**, 687–720.

Lawler, John (1974). Ample negatives. In *Papers from the Tenth Regional Meeting, Chicago Linguistic Society* (ed. M. La Galy, R. Fox, and A. Bruck), pp. 357–77. Chicago Linguistic Society, Chicago, IL.

Lebeaux, David (1988). *Language Acquisition and the Form of the Grammar*. Ph.D. thesis, University of Massachusetts, Amherst.

Lechner, Winfried (2007). Interpretive effects of head movement. Ms., Universität Stuttgart.

Levine, Robert (2001). The extraction riddle: Just what are we missing? *Journal of Linguistics*, **37**, 145–74.

Levine, Robert and Sag, Ivan (2003). Some empirical issues in the grammar of extraction. In *Proceedings of the 10th International Conference on Head-Driven Phrase Structure Grammar* (ed. S. Müller), pp. 236–56. CSLI, Stanford, CA.

Lin, Vivian (2001). A way to undo A-movement. In *WCCFL 20: Proceedings of the 20th West Coast Conference on Formal Linguistics* (ed. K. Megerdoomian and L. Bar-el), pp. 358–71. Cascadilla Press, Somerville, MA.

Lin, Vivian (2002). *Coordination and Sharing at the Interfaces*. Ph.D. thesis, Massachusetts Institute of Technology.

Link, Godehard (1983). The logical analysis of plural and mass terms: A lattice-theoretical approach. In *Meaning, Use and the Interpretation of Language* (ed. R. Bäuerle, C. Schwarze, and A. von Stechow), pp. 303–23. De Gruyter, Berlin.

Lipták, Anikó (2009). *Correlatives Cross-Linguistically*. John Benjamins, Amsterdam.

Longacre, Robert (1983). *The Grammar of Discourse*. Plenum Press, New York.

Lyskawa, Paulina (2021). *Coordination without Grammar-internal Feature Resolution*. Ph.D. thesis, University of Maryland.

Maier, Emar and Bimpikou, Sofia (2019). Shifting perspectives in pictorial narratives. In *Proceedings of Sinn und Bedeutung 23* (ed. M. T. Espinal, E. Castroviejo, M. Leonetti, L. McNally, and C. Real-Puigdollers), pp. 91–105. Universitat Autònoma de Barcelona, Barcelona.

Manetta, Emily (2006). *Peripheries in Kashmiri and Hindi–Urdu*. Ph.D. thesis, University of California, Santa Cruz.

Mann, William and Thompson, Sandra (1986). *Rhetorical Structure Theory: Description and Construction of Text Structures*. Information Sciences Institute, Nijmegen.

Marcus, Mitchell, Santorini, Beatrice, Marcinkiewicz, Mary Ann, and Taylor, Ann (1999). Treebank-3. Linguistic Data Consortium item LDC99T42.

Martin, James (1992). *English Text: Systems and Structure*. John Benjamins, Amsterdam.

May, Robert (1977). *The Grammar of Quantification*. Ph.D. thesis, Massachusetts Institute of Technology.

May, Robert (1985). *Logical Form: Its Structure and Derivation*. MIT Press, Cambridge, MA.

Mayr, Clemens and Schmitt, Viola (2017). Asymmetric coordination. In *The Wiley Blackwell Companion to Syntax, Volume 1* (2nd edn) (ed. M. Everaert and H. van Riemsdijk), pp. 1–32. Wiley Blackwell, Hoboken, NJ.

McCawley, James (1968). Lexical insertion in a transformational grammar without deep structure. In *Papers from the Fourth Regional Meeting, Chicago Linguistic Society, April 19–20, 1968* (ed. B. Darden, C.-J. Bailey, and A. Davison), pp. 71–80. Chicago Linguistic Society, Chicago, IL.

McCawley, James (1993). Gapping with shared operators. In *Proceedings of the Nineteenth Annual Meeting of the Berkeley Linguistics Society: General Session and Parasession on Semantic Typology and Semantic Universals* (ed. J. Guenter, B. Kaiser, and C. Zoll), pp. 245–53. Berkeley Linguistics Society, Berkeley, CA.

McCloskey, James (2001). The morphosyntax of WH-extraction in Irish. *Journal of Linguistics*, **37**, 67–100.

McNally, Louise (1992). VP-coordination and the VP-internal subject hypothesis. *Linguistic Inquiry*, **23**, 336–41.

McNally, Louise (1995). On recent formal analyses of Topic. In *The Tbilisi Symposium on Language, Logic and Computation* (ed. J. Ginzburg), pp. 140–62. CSLI, Stanford, CA.

Merchant, Jason (2008). Variable island repair under ellipsis. In *Topics in Ellipsis* (ed. K. Johnson), pp. 132–53. Cambridge University Press, Cambridge.

Mitrović, Moreno (2014). *Morphosyntactic Atoms of Propositional Logic: A Philo-logical Programme.* Ph.D. thesis, University of Cambridge.

Moens, Marc and Steedman, Mark (1988). Temporal ontology and temporal reference. *Computational Linguistics*, **14**, 15–28.

Moltmann, Friederike (1992). *Coordination and Comparatives.* Ph.D. thesis, Massachusetts Institute of Technology.

Morgan, Jerry (1975). Some interactions of syntax and pragmatics. In *Syntax and Semantics 3: Speech Acts* (ed. P. Cole and J. Morgan), pp. 289–304. Academic Press, New York.

Muadz, Husni (1991). *A Planar Theory of Coordination.* Ph.D. thesis, University of Arizona.

Müller, Christiane (2019). *Permeable Islands: A Contrastive Study of Swedish and English Adjunct Clause Extractions.* Ph.D. thesis, Lund University.

Munn, Alan (1992). A null operator analysis of ATB gaps. *The Linguistic Review*, **9**, 1–26.

Munn, Alan (1993). *Topics in the Syntax and Semantics of Coordinate Structures.* Ph.D. thesis, University of Maryland.

Munn, Alan (1999). First conjunct agreement: Against a clausal analysis. *Linguistic Inquiry*, **30**, 643–68.

Munn, Alan (2000). Three types of coordination asymmetries. In *Ellipsis in Conjunction* (ed. K. Schwabe and N. Zhang), pp. 1–22. Max Niemeyer Verlag, Tübingen.

Munn, Alan (2001). Explaining parasitic gap restrictions. In *Parasitic Gaps* (ed. P. Culicover and P. Postal), pp. 369–92. MIT Press, Cambridge, MA.

Na, Younghee and Huck, Geoffrey (1992). On extracting from asymmetrical structures. In *The Joy of Grammar: A Festschrift in Honor of James D. McCawley* (ed. D. Brentari, G. Larson, and L. MacLeod), pp. 251–74. John Benjamins, Amsterdam.

Neeleman, Ad, Philip, Joy, Tanaka, Misako, and van de Koot, Hans (2021). Subordination and binary branching. Ms., University College London.

Neeleman, Ad and Tanaka, Misako (2020). On the relation between adjunction and type A coordination. Ms., University College London.

Newton-Haynes, Blythe P. and Altshuler, Daniel (2019). Analyzing ballet mime at the semantics/pragmatics interface. Paper presented at GLOW 42, Generative Linguistics beyond Language: Shared Modules for Rhythm, Narration and Emotion across Domains.

Nissenbaum, Jon (2000). *Investigations of Covert Phrase Movement.* Ph.D. thesis, Massachusetts Institute of Technology.

Nunes, Jairo (2005). *Linearization of Chains and Sideward Movement.* MIT Press, Cambridge, MA.

Nunes, Jairo and Uriagereka, Juan (2000). Cyclicity and extraction domains. *Syntax*, **3**, 20–43.

Oda, Hiromune (2017). Two types of the Coordinate Structure Constraint and rescue by PF deletion. In *Proceedings of NELS 47, Volume 2* (ed. A. Lamont and K. Tetzloff), pp. 343–56. GLSA, Amherst, MA.

Oehrle, Richard (1987). Boolean properties in the analysis of gapping. In *Syntax and Semantics 20: Discontinuous Constituency* (ed. G. Huck and A. Ojeda), pp. 203–40. Academic Press, San Diego, CA.

Onea, Edgar (2013). *Potential Questions in Discourse and Grammar.* Ph.D. thesis, University of Göttingen.

Page, Anna Katarina (2017). Information structure and the Coordinate Structure Constraint: Two corpus studies. Master's thesis, University of Edinburgh.

Parsons, Terence (1990). *Events in the Semantics of English: A Study in Subatomic Semantics.* MIT Press, Cambridge, MA.

Partee, Barbara (1973). Some structural analogies between tenses and pronouns in English. *The Journal of Philosophy*, **70**, 601–9.

Partee, Barbara (1984). Nominal and temporal anaphora. *Linguistics and Philosophy*, **7**, 243–86.

Partee, Barbara and Rooth, Mats (1983). Generalized conjunction and type ambiguity. In *Meaning, Use, and Interpretation of Language* (ed. R. Bäuerle, C. Schwarze, and A. von Stechow), pp. 361–83. Walter de Gruyter, Berlin.

Pavese, Carlotta (forthcoming). The semantics and pragmatics of argumentation. In *Linguistics meets Philosophy* (ed. D. Altshuler). Cambridge University Press, Cambridge.

Perlmutter, David (1968). *Deep and Surface Constraints in Syntax*. Ph.D. thesis, Massachusetts Institute of Technology.

Perrault, R. and Allen, J. (1980). A plan-based analysis of indirect speech acts. *American Journal of Computational Linguistics*, **6**, 167–82.

Pesetsky, David (1982). *Paths and Categories*. Ph.D. thesis, Massachusetts Institute of Technology.

Pesetsky, David (1987). *Wh*-in-situ: Movement and unselective binding. In *The Representation of (In)definiteness* (ed. E. Reuland and A. ter Meulen), pp. 98–129. MIT Press, Cambridge, MA.

Pesetsky, David and Torrego, Esther (2001). T-to-C movement: Causes and consequences. In *Ken Hale: A Life In Language* (ed. M. Kenstowicz), pp. 355–426. MIT Press, Cambridge, MA.

Peters, Stanley and Ritchie, Robert (1973). On the generative power of transformational grammars. *Information Sciences*, **6**, 49–83.

Peterson, Peter (2004). Coordination: Consequences of a Lexical–Functional account. *Natural Language & Linguistic Theory*, **22**, 643–79.

Polanyi, Livia (1985). A theory of discourse structure and discourse coherence. In *Proceedings of the 21st Meeting of the Chicago Linguistic Society* (ed. W. Eilfort, P. Kroeber, and K. Peterson), pp. 306–22. Chicago Linguistic Society, Chicago, IL.

Polanyi, Livia (1988). A formal model of the structure of discourse. *Journal of Pragmatics*, **12**, 601–38.

Polinsky, Maria (2001). Information structure and syntax: Topic, discourse-linking, and agreement. In *Proceedings of the Third Workshop on Spoken and Written Texts*. Texas Linguistic Forum, Austin, TX.

Pollard, Carl and Sag, Ivan (1992). Anaphors in English and the scope of the binding theory. *Linguistic Inquiry*, **23**, 261–305.

Pollard, Carl and Sag, Ivan (1994). *Head-Driven Phrase Structure Grammar*. CSLI, Stanford, CA.

Portner, Paul and Yabushita, Katsuhiko (1998). The semantics and pragmatics of topic phrases. *Linguistics and Philosophy*, **21**, 117–57.

Portner, Paul and Yabushita, Katsuhiko (2001). Specific indefinites and the information structure theory of topics. *Journal of Semantics*, **18**, 271–97.

Posner, Roland (1980). Semantics and pragmatics of sentence connectives in natural language. In *Pragmatics and Speech Act Theory* (ed. J. Searle, F. Kiefer, and M. Bierwisch), pp. 169–203. Reidel, Dordrecht.

Postal, Paul (1993). Parasitic gaps and the Across-The-Board phenomenon. *Linguistic Inquiry*, **24**, 735–54.

Postal, Paul (1998). *Three Investigations of Extraction*. MIT Press, Cambridge, MA.

Progovac, Ljiljana (1998a). Structure for coordination, part I. *Glot International*, **3**(7), 3–6.

Progovac, Ljiljana (1998b). Structure for coordination, part II. *Glot International*, **3**(8), 3–9.

Reich, Ingo (2007). From phases to ATB-movement. In *Proceedings from the Annual Meeting of the Chicago Linguistic Society 43* (ed. M. Elliott, J. Kirby, O. Sawada, E. Staraki, and S. Yoon), pp. 217–32. Chicago Linguistic Society, Chicago, IL.

Reich, Ingo (2009). *"Asymmetrische Koordination" im Deutschen*. Stauffenburg, Tübingen.

Reinhart, Tanya (1982). Pragmatics and linguistics: An analysis of sentence topic. *Philosophica*, **27**, 53–94.

Reinhart, Tanya and Reuland, Eric (1993). Reflexivity. *Linguistic Inquiry*, **24**, 657–720.

Rizzi, Luigi (1990). *Relativized Minimality*. MIT Press, Cambridge, MA.

Rizzi, Luigi (1997). The fine structure of the left periphery. In *Elements of Grammar* (ed. L. Haegeman), pp. 281–337. Kluwer, Dordrecht.

Rizzi, Luigi (2013). Locality. *Lingua*, **130**, 169–86.

Roberts, Craige (1996). Information structure in discourse: Towards an integrated formal theory of pragmatics. In *Ohio State University Working Papers in Linguistics Volume 49* (ed. J. H. Yoon and A. Kathol), pp. 91–136. Ohio State University, Columbus, OH.

Rodman, Robert (1976). Scope phenomena, "movement transformations," and relative clauses. In *Montague Grammar* (ed. B. Partee), pp. 165–76. Academic Press, New York.

Roelofsen, Floris and van Gool, Sam (2010). Disjunctive questions, intonation, and highlighting. In *Logic, Language and Meaning* (ed. M. Aloni, H. Bastiaanse, T. de Jager, and K. Schulz), pp. 384–94. Springer, Berlin.

Rögnvaldsson, Eiríkur (1982). We need (some kind of a) rule of conjunction reduction. *Linguistic Inquiry*, **13**, 557–61.

Rohde, Hannah and Horton, William (2014). Anticipatory looks reveal expectations about discourse relations. *Cognition*, **133**, 667–91.

Ross, John Robert (1967). *Constraints on Variables in Syntax*. Ph.D. thesis, Massachusetts Institute of Technology.

Ross, John Robert (1970a). Gapping and the order of constituents. In *Progress in Linguistics* (ed. M. Bierwisch and K. Heidolph), pp. 249–59. Mouton, The Hague.

Ross, John Robert (1970b). On declarative sentences. In *Readings in English Transformational Grammar* (ed. R. Jacobs and P. Rosenbaum), pp. 222–72. Ginn, Waltham, MA.

Ruys, Eddy (1992). *The Scope of Indefinites*. Ph.D. thesis, Universiteit Utrecht.

Sag, Ivan (1976). *Deletion and Logical Form*. Ph.D. thesis, Massachusetts Institute of Technology.

Sag, Ivan (1982). Coordination, extraction, and generalized phrase structure grammar. *Linguistic Inquiry*, **13**, 329–36.

Sag, Ivan, Gazdar, Gerald, Wasow, Thomas, and Weisler, Steven (1985). Coordination and how to distinguish categories. *Natural Language & Linguistic Theory*, **3**, 117–71.

Sanders, Ted, Spooren, Wilbert, and Noordman, Leo (1992). Toward a taxonomy of coherence relations. *Discourse Processes*, **15**, 1–35.

Schank, Roger and Abelson, Robert (1977). *Scripts, Plans, Goals, and Understanding: An Inquiry into Human Knowledge Structures*. Lawrence Erlbaum, New York.

Schlöder, Julian (2018). *Assertion and Rejection*. Ph.D. thesis, ILLC, University of Amsterdam.

Schlöder, Julian, Breitholtz, Ellen, and Fernández, Raquel (2016). Why? In *Proceedings of the 20th Workshop on the Semantics and Pragmatics of Dialogue* (ed. J. Hunter, M. Simons, and M. Stone), pp. 5–14. SEMDIAL, New Brunswick, NJ.

Schlöder, Julian and Lascarides, Alex (2015). Interpreting English pitch contours in context. In *Proceedings of the 19th Workshop on the Semantics and Pragmatics of Dialogue* (ed. C. Howes and S. Larsson), pp. 131–9.

Schlöder, Julian and Lascarides, Alex (2020). Understanding focus: Pitch, placement, and coherence. *Semantics & Pragmatics*, **13**, 1–48.

Schmerling, Susan (1972). Apparent counterexamples to the Coordinate Structure Constraint: A canonical conspiracy. *Studies in the Linguistic Sciences*, **2**, 91–104.

Schmerling, Susan (1975). Asymmetric conjunction and rules of conversation. In *Syntax and Semantics 3: Speech Acts* (ed. P. Cole and J. Morgan), pp. 211–31. Academic Press, New York.

Schriffin, Deborah (1986). Functions of *and* in discourse. *Journal of Pragmatics*, **10**, 41–66.

Schwarz, Bernhard (1998). On odd coordinations in German. *Journal of Comparative Germanic Linguistics*, **2**, 191–219.

Schwarzschild, Roger (1992). Types of plural individuals. *Linguistics and Philosophy*, **15**, 641–75.

Schwarzschild, Roger (1996). *Pluralities*. Kluwer, Dordrecht.

Shieber, Stuart (1985). Evidence against the context-freeness of natural language. *Linguistics and Philosophy*, **8**, 333–43.

Siegel, Muffy (1987). Compositionality, case, and the scope of auxiliaries. *Linguistics and Philosophy*, **10**, 53–75.

Simmons, Mandy (2001). Disjunction and alternativeness. *Linguistics and Philosophy*, **24**, 597–619.

Smyth, Ron (1994). Grammatical determinants of ambiguous pronoun resolution. *Journal of Psycholinguistic Research*, **23**, 197–229.

Sporleder, Caroline and Lascarides, Alex (2008). Using automatically labelled examples to classify rhetorical relations: An assessment. *Natural Language Engineering*, **3**, 369–416.

Stalnaker, Robert (1978). Assertion. In *Syntax and Semantics 9: Pragmatics* (ed. P. Cole), pp. 315–32. Academic Press, New York.

Starke, Michal (2001). *Move Dissolves into Merge: A Theory of Locality*. Ph.D. thesis, Université de Genève.

Steedman, Mark (1985). Dependency and coördination in the grammar of Dutch and English. *Language*, **61**, 523–68.

Steedman, Mark (1989). Constituency and coordination in a combinatory grammar. In *New Conceptions of Phrase Structure* (ed. M. Baltin and A. Kroch), pp. 201–306. University of Chicago Press, Chicago, IL.

Steedman, Mark (1990). Gapping as constituent coordination. *Linguistics and Philosophy*, **13**, 207–63.

Steedman, Mark (1996). *Surface Structure and Interpretation*. MIT Press, Cambridge, MA.

Steedman, Mark (2000). *The Syntactic Process*. MIT Press, Cambridge, MA.

Steedman, Mark (2011). *Taking Scope: The Natural Semantics of Quantifiers*. MIT Press, Cambridge, MA.

Steedman, Mark (2014). The surface-compositional semantics of English intonation. *Language*, **90**, 2–57.

Stepanov, Arthur (2007). The end of CED? Minimalism and extraction domains. *Syntax*, **10**, 80–126.

Stjepanovic, Sandra (2014). Left branch extraction and the Coordinate Structure Constraint. In *Proceedings of NELS 44, Volume 2* (ed. J. Iyer and L. Kusmer), pp. 157–70. GLSA, Amherst, MA.

Stojnić, Una (2016). *Context-sensitivity in a Coherent Discourse*. Ph.D. thesis, Rutgers University.

Stojnić, Una (2017). One's *modus ponens*: Modality, coherence and logic. *Philosophy and Phenomenological Research*, **36**, 167–214.

Stojnić, Una and Altshuler, Daniel (2021). Formal properties of *now* revisited. *Semantics & Pragmatics*, **14**, 1–44.

Stojnić, Una, Stone, Matthew, and Lepore, Ernie (2013). Deixis (even without pointing). *Philosophical Perspectives*, **27**, 502–25.

Stojnić, Una, Stone, Matthew, and Lepore, Ernie (2017). Discourse and logical form: Pronouns, attention and coherence. *Linguistics and Philosophy*, **40**, 519–47.

Stone, Matthew and Lascarides, Alex (2010). Coherence and rationality in grounding. In *Proceedings of the 14th Workshop on the Semantics and Pragmatics of Dialogue: Full Papers* (ed. P. Łupkowski and M. Purver), pp. 51–8. SEMDIAL.

Stone, Matthew and Stojnić, Una (2015). Meaning and demonstration. *Review of Philosophy and Psychology*, **6**, 69–97.

Stump, Gregory (1978). Interpretive gapping in Montague Grammar. In *CLS 14: Papers from the 14th Regional Meeting of the Chicago Linguistic Society* (ed. D. Farkas, W. Jacobsen, and K. Todrys), pp. 472–81. Chicago Linguistic Society, Chicago, IL.

Sturt, Patrick, Keller, Frank, and Dubey, Amit (2010). Syntactic priming in comprehension: Parallelism effects with and without coordination. *Journal of Memory and Language*, **62**, 333–51.

Szabolcsi, Anna and Zwarts, Frans (1993). Weak islands and an algebraic semantics for scope taking. *Natural Language Semantics*, **1**, 235–84.

Takahashi, Daiko (1994). *Minimality of Movement*. Ph.D. thesis, University of Connecticut.

Takahashi, Shoichi and Fox, Danny (2005). MaxElide and the re-binding problem. In *Proceedings of SALT XV* (ed. E. Georgala and J. Howell), pp. 223–40. CLC Publications, Ithaca, NY.

Takami, Ken-Ichi (1989). Preposition stranding: Arguments against syntactic analyses and an alternative functional explanation. *Lingua*, **76**, 299–335.

Talmy, Leonard (1988). Force dynamics in language and cognition. *Cognitive Science*, **12**, 49–100.

Taylor, Heather Lee (2006). Moving out of *if*-clauses: If an *if*-clause is sentence-initial … Paper presented at GLOW 28, Universitat Autònoma de Barcelona.

te Velde, John (2006). *Deriving Coordinate Symmetries: A Phase-based Approach*. John Benjamins, Amsterdam.

Toosarvandani, Maziar (2014). Contrast and the structure of discourse. *Semantics & Pragmatics*, **7**, 1–57.

Travis, Lisa (1984). *Parameters and Effects of Word Order Variation.* Ph.D. thesis, Massachusetts Institute of Technology.

Trnavac, Radoslava and Taboada, Maite (2016). Cataphora, backgrounding and accessibility in discourse. *Journal of Pragmatics*, **93**, 68–84.

Truswell, Robert (2007). *Locality of Wh-movement and the Individuation of Events.* Ph.D. thesis, University College London.

Truswell, Robert (2008). Preposition stranding, passivisation, and extraction from adjuncts in Germanic. In *Linguistic Variation Yearbook 8* (ed. J. van Craenenbroeck and J. Rooryck), pp. 131–78. John Benjamins, Amsterdam.

Truswell, Robert (2011). *Events, Phrases, and Questions.* Oxford University Press, Oxford.

Truswell, Robert (2019). Event composition and event individuation. In *The Oxford Handbook of Event Structure* (ed. R. Truswell), pp. 90–122. Oxford University Press, Oxford.

Txurruka, Isabel (2003). The natural language conjunction *and. Linguistics and Philosophy*, **26**, 255–85.

Umbach, Carla (2005). Contrast and information structure: A focus-based analysis of *but. Linguistics*, **43**(1), 207–32.

Uriagereka, Juan (1999). Multiple spell-out. In *Working Minimalism* (ed. S. Epstein and N. Hornstein), pp. 251–82. MIT Press, Cambridge, MA.

van Koppen, Marjo (2005). *One Probe—Two Goals: Aspects of Agreement in Dutch Dialects.* Ph.D. thesis, Universiteit Leiden.

van Kuppevelt, Jan (1995). Main structure and side structure in discourse. *Linguistics*, **33**, 809–33.

van Oirsouw, Robert (1987). *The Syntax of Coordination.* Croom Helm, London.

van Valin, Robert (1986). An empty category as the subject of a tensed S in English. *Linguistic Inquiry*, **17**, 581–6.

Velleman, Dan, Beaver, David, Destruel, Emilie, Bumford, Dylan, Onea, Edgar, and Coppock, Elizabeth (2012). It-clefts are IT (inquiry terminating) constructions. In *Proceedings of SALT 22* (ed. A. Chereches), pp. 441–60. CLC Publications, Ithaca, NY.

Vieu, L., Bras, M., Asher, N., and Aurnague, M. (2005). Locating adverbials in discourse. *Journal of French Language Studies*, **15**, 173–93.

von Fintel, Kai (1994). *Restrictions on Quantier Domains.* Ph.D. thesis, University of Massachusetts, Amherst.

von Prince, Kilu (2013). Daakaka. The Language Archive. Available at https://hdl.handle.net/1839/00-0000-0000-000F-4E20-B. Last accessed Dec 7 2021.

Wälchli, Bernhard (2005). *Co-compounds and Natural Coordination.* Oxford University Press, Oxford.

Wasow, Thomas (1972). *Anaphoric Relations in English.* Ph.D. thesis, Massachusetts Institute of Technology.

Webber, Bonnie (1988). Tense as discourse anaphor. *Computational Linguistics*, **14**, 61–73.

Weir, David (1988). *Characterizing Mildly Context-Sensitive Grammar Formalisms.* Ph.D. thesis, University of Pennsylvania.

Weisser, Philipp (2015). *Derived Coordination: A Minimalist Perspective on Clause Chains, Converbs and Asymmetric Coordination.* De Gruyter, Berlin.

Westera, Matthijs (forthcoming). Alternatives. In *Linguistics meets Philosophy* (ed. D. Altshuler). Cambridge University Press, Cambridge.

Wilder, Chris (1994). Coordination, ATB and ellipsis. *Groninger Arbeiten zur germanistischen Linguistik*, **37**, 291–329.

Williams, Edwin (1977). Discourse and logical form. *Linguistic Inquiry*, **8**, 101–39.

Williams, Edwin (1978). Across-the-board rule application. *Linguistic Inquiry*, **9**, 31–43.

Williams, Edwin (1981). Transformationless grammar. *Linguistic Inquiry*, **12**, 645–53.

Williams, Edwin (1990). The ATB theory of parasitic gaps. *The Linguistic Review*, **6**, 265–79.

Winter, Yoad (1995). Syncategorematic conjunction and structured meanings. In *Proceedings of SALT 5* (ed. M. Simons and T. Gallaway), pp. 387–404. CLC Publications, Ithaca, NY.

Wolf, Florian, Gibson, Edward, and Desmet, Timothy (2004). Discourse coherence and pronoun resolution. *Language and Cognitive Processes*, **19**, 665–75.

Woodgate, Amy (2010). This is the linear order which if we use, most people will be happy. Honours dissertation, University of Edinburgh.

Wunderlich, Dieter (1988). Some problems of coordination in German. In *Natural Language Parsing and Linguistic Theories* (ed. U. Reyle and C. Rohrer), pp. 289–316. Reidel, Dordrecht.

Zeevat, Henk (2011). Rhetorical relations. In *Semantics: An International Handbook of Natural Language Meaning* (ed. C. Maienborn, K. von Heusinger, and P. Portner), pp. 946–68. De Gruyter Mouton, Berlin.

Zhang, Nina Ning (2009). *Coordination in Syntax*. Cambridge University Press, Cambridge.

Zimmermann, Thomas Ede (2000). Free choice disjunction and epistemic possibility. *Natural Language Semantics*, **8**, 255–90.

Zoerner, Cyril (1995). *The Syntax of &P*. Ph.D. thesis, University of California, Irvine.

Zwart, Jan-Wouter (2009). Prospects for top-down derivation. *Catalan Journal of Linguistics*, **8**, 161–87.

Index

OXFORD SURVEYS IN SYNTAX AND MORPHOLOGY

General Editor
Robert D Van Valin, Jr.
Heinrich-Heine University and the University at Buffalo, State University of New York

Advisory Editors
Guglielmo Cinque, University of Venice; Daniel Everett, Illinois State University;
Adele Goldberg, Princeton University; Kees Hengeveld, University of Amsterdam;
Caroline Heycock, University of Edinburgh; David Pesetsky, Massachusetts Institute of
Technology; Ian Roberts, University of Cambridge; Masayoshi Shibatani, Rice University;
Andrew Spencer, University of Essex; Tom Wasow, Stanford University

PUBLISHED

1. Grammatical Relations
Patrick Farrell

2. Morphosyntactic Change
Olga Fischer

3. Information Structure
The Syntax–Discourse Interface
Nomi Erteschik-Shir

4. Computational Approaches to Syntax and Morphology
Brian Roark and Richard Sproat

5. Constituent Structure
(Second edition)
Andrew Carnie

6. Processing Syntax and Morphology
A Neurocognitive Perspective
Ina Bornkessel-Schlesewsky and Matthias Schlesewsky

7. Syntactic Categories
Gisa Rauh

8. The Interplay of Morphology and Phonology
Sharon Inkelas

9. Word Meaning and Syntax
Approaches to the Interface
Stephen Wechsler

10. Unbounded Dependency Constructions
Theoretical and Experimental Perspectives
Rui P. Chaves and Michael T. Putnam

11. Gradient Acceptability and Linguistic Theory
Elaine J. Francis

12. Coordination and the Syntax–Discourse Interface
Daniel Altshuler and Robert Truswell

IN PREPARATION

Complex Sentences
Toshio Ohori

Periphrasis
Gergana Popova and Andrew Spencer